# THE PARIS COMMUNE
## 1871

by the same author

*(ed.)* PIERRE-JOSEPH PROUDHON: SELECTED WRITINGS

# THE PARIS COMMUNE
# 1871

## Stewart Edwards

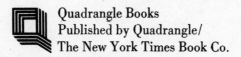

Quadrangle Books
Published by Quadrangle/
The New York Times Book Co.

First paperback printing, September 1977
First published in England in 1971
by Eyre & Spottiswoode, Ltd.
First Quadrangle edition, 1973

Quadrangle Books are published by
Quadrangle/The New York Times Book Co., Inc.,
Three Park Avenue, New York, N.Y. 10016.


Library of Congress Cataloging in Publication Data

Edwards, Stewart, 1937–
    The Paris Commune, 1871.

    Bibliography:    p. 392–403.
    1.    Paris—History—Commune, 1871.    I.    Title
DC316.E3    1973        944′.36′081        72–80213
ISBN 0–8129–6277–X

# CONTENTS

———◆———

# ILLUSTRATIONS

### Acknowledgements for the Illustrations

Acknowledgement and thanks for permission to reproduce photographs are due to the Bibliothèque de la Ville de Paris for Plates 1a, 1c, 1d, 6a, 6b, 6c, 8b, 8c, 8e, 8f, 9a, 9e and 9g; to the Bibliothèque Nationale for Plates 1b, 5, 8g, 10, 13a and 14a; to Murailles politiques françaises for Plate 4a; to Le Monde Illustré for Plate 7a; to the Illustrated London News for Plate 7c; to H. Roger Viollet for Plates 9b, 9c, 9f, 11b and 15c; to Photo Combier for Plate 12a; to Photographie for Plate 12b; to the Mansell Collection for Plate 14b; and to the Musée Carnavalet for Plate 16. Jennifer Pozzi kindly helped to gather illustrations.

# ACKNOWLEDGEMENTS

I have benefited greatly in writing this book from discussion with other students in the field, to whom I am most grateful, though this does not at all imply that they share the views expressed here. In particular to James Joll, who helped me in the first stages and encouraged me throughout; to Chimen Abramsky, with his hospitable generosity and extensive knowledge of the bibliographical material on European socialism; to Eugene Schulkind, who enthusiastically helped me round the University of Sussex Special Collection on the Commune; to Gerald Hoeffel, who was especially helpful with regard to the 17th arrondissement during the Commune; to Robert Wolfe, who also let me consult his thesis at Harvard on the popular movements; and to Charles Posner, particularly for his help on some of the theoretical aspects of the Communal revolution. Charles Tilly of the Center for Advanced Study in the Behavioural Sciences at Stanford, Gordon Lewis of the University of Puerto Rico and Roger Price of the University of East Anglia kindly let me have copies of their papers relating to the subject. Michelle Perrot, Jacques Rougerie and Jean Maitron of the Institut d'histoire économique et sociale de la Sorbonne helped me with my researches in Paris, as did Tristan Haan at the International Institute for Social History in Amsterdam. The Nuffield Foundation assisted generously with a grant towards travelling costs. Finally the Department of Politics of Southampton University was most understanding in enabling me to complete my writing while I was teaching there.

# ABBREVIATIONS

———◆◆◆◆———

A.H.G.     Archives Historiques de la Guerre, Vincennes.

A.N.     Archives Nationales, Paris.

B.N.     Bibliothèque Nationale, Paris

*Dépositions*     *Les Actes du Gouvernement de la défense nationale. Enquête parlementaire. Dépositions*, 5 vols., Versailles, 1872–5.

*Dictionnaire*     *Dictionnaire biographique du mouvement ouvrier français*, edited by Jean Maitron. Part 2, 1864–1871, vols. 4 ff., Paris, 1967–71.

*Enquête*     *Enquête parlementaire sur l'insurrection du 18 mars*, 3 vols., Versailles, 1872

I.I.S.H.     International Institute of Social History, Amsterdam.

J.O.     *Journal Officiel de la République Française* (of the Commune).

MESW     *Marx–Engels: Selected Writings*, 1 vol. edn., London, 1968.

M.P.     *Les Murailles politiques françaises*, 2 vols., Paris, 1871.

P.V.C.     *Procès-Verbaux de la Commune de 1871*, ed. G. Bourgin and G. Henriot, 2 vols., Paris, 1924, 1945.

# PREFACE

This is not an objective history, although I hope it is an accurate one. Objectivity is not to be expected of mortals writing their own story, the history of the events that have constructed the world they live in. Even history that is thought to be dead needs but the right wind to rouse its embers. A revolution, successful or failed, is but a particularly clear case of this general truth.

A hundred years after the Commune it is still not possible easily to assign the events of 1870–71 a place in the history either of France or of the European socialist movement. The numerous detailed contemporary accounts have more recently been modified and expanded by later historians, and the present work seeks to include their findings. But much more work needs to be done, both on the composition of the popular forces within Paris and on the provincial movements. Socialist, anarchist and conservative interpretations of the Communal revolution appeared at the time and have continued ever since. The revolutionary movement that culminated in the European revolutions at the end of the First World War have given way more recently to the development of guerrilla resistance wars and of new forms of urban revolutionary experiences, which have only added to the possible readings that can be drawn from the Franco-Prussian war and the Commune. In a country such as England where revolution has largely been excised out of the national consciousness, it is that much more difficult to be able to understand Paris during the time of the Commune. But contemporary French experience should be of some help. The barricades in the Latin Quarter in May '68 were identical to many of those of May '71, down to the metal grilles thrown on after the *pavés* had been dug up. Only the overturned cars distinguished them from the horse-drawn buses and cabs of the earlier epoch.

The international revolutionary movement, as set in motion over a century ago by the western proletariat, failed. Its so-called 'victories' and 'defeats', if judged in the light of their historical consequences, tend to confirm Liebknecht's remark, the day before his assassination, that 'some defeats are really victories, while some victories are more shameful than any defeats'. Thus the first great 'failure' of workers' power, the Paris Commune, is in fact its first great *success*, whereby the primitive proletariat proclaimed its historical capacity to organize all aspects of social life *freely*.

*The International Situationists*

# Chapter 1

# PARIS AT THE END OF THE EMPIRE

It would be misleading to say that the Commune was an accident, but it would not be wholly untrue. The cause of the Paris Commune was the complete defeat of the French army by Prussia in the autumn of 1870 and the ensuing four-month siege of the capital. This brought about the downfall of the political regime and its replacement by nothing stronger than a self-confessed provisional power. The effect of the unexpectedly long siege, unexpected that is to everyone except the patriotic Paris population (and probably the Prussians), was to drive a wedge between most of the inhabitants of the capital and the rest of the country, including those claiming authority. The structure of society, in Paris at least, was broken apart; this was the situation in which a revolt could be expected to occur. To explain what happened when this did break out, when Paris declared itself an independent Commune, means examining a different set of circumstances, antedating the war. For the problem then is, given that a revolution is probable, what form will this take? And the answer to this can only be found by looking at the economic and social structure of France at the time and how this had developed.

The most obvious but nonetheless very important fact about the Paris Commune was that it was restricted to the capital, unlike, for example, the revolution of 1789. There had been two successful previous revolutions in Paris since the first French Revolution, that of 1830 and that of 1848. In 1830 the Paris workers who had helped overthrow the Monarchy, which had been restored following the defeat of Napoleon, received no benefits from their action. But it did mark a period of industrial agitation and the spread of socialist ideas. The first revolts against industrial conditions occurred not in Paris but among the Lyon silk workers in 1831. These disturbances had a big influence on contemporary opinion and for the first time the existence of a 'social problem' was openly recognized. Further uprisings occurred in Lyon in 1834 and there were a number of riots in Paris. The revolution of 1848 did not begin as a workers' uprising, having its origins rather in the discontented bourgeoisie's campaign for greater political liberties. But again it was the working population of Paris that fought in the streets. This time it was consciously felt the working class should gain some rewards for their part in overthrowing the monarchy of Louis-Philippe. The effect of this attempt was to divide the workers from the republican bourgeoisie. The latter were fearful of such signs as 'the workers' parliament' at the Luxembourg Palace and the continuing demonstrations in the streets pressing the Provisional Government to form a 'democratic Republic' that would abolish 'the exploitation of man by man'. Finally, on 21 June 1848, the moderate Republican majority in the newly elected National Assembly closed down the National Workshops, which at least had provided a form of public subsistence for the thousands of unemployed. This provocation led to an uprising in the popular quarters to the east of Paris on both the Left and Right Banks. There may well have been up to 100,000 insurgents, who were finally crushed after a three-day battle with the army, reinforced by volunteers and reserves from the provinces. It was a foretaste of 1871 – as was the repression, which was without mercy.

This reaction was completed when Louis-Napoleon, the nephew of Napoleon I, who had been elected for a three-year term of office as the first President of the new Republic, dissolved the National Assembly by a *coup d'état* in December 1851 and subsequently proclaimed himself Emperor. A plebiscite was held in 1852 which gave the new Napoleon III a huge majority, thereby endorsing the new regime and bringing to an end the uncertainties of the previous few years. The spectre that had been haunting Europe, and which between February and June of 1848 had seemed frighteningly imminent, was banished, even though political liberty and parliamentary government had also had to be abandoned in the process. The countryside had again asserted itself over Paris. The confidence of the upper ranks of the bourgeoisie in Napoleon's assurance that the Empire meant peace was expressed in an outflow of capital investment that made 1852 a boom year on the French stockmarket, and heavy industry soon had its order books full.

The industrialization of France had begun in the reign of Louis-Philippe in the 1840s when the first railways were constructed. In the February and June days of 1848, for the first time in French history, industrial workers (from the railway workshops of Paris) were among the arrested insurgents.[1] The full expansion of French industrial capitalism did not come until after 1880, but the twenty years of the Second Empire mark an important step forward. The first stage of the railway network was completed, linking up the major cities. Mechanization of industry took place: the number of machines used in industry in 1850 was 5,332; in 1870 this number was 27,958 (in 1890 it was 64,000). Sainte-Beuve called Napoleon III 'Saint-Simon on horseback', and under the Second Empire the emphasis was on public works – canals, roads, railways. The Duc de Morny, the Emperor's illegitimate half-brother, had his hand in many of these developments, and the assurance that Morny *est dans l'affaire* was good security for other investors.

Above all, the Second Empire was a great period of accumulation of capital, of expansionist though speculative financing. The most important native socialist writer of the time, Pierre-Joseph Proudhon, called it an epoch of 'industrial feudalism'. The Banks were the motor of industrial expansion. Under the previous regime financing was in the hands of a few conservative private bankers, the Rothschilds being the largest and most influential. To meet the expanded need for credit, a more audacious group of bankers and political figures founded the Crédit Mobilier and Crédit Foncier in 1852. The former was established by Imperial decree, and its starting capital came from a group of private bankers led by the Péreire brothers. The latter received an initial subvention from the Government, and its purpose was to give loans on landed securities. Other banks were formed in the provinces, such as the Crédit Lyonnais in 1863, and in 1856 the Odéon Theatre celebrated this credit expansion by putting on a play entitled *La Bourse*.

The 1850s and 1860s in France, however, were not a period of *laisser-faire* capitalism on the British model. The absence of parliamentary government during much of the regime contrasts with the growth of influence of the British manufacturers in municipal government and in the House of Commons. In France both then and now capitalism depended considerably on help and support from the State, which often undertook projects that private speculators were too timid to develop. The first iron works in France were started in 1785 under the patronage of Louis XVI at Le Creusot in Burgundy.

[1] G. Rudé, *The Crowd in History*, London, 1964, p. 177.

By the end of the Second Empire these same works were the biggest iron and steel works on the Continent, employing some 10,000 workers, being by then privately owned by the Schneiders. But the family still looked to the State, from which it had benefited greatly in arms production for the Crimean War, and E. Schneider ruled not only over the local municipality but was made President of the National Legislative Body as well as being President of the organization of iron and steel owners, the Comité des forges, founded in 1864.

If France was moving on the path of industrialization, the pace was only moderate. In contrast to England, there was no 'take-off' period of rapid industrial expansion in a few leading industries.[1] France remained primarily a rural country, and the railway expansion prevented the rapid urbanization of the economy by linking up rural markets. Some seventy per cent of the population lived in the countryside in the 1860s (the real agricultural revolution of France only began in the 1950s), though only fifty per cent of the total population was directly engaged in agriculture. In the period 1850–80 industry represented thirty-four per cent of France's total production, with another twelve per cent in the building industry. The concentration of industry was localized in a few industries around the big cities in the north and along the Rhône valley, down which since 1856 a railroad connected Paris to Marseille. But to the west of this corridor the countryside was hardly touched by the industrial expansion of the Empire, and even today this is an 'underdeveloped' region industrially.

In the capital, industry supported itself to a great extent off the large consumer market that the city provided, and the luxury trades were able to thrive off the re-establishment of a court life and the conspicuous spending this encouraged, aided not a little by the influx of rich foreign visitors. For if under the Second Empire Paris was not quite the stage it was to become during the 'banquet years' of the turn of the century, it was well started on this path by the time of the Universal Exhibition held there in 1867. Garnier's new Opera House was never completed in time for the Emperor and Empress to make use of the special entrance being built for them. Instead, it was in the old Opéra Comique or in the smaller theatres along the Champs Elysées that the *beaumonde* displayed itself, houselights being left on during performances since the public had pri-

[1] See M. Lévy-Leboyer's comments on J. Marczewski's 'The Take-Off Hypothesis and French Experience', in *'La Croissance économique en France au XIXe siècle'*, *Annales E.S.C.*, July–August 1968, pp. 788–807.

marily come to see each other. Offenbach's operettas suited this mood much more than Wagner, whose only success in getting one of his operas staged was a flop, for the men of the Jockey Club and their mistresses howled down *Tannhäuser*, which did not include the usual ballet entertainment to show off the legs of the dancers. The perpetual frivolity of the capital caused doubt as to the seriousness of the nation and its Emperor; 'we are hastening to our decline', wrote one acute observer, de Viel Castel, in 1864.

Away from the centre, particularly in the communes lying outside the old city boundaries, Paris was sharing in the general industrial development of the north of France. Between the *octroi*[1] wall encircling the old nine arrondissements[2] of Paris, which included amongst its customs gates the Porte Saint-Martin and the Porte Saint-Denis, and the fortified wall completed in 1844, lay a sort of no-man's land. It was here that most of the heavy industry had grown up, particularly in the new arrondissements on the Left Bank; the railroad repair shops, yards and freight stations; the locomotive works; the chemical works; the big metallurgical works of the Cail family, with two factories, one on the Quai de Grenelle in the south-west of Paris and the other behind the Gare du Nord. This industrialization also threatened some of the traditional craftsman industries, both employees and their patrons alike: the Godillot shoe factory, for example, which later became so well known that it gave its name to a military boot type of shoe.

The population of the city increased by about half as much again between 1851 and 1872 (from 1,200,000 in 1851, including the outlying communes annexed in 1860, to 1,850,000 in the 1872 census). Two-thirds of this expansion was due to immigration from the provinces, and to a lesser extent from bordering countries such as Belgium and Germany. Immigration into Paris was nothing new, of course, though the scale of it caused much discussion at the time of the need for possible remedies. Sometimes immigrants did settle around the stations of their arrival – for example, the Breton community around the Gare Montparnasse – but statistics belie the literary notion that Paris was marked by strongly regional quarters.

---

[1] The *Octroi* was a well-established tax levied on goods coming into Paris to be sold. To enforce this there was a wall round the city with customs gates, which also marked the city's administrative boundary.

[2] An arrondissement is the unit of local government in Paris, each with its own mayor. In 1860, when the city boundaries were extended, the number of arrondissements was raised from nine to their present figure of twenty.

With exceptions such as the workers in the wine depots at Charenton and Bercy, who often returned to their Burgundian villages, most immigrants were absorbed by the city and became Parisians.[1]

The proportion of industrial workers arrested in 1871 after the Commune was higher than after the 1848 Revolution, reflecting the industrial development of the outer suburbs of Paris.[2] But the Parisian working population of the end of the Empire was still far from being an industrial proletariat. The 1872 census gave forty-four per cent of the working population as industrial, a drop from the figures given in the previous censuses of 1866 and 1856. Rather than an actual decline, this shows the sharpening of the distinction between the categories of commercial and industrial. The term *ouvrier* was likewise just beginning to be restricted to those who were wage earners. In Paris itself, one count for around 1870 gives some fifteen factories employing more than a hundred workers each, and a further hundred factories each employing between twenty and fifty workers.[3] But throughout France, Paris included, small-scale production remained the norm – sixty per cent of the industrial work force in 1866 was in workshops employing less than ten workers. Accordingly it was not easy to make sharp distinctions because of the many small workshops run by the master-owner with one or two employees occupying just a shop front, where were sold the goods produced at the rear. The most solidly working-class district in all of Paris, Belleville, consisted of workers in traditional Parisian crafts and traditions, rather than in the new factory industries.[4]

The most dramatic change in Paris, for all classes, was brought about not by the slow process of industrialization but by the Emperor's ambition to complete and expand the work of his uncle of 'beautifying' Paris, giving it the monumental character considered

---

[1] See L. Chevalier, *La Formation de la population parisienne au XIXe siècle*, Paris, 1950, pp. 44, 238–40. Georges Duveau, *La Vie ouvrière en France sous le Second Empire*, Paris, 1946, p. 218, says of Paris that it was not a city of big industrial factories but 'a factory of dreams'.

[2] See J. Rougerie, *Procès des Communards*, Paris, 1964, p. 128; Charles Tilly, 'How Protest Modernized France, 1845–1855', Conference on Applications of Quantitative Methods to Political, Social and Economic History, University of Chicago, June 1969.

[3] J. Rougerie, '*Les Elections du 26 mars à la Commune de Paris*', D.E.S. of the Sorbonne, 1955, pp. 128–44.

[4] See J. Rougerie, '*Belleville*', in L. Girard, *Les Elections de 1869*, Paris, 1960, p. 21; Duveau, op. cit., pp. 197–9.

fitting for an Imperial capital. The 'Haussmannization' of Paris, as contemporaries called it, thereby honouring the name of Napoleon's chosen Prefect of the Seine, served several purposes beyond that of the Emperor's dream of being a 'Second Augustus, because Augustus made Rome a city of marble'. There were good public health reasons for improving the city's water supply and sewerage system, and for providing more open spaces and parks. In London, where Napoleon had lived in exile, such issues were a matter of administrative concern. Also it had long been a policy of Paris's rulers to undertake construction to try to reduce unemployment. Napoleon and Haussmann simply increased the pace, thereby providing not only employment for those already in Paris, which had been one of the aims of Haussmann's predecessor in the 1840s, but attracting to Paris many additional masons, carpenters and unskilled labourers. After the Commune contemporaries were wont to blame Haussmann for having in this way increased rather than decreased the revolutionary potential of the city.[1] To offset this charge, the cutting of wide boulevards through the narrow winding streets of the most populous quarters opened up a clear field for artillery fire and for the quick movement of troops to outflank any insurrectionary barricades. Haussmann recounts, for example, the enthusiasm with which Napoleon III greeted his Prefect's proposal to cover the Canal Saint-Martin by the boulevard Richard Lenoir. For to do this would remove a good line of defence for the inhabitants of the Faubourg Saint-Antoine, giving a clear run from the Place de la Bastille to the new Boulevard Prince-Eugène (now Boulevard Voltaire) and then on to the enlarged Place du Château-d'Eau (now Place de la République), where a large barracks was strategically sited. As Haussmann said, 'one cannot deny that a very fortunate consequence of all the big constructions conceived of by His Majesty was to rip open the Old Paris, the district of insurrections and barricades'.[2]

The task of rebuilding Paris by autocratic decree was far from completed by 1870, and the Communards were not prevented from raising barricades. But as the demolitions were mainly in the poorer areas, such as the vicinity of the Tuileries Palace (where Auguste Renoir grew up with fond memories – an area that Balzac described as a slum) to extend the rue de Rivoli, or in the old central market place to make way for the expanded Les Halles, the population of

[1] Louis Lazare, *La France et Paris*, Paris, 1872, p. 84.
[2] Haussmann, *Mémoires*, Paris, 1890, vol. 2, p. 318; vol. 3, pp. 54–5.

these areas had been forced to emigrate to the communes of the 18th, 19th and 20th arrondissements in the north. The construction of Les Halles, a case in point, cut the population of that district by almost a half in a period of six years. The population of the Faubourg Saint-Honoré likewise fell by about a third, whereas during the same period the population of the outlying communes rose by 140,000 new inhabitants. This new working-class area of the north lacked many of the amenities that had made life durable in the dark, overcrowded central area. There were fewer public fountains (the main source of water in mid-nineteenth-century Paris), and no hospitals, schools or charitable institutions, and the whole area had the appearance of a shanty town. But at least at first prices were cheaper since they did not have to pay the Paris customs taxes (the *octroi*). The annexation of the outlying communes in 1860 removed even this advantage and only increased discontent since the expenditures proposed by Haussmann were not sufficient and took time to take effect. It was the common story of urban development forcing out the indigenous population. Haussmann claimed he built more accommodation than he destroyed, but the new apartments along the boulevards were too expensive for most workers to afford. The idea of rent control was rejected as a fallacious socialist theory. One conservative journalist claimed that the return on workers' shanty places was greater than that on the bourgeois apartments.[1] Thus began the division of Paris, along with most modern cities, into class districts in place of the earlier vertical division into middle class on the first and second floor, with servants in the basement or at the top along with artists, writers, students and workmen's families.[2] This new geographical separation of the different classes in turn only increased the need for further road construction to enable the population to

---

[1] M. Hervé before the Commission of Inquiry into the Commune: *Enquête*, II, p. 175.

[2] Cf. J. Renoir, *Renoir, My Father*, Eng. trans. London, 1962, p. 14, who says that his father 'hated the division of modern cities into slums, middle-class, quarters, workers' sections, and so on'. Renoir disliked Haussmann's plans, and it was one of his regrets that during the bombardment of Paris the new Opera House was not hit. Picard, a Minister in the Government after the fall of the Empire, said that the effect of the rebuilding of Paris was noticeable in the formation of the National Guard battalions in September 1870. There were, as a result, battalions of rich and poor instead of the socially mixed battalions of 1848, where everyone knew each other, 'watched over each other, controlled one another': *Dépositions*, I, pp. 489–90.

get about the city. In old Paris most people lived and worked in the same district, and journeys outside of this were infrequent.

This shift of population would be shown in the Commune, for instead of the crowds massing in the old quarters around the Bastille it was from the north and north-east that the revolutionary battalions descended on the Hôtel de Ville. The new arrondissements, particularly those of the Right Bank, were not cut off from the life of the city. Though there was no Métro, and the buses were far too dear, the Parisian working class was accustomed to making the journey between the centre and Belleville, Montmartre or La Villette. At one time this had been an area to be visited on holidays, a 'Garden of Eden' as one writer called it,[1] for those seeking a bit of countryside. Now, most of those who had been expropriated from their homes still had to make a daily journey back to the centre where they had kept their old jobs, adding an hour's journey by foot to their working day. This link between the old and the new Paris is brought out by the fact that Belleville and Montmartre were the only districts in the whole of the city where the number of Parisian-born inhabitants exceeded the number of immigrants from the provinces. As a result of such continuities the Paris revolutionary traditions were not broken, and the memories of 1848 and before were continued in the revolutionary consciousness of Belleville or Montmartre. Also, the sense of intense life that had marked the old central districts was retained, and this continuing sense of *quartier* explains how the local population would fight very fiercely for their own areas, but disliked being sent off outside them; and how the National Guard fought so well to defend itself in the Commune but not on the battlefields during the siege of Paris. The natural instinct was that of the barricade – that is, to defend the *quartier* or at the most to take the Hôtel de Ville, but not to march into strange territory, as would have been involved in attacking the Government at Versailles in 1871.

The *coup d'état* of Louis-Napoleon had been against a conservative bourgeois National Assembly, something Marx emphasized in his 1852 pamphlet on these events, *The Eighteenth Brumaire of Louis Bonaparte*. Few workers had been willing to fight in the streets to oppose this takeover of power. It was left to liberal republicans of the professional classes and a few artisans such as shoe-makers to

[1] E. de Labedollière, *Le Nouveau Paris*, Paris, 1860: quoted in Rougerie, '*Belleville*', p. 20.

try to defend parliamentary rule. Many workers had been killed or imprisoned following the June days of 1848. The rest, as Flaubert expressed it in his novel of the period *L'Education sentimentale*, did not intend to be 'so stupid as to get themselves killed for the bourgeoisie. They can settle their own affairs.' The first interest of the new Emperor naturally enough was to establish his personal position, and he sought to win support from whatever sources were available. These included the Left, the working classes, as well as the Right, the Church and the army. Before he came to power, whilst a prisoner at Ham for having tried to overthrow the throne, Louis-Napoleon had published a short book entitled *The Extinction of Poverty*. It was mainly based on Saint-Simon's writings, and Louis Blanc, from whose best-selling *The Organisation of Labour* some of its ideas had been taken, was sufficiently impressed to go and spend three days discussing social problems with the future Emperor. The *coup d'état* signalled not only the end of the constitutional monarchy of Louis-Philippe, but a change in the conservative protectionist economic policies of the Orleanist bourgeoisie. Guizot, recently deposed as Prime Minister along with his Monarch, was convinced that the *coup d'état* marked 'the complete and definite triumph of socialism'. He need not have feared. But the new Emperor was determined to do something for what Saint-Simon had called 'the poorest and most numerous class'. As Napoleon said in 1857, the State must 'come to the aid of those who cannot keep up with the increased pace of progress'. Then there were good political reasons for making some concessions to the bulk of his citizens, in the hope of winning working-class support for his throne against the monarchists of the Right and republicans of the Left who opposed his dynasty.

In his youthful pamphlet on poverty the future Emperor had written that 'one can govern only with the aid of the masses; they must be organized so that they can formulate their wishes and be disciplined so that they may be directed and enlightened concerning their own interests'. In the first year of his reign, amongst several social measures, he granted a reform of the local labour courts, the councils of *Prud'hommes*, which had been demanded in the 1840s by the first working-class paper, *L'Atalier*. But the real crux was the question of workers' organizations, and how to allow these to develop without their becoming sources of disaffection. Napoleon III favoured, for example, the setting up of mutual security societies, which were a form of workers' pension and sickness benefit schemes.

But the Government decree of 1852 said such organizations had to have the patronage of the local mayor and priest, and the Government appointed the president. A Paris wholesale merchant, commenting on the events of 1870-1, said these societies had as their aim 'order, work and harmony'.[1] A struggling co-operative movement was given Government assistance by the law of 1867, but again within limits, in this case that they should not hold public meetings to propagate their views or to recruit members. In 1864, Napoleon went so far as to force through a reluctant Legislature a measure legalizing strikes by a repeal of the Le Chapelier Anti-Combination Act of 1791, though the Legislature did succeed in making sure that any violence or 'fraudulent manœuvres' to bring about wage increases or a stoppage of work would result in prosecution.

The Emperor's social policy, however, was hardly sufficient to create enthusiasm for his regime. The greatest show of popular support came over foreign affairs in 1859, the year of the Italian Campaign. This was also a prosperous year, but from the early 1860s it was clear that the workers were against the Empire. They had not shared in the wealth created by the economic expansion of the first years of the Empire, which had been accompanied by a sharp price rise – prices rose by more than fifty per cent between 1850 and 1857. Wages had lagged behind prices, with the effect that there was a redistribution of income in favour of the propertied classes, which in turn was an additional factor contributing towards the stagnation of the economy during the second half of the reign.[2] The misery of the poor was put into sharper relief by the ostentatious display that many of the rich made of their wealth. The bronze-worker and later Communard, Louis Chalain, on trial in 1870 for belonging to the International, said to his accusers that 'When you see a fabulous fortune built up in a few years, you say "National prosperity". We say, "waste of capital, robbery and abasement of the working class", for the one goes with the other.' Chalain spoke of the 'immorality' and 'obvious greed' of the capitalists in their 'frenzied' competition

---

[1] Frère before the Commission of Inquiry into the Government of National Defence, *Dépositions*, II, p. 260.
[2] Cf. R. E. Cameron, 'Economic Growth and Stagnation in France, 1815-1914', *Journal of Modern History*, March 1958, p. 5; 'French Finance and Italian Unity: The Cavourian Decade', *American Historical Review*, April 1957, pp. 553-4; D. I. Kulstein, 'The Attitude of French workers towards the Second Empire', *French Historical Studies*, Spring 1962, pp. 367-70.

between themselves at the expense of the worker.[1] At an earlier trial Eugène Varlin, also later a Communard, in the collective defence of the Internationalists spoke of their class hatred for those who wanted to conserve what they had taken from others, and Varlin warned his judges to beware because 'the ground is crumbling under your feet'.[2]

The Government's attempt at 'tutelage' found little support. In 1861 Henri Tolain, an engraver and one of the founders of the Paris International, wrote in a public letter that 'when the initiative comes from above, from the Government or from the employers, this inspires in the workers only a small degree of confidence'.[3] The Emperor's attempt to 'direct' the masses was resented as 'Social Caesarism', and an *ouvriériste* sentiment developed, which was the meaning given by the French to the device of the International 'that the emancipation of the working classes must be the work of the working classes themselves'. The anarchism of Pierre-Joseph Proudhon can also be seen as a formulation of this common desire, which continued in the French Trade Union movement, the Syndicalists of the end of the century, to separate the working class from the bourgeoisie and its State. Proudhon, who died in 1865, was more concerned with the peasantry and the artisanal tradition than the newer factory workers. Hence his social theories sought to protect the small independent producer from the encroachments of large-scale capitalism and its ally the State. In the 1863 elections Proudhon supported the campaign in favour of non-voting, though the following year he was greatly impressed when Tolain stood as a specifically working-class candidate. The committee supporting Tolain published a Manifesto arguing that only members of the working class could represent the interests of that class, a rejection of the doctrine that the Republicans represented all forms of opposition to the Empire. Proudhon took these events, though Tolain came nowhere near to being elected, as a sign that at last the working class was developing its own self-consciousness and would henceforth assert its independence of a decadent bourgeoisie.

[1] *Troisième procès de l'Association Internationale des Travailleurs à Paris*, Paris, 1870, p. 164.

[2] *Procès de l'Association Internationale des Travailleurs. Première et deuxième commissions du bureau de Paris*, Paris, 1870, p. 102.

[3] *L'Opinion Nationale*, October 15 1861: quoted by Murat at the Third Trial of the International, op. cit., p. 109.

Political action, according to Proudhon and the first Internationalists and mutualists (as the co-operative movement was called) should give way to economic activity.[1] The organization of labour in the form of associations of workshops would come to replace the organization of government. The value of labour was extolled – that is labour in an artisanal or agricultural form – as against the corrupting and parasitical nature of finance and trade, with the concomitant political jobbery of parliaments. Irrespective of the scale of production in France in the 1860s, the working-men's mentality remained primarily that of the artisan. In heavy industry, most workers were first generation, who had immigrated to the town and worked at first in a small workshop before being forced to seek employment in a large factory. The discipline of factory production had hardly had time to become internalized. Throughout the century there are constant complaints by industry and public officials of workers taking unofficial holidays, extending their Sunday rest-day through to Monday or Tuesday, being insubordinate and not turning up on time.[2]

If some tried to escape from the appalling conditions (doubly so

[1] Proudhon's notion of 'mutualism' differed from the common co-operative or associationist idea. Associations of producers, according to Proudhon, should only be formed in the few industries where large-scale production could not be avoided or in certain public utilities such as the railways. But in general he was in favour of production being limited to units small enough to be owned and run by one man. 'Mutualism' in Proudhon becomes identical with 'Federalism'. The State should give way to federations of communes of small-scale producers and consumers: cf. *Selected Writings of P.-J. Proudhon*, ed. S. Edwards, New York/London, 1969–70, pp. 58–63, 111.

[2] This is a general feature of the introduction of industrial forms of production; as Max Weber put it in his classic discussion of the spirit of Capitalism: 'Wherever modern capitalism has begun its work of increasing its intensity, it has encountered the immensely stubborn resistance of this leading trait of pre-capitalist labour' (*The Protestant Ethic and the Spirit of Capitalism*, Eng. trans. 1930, p. 60). In *Capital* (vol. 1, Pt. IV, ch. 14), Marx points out that 'throughout the whole manufacturing period, there runs the complaint of want of discipline among workmen'. Edward Thompson's study of *The Making of the English Working Class* (London, 1963, p. 357) substantiates these remarks in detail, noting that 'the deep-rooted folk memories of a "golden age" or of "Merrie England" derive not from the notion that material goods were more plentiful in 1780 than in 1840, but from nostalgia for the pattern of work and leisure which obtained before the outer and inner disciplines of industrialism settled on the working man'.

because so new) of the factory and from their poor and often distant lodgings by spending most of their wages in cabarets and cafés, others were proud of the tradition of their craft and sought to improve their lot by diligent saving and education. Thus the two big demands constantly being raised were for education and credit. It was a question of dignity and justice. Of dignity, because the wage-earner in a factory was an 'automaton' losing all sense of 'the value of what he was producing with his hands'; he was simply, 'in one word, a machine'. The proposed remedy was that the worker should be able to obtain capital for himself by 'mutualist' or State free-credit schemes; or, at least, machine production, since it enabled the same amount to be produced in less time, should be used to give workers more freedom to devote to other pursuits – such as the furtherance of their education and a more active interest in public affairs – and above all to leisure so that 'at least one can live, and live as a family'.[1] Of justice, because the existing system of unregulated competition, together with the theoretical liberty and equality of the legal code since the French Revolution, in practice grossly favoured the industrialist with his capital and the State behind him against the individual working man. The demand for the right to associate, to form Trade Unions or to establish workers' co-operatives was intended to reduce this imbalance.

For most of the twenty years of Napoleon's rule political censorship made almost impossible any form of political activity. But this did not mean that the purely economic reform movement was able to make great progress. A delegation of Paris workers had been willing to accept Government funds to travel to England for the London Exhibition of 1862. The occasion was used to make contacts with English trade unionists, which led to the founding of the International Workingmen's Association at St Martin's Hall two years later. But one of the first actions of the newly-formed Paris branch of the International was to hold a public meeting to explain that the new workers' Association was completely independent of the Government, and it was only after this assurance had been given that they were able to attract many recruits. The Government took its revenge for such a sign of independence by banning publication

---

[1] *Exposition Universelle de 1867 à Paris: Rapports des délégations ouvrières, dirigées par M. Arnould Desvernay*, Paris, 1869, vol. 1, *Rapport des ouvriers en cuirs et peaux*, p. 16; vol. 2, *Rapport des mécaniciens*, pp. 155–6. See also Duveau, op. cit., pp. 506–9.

in France of the *Memoir* the French delegation had presented to the International's first Congress held in Geneva in 1866. This was mainly a restatement of Proudhonist mutualist views, and far from containing any call to 'political action' came close to condemning strikes. The Government would have been willing to lift its ban if the French Internationalists had been willing to insert a few phrases in favour of the Emperor 'who had done so much for the working-classes'.[1] Tolain, Fribourg and the other French delegates had no desire to do this, as it would have been contrary to their notion of the working class working out its own salvation separately from the bourgeoisie. Also to have done so would have lost them most of their support, providing justification for the accusation that they were agents of the Emperor.

This same *ouvriériste* tendency was expressed in the first French edition of the rules of the International, which immediately marked the split between the Proudhonist French section and the Marxist General Council. The French interpreted the declaration that 'the economical emancipation of the working-classes is the great end to which every political movement must be subordinated' as support for their own preference for economic rather than political action. Marx of course was furious with the French for having omitted his qualifying phrase 'as a means', which was not included in the official version of the rules until the London Conference of 1871. But this moderate tendency in the French International and amongst the co-operative movement was soon forced into a greater involvement in politics. The Imperial police would not let the Internationalists peaceably pursue their own affairs, and in 1868 Tolain and the other founders of the International were arrested. The new leadership that took over was more politically orientated, but they too were almost at once arrested. The two trials of 1868 practically finished off the Paris section, and it was not until a year later that a third attempt was made to form a branch in Paris. This time Blanquists and revolution-aries were much better represented than before. Again the police prosecuted the leaders, on the eve of the outbreak of the war against Prussia.

The increasing willingness of the Internationalists to move away from the Proudhonist and *ouvriériste* notion of economic action corresponded to the renewal of political activity during the last two

[1] Reported by Murat at the First Trial of the International: *Procès*, op. cit., p. 74.

years of Napoleon's regime. The most pressing issue for the International was the outbreak of strikes, which following the mild recession of 1867–8 had become very numerous. These had no common origin apart from the working conditions and low wages, nor any clear ideology. This did not prevent the Government and police seeing everywhere in them 'the hand of the International'. In 1867 the International and workers' organizations supported the strike of the Paris bronze workers for higher wages and the right to organize their own Mutual Credit Society, which had some 5,000 members. The strikers eventually won a twenty-five per cent increase and the recognition of their society. Troops were sent in against strikers at Saint-Etienne and Aubin in June 1869, giving the movement its 'martyrs'.[1] Two of the Republican Deputies visited the wounded workers but the Parliamentary Opposition did not mount an attack on the Government, which instead decorated the captain who had given the order to fire. In January 1870 the mighty Schneider had to summon two infantry regiments and forty police to intimidate the striking steel workers of Le Creusot and in March this had to be increased to a brigade and two generals when the miners went on strike. This time the fiery republican Deputy Gambetta accused the Government of having used 'bayonets to support the employers' but was told by the Minister that this was necessary in order to defend 'order, property, freedom of work and respect for the law'.

As *Le Temps* noted on 8 June 1870, 'This movement is overwhelming us', with strikes at Le Mans, Albi, Saint-Etienne, Lyon, Marseille, Rouen, etc. On 13 April 1870, the leading left-wing paper, *La Marseillaise*, published a 'manifesto of the workers of Mulhouse' calling on their 'brothers' to march forward 'in a war on capital and for the emancipation of the workers'. Federations of regional workers' associations were formed in Marseille, Rouen, Lyon, and above all in Paris, where the federation linked up sixty workers' associations and had its headquarters in the same building as the International, Place de la Corderie. The Paris sections of the International tried to follow this example, but their federation was barely formed before the outbreak of the war. On 10 April 1870, the *procureur général* of Lyon reported that 'the firmness with which workers maintain their demands in spite of the misery caused by unemployment, which is barely relieved by any forms of assistance...

[1] As Chalain called them at the third trial of International, op. cit., p. 106.

is a sign of their strength and power. This the workers are perfectly
well aware of and it gives them a remarkable organization.' In the
end the war alone put an end to the movement, especially after the
overthrow of the Empire, and many workers enlisted and the troops
were withdrawn to fight the Prussians.

By 1870 the industrial action and various workers' movements of the
past ten years showed, as Proudhon had said a few years earlier, that
the working class had arrived on the political scene.[1] The existing
regime was strongly criticized, and the State was seen as the ally
of industrial capitalism against the worker. If this criticism was not
always clearly formulated, this had not prevented the development
of the beginnings of a working-class political consciousness and a
sense of differentiation from the rest of the nation. It was realized
that the 'fourth estate' had made its presence felt, had tested its
strength, and shown a sense of class unity in the mutual support
given to those on strike and to those arrested. But in spite of the
violence with which it was met and with which it denounced big
finance and factory production, such demands as were made were for
very moderate reforms. Even many of the Communards, when they
were allowed during the Third Republic to return from exile, found
that they were to the right of the socialist movement that had developed by the 1880s. And during the civil war of the Commune
some of the early leaders of the International, notably Tolain,
Fribourg and Murat, did not support Paris and afterwards became
radical rather than socialist Deputies.

The revolutionary tradition was maintained less at the Corderie,
where the Paris branch of the International had its offices, than by
the students and journalists who frequented the boulevard cafés,
such as the Brasserie on the corner of the rue Saint-Séverin and the
Boulevard Saint-Michel, whose patron had lost his school-teaching
job because of his republican sympathies. Memories of the Paris
'*journées*' were handed down from generation to generation. An early
member of the International and later opponent of the Commune,
Héligon, as a young apprentice had often heard of 'the uprisings of
1834, 1835, of the barricade of the rue Saint-Méry', with the result
that they all expected that their turn too would come to build barricades. 'Children,' said Héligon, 'are brought up hearing revolutions
glorified . . . boys who cannot work out their own pay, who do not

[1] In his last book, *On the Political Capacity of the Working Classes* (1864).

read any newspapers, rush out as soon as there is a disturbance in the street'.[1] Maxime Vuillaume with some of his Blanquist friends used to meet an old painter, Jules Vialle, in one of their favourite cafés, Chez Hoffmann, on the corner of the Boulevard Montparnasse and the Avenue de l'Observatoire. Vialle had fought in 1848 and would show visitors to his studio a bullet that had just missed him in the Royal Palace and which he had prised out of the doorpost where it had lodged.[2] The young student revolutionary Jules Vallès, when studying the history of 1848, was invited to dinner by père Gros, a rag-and-bone man. Over the soup in his garret on the rue Mouffetard Gros expressed his pleasure that 'educated men' such as Vallès were on 'the side of the proletarians', and made Vallès promise to join him on the barricades 'if ever it was necessary to go and find the rifle buried on the evening of 24 June behind the Gobelins'.[3] Workers sometimes joined the café groups, having often come across the revolutionary Auguste Blanqui or his followers during a term in prison.

Imprisonment had made 'the old one' into a legend, and De Tocqueville could only feel 'disgust and horror' when Blanqui appeared at the tribune of the National Assembly in May 1848. This 'strangely cold fanatical figure of savage grandeur', as Victor Hugo called him, invariably clad in black down to the gloves he always wore, had devoted himself to preparing for the Revolution. He had been a pupil of Buonarotti, who transmitted the doctrines of Gracchus Babeuf and his 'conspiracy of equals' of 1796 against the Directorate to groups of young men organized into secret societies calling themselves the 'Families' or the 'Seasons'. Blanqui's social and political ideas developed over his lifetime, especially after the failure of the 1848 Revolution. But he always retained an atmosphere of conspiracy, believing in the necessity for a dedicated minority to make a successful revolution. The Blanquists' revolutionary theory was based on the great 'days' of the first French Revolution. This was understood in terms of the events in Paris itself, for, as Blanqui wrote in November 1848, 'what would have become of French society without this initiative of Paris, which has always acted on

---

[1] *Enquête*, II, p. 544 (70 troops, 80 insurgents were killed in the two-day battle of June 1832 in the rue Saint-Méry).

[2] M. Vuillaume, *Mes Cahiers Rouges au temps de la Commune*, Cahiers de la Quinzaine, Paris, 1908–14, IV, pp. 75–6.        [3] J. Vallès, *L'Insurgé*, ch. 11.

its own authority without consulting anyone?'[1] By this he meant that on 14 July 1789, it had been the people of Paris whose action in taking the Bastille had set in motion the first stage of the French Revolution. It was the Paris crowd that had brought back the king from Versailles to Paris, and then on 10 August 1792 had invaded the Tuileries, leading to the trial and execution of the king. It was the Paris 'sections' gathered in the revolutionary Commune at the Hôtel de Ville in 1793 which had saved the Revolution from a moderate Assembly and from foreign invasion. This, at least, was the mythology that had been developed around the Revolution. Thus, for the Blanquists revolutionary action was centred on Paris, a conclusion that the 1848 Revolution seemed to bear out. The mistake on that occasion, according to Blanqui, had been the appeal from the Paris crowds to the provinces, that 'blind tribunal' of reactionary because unenlightened opinion. Instead there ought to have been a 'dictatorship of Paris'.

The *'enfermé'*, as Blanqui was often called because of his years behind prison walls, did not publish his views; ideology gave place to action – or at least to organizing for action. But Blanqui as revealed by his manuscripts did hold advanced socialist views, and most of his followers could be and usually were called communists in a fairly general sense. Although Blanqui did devote time to studying the economics of capitalism, he was too much of a voluntarist to believe in any notion of economic determinism and too deeply an atheist to accept any idea of providence or fate. The evils of society sprang out all around one, and the immemorial injustice and exploitation of man by man would only cease when the revolution put an end to all forms of slavery, completing finally the work begun by Spartacus. Existing society was divided by the class war between 'the bourgeoisie' and the '32 millions [the population of France as it then was] of proletarians, without property, or at least without any serious property, living only off the meagre product of their arms'.[2]

Blanqui himself came to prefer Hébert to Robespierre, whom he saw as the bloody agent of the bourgeoisie, thus marking his development from the Jacobin tradition. One of his followers, Gustave

---

[1] Blanqui MSS in B.N.: quoted in M. Dommanget, *Les Idées politiques et sociales d'Auguste Blanqui*, Paris, 1957, p. 177. This was Blanqui's equivalent to Marx's dictatorship of the proletariat.

[2] Letter to Maillard, June 1852: Dommanget, op. cit., p. 242.

Tridon, the son of a wealthy Burgundian landowner, sought to rescue what he called the *damnés de l'histoire*, and published in 1865 a series of articles on the *Hébertistes* in Vermorel's paper, the *Rive Gauche*, which otherwise was largely given to publishing news of the co-operative movement. Later in the year Tridon gathered his articles into a brochure, whose defence of the *bras nus*, the *enragés* of the Revolution, slowly won a wide circulation amongst the students and educated workers, as well as more respectable circles. Sainte-Beuve and the Goncourts debated its merits on one occasion.

Another Blanquist who studied Hébert was Raoul Rigault, the future head of police during the Commune. Rigault would spend hours watching the comings and goings at the Prefecture of Police and attending the political trials in order to discover the names of the informers. Then by going through the electoral register he found out their addresses, thus completing his dossiers. Both Tridon and Rigault studied the Hébertist newspaper, *Le Père Duchêne*, which was resuscitated during the Commune. Hébert was praised too for his atheism, in contrast to Robespierre's 'bourgeois metaphysics' (Blanqui), and for his attention to the question of educating the poor. Rigault gave lectures on Hébert's educational ideas at several public meetings in 1868, and atheism was one attribute that united workers, revolutionaries and more moderate republicans in a common opposition to the Church, which was so openly on the side of the status quo. The occasion of a civic burial (as opposed to a religious one) was a frequent meeting ground for students from the Latin Quarter and workers from the outer suburbs to meet and exchange addresses in a café afterwards.

By the late 1860s the Blanquists numbered possibly some 3,000 members, organized into companies of ten, who would assemble at selected street corners to be reviewed secretly by Blanqui (carrying as his 'safe conduct' a copy of *Le Pays* or *Le Constitutionnel*), or who would mingle, often armed, with crowds at any demonstration. They tried to spread their views and win recruits at all occasions. Some members, for example, joined the Paris branch of the International, and helped to give it a more revolutionary flavour. It was at a meeting at a café on the Boulevard Saint-Michel, the *Renaissance*, held to discuss the Blanquists' position with regard to the International, that in 1866 the police made their spectacular coup of arresting everyone assembled there. Of the forty-one so caught, there were fifteen workers, chiefly artisans, and a few traders, whilst the rest were students.[1] The Government press and the police did not discriminate between the Blanquists and the far more peaceful members of the International. Both alike were regarded as the surface agitators of those lower depths of French society, lurid descriptions of which were to be found in the pages of Eugène Sue, Victor Hugo and Balzac. In truth, however, the International did not take the lead of any of the strikes of the last years of the Empire, and none of the Blanquist attempts at insurrection came at all close to success. But although the major popular upheavals were on a scale that surpassed the Blanquists, they did represent the only organized revolutionary group and one that was in the front of all the movements during 1870–1.

The Blanquists were not the only partisans of revolution, simply the most determined. There was no common agreement in France on the results of the first Revolution. Louis-Philippe's chief minister in the 1840s, Guizot, had sadly regretted that whereas in England M.P.s had 'only committed themselves for or against the ministry; there is no question of changing institutions', this was not so in France. Here, until the bourgeoisie found a certain class unity in repressing the Commune, political differences expressed themselves as challenges to the political institutions themselves. Legitimists, claiming power and privilege for the *émigré* nobility that had returned with the Allies after the defeat of France in 1815, harked back to the Restoration, if not to the Ancien Regime itself. Those members of the bourgeoisie who had held power and benefited under the Monarchy of Louis-Philippe formed 'an intellectual and financial *élite*',[2] the Orleanists, that continued to hold important posts under the Second Empire, in spite of their professed opposition to Bonapartism. More complex than either of the two monarchist groups were the republicans. Republicanism meant accepting at least part of the work of the first Republic of 1792–4, though many moderate republicans rejected Robespierre and the 'Terror'. Republican ideas had been revived by middle-class students in opposition to the Restoration, and republicans had taken the initial role in both the 1830 and 1848 revolutions. But apart from opposing the monarchical regimes that governed France from 1815 to 1848 there was no unity about what a successful revolution should accomplish, for men of very different political and social persuasions called themselves republicans. One division between the radicals and the moderates

[1] Charles da Costa, *Les Blanquistes*, Paris, 1912, pp. 19–24.
[2] T. Zeldin, *Emile Ollivier*, Oxford, 1963, p. 156.

coincided, though with important exceptions, with a difference between the more ardent younger students and journalists and those whose revolutionary enthusiasm had declined with age. More fundamental was the problem of how far republicans were willing to go towards accepting the importance and urgency of the workers' demands. For the growth of a working class and its expression in the form of strikes and various co-operative movements had challenged the basic republican doctrine of the unity of the Third Estate against the other orders in society. This feudal language was giving way to a language of class in which the bourgeoisie were pitted against the proletarians, or workers. Already it was becoming common to refer to the French Revolution not as the victory of the whole *peuple*, but only of a section of it, the bourgeoisie. What the bourgeoisie had won in 1789 the working class still had to attain. The issue was how far would republicans be willing to go in meeting this new challenge to their ideals of equality and fraternity.

In the 1840s among the radical republicans were included both political revolutionaries such as the future Communard Charles Delescluze and socialist theorists such as Louis Blanc, whose book on the *Organization of Labour* represented the most advanced socialist position of that time and, as has been seen, had been read by the young Louis-Napoleon. The radicals formed societies to spread their ideas and plot revolution, whilst their spokesman in Parliament was that powerful orator, Ledru-Rollin. This group of radicals were exiled after the *coup d'état* and when they returned to France after the political amnesty of 1859 or on the fall of the Empire in 1870, though still to the left of the more moderate republicans, they were largely out of touch and sympathy with the labour movement as it had developed during the Second Empire. The more moderate republicans, who had not been tempted by socialist ideas, at first kept their distance from the new regime. Many lost their State teaching posts and had to rely on the few private colleges. But they continued to have a dominant influence on the rising generation of students and propagated their ideas to a wider public through the press, both in the provinces and the capital. In the 1857 elections, the first since those of 1852, the Republicans gained seven seats. This posed the problem of whether they would take the loyalty oath or resign. Two did resign, one died, one went over to the Government, but the three others decided to sit in the Parliament. Two more Republicans were added to this number in the subsequent by-elections, and these five, *les Cinq* as they were called, became the nucleus of the parliamentary Republican opposition. Of these three were to play important roles in the future. Emile Ollivier, a brilliant orator, had through the influence of his radical father been put in charge of the Marseille region after the 1848 Revolution. The son proved to be more conservative than his father, though not sufficiently so to enable him to keep this important post for long. Jules Favre, another eloquent lawyer who had briefly been a Minister after 1848, had made his reputation in Paris by his defence of Orsini, who had tried to blow up the Emperor's coach when it arrived at the Opera. Ernest Picard, wealthy and witty in an eighteenth-century sceptical manner, was typical of conservative republican circles.

In the next elections in 1863 the Republicans triumphed in Paris, winning eight out of the nine seats; the Orléanist Thiers gained the remaining seat for the opposition. Similar results occurred in the other major cities, and the 1869 elections were still more decisive. As a result the Emperor decided to move towards giving Parliament greater power, and the beginning of 1870 saw the brief attempt at a Liberal Empire, with Ollivier in effect as Prime Minister.

This growing electoral strength of the opposition groups was marked by a move away from the revolutionary ideology that had been so often evoked by the earlier more romantic republicans. In July 1847, for example, Lamartine had told his audience at a banquet celebrating the publication of his *History of the French Revolution* that 'my book required a conclusion: it is you who are making it'.[1] By the late 1860s such calls to revolution were seldom any longer heard from the ranks of the discontented middle classes. The senior Republicans, members of the original 'Five' such as Ollivier, Favre and

---

[1] D. Johnson, *Guizot: Aspects of French History 1787–1874*, London, 1963, p. 244. Cf. too the article of E. Caro, 'La Fin de la bohème', *Revue des Deux Mondes*, vol. 94, July 1871, pp. 262–3: 'We more or less know only two kinds of history: that of classical antiquity and that of the French Revolution. Everything else has been gradually forgotten; but these two groups of events and characters still excite and live in our imagination . . . The heroes of the ancient republics intermingle with those of our recent history; it is a sort of illustrious company that haunts our minds in choice attitudes, with sublime speeches about republican virtue, liberty and country. . . . Everything there is seen from the standpoint of immortality, illuminated by a light far too brilliant. It is a world somewhat overpraised, a little too declamatory, that does not resemble anything that ever really existed, a result of our classical education combined with legends based on that inexhaustible theme, the French Revolution.'

Picard, were ceasing to challenge the very basis of the regime and their policy in Parliament was to press for its liberalization rather than its overthrow. In this they were closer to some of the Orléanists, who likewise were reconsidering their dynastic preference, than to some of the younger members of their own party. Léon Gambetta, for example, or Jules Simon, an ex-professor of the Sorbonne who later became the first Minister of Education of the Third Republic, remained sceptical of the liberal intentions of what they regarded as an irrevocably authoritarian system. But one republican banker was not far wrong when he wrote to a friend that 'there will be few who have taken the oath who will be capable of remaining irreconcilable to the end . . . We shall see . . . if God gives life to the Empire, Picard after Ollivier, Jules Ferry after Picard, Gambetta after Jules Ferry.' Picard himself later claimed that the opposition Deputies in entering electoral politics had broken with 'the revolutionary school' and had become an 'extremely moderate' legal opposition.[1] In reality their position was that of Adolphe Thiers' 'Third Party', or as wits called it after the 1869 election, '*le Thiers parti*', a party of the centre. This stood for what Thiers had called 'the necessary freedoms', freedom of the Press, electoral freedom, and ministers responsible to an elected Assembly. Thiers, though officially the leader of the Orléanists in the Legislature, having been a Minister under Louis-Philippe, gave cautious support to Ollivier's Liberal Government, hoping that if it succeeded then, as the Duc de Broglie had said, 'one will have economized on a revolution'.[2] Thiers' position represented that of many *gens d'affaires*, who were not interested in the title of the regime, whether it be Liberal Empire, Orléanist or Republican (so long as this latter meant Thiers' later 'conservative Republic'), but wanted an order that would 'let them get on with their business affairs' in peace.[3]

Outside of the Legislative Body itself, a growing republican movement was making itself heard, aided by the lifting of some of the restrictions on political activity. Both in Paris and in the main provin-

---

[1] *Dépositions*, I, p. 473. For letter of the banker Cernuschi see J. Adam (Lamber), *Mes Sentiments et nos idées avant 1870*, Paris, 1905, p. 425: January 1870.

[2] Quoted by Thiers, *Dépositions*, I, p. 3.

[3] Letter of a French representative in New York of the Loire iron and steel industry to the sub-manager of the Crédit Lyonnais Bank: J. Bouvier, '*Des Banquiers devant l'actualité politique en 1870–71*', *Revue d'Histoire Moderne et Contemporaine*, 1958, pp. 138, 151.

cial centres there were demands for press, municipal and national electoral liberties. Anti-clericalism rather than any socialist doctrines gave a strident tone to this movement, which appealed to many lawyers, doctors, journalists, teachers and artisans. Bançel, deputy for Lyon in 1869, set out the typical republican view when he wrote in his electoral address that 'social problems can only be resolved through the free initiative of citizens, outside of any direction or support from the State'. He received the votes of the workmen who belonged to the co-operative movement, just as in Paris in 1864 the working-class districts elected the Republican Garnier-Pagès in preference to the bronze-worker Tolain and in 1869 the future leaders of the Government of National Defence, Gambetta, Picard, Favre and Jules Simon. The *ouvriériste* notion of abstention never found much support, the working class preferring to exercise their sacred right to vote by supporting the most extreme political opponents of the Empire. This 'tail' of republicanism, as Picard put it, sometimes swept along the parliamentary moderates, especially at election times. M. Frère, a Paris trader and admittedly a very conservative witness, was shocked by the speeches of Jules Simon during the 1869 election campaign, which Frère regarded as inciting the workers against their employers. Frère showed more perception when he said that he thought the parliamentary republicans were using the people as a 'step-ladder' to power.[1]

Another source of opposition to the Empire was the movement for municipal liberties. To the Jacobins the Commune meant Paris dictating the revolution to France. But to others the demand for greater Communal liberties meant the transfer of power to local authorities. As a liberal doctrine it went back to the Restoration Monarchy and was best expressed in Augustin Thierry's historical essays and by de Tocqueville's writings on the *Old Regime in France* and on *Democracy in America*, which extolled the merits of corporate and local liberties. De Tocqueville's writings had little immediate influence, though Edouard Laboulaye's *The State and its Limits* (1863) did directly take up de Tocqueville's arguments. Against the centralization of Napoleon III, who in this was following his uncle, demands arose for elected mayors, control over local budgets, freedom from subservience to Paris, for as Marx had said, 2 December had represented the victory of 'the executive power over the legislative power . . . the State had made itself completely independent'. Paris

[1] *Dépositions*, II, p. 261.

had lost its municipal council after the June revolt of 1848; Lyon shared this distinction of being with Paris the only city without an elected municipal council, though Marseille and other large cities feared that they might well become included in this number. In 1868 there was a three-day riot when the Government tried to suppress the local council in Toulouse.

In fighting for local liberties the republicans in one respect were simply trying to attain at the local level the political freedom they were unable to get at the national level. But there were also some supporters of a republic who ideologically preferred the countryside to Paris. Michelet in his little book *Le Peuple* (1846) had picked out the peasants as being the only representatives of the true spirit of France. The artistic and literary movement of 'realism' revived popular and rural traditions. Proudhon's 'peasant socialism' expressed a preference for small-scale production and a strong sentiment in favour of the land. Against the State with its wasteful bureaucracy and its extravagant wars, and against the European nationalists, he envisaged a federation of small communes and independent proprietors. The reduction of scale that could be expected from a federation, Proudhon thought, would increase men's liberty and restore a sense of value to their work. But among the working classes the Jacobin republican tradition was dominant, even amongst the self-styled anarchists. The leading follower of the exiled Russian anarchist Bakunin, Albert Richard of Lyon, admitted that in France 'the masses stubbornly rejected the spread of opinions so contrary to the old Jacobin or parliamentary tradition of French democracy. And as the heads of [Bakunin's] *Alliance* themselves were not very imbued with the doctrine, or rather the spirit of Bakunin, there was never, in spite of great efforts, complete understanding.' Richard himself was accused by Bakunin of 'remaining as much as ever a supporter of the centralized revolutionary State'.[1]

The provincial movement for decentralization was dominated rather for the most part by Legitimists, who saw in greater local autonomy a way for them to exercise the influence of their family position. This was developed into a general critique of the first Revolution as being responsible for the 'decadence' of France – a view developed later at great length by the historian Taine in re-

---

[1] A. Richard, *Revue de Paris*, September 1896: quoted by J. Rougerie, '*La Première Internationale à Lyon (1865–70)*', Istituto Giangiacomo Feltrinelli, *Annali*, 1961, pp. 143–4.

action to the events of the Commune. Ignoring de Tocqueville's evidence that it was the Monarchy that had first established the dominance of Paris, the Legitimists attacked the supremacy of Paris as Jacobin and anti-monarchical.[1] In 1865 a group of local landowners and politicians in the region around Nancy published a *Project on Decentralization*, and a conference of journalists was held at Lyon in September 1869. The Provençal poets around Frédéric Mistral represented an assertion of the values of ancient France against the cultural preponderance of Paris. Because of the aristocratic and monarchist sympathies of such writings not all republicans were willing to support the municipal movement, but Jules Favre, Jules Simon and Garnier-Pagès praised the Nancy document, and Jules Ferry defended the notion of local liberties at the Second International Congress of Peace at Lausanne in 1869. By this time the *Siècle*, the leading moderate republican paper, had come out in support and was petitioning the Senate in favour of local liberties. When Ollivier came to power in January 1870 he tried to placate this pressure by forming a 'Committee on Decentralization,' but the Cabinet rejected its most important recommendation, that mayors should cease to be Government nominees and instead be chosen by local elections. It is significant that the Republicans refused to change the nomination system when their turn came to be in power, and this became one of the points of the dispute at the time of the Commune.

In turn Paris scorned '*les ruraux*' who, led by their priests to the polls, gave Napoleon his plebiscitary majorities over republican Paris. It was the countryside that was held responsible for the overthrow of the Republic established in 1848. Paris resented also the loss of its elected municipal council, and this feeling was intensified by the dictatorial way in which Haussmann exercised his prefectorial powers. Haussmann saw the Emperor every day, and was made a Baron and a Senator to increase his prestige and domination over the nominated city council that was supposed to keep a check on the government of the capital. Paris, according to Haussmann, had no need for its own government as it was a city without any real inhabitants of its own. The population, in Haussmann's view, was

[1] The Monarchists tended to ignore Louis XIV and looked back to an ideal picture of Henry IV; cf. letter of the Comte de Chambord, 14 November 1862, quoted in L. M. Greenberg, 'The Commune of 1871 as a decentralist reaction', *Journal of Modern History*, September 1969, p. 305.

made up entirely of foreigners and immigrants from the provinces who needed simply 'a huge consumer market, an immense workshop, an arena for ambition, or simply a rendezvous for pleasure'. This view excluded the indigenous population which, as has been seen, was particularly strong in certain of the northern working-class districts. Amongst many members of the bourgeoisie Haussmann's high-handed approach simply created a favourable atmosphere for the idea of Communal liberties.

Both within and outside Paris, therefore, in opposition to the centralization and dictatorial rule of the Empire, there continued the old demand for municipal liberties. For the liberal middle classes this meant their gaining control over the affairs of the capital and of the major provincial centres such as Lyon, Marseille and Toulouse. After all, as Augustin Thierry's historical studies had sought to show in the period following the revolution of 1830, the bourgeoisie could claim to have first won its own political liberties in the medieval free city communes. Thierry had developed a history of the Third Estate in opposition to the Monarchist and aristocratic traditions, and had argued that 'the municipal revolutions of the twelfth century' were 'the source of the social order of modern times' and 'the cradle of our modern liberty'.[1] But the historical antecedents of the communal idea were not a single legacy, since there was also the tradition of the revolutionary Commune, established after the uprising of 10 August 1792, which had become the centralizing Jacobin Commune of Year II of the Revolution. This, together with the Convention's Committee of Public Safety eventually headed by Robespierre, had saved France from foreign invasion and the revolution from aristocratic reaction. Although in the end, as Blanqui, Tridon and the other latter-day *Hébertistes* had realized, Robespierre had crushed the social and political extremists of the capital and its Commune, the *enragés*, the *bras nus*, before in turn being overthrown preparing the way for the reaction of the Directory and Empire, '93 marked the high point of the popular movement. Commune could mean, therefore, both municipal franchises and revolutionary dictatorship; the autonomy of the bourgeoisie or the triumph of the

---

[1] A. Thierry, *Formation and Progress of the Tiers Etat in France*, Eng. trans. London, 1855, vol. 1, pp. 41–2; see too his *Narratives of the Merovingian Era* and *Historical Essays*, which were reprinted in France in 1868; cf. H. Lefebvre, *La Proclamation de la Commune*, Paris, 1965, p. 142; C. Rihs, *La Commune de Paris, sa structure et ses doctrines*, Geneva, 1955, pp. 179–84.

popular forces. Such disparate tendencies enabled the magic name of the Commune to become the obvious cry of Paris, just as it had been of the slate-quarrymen of Trelazé who had marched on Angers in 1855 demanding the Commune,[1] and of the popular classes in Le Creusot, Lyon, Marseille, Toulouse and other large French cities on the news of the fall of the Second Empire.

[1] Duveau, op. cit., p. 543.

# Chapter 2

# WAR AND THE FALL OF AN EMPIRE

The year 1868 marked the beginning of the two years of crisis that resulted in the downfall of the regime. This was the year of the liberalization of the Press and of the law making public meetings legal again so long as they avoided politics, a measure that was meant to help the co-operative movement by allowing public discussion of 'social' and 'economic' matters. In the first issue of the *Lanterne* (which was to pillory Napoleon III's declining Empire) Rochefort defined France as having 'thirty-six million subjects, not counting the subjects of discontent'. The bourgeoisie showed its dissatisfaction by withdrawing its confidence: savings increased as investors hoarded their money rather than risk it in speculating on the unclear future of the regime – *la grève du milliard*. Conservatives again raised their voices against the Saint-Simonian expansionist financial policies of the Government, and the recession of 1867–8, though relatively mild, gave strength to their arguments against the Emperor's free-trade and public works' policies. This same year one of the bastions of Imperial financing, the Crédit Mobilier, went out of business. This had been created in the optimism at the beginning of the regime to meet the new demand for credit. And even Haussmann was running into difficulties. The parliamentary Opposition had at last begun to discover details of Haussmann's schemes, which, though not as corrupt as was rumoured, had increasingly been forced to rely on barely legal methods. He had side-stepped the statutory powers of control of the Legislative Body and relied on outside banks (mainly the Crédit Foncier, which of course had profited greatly from the loans. Certainly the total expenditures resulting from Haussmann's office were immense, amounting to almost fifty times the normal annual expenditure of the city. The republican Deputy Jules Ferry published in 1868 his *Fantastic Accounts of Haussmann*; a pun on the *Contes fantastiques d'Hoffmann*, which Offenbach had yet to make popular as operettas. Although by no means accurate, the book was a best-seller. Haussmann eventually and reluctantly had to agree to submit to proper parliamentary accounting controls, and the effect of his difficulties was to slow down the building industry in Paris. In 1861 the English economist Nassau Senior had reported that 'a week's interruption of the building trade would terrify the Government'.[1] What now occurred was aggravated by the fact that Haussmann's operations had encouraged immigration of building workers into Paris, whereas previously Government public works projects had been on a scale limited simply to taking up unemployment.

In this same year the second (the first was in 1866) of Eugène Ténot's histories of the *coup d'état* of 1851 was published, Ténot being an editor on *Le Siècle*.[2] This revived memories of the massacres that had inaugurated the Second Empire and showed up the bloody nature of what by means of censorship had been presented as 'the deliverance of 1851'. Charles Delescluze, one of the radical republicans of 1848 returned from exile, opened up in his paper, *Le Réveil*, a subscription for a monument to the Deputy Baudin, who had been killed on the barricades of 1851. Demonstrations were held at his tomb, and when the Government arrested Delescluze, Gambetta made his name as Delescluze's counsel by a brilliant and powerful indictment of the Government. The Government found to its own cost that there was growing up a new electorate that had not known the fears of 1848.

The public meetings permitted by the legislation of 1868 started a period of continuous public discussion in Paris that went on until the fall of the Commune. At first liberal classical economists and mutualists put forward their suggestions for the 'solution of the social problem'. 'Mutualists' such as Vermorel, Tolain and Langlois presented the ideas of Proudhon. An old Babeuvist cobbler, Gaillard, spoke of the Spartacist revolt. Blanquists too were among the public speakers and before long the meetings had been taken over by the revolutionaries and their venue moved from the middle-class Vauxhall to the halls in the working-class areas. After the Commune,

[1] Nassau Senior, *Conversations with distinguished persons*, London, 1880, p. 193.
[2] Cf. Marx's letter to Kugelmann of 3 March 1869, in which referring to Tenot's two books he says 'a very interesting movement is going on in France. The Parisians are making a regular study of their recent revolutionary past, in order to prepare themselves for the business of the impending new revolution.'

one police Commissioner described them as 'a permanent attack on religion, property and the family', and another said all the theories later found in the Commune were aired in these meetings.[1] Marx thought it worthwhile to visit Paris in July 1869. So far as the police were concerned, and probably with reason, workers' strike associations, mutual-help societies, public meetings and even the International by now were all alike uniting political and social demands in a common attack on the Empire. The police tried to break up the meetings, and overcame the frustration of having to force their way in along narrow passages in un-Haussmannized buildings by 'mounting an assault from the windows'.[2] But the Press and Deputies forced the police to abandon their attacks, and the meetings flourished more vigorously than ever. Those who were arrested seem to have remained indifferent to police Commissioner Mouton's lectures that they should not be full of hatred for society but take inspiration from the 'fact' that many 'simple workers' had worked their way up to becoming 'millionaires'.

In the spring of 1869, the first comparatively free elections were held since the establishment of the Empire. The weakening of the Government's confidence in the face of pressure from moderate opinion was shown by the widespread abandonment of the term 'official candidate', which in the past had been the way to victory. One Prefect suggested to his candidate the title 'candidate of the Government' and then had second thoughts that this also might be too strong and telegrammed: 'Liberal Conservative Candidate'.[3] The result of the elections showed how far the Government's popularity had fallen. The Opposition increased its votes by 1½ million over the last election of 1863 to 3,258,777 and the Government vote dropped to 4,477,720, which would be a sizeable majority under a modern two-party system, but elections in the Second Empire were a vote of confidence in the regime itself. All the major cities, including Paris, voted for the Opposition by large majorities. In Paris the Government received only 77,000 votes to the Opposition's 234,000. Clearly the Empire could not resist moving towards a parliamentary system of government, and in January 1870 Ollivier formed his own Cabinet (instead of having the posts nominated by the Emperor) except for War and the Navy, the Emperor consider-

---

[1] *Dépositions*, II, p. 177; *Enquête*, II, p. 227.
[2] *Enquête*, II, p. 228 (Commissioner Mouton).
[3] T. Zelden, *The Political System of Napoleon III*, London, 1958, p. 137.

ing himself still personally responsible for National Defence. One of the first to suffer from the new order of things was Haussmann, whose dismissal order, since he refused to resign, Napoleon signed with tears in his eyes (so Napoleon said). Although there was still a republican Opposition, Thiers, who was not a man to allow his dynastic preferences to outweigh his political empiricism, supported the new Government in the Chambre, and republicans such as Ferry, Favre and Picard were willing to give the Government a chance. The bourgeoisie breathed a sigh of relief, which was registered by a rise on the Bourse.

In Paris the election campaign of 1869 gave full opportunity for opinion in the popular districts of Paris to express its hostility to the Empire. Several public meetings considered putting up their own candidates. Jules Vallès, a future member of the Commune, for example, was chosen as the 'revolutionary socialist democratic' candidate against Jules Simon by a meeting in the Faubourg Saint-Antoine.[1] The conservative paper *Le Pays* quoted the claims of a blacksmith named Harvey to show that 'everywhere you will find the bourgeoisie in combat against the workers; the working class must have its own representatives'.[2] But generally class lines were not drawn in this *ouvriériste* fashion. The most politically radical electoral district was the first circumscription of the 17th to 20th arrondissements. Here in the first round most of the public meetings adopted the arch-republican Gambetta as their candidate, in preference to the mutualist worker Henry. Gambetta was popular because of his defence of Delescluze and because of his attacks on the Empire, whereas Henry was considered tainted with Napoleon's 'social Caesarism' as he had been a member of the Workers' Delegation to the Universal Exhibition of 1867. Gambetta was an out-and-out republican, refusing all notions of a parliamentary alliance between the republican and Orléanist opposition parties. But Gambetta considered that social questions were secondary to political ones, since the problem was that of political liberty, after which a solution would be found to social issues. Nor was he in favour of revolutionary methods to topple the regime he so strongly disliked. This election of Gambetta showed the strength of Jacobin sentiment in this solidly working-class district of Paris. It also showed how closely the idea of social reform was linked with political opposition to the Empire. It was Napoleon III who personified the rule of the privileged, and

[1] *L'Insurgé*, ch. 12.                              [2] 21 February 1869.

gave them the protection of his police and army, at least the professional soldiers. The Empire too was the ally of the Church. Thus the recurrent demands of working-class Paris were for the separation of Church and State, together with the establishment of a public system of non-religious education, the abolition of the Paris Prefecture of Police, and an end to a permanent standing army.

The campaign of 1869 in effect opened the eyes of the republican party, with its revolutionary rhetoric but conservative social basis. Jules Ferry later pointed to this period as marking the development of an extremist republican movement that 'dreamed only of demonstrations modelled on the first Revolution' and which followed the promptings of certain newspapers and public meetings. Such men, said Ferry, were 'a perpetual torment'[1] to the parliamentary republicans. Gambetta was not alone among the republican Deputies elected by Paris who preferred to take up a quieter seat than that provided by the capital. The Government hoped that this reappearance of the 'red spectre' would frighten many liberal bourgeois back into its fold. In turn Republicans like Jules Simon were worried that if the Government remained adamant in refusing any political reform a 'fine opportunity of gaining liberty and guaranteeing order' would be lost, and the revolutionaries would be presented with a turbulent Paris.[2] The by-election of November 1869 only increased the fears of the moderate republicans. Gambetta's seat was filled by Rochefort, the bitterest journalistic opponent of the Empire. His Bonapartist preference, he had once written, was for the peaceful and economical reign of Napoleon II! Rochefort's election was assured when the police arrested him as he crossed the frontier as the cry then was 'to vote for Rochefort because the Government doesn't want him'. This election was followed by the founding of a newspaper to represent what was already being called the 'socialist party'. The mutualist journalist Vermorel, for instance, published a book of this title in 1870. The *Marseillaise*, as the paper was called, became the organ for the workers' societies and in particular for the International, though its editorial board had been chosen at a public meeting in La Villette and included a number of Blanquists. At the beginning of 1870 the bookbinder Eugène Varlin felt able to write to a fellow

---

[1] *Dépositions*, I, p. 382.
[2] I. Tchernoff, *Le Parti républicain au coup d'état et sous le Second Empire*, Paris, 1906, pp. 561–2.

Internationalist, the printer Emile Aubry in Rouen, that 'feeling is mounting and the revolution is advancing.'[1]

The Emperor, in face of this mounting opposition, decided to re-affirm his own position and thus the future of his line by agreeing to the holding of a plebiscite on the 'liberal reforms' carried out since 1860. The result, in contrast to the elections of the previous year, was a massive majority – 7.3 million yes's, not far short of the majority of the first plebiscite establishing the Empire in 1852. Because the plebiscite was really asking two questions at the same time this majority included many who held opposing views. But it could easily be taken to show that the desire for change as shown by the elections did not mean the country rejected the regime itself. For the Opposition the result, as Thiers said, was 'discouraging'; downright fatal according to Jules Ferry because it restored the confidence of the conservative Bonapartists who now sought to overthrow Ollivier and his more liberal regime. But it had still been the countryside that had given the Emperor his majority; Paris had voted no. Only in the more predominantly bourgeois arrondissements had there been a substantial proportion though still not a majority in favour of the Empire. In the north and north-east seventy-two to seventy-seven per cent of the vote had been against the Emperor, and to a slightly lesser degree the same was true for the revolutionary faubourgs on the Left Bank and the district around the Bastille. Even Schneider could not prevent his workers in Le Creusot from voting three to one against his Emperor.

The International had published a Manifesto against the plebiscite calling for abstention and reminding the workers of the different treatment meted out to the Le Creusot strikers in the courts at Autun and to the Emperor's cousin in the court at Tours. This latter was a reference to an incident that had marred the beginning of the new Liberal ministry. The Emperor's youngest cousin, Prince Pierre Bonaparte, who had never been very popular at the Court, had shot and killed Victor Noir, a journalist on the staff of Rochefort's *Marseillaise*. Noir had gone to visit the Prince as a second of a fellow journalist on the same paper, Paschal Grousset, of whom more will be heard later, in order to arrange a duel. Rochefort naturally enough took up the affair both as editor of the offending paper and in his new role as Deputy for the first circumscription of Paris.

[1] 19 January 1870: quoted in Bruhat, J., Dautry, J., and Tersen, E., *La Commune de 1871*, Paris, 1960, pp. 51–2.

Particular exception was taken to the law of 1852, which decreed that only a special court could try a member of the Imperial family. This court in the end simply imposed a fine of 20,000 francs. Rochefort did not hesitate to compare the murder to that of the mass-murderer Troppmann, whose crimes had been followed with morbid fascination by the Paris population until finally he was tracked down by the police. That winter of 1868-9 cartoons were openly sold on the streets depicting the 'Imperial Troppmann', a reference this time to the head of State himself. In the Legislature Ollivier warned Rochefort and through him the outside opposition that 'we are moderation, we are liberty, and if you so compel us, we will be force'.

The funeral of Victor Noir on 11 January in driving rain united 100,000 Parisians in the biggest demonstration that occurred during the Second Empire. The Blanquists, some 2,000 of them, all armed, wanted to lead the crowd down the Champs-Elysées and across Paris to the cemetery of Père Lachaise, and even tried to turn the horses of the funeral bier that way. But Delescluze and Rochefort (before he collapsed on top of the hearse exhausted and faint from hunger) persuaded the crowd to go to the cemetery at Neuilly. Fortunately so, for troops were ready to fire on the crowd if they had tried to attack the Hôtel de Ville or the Tuileries Palace. Rochefort declared at the funeral that 'we are no longer ruled by Bonapartes, but by the Borgia'. The police retaliated shortly afterwards by picking up Rochefort right in the middle of his own constituency at the Hall of the Marseillaise in La Villette. And as an additional measure to try to stem this mounting agitation the council of the International was arrested for a third time. At the trial, one member of the accused, the jeweller Combault, shouted out 'we want the social revolution and all that follows'.[1]

The political ferment, the strikes throughout the industrial regions of France, and the economic recession brought about a crisis that reflected upon the whole future of the Imperial regime. The seeming consolidation of the Liberal Empire by the 1870 plebiscite could not cover up the dissension within the Court itself. The Emperor was very ill, suffering from bad attacks of the stone, which finally killed him in 1873. The orthodox authoritarian Bonapartists, the Arcadians as they were called, who were centred around the 'legitimist' Empress, as Napoleon III quipped, disliked Ollivier and the concessions made to Parliament. Their answer to the question that was increasingly

[1] Quoted in L. Michel, *La Commune*, Paris, 1898, p. 21.

on everyone's lips as to what would follow Napoleon III was a regency under the Empress. This prospect was viewed with great distaste by the majority of Frenchmen, who had never taken to their Spanish-born Empress. The Arcadians thought that the way back to power lay in restoring France's international prestige. Internal liberties could then be exchanged for the glory of a victorious war. The enemy ever since Sadowa had been marked out as Prussia. In Prussia itself it was now being more openly said that the defeat of Jena at the hands of the first Napoleon had to be revenged, and Moltke had advocated an immediate war against France following the defeat of Austria in 1866. Napoleon III in turn had demanded compensation on the Rhine for Prussian acquisitions from Austria, as these had changed the balance of power in Europe. But Bismarck rebuffed Napoleon suggesting Belgium instead, which England would not have allowed. The situation in France was hardly improved when in 1867 the attempt at establishing French control in Mexico finally had to abandoned. The French expeditionary troops were withdrawn and Napoleon's protégé, the Emperor Maximilian, was shot by the victorious Mexicans.

The crisis between France and Prussia came to a head in the summer of 1870, giving both the Right at the French court and Bismarck the opportunity for war. At the beginning of July the news hit Paris that the vacant Spanish throne had been offered to a Hohenzollern prince. At once the Press and the Government put this down to Bismarck's intrigues, though in fact he had not originated the proposal. Ollivier's ministry, until then more intent upon domestic reform than foreign affairs, afraid that it would be overthrown if it did not react strongly, protested to Prussia. Ollivier and his Foreign Minister backed this up by patriotically declaring in the Legislature that if France's protests were not heeded then 'we shall know how to fulfil our duty without hesitation and without weakness'. At first it seemed as if this sudden firmness on France's part had paid off, for shortly after the King of Prussia had received the French ambassador, Benedetti, Prince Leopold von Hohenzollern's candidacy was withdrawn. But now the Empire overplayed its hand by trying to turn this victory into an assertion of France's diplomatic supremacy in Europe. Again as a result of pressure from the Right surrounding the Empress, though political opinion in the form of the main papers and the Legislature also probably favoured some further action, Benedetti was instructed by his Foreign

Ministry to get an assurance from the King of Prussia that 'he would never again authorize this candidacy'. To have done this would have implied that Prussia had behaved improperly in the first place. The King of Prussia left it to Bismarck's discretion as to whether news of this second interview should be made public or not. This was Bismarck's chance, and he published the news in such a way that by abbreviating the conversations he made it appear that the Prussian King had rebuffed the French ambassador. This was the famous Ems telegram. When a frenzied Paris received the news of this supposed snub of the French ambassador Ollivier had no choice but to declare war with, as he foolishly put it, 'a light heart'. This he instantly qualified as meaning 'a confident heart'; but the phrase stuck to hound him for the rest of his long life. War, as *Le Pays* said on 13 July, was necessary in order to clear the path for Napoleon IV.

The Emperor probably alone amongst his ministers knew the political and military seriousness of declaring war. The army, for all its legendary dash and élan, was ill-equipped, untrained and lacking in generals capable of organizing a European campaign. The earlier glamorous victories in Algeria were to be paid for now. The Emperor had been so worried by the state of the army that he had forced a series of reforms through a reluctant Legislature, but these, insufficient in any case, had hardly begun to be carried out by the summer of 1870. There were no firm alliances with Austria or Italy, who had so far only promised neutrality. It would have needed a few quick victories to decide them to enter in on the side of France. The Government tried to sample public opinion on the war, and the reports of the *procureurs généraux* and the Prefects could be taken as indicating that there was support for a war against Prussia.[1] But there was little reason to believe that the peasants wanted to be dragged away from their land and it was they who provided the main body of the infantry, the rich being always able to buy their way out of a 'bad number', whilst the town workers often were too

---

[1] L. M. Case, *French Opinion on War and Diplomacy during the Second Empire*, Philadelphia, 1954, pp. 250–62. But St Marc-Girardin, the President of the Commission of Inquiry, *Dépositions*, I, p. 252, who had seen these reports, doubted that opinion was all that favourable, especially in the countryside. George Sand wrote from Nohant on 13 August that the peasantry did not want a war. E. Ranc, a republican opponent of the Empire, *Souvenirs-Correspondance*, Paris, 1913, p. 146, argued that in voting for the Empire in the plebiscite the peasants thought they were voting for peace.

unfit to pass the medical. In the Legislature, Thiers and a few republicans, including Favre and Gambetta, questioned the wisdom of the war. They did not accept the justification of the *casus belli* and wanted to await the arrival of an explanation from Benedetti, the French ambassador concerned. As Favre said, 'the French nation does not know why it is being sent to die'. This did not prevent large crowds cheering the troops off from Paris, though the Emperor departed straight for the front from his chateau outside Paris. The Opposition said he dared not test his popularity by a journey across Paris; Ollivier, more rightly, that he was too ill to do so. General Jules Trochu, the future Governor of Paris, who had pointed out the faults of the army in a book in 1867, wrote down his testament to the effect that the French would be easily defeated.

Vocal working-class and republican opinion expressed its anti-war sentiment. Louis Blanc condemned the Government for attempting to rouse the chauvinism of the population to support a war that was undertaken, according to Blanc, by a despot to cover up the faults of his own regime.[1] In the same paper, Félix Pyat, a popular journalist and future Communard, blamed the likelihood of war on the despotic nature of the Empire, with its huge regular army cut off from the people. The *Rappel* also argued that a war against Prussia would only intensify Prussia's hold over the rest of Germany.

At the outbreak of the war, the Government suspended the *Marseillaise* because it had so consistently opposed the Government's policy towards Prussia. And in its last number that appeared under the Empire, the paper gave a report from Lyon of how a crowd crying 'Long Live Peace!' had been repulsed by the troops.[2] Nor did the threat of war put a stop to all working-class agitation. There were strikes in Colmar, Marseille and Saint-Etienne, and the striking Paris ironmoulders appealed to the International for help. Their appeal to 'all the workers in France and abroad' was published in the *Rappel*, which also announced that 105 francs had been sent to them by workers in Hamburg. The paper took this as evidence that the war was not preventing the workers from continuing the struggle for their own betterment.[3]

At the beginning of July, the French Internationalists published

[1] *Le Rappel*, 14 July 1870.   [2] 25 July.
[3] 26 July. The British Amalgamated Society of Engineers sent £264 to the Parisians, and the Ironfounders £25, with apologies for the smallness of the sum: H. Collins and C. Abramsky, *Karl Marx and the British Labour Movement*,

an appeal to the workers of all countries, which protested against the threat of war. This concluded by affirming the desire of the French people for peace, and called on the German workers to resist all attempts to provoke them into supporting a war against France. It had some 180 signatures, including those of Tolain, Malon and Eugène Pottier, who was to commemorate the Commune in the words of the 'Internationale', written during the week after its final defeat. This address received the support of eighty workers from Neuilly-sur-Seine condemning the war as neither just nor in the national interest. It was simply dynastic. The Berlin branch of the International replied supporting the appeal of the French.

If these manifestoes are taken as showing that the International maintained its anti-war principles at the outbreak of the Franco-Prussian war, it did so only by protests; the resolution of the Brussels International Congress of the previous year in favour of a general strike was never mentioned in the summer of 1870. There was no call to action, and even the protests showed little hope that the workers would be able to do anything very effective to prevent a war. The Brunswick declaration against the war could say only that 'With deep sorrow and grief we are forced to undergo a defensive war as an unavoidable evil.' In France, the Paris branch of the International had been disorganized by the trials of June and July, which had condemned thirty-eight of its members to prison, and the Government had also arrested at the same time seventy-two Blanquists. There was, therefore, little danger of a revolt against the war, although there were some popular demonstrations. The *Rappel*, for example, reported that when attempts were made to rouse chauvinistic feelings among the population of Belleville, the crowd replied only with shouts of 'Long Live Peace!', and the police then had no choice but to break up the crowd.[1] Another peace demonstration was broken up by the police when it reached the Boulevard Montmartre. Arthur Ranc, a left-wing republican, said that these demonstrations were meant to show that Napoleon was not being pushed into war by popular opinion and, therefore, that the responsibility for such a calamity was the Emperor's alone.[2] If Ranc

---

London, 1965, p. 172. One of the French delegates sent to collect these sums was Emile Duval, future member of the Commune: *Dictionnaire*, V, p. 448.

[1] 17 July.

[2] Ranc, op. cit., pp. 146–7; see too J. Claretie, *Histoire de la Révolution de 1870-71*, Paris, 1872, vol. 1, p. 116.

was right, then protest meant dissociation from responsibility – such was the debilitating effect of nearly twenty years of dictatorship. But little could be expected of the ill-organized and still numerically small French working class of 1870, whose chauvinism in any case was easily aroused, and in 1914 the much more powerful C.G.T. felt that it would not have received much support if it had tried to oppose that war.

Such hostility as was expressed to the prospect of war soon disappeared before its actuality, and from the latter part of July and into August Paris was gripped by the excitement of expected victory, for it was inconceivable that the French armies could be defeated. The 'Marseillaise', which had been forbidden previously because it was a republican song, was sung again in public. The first occasion was at the Opera, when the audience rose to demand it in the middle of a performance. Maps were bought – but only of Germany, across which imaginary French victorious advances on Berlin were plotted. Similarly the maps given to the troops were of Germany and not of Eastern France. Any officer who went and asked for a map of Alsace-Lorraine was given such looks as to soon make him feel ashamed. Railway companies were taking bookings to Berlin to see the French Emperor's triumphal victory. In cafés people made rendezvous for a month ahead – in Hamburg and other German cities. So impatient was popular opinion for success that on Sunday, 6 August, a crowd outside the Bourse celebrated with shouts and flags the news of a supposed victory, and seeing a popular singer from the Opera in her coach called on her to lead them in the 'Marseillaise'.

This enthusiasm over the war extended to all sections of the population. The *Rappel* reported on 19 July that the war had disorganized the strikes at Mulhouse and that the workers preferred to join the army because it promised them better conditions than if they went back to work. The *procureur général* for that region reported on 21 July that the war had reunited the various parties and classes 'in a single patriotic enthusiasm'.[1] Republican papers like the *Rappel* and the *Reveil* were soon caught up in this popular chauvinism. An editorial in the *Rappel* on 23 July warned the German Emperor not to expect that 'the legitimate resentment of the French democrats against the Imperial Government will profit the foreigner . . . before the enemy the republicans have for the present

[1] Cour de Colmar, 21 July (A.N.: BB/30,390).

only one thought: our country'. Delescluze, who had earlier condemned the prospect of war, allowed his Jacobin patriotism to overcome his hatred of the Empire. The radical democrats, he wrote in
the *Reveil* on 20 July, would never abandon 'the home of European
liberty to M. de Bismarck'.[1] The socialist ex-school teacher, Gustave
Lefrançais, afterwards blamed the republicans for being swept away
by their patriotic feelings and for accusing those socialists who
opposed the war of having sold out to the Prussians.[2] Arthur
Arnould, later to be both a member and an historian of the Commune, also witnessed to the strength of this patriotic feeling when
he regretted that the war had put an end to the social movement.
'Yesterday,' he wrote, 'there was in face of one another a people
longing for liberty and a Government greedy for power . . . Today,
there is only a general who leads his army to combat, and a crowd
that thinks only of the safety of the country.'[3] Jules Vallès described
how the opposition to the war on the part of some socialists and
revolutionaries met with hardly any support from the population at
large. A crowd broke Thiers' windows, and Vallès was almost
mobbed when he opposed the cries of 'To Berlin! To Berlin!' Only
his reputation as a revolutionary and a friend of the people saved
him from being badly manhandled.

But no news came of dashing French advances, and instead in
early August there came reports of the first defeats. The Government could not prevent the recalling of the Legislature, which immediately ousted Ollivier, and the Empress appointed General de
Montauban, Comte de Palikao (who had gained his title as a result
of a victorious campaign in China), as President of the Council and
Minister of War. The workers knew Palikao as a general who had
been praised for his command of troops against strikers. The Empress then summoned Napoleon to make Bazaine Commander-in-
Chief and leave for the front, although he was too ill to command.
Napoleon set off to Châlons where MacMahon was with the Second
French army. In effect this was his abdication, for he was neither
Commander-in-Chief on the front nor ruling from the Palace at home.

[1] Cf. too issues of 28 July, 1, 5 August. Marx described Delescluze's attitude
as 'the most complete expression of chauvinism because France alone is the
home of ideas': Marx to Engels, 20 July. See too M. Dessal, *Un Révolutionnaire
jacobin: Charles Delescluze*, Paris, 1952, pp. 275–6.
[2] G. Lefrançais, *Etude sur le mouvement communaliste à Paris*, Neuchâtel, 1871,
pp. 27–9.                                    [3] *La Marseillaise*, 24 July.

In Paris the truce between the republican Opposition and the Government that had been established by Ollivier was now góne. The Opposition had been willing to grant the new Government a chance to prove itself. But the absence of the Emperor, the news of French losses and the appointment of Palikao convinced republicans that the Empire was leading the country to the brink of an abyss. Picard, looking back, said that 'it was evident to all serious observers that there were going to be some grave events'.[1]

Sharing this view was General Trochu. Trochu, fifty-five years old in 1870, was one of the best French generals, having been with the great Bugeaud in Algeria. But instead of becoming a marshal, he remained a general of a division. He refused the mission to China that won Palikao his title, and a certain Catholic pessimism (he was fond of referring to his 'old Breton faith' and 'pessimistic' philosophy), together with his monarchist preferences, had resulted in his being left out of the promotions in the Imperial Army. But now he was becoming clearly the man of the hour. As a conservative military figure, not closely personally attached to the regime, he came to represent an alternative figure of authority. Even the Empress had to admit this, and offered him the Ministry of War in the new Government. He refused, Palikao again having to take Trochu's place, and instead Trochu went off to join MacMahon at Châlons.

The day after his arrival Napoleon came to the camp, along with Prince Jérôme Napoleon. Neither Napoleon nor MacMahon knew what to do, and Trochu was able to convince them of the soundness of his plan, which was directly opposite to that of Palikao at the Ministry of War. Trochu argued that the system of fortifications surrounding Paris could only be effective if used as a base for an army operating in front of the city. This had been the military plan behind the building of the fortifications some twenty-five years ago. In this way, Trochu suggested, the Second Empire could avoid the disaster of the First. Paris would not fall and an armistice could be negotiated with the enemy. Trochu's pessimism rightly judged that Bazaine would not be able to break out of the 'circle of steel', as Thiers called it, that Moltke had thrown round the first French army at Metz.

Trochu was then appointed by the Emperor as Governor of Paris, to which he repaired, taking with him the 15,000 Parisian *gardes mobiles*, whose indiscipline was notorious. It was precisely because

[1] *Dépositions*, I, p. 473.

of their indiscipline that the Government had sent them away from Paris, fearing for its own safety if they stayed. Sinister stories about their conduct had filtered back to Paris of how, for example, whenever a group of them passed the sumptuous tent awaiting the Emperor, to the shout of 'Long Live the Emperor!' would come the reply 'One, two, three, *Merde!*' Trochu's arrival back in the capital caused consternation at the Court. His appointment as Governor of Paris was taken as a direct challenge to Palikao's supremacy at the Ministry of War; his bringing back of the *gardes mobiles* against Palikao's wishes was seen as his own 'praetorian guard' in case the Government resisted his appointment. Meanwhile, as extra forces of order 'to hold in check the political passions'[1] the Government summoned firemen and *gardes mobiles* from the provinces, and Trochu published a decree expelling 'anyone who had no visible means of support, whose presence in Paris would constitute a danger to public order'.

Following Trochu's arrival there came the news that the Emperor himself was going to return to Paris. The Empress and Palikao at once told him not to, fearing there would be a revolt in Paris if the Emperor returned unvictorious. The Government was relying totally on the 'glorious' Bazaine (as he was known after the Mexican expedition), and the ex-Prime Minister Rouher was sent to back up the Council's decision. MacMahon also received news from Bazaine, now his Commander-in-Chief, that he was going to move north and so MacMahon could satisfy his military conscience and please the Government by 'flying' towards Bazaine.

The lines therefore were drawn. On the one side was the Empress, and her Ministers seeking to conserve the future of Bonapartism. Their only hope lay in a victory over the Prussians and the triumphal return of both armies under Bazaine. On the other side was the parliamentary Opposition. They were not able to judge the situation accurately, and they could hardly wish for a military disaster when the Paris population, especially the Bellevillois, were expecting great news as a result of what *The Times* had called 'the imminence of some great movements'.[2] But they had not wanted the war, fearing that victory would bring back the worst of Bonapartism, and had supported Trochu's plan over that of the Government. What now united them to Trochu was the common fear that the regime would

[1] Baron Jérôme David, *Dépositions*, I, p. 161.
[2] 23 August.

be brought down by a revolution and not by the gradual process of parliamentary reform. Both Government and Opposition knew the danger of a revolution in Paris. Both wanted to avoid it, the Government by sending the army off to a glorious victory, the Opposition by bringing it back to the walls of Paris. As the President of the Chambre, Schneider, told Jules Favre, the Government thought that only they could save France, whereas, as Favre said, the Opposition was convinced the Government was in the midst of losing it. The Opposition's aim, therefore, according to Favre was 'to prevent the Emperor from preserving his command and to prevent a revolution from breaking out'.[1] The danger of this latter occurring had been increased by the news of the reverses of the French army, opening up the prospect of invasion. For this turned the war into a war for France's national independence instead of a dynastic war of conquest, and the symbol of the successful defence of France against invasion was the Republic and the Commune. Louise Michel, soon to be a leading woman revolutionary in the Commune, says that those who had earlier shouted for peace were now roused up at the prospect of invasion.[2] The successful light dramatist Ludovic Halévy, who had at one time helped Morny in his literary efforts, reported hearing a group of workers saying 'it would be with the Republic that they would march against the enemy'.[3]

The day of Ollivier's replacement by Palikao, 9 August, a large crowd had assembled on the Place de la Concorde demanding the abdication of the Emperor and the arming of the population. But the crowd was not armed and the police were able to disperse it easily. A delegation from the International and the Workers' Federation visited some of the Paris republican Deputies to try to get their support for the overthrow of the Empire. This the Deputies refused, arguing that since the Paris populace had not supported the Republic in 1851 against the *coup d'état* they would not act until further military disasters had made the danger of a Prussian occupation even more obvious.

The real problem now for the Deputies of the centre-left was how to prepare the way for a transfer of power that would not give the revolutionary forces the chance to form a government of their own choosing in the capital. For increasingly the control of Paris lay

---

[1] Favre, *Dépositions*, I, p. 330.
[2] L. Michel, op. cit., p. 51.
[3] L. Halévy, *Carnets*, Paris, 1935, vol. 2, p. 219.

with the armed battalions of the National Guard. This body had its
origins in the days after the fall of the Bastille in 1789. It had sprung
up as a citizen militia of the bourgeoisie, committed to defending
their rights against the despotism of the State or the passions of
the mob. It had played a leading role in the token defence of Paris
in March 1814, when at the legendary *barrière de Clichy* it had held off
the Russians. The popular classes had spontaneously thrown up
barricades in the city and demanded arms to join in this defence.
But a truce had been quickly agreed on, leaving the bourgeois
Guardsmen as the only armed forces in the capital to maintain order.
In the poorer districts the rumour of treason was easily given
credence. During the Hundred Days the Paris National Guard played
a neutral role between Napoleon I and the Allies, and so Napoleon
had had to arm the populace. But after Waterloo it was the National
Guard who ensured that Paris surrendered peacefully. Charles X
disbanded the National Guard, which helped him lose his throne in
1830 when under Lafayette the National Guard played a major role
in bringing Louis-Philippe to power. The first time popular battalions were formed in the Paris National Guard was after the
Revolution of 1848, and this meant that it was no longer reliable as
a force on the side of order. The workers' revolt of June 1848 had
had to be suppressed by the army, and when Napoleon III seized
power he let the National Guard fall into abeyance.[1]

At the beginning of the 1870 war after the departure of the troops
to the front the Government had had to call up the sixty battalions
of the National Guard to defend the Paris fortifications. But the
republicans demanded the opening up of the National Guard to all
citizens and the arming of the population. These demands were
opposed by Palikao and the Government, who wanted to keep the
distribution of arms strictly limited to the trustworthy bourgeois
battalions. Clearly there was a well-justified fear, as one Minister
later put it, that 'the agitators would use their arms more for social
upheaval than for national defence'.[2] But the Chambre as a whole
took the patriotic view that as in 1814–15 it was up to the National

---

[1] See L. Girard, *La Garde Nationale, 1814–1871*, Paris, 1964, *passim*.
[2] Baron David, *Dépositions*, I, p. 149. Pyat in *Le Combat*, 16 September, had
said 'when we cease firing we will take up our tools again – keeping our rifles';
Favre, *Enquête*, II, p. 43, had heard it rumoured that in Belleville the National
Guards were saying 'we have our rifles, but it won't be against the Prussians
that we shall be using them'.

Guard to defend Paris against invasion. Accordingly sixty more battalions were created, and within a few weeks the number of new battalions had risen to 134, making a total of around 300,000 Parisians in the National Guard. 'No one could call himself a citizen,' it was being said, 'unless he had a rifle.'[1] The cry was for more arms, and the authorities were forced to distribute hundreds of thousands of weapons to those flocking to join the newly formed battalions. This developed into a scramble for weapons which did not always stop short of a little pillaging, though only a few of the most revolutionary battalions were fortunate enough to be able to lay their hands on chassepots, the best rifle in the army. Flintlocks were probably no rarer. Soon the distinction was being made between the 'good battalions', the original sixty drawn from the ranks of the bourgeoisie, and the 'bad', the new battalions to which the lower classes had flocked. Often, however, even within the same battalion there were 'good' and 'bad' elements, and the authorities found it increasingly difficult to know which battalions, if any, they could rely on.

By now most people considered the Empire was lost and its fall only a matter of time, a situation the Blanquists tried to take advantage of. They rightly considered that Paris was ready to welcome the Republic, but judged wrongly that this could be accomplished through them leading an armed insurrection. As Blanqui himself later admitted, it was either too early or too late. They should have tried to lead the crowd on 9 August, or await some other military disaster to cause a popular mood which they could then try to use, as was to happen on 4 September. But the young Blanquist revolutionaries could not wait and, needing arms for the National Guard, plans were made to stage an attack on the fort at Vincennes. Not having time to get to know the soldiers this was then changed to the fire-station at La Villette. On 14 August Eudes gave the cry 'Forward' and the armed Blanquists descended on the fire-station. A guard was lightly wounded as they forced their entrance, but the firemen would not surrender their arms. Blanqui had expressly forbidden any bloodshed, so after more parleys the Blanquists withdrew. They marched back to Belleville, unmolested but unsupported, through the astonished Sunday crowd who did not take up their cry of 'Long live the Republic! Death to the Prussians! To arms!'

The two student Blanquist revolutionaries Eudes and Brideau were later caught by the police and charged with being traitors, paid

[1] M. Marseille, Prefect of Police, Enquête, II, p. 196.

by Prussian money. Gambetta in the Assembly demanded the death sentence. The *Temps* and other papers spread the false news that a fireman had been killed,[1] along with a woman and a five-year-old child. The Blanquists agitated vigorously to get the death sentence remitted, Eudes and Brideau refusing to appeal to the Emperor for a pardon. Jules Vallès and others persuaded Michelet to write an open letter asking for a reprieve of the death sentence. Gambetta, now better informed, went to see Palikao, and Ranc went to see the Minister of Commerce, where he argued that 'since it was probable that in two weeks there would be no more Empire' it would be wrong to shed blood that would later demand reprisals. On 2 September Ranc received a letter from Blanqui thanking him for having saved the two 'benjamins' (Eudes and Brideau were twenty-five and twenty-six years old). At his defence Eudes had of course denied that he had wanted to help the Prussians, insisting rather that he had wanted to 'repel the invaders' by first 'overthrowing the Empire . . . I acted with all my patriotic ardour for France and for the Republic'.

Then on 3 September catastrophic news reached Paris. At Sedan the whole of MacMahon's army had been captured, some 100,000 troops, and the Emperor himself had had to surrender 'his sword into the hands' of King Wilhelm. To the consternation of the Government the Opposition demanded a special session of the Legislature that night to try to settle affairs at once. The next day was a Sunday and there would certainly be disturbances when the news of Sedan was posted up on the streets of Paris. But Palikao had no sense of political finesse; as a General, as the Minister of War and as the President of the Council he refused to admit to the Deputies that there was a problem. Above all, he said, this was 'not the time' to raise the question of abdication. Against the Government, only a few members of the Legislature were willing openly to demand the abdication of the Empress. The majority after all had been elected by the countryside to preserve the Empire, and the plebiscite of 1870 had made clear that the opposition sentiments of Paris and the other big cities were not those of the majority of Frenchmen. The Government for its part even seems to have considered dissolving the

[1] At the trial it was shown that neither of the revolvers had been fired. Standing as a Deputy in 1887 Eudes was visited by the police agent he had supposedly killed seventeen years earlier: M. Dommanget, *Blanqui, la Guerre de 1870-71 et la Commune*, Paris, 1947, p. 13.

Chambre and enforcing order in Paris.[1] The session therefore was adjourned until the following day.

By the time Parliament reassembled on the fourth, the position of the centre-left had become very difficult. They saw clearly that the regime was finished and were glad that this was so, though the republicans amongst them did not want their long-awaited Republic to inherit a disastrous defeat. More to the point they did not wish the Republic to be established at the dictatorship of Paris, fearing that this would only cause a reaction in the provinces and destroy the support they had been patiently building up throughout the country. The only solution therefore, in Thiers' words, would be for the Legislative Body, representing all of France, to 'declare the throne vacant, form a governmental commission, try to sign an armistice with the enemy, then convoke an Assembly that would reunite all those who were capable and devoted, and from which could emerge a remedy for our misfortunes'. The majority, hesitantly, were willing to accept this plan, though they would not go so far as to declare the throne vacant. So Thiers modified his resolution to 'In view of the circumstances...' This was the only possible solution, as all sides came to realize; even the Government dare not resort to the plan of leaving Paris and setting up a government in the provinces, where already Lyon had proclaimed the Republic, nor were they sure they could use the troops to subdue Paris. For, as Trochu afterwards insisted, it was doubtful if the troops would have fired, and no one would take the responsibility of starting a civil war in France on top of Sedan and in face of the Prussian invasion.[2] At least, so it seems to have been tacitly half-felt, they should wait until the war with Prussia was over.

The Chambre's timid hesitations were ended when the crowd, which had slowly been infiltrating, finally burst in and descended from the Tribunes, in spite of efforts by Gambetta and others to check them. Two Blanquists, Granger and Levraud, reached Schneider's Presidential chair and Granger declared that 'in the presence of our disasters and in the face of the misfortunes of the country the people of Paris had invaded this place to proclaim the Republic and the downfall of the Empire'. Schneider hastily declared the session closed, and escaped. Jules Favre, seeing that there was about to be a popular takeover of the Chambre and remembering

---

[1] Baron David, *Dépositions*, I, p. 161.
[2] Trochu, *Pour la Verité et pour la Justice*, Paris, 1873, pp. 27–8.

with horror the similar situation of 15 May 1848, when Barbès had
led an invasion of the Assembly and voted the abolition of property,
declared that 'it is not here that you should proclaim the Republic
but you must go to the Hôtel de Ville if you want to proclaim it'.
It was, as he said afterwards, the 'only means to obtain a little order'.[1]
This had the desired effect and Favre and Ferry, arm in arm, followed
by some of the other Deputies, led the crowd to the Hôtel de Ville,
the traditional centre for all Paris revolutions.

The invasion of the Palais Bourbon was not just the result of a
spontaneous movement, but had been partly prepared for by the
Left opposition and by the Paris revolutionaries. Every one knew
that there would a a big demonstration in the Place de la Concorde
on the Sunday. Already on the previous evening an unorganized
crowd from the working-class suburbs had invaded the boulevards.
Later that night Blanquists had toured the popular quarters making
preparations for the coming demonstration. It was on their initiative
that a number of the popular battalions arrived armed on the
Sunday morning. On the other side, several Opposition Deputies
and certain journalists had agreed that the National Guard would
turn out, though without arms,[2] more to prevent or at least to control
a revolution than to cause one. When they saw that other Guardsmen
were armed they went and fetched their rifles. The Opposition also
feared that the Government might try to use certain army regiments
or the police to repeat the *coup d'état* that had inaugurated the Empire.
For this reason Palikao seems to have been forced to withdraw the
police from around the Palace itself. Instead, the security of the
Legislature was entrusted to a specially selected National Guard
regiment from the Sixth arrondissement, one that was considered to
be a 'good battalion'.

The crowd in the square, which by late morning included many
workmen who had descended from the North and groups of armed
Blanquists who raised the cry of 'Down with the regime' and 'Up
with the Republic', broke through the line of troops – the soldiers

---

[1] *Dépositions*, I, 331–2.
[2] Cf. Kératry, *Dépositions*, I, pp. 648, 656; *Le Siècle*, on the morning of 4 September, wrote that 'A rendez-vous is given for the thousands of National
Guards to turn up, without arms, in front of the Legislative Body at 2.0 p.m.'.
The most detailed account of 4 September is that by R. Gossez, '*Le 4 Septembre
1870*', *Actes du 77e Congrès des Sociétés savantes. Grenôble 1952*, Paris, 1952,
pp. 505–31.

refusing to fire – and pushed across the bridge between the square and the Palais Bourbon. The Blanquist historian, Gaston da Costa, claims the Blanquists led this march, and when the crowd came up against the police lines with their drawn sabres it was the Blanquists who helped persuade the police of the futility of further defence.[1] In any case the police felt uneasy, knowing that the troops would not back them up, and a few sections of the crowd were able to squeeze past them. The police then withdrew, leaving the way open to the gates of the Legislature, and the troops raised the butts of their rifles in the air rather than fire on the National Guard. The Chambre therefore was invaded by a mixture of bourgeois National Guards and National Guards from the working-class districts, and it was this alliance that was fatal to the Government. Thiers noted that amongst the invaders of the Chambre 'there were many men who were quite well dressed'. It was not, he said, 'like I had seen on previous occasions, a revolt made by the populace'.[2] One Deputy, when he had presented his Deputy's badge to pass through the lines on the way to the Chambre, had been greeted by the officer who let him through with the wish that 'he was on his way to declare the downfall of that swine'.[3] But it was the Blanquists who, having caught up with the moderate Guardsmen in the Assembly, demanded the Republic. This forced Favre's hand, for the Opposition Deputies had not wanted to take over the Government in these circumstances and had been doing all they could precisely to avoid such a situation.

At the Hôtel de Ville the crowd was well in charge by the time Favre and the other Deputies arrived, and the situation was, as Ferry described it, 'a little different',[4] than in the Chambre. On the way Favre and Ferry had met Trochu, riding slowly through the crowd to see what was going on. Palikao and other ex-Ministers tried in the official inquiry after the Commune to blame Trochu for not fulfilling his duties as Governor of Paris and defending the Government and the Empress. But Trochu had been ignored by the Government and so had retired, Achilles-like, to his rooms in the Louvre. Certainly no one wanted him to bring his *gardes mobiles* into Paris, as on the morning of 4 September news had reached the

---

[1] G. da Costa, *La Commune vécue*, Paris, 1903–5, vol. 3, p. 320; cf. Ranc, op. cit. p. 158.

[2] *Dépositions*, I, p. 17; cf. Ferry, *Dépositions*, I, p. 381.

[3] Guyot-Montpayroux, *Dépositions*, II, p. 199.

[4] Ferry, *Dépositions*, I, p. 382.

Government that they were mutinous and threatening to march on Paris of their own accord. Favre called on Trochu to follow them to the Hôtel de Ville. There the Jacobin revolutionaries were already forming their own government and tossing out from windows lists to the crowd below, who were cheering the names of Blanqui, Delescluze, Rochefort and other radical figures. Jules Favre, Ferry and a few other Deputies closeted themselves away with Trochu and hit on the solution of proclaiming a provisional government composed of the Deputies of Paris. Paris had made the revolution and so the elected representatives of Paris should head it, which would have the added value of seeming to restore to Paris its municipal liberties. Such was how the new government would present itself, though their motives were more direct. By this means they would prevent anyone else from 'touching power', as Favre put it; it was a 'polite way of excluding certain names' as Picard said.[1] The addition of Trochu, as the anti-republican General Ducrot said, was the Left's pledge to the 'conservatives' and a means of assuring itself the support of the army.[2]

Then Rochefort arrived, having been freed from prison by a section of the crowd under the leadership of Paschal Grousset of the *Marseillaise*. The prison guards had been too frightened to resist as the prisoners broke out. As a Deputy for Paris, his name could hardly be kept off the list, especially as several of the Deputies who had been included, namely Gambetta, Picard and Jules Simon, had never actually taken up their Paris seats, preferring the relative quiet of representing the provinces. When Trochu saw the name of Rochefort on the list he nearly became choleric but was convinced that 'it was to our interest that this man be included among us'.[3] Favre had astutely realized that Rochefort would 'be very wise, and that it would be better to have him inside than outside' of the Government.[4] Later Trochu paid Rochefort the tribute of saying that 'he showed a spirit of sincere patriotism . . . supporting the measures of order'.[5] As Vallès said, Rochefort's popularity would be a 'cloak' for the far from revolutionary acts of the Government.[6]

The newly formed Government met with the rump of the

[1] *Dépositions*, I, pp. 383, 476.

[2] *Dépositions*, III, p. 83.                    [3] *Dépositions*, I, p. 280.

[4] *Dépositions*, I, p. 383; G. Flourens, *Paris livré*, Paris, 1871, p. 61.

[5] Trochu, *La Politique et le siège*, Paris, 1874, p. 83.

[6] *L'Insurgé*, Ch. 18.

Chambre, who had not been in favour of the declaration of a Republic. But Thiers dominated the hundred or so Deputies, and he realized that if the Assembly tried to oppose what had occurred they would 'spoil everything'.[1] So he persuaded them that they 'had nothing further to do' and he himself 'retired' to his scientific studies. Thiers' own position was consistent with what he had tried to organize before the invasion of the Chambre. He had not joined the other Paris Deputies in forming a provisional Government, being too wily for that. But the Orleanist Comte D'Haussonville reports a conversation with him on the morning following 4 September in which Thiers said that the Republic must be accepted as an accomplished fact. The important issue for the time being was to support the new Government, and in particular Trochu, to enable it 'to resist the enemy invaders, and also all the bad passions that were swarming and fermenting behind the Government'.[2]

The Orleanist party in Paris even thought that the overthrow of the Empire was the opportunity for a restoration of the monarchy. Three of the Orleanist princes left London as soon as they heard the news from Paris. But Thiers, the elder statesman of the party, was insistent that it would be foolish to try to effect a restoration. When a group of nobles went to see Trochu, Favre and other members of the new Government, they were met with polite refusals even from the Orleanists amongst them, who rightly realized that Paris would never accept a monarchical restoration. So after having made a tour of the city of their ancestors, which they had not seen for over twenty years, and having bought souvenirs, the princes returned by the next train to London.

All the contemporary accounts emphasize the joyous, festive nature of the crowd on this day. Arnould described it as a 'public celebration' in which the population 'enjoyed the word Republic and the absence of the police, who had disappeared from the streets'.[3] Ranc called it 'a festive day'.[4] Francisque Sarcey, the theatre critic of one of the Paris dailies, Le Temps, said the proclamation of the

[1] Dépositions, I, p. 19.
[2] Comte D'Haussonville, Mon Journal pendant la guerre (1870–71), Paris, 1905, pp. 110–11.
[3] A. Arnould, Histoire populaire et parlementaire de la Commune de Paris, Brussels, 1878, vol. 1, p. 18. Cresson, Dépositions, II, p. 34, said that the police had to go into hiding for fear of their lives; cf. Kératry, I, p. 661.
[4] E. Ranc, Sous l'Empire, Paris, 1872, p. 176.

Republic was welcomed as 'an old friend, there was only the peaceful animation in the streets of a completely joyous population . . . an
atmosphere of exuberant gaiety'.[1] Washburne, the American ambassador, said that the proclamation of the Republic was 'received
by every possible demonstration of enthusiasm'.[2] People were everywhere. Juliette Adam, long an enthusiastic republican, described the
Place de la Concorde as 'a marvellous spectacle. From the chestnut
trees of the Tuileries just as far as the horizon of Mont-Valérien and
the hills bathed by the Seine, the scene is on so grand a scale, the
crowd feels such a real communion of ideals and desires, that poetry
and enthusiasm invade even the coldest and most insensitive hearts.'[3]
The weather was glorious, though Edmond de Goncourt, still
mourning his brother's death, had found the skies grey that morning.
Juliette Adam noticed a young worker in a red fez who had been
singing the 'Marseillaise' non-stop for the past three hours, clinging
to one of the candelabra on the bridge. As Ferry said, it was a
'carnival; never was a revolution carried out with such gentleness'.[4]

In such an atmosphere Gambetta had little difficulty in persuading
the crowd at the Hôtel de Ville, as Lamartine had done in 1848, that
the new Republic should keep the Tricolor rather than adopt the
Red Flag. Trochu later remarked on the similarities with 1848,
saying that the Provincial Government 'played the same role on
4 September as did Lamartine's Government in February 1848. The
Provisional Government saved the situation, which otherwise would
have been lost. It prevented the demagogues from taking over the
defence of Paris and from producing an immense social upheaval
throughout France.'[5]

It was only a minority of Blanquists, Jacobins and socialists who
realized that the revolutionary movement had been duped. When
Delescluze met Arthur Arnould, a fellow radical journalist, in the
streets that evening he said sadly, 'We are lost.'[6] Gustave Flourens,
another revolutionary figure, looking back after the siege was over,
felt that the Republic had been proclaimed 'so as to be able to better

[1] F. Sarcey, Le Siège de Paris, Paris, 1871, pp. 26, 28.

[2] E. B. Washburne, Recollections of a Minister to France 1869–1877, New York,
1887, vol. 1, p. 63.

[3] Juliette Lamber, Le Siège de Paris, Paris, 1873, p. 30; quoted in A. Horne, The
Fall of Paris, London, 1965, p. 59.

[4] Dépositions, I, p. 381.                                    [5] Dépositions, I, p. 281.

[6] Arnould, op. cit., p. 26.

finish it off',[1] by which he meant the revolutionary conception of the Republic. Arnould considered that the parliamentary Left had been completely able 'to fool the revolutionary socialist party'[2] because it alone had organized itself to take over power as soon as it was realized that the Empire was about to go. Paris, said Lissagaray, both future member and historian of the Commune, 'gave herself up without reserve to that same Left to which she had been forced to do violence in order to make her revolution'.[3]

Arnould took the festive atmosphere as a sign that 4 September was 'not a revolution'. But it was not the festive spirit that had betrayed the social revolution. In a sense, as the whole agitation during the siege against the Government of National Defence was to reveal, the population did believe that Paris had carried out a real revolution. This was what was being celebrated. The deception arose because the Imperial regime fell so quickly that when the Opposition Deputies proclaimed the Republic it was not immediately seen that there was still anything left to fight for. All energies, it was thought, could now be turned to reversing the French losses against the Prussians. This popular patriotism and preoccupation with the war was used by the bourgeois Deputies to safeguard their own rule and prevent any immediate movement towards establishing a more socially revolutionary Republic. Trochu, looking back, could defend his support of the new government by saying it had not been 'the Government that on that day had made unfortunate concessions to the demagogues. It was the demagogues who had made the fortunate concession of letting the Provisional Government install itself in place of the Commune.'[4] It was yet another example of what the young Blanquist revolutionary Gaston da Costa called that 'strange phenomenon'[5] whereby each time the country was in danger the masses could be relied on to be more patriotic than the privileged. The 'national *souvenirs*' that Marx had warned the French workers to beware of had carried the day.[6]

[1] Flourens, op. cit., p. 59.

[2] Op. cit., p. 23.

[3] P.-O. Lissagaray, *History of the Commune of 1871*, Eng. trans by Eleanor Marx Aveling, 2nd edn. New York, 1898, p. 14. The first French edition was published in Brussels, 1876; English translation first published 1886.

[4] Trochu, *La Politique*, p. 82.

[5] Da Costa, op. cit., p. 320.

[6] *Second Address on the Franco-Prussian War*, MESW, p. 272.

Chapter 3

# A GOVERNMENT OF NATIONAL DEFECTION

———— ◆◆◆ ————

The war had been entered upon for reasons of internal politics; its conduct and conclusion were to be likewise determined. It is a story on the French side of a Government seeking peace whilst trying to keep at bay the popular forces patriotically pressing for more determined action. Particularly noticeable is how the latter were organizing into clubs and committees that became a real threat to the new Provisional Government's authority in the capital. The Civil War of 1871 was fought in a mould prepared for it by the defeat of France by Prussia. It was the war that provided both the special circumstances favouring the outbreak of a revolution as well as limiting its chances of success. The main emphasis in what follows is on these internal effects in Paris of the war and the siege.

. The Republicans who had seized power to prevent the revolutionaries from taking over did not for the most part relish their new position. They knew that without the Orleanist General Trochu at their head the army would not have obeyed them. All the leading generals owed their position to the Emperor and were solidly Bonapartist, though only Bazaine, isolated on the eastern frontier at Metz, actually tried to negotiate the evacuation of his beseiged army in the name of the ex-Emperor. But as Trochu said, 'none of the generals had any taste for the republican form of government, nor had they any sympathy for the politicians who were its representatives'. Some, he said, 'even hated them'.[1] General Vinoy, who later replaced Trochu as head of the Government, General Ducrot, the most vigorous of the commanders in Paris, and most of the others did not distinguish between moderate and radical republicans.

[1] Trochu, *Oeuvres posthumes*, Vol. 1, *Le Siège de Paris*, Paris, 1896, p. 268. For a fuller account of the military side of the war there is the excellent history by Michael Howard, *The Franco-Prussian War*, London, 1961.

During the siege Ducrot could not understand why Trochu did not take more forcible measures in order to crush all incipient revolts, and when during the most serious of these the revolutionaries imprisoned several members of the Government in the Hôtel de Ville Ducrot started to march his troops back into Paris and was only stopped by Trochu himself. Ducrot later claimed that if he had been allowed to have his own way his method of repression would have been so 'terrible' as to put an end to all further revolts, even at the cost of a few members of the Government being shot by the revolutionaries as hostages.[1] What after all did a few republicans, more or less, matter?

The Government itself avoided such extreme measures. The republican Deputies had too many links with at least some of the more radical republicans to share the military's reflex of using troops to put down the Paris crowds. Above all, Trochu himself was against blood being shed between Frenchmen. Trochu was not a Bonapartist. His preference was for the Orleanist monarchy but, like Thiers, he was more concerned with the substance than the form. When he was first appointed Governor he had surprised official opinion by announcing in a letter to the Press that he would use only 'moral force' to maintain order in Paris: 'the idea of maintaining order by the force of the bayonet and the sword in a Paris suffering from the most well-founded fears fills me with horror and disgust'. To the Imperial Government this had seemed like a renunciation of his duty to protect the Empire. But after 4 September Trochu maintained the same position, and defended his policy very forcefully before the Commission of Inquiry into the Commune. Trochu's 'old Breton faith' was fatalistic and pessimistic. The expression he returned to time and again to explain his actions, or lack of them, was 'the force of circumstances'. The revolution of 4 September was, in Trochu's view, inevitable, as was the constant excitement and attempt at revolt of Paris during the siege, or the final capitulation of Paris to the Prussian army. Since none of these ills could be avoided, the best that could be hoped for was to manage events so as to cause least suffering whilst preserving the foundations of order, 'religion, property and the family'.[2] On this latter point he had insisted on receiving a solemn assurance from the Paris Deputies before he would accept office in their Provisional Government. This same

[1] *Dépositions*, III, p. 88.
[2] Trochu, *La Politique*, p. 73.

concern for moral sentiment had marked his book on the French army of 1867 where he had shown himself greatly concerned about the military spirit of the nation, considering in effect that a country gets the army it deserves. As Governor of Paris, he realized that the morale of the troops was not such that they could be relied on to fire on the Paris crowd, especially not on the National Guard. The troops had become affected by the atmosphere in which they lived and by the populace on whom they were billeted.[1]

This same Cassandra-like spirit marked Trochu's conduct of the defence of Paris, though in this he was not alone. In his book of 1867 Trochu had condemned the existing organization of the army as completely inadequate for the needs of the defence of France. The best means of defence would be to train up a professional long-service army of some 500,000 men. The Prussian *landwehr* system of a big trained reserve army was excellent, but would take too long, whilst to maintain a large permanent army would disturb the peace of the existing social order.[2] The Imperial Government had not heeded Trochu's advice and had rather tried to form a conscripted reserve army. At the beginning of the war, Trochu had advised the Emperor against the march towards Bazaine, considering that Paris could only be defended by an army manœuvring outside of its fortifications. After Sedan, therefore, so far as Trochu was concerned, the war was over – though right from the start he had never had any faith in a French victory. For with both armies defeated and no trained reserve, how could Paris be defended any further? At the first meeting of the Government of National Defence Rochefort proposed the revolutionaries' solution of a *levée en masse*. Trochu politely and firmly scotched this idea, adding that 'for a long time the French army has been only an anachronism'.[3]

Throughout the siege, Trochu's constant theme to the civilian Government of National Defence was that they should have 'no illusions'; they were there 'simply to accept defeat on the field of battle'. All that could be done was to wait the inevitable end: 'we will defend ourselves, but it is a heroic folly'. His favourite expression

[1] *Dépositions*, I, pp. 312–13. After the Commune Trochu claimed he had warned Thiers that the attempt to use troops to seize the cannons, which gave rise to the revolution of 18 March, would fail if the National Guard resisted, as indeed proved to be the case.
[2] Trochu, *L'Armée française en 1867*, Paris, 1867, pp. 278–85.
[3] H. Guillemin, *Les Origines de la Commune*, Paris, 1956–60, vol. 2, p. 14.

was that they could only 'chicaner l'ennemi'.[1] General Totlebon, famous from his defence of Sebastopol, made no secret of his opinion that the Paris fortifications could not hold out for forty-eight hours, and Trochu said to a friend that the Prussians could enter Paris 'when and how they liked'.[2] So far as Trochu was concerned, and on this he stood firm against Thiers, Favre, Picard and the other members of the Government who were more impetuous in their desire for peace, the important point was that this 'heroic folly' of a defence should at least 'save the honour' of France and of the army. Trochu intended to do his duty. The siege would be conducted according to the customs of war. So too would its surrender, especially after Bazaine surrendered Metz in what were regarded as treacherous conditions (Bazaine was later court-martialled). His punctiliousness regarding honour in the end caused his colleagues trouble, and afterwards Trochu was attacked by Comte Daru, Chairman of the Commission of Inquiry into the Acts of the Government of National Defence, who said that he allowed his military sense of honour to override his political duties as Governor.

The rest of the Government had fewer scruples. They feared the forces that had carried them to power, and which threatened constantly to sweep them away. 'The object of our greatest concern, for me as for my colleagues,' said Jules Favre, 'was to repel the forces of anarchy and to prevent there being a shameful revolt in Paris.'[3] The fourth of September marked the beginning, as Trochu said, 'of the struggle between the Provisional Government and the demagogues'.[4] Ducrot later said that 'the diplomacy of the Government and almost all the defence revolved around one thing: *the fear of a revolt*'. Of the two enemies it was 'not always the most distant one that was the most feared'.[5] The Bonapartist man of letters Eugène Balleyguier, who wrote under the pen-name of Fidus, was of the same opinion, and noted on 14 September in his diary that among his

---

[1] Kératry, *Dépositions*, II, p. 668; Garnier-Pagès, *Dépositions*, I, p. 445: Trochu similarly described the siege as a 'heroic folly' to a meeting with the Mayors in January 1871: cf. Corbon, *Dépositions*, IV, p. 329, and *Le Rappel*, 17 March 1871.                                                       [2] Sarcey, op. cit., p. 44.
[3] *Dépositions*, I, p. 336.                            [4] *Dépositions*, I, p. 279.
[5] General Ducrot, *La Défense de Paris (1870–1871)*, Paris, 1877, vol. 1, p. 215; cf. Jules Simon, *Histoire du Gouvernement de la Défense Nationale*, Paris, 1874, p. 12, 'from that day (4 September) until the end of the siege our constant concern was the question of a revolt'.

circle 'the internal dangers were dreaded as much as the Prussians'. Conservatives who had at first supported the war had now turned against it, for victory, unlikely as that seemed, could only mean a triumph for the Republic. The respectable papers were primarily concerned about the 'ultra-red Government of Rochefort and Arago', as the *Gazette de France* of 5 September characterized the new Government. Sarcey summarized the situation of the bourgeoisie as being caught between the Prussians and the reds, adding that he did not know 'which of the two evils the bourgeoisie most feared: they hated the foreigner most, but were more fearful of the Bellevillois'.[1]

The task of the new Government was therefore clear. It had to put an end to these twin evils by making peace as quickly as possible. For with peace would also come an end to the isolation of Paris. An Assembly could be elected in which a rural majority would put a stop to the dictatorship of Paris over France. In his second circular as Minister of Foreign Affairs Favre told his diplomats that 'the determination to convoke a National Assembly as soon as possible sums up our entire policy', and Favre repeated this assurance to the Commission of Inquiry. Elections for all of France were at first fixed by the new Government for 2 October, though Gambetta did manage to insist that municipal elections be held in advance of the national elections, and for Paris these were fixed for 28 September. The inner council of the Government, and the Governor himself, as well as all conservative opinion, saw the forthcoming elections as a means to peace. Gambetta, however, wrote to his Prefects telling them to use the campaign to stir up public opinion in favour of the war, which also implied a preference for Republican rather than Monarchist or Bonapartist candidates. In Paris popular opinion was overwhelmingly in favour of such an unyielding resistance. The most working-class sections of the city were also the most violently pro-war, and this sentiment was a constant threat to the Government's continued existence. The Government therefore had to be Janus-faced and dared not make its actual policy public. Favre's summary of the situation was that he 'doubted whether it would have been possible to have told Paris that it was seriously intended to convoke a National Assembly, because the very idea of doing this would have appeared as a move towards peace'.[2] That this was so became apparent when it was realized that national elections could not be held

[1] Op. cit., p. 87.                    [2] *Dépositions*, I, p. 336.

whilst fighting was still going on. Peace, or at least a truce, became necessary before anything further could be done. But to delay the national elections also meant postponing the municipal elections, for, as was said in Council at the end of September, to hold elections in Paris without there being any national elections would be a victory for the revolutionary forces, as this would in effect be to grant the Commune. This was the dilemma around which the policies of the new Government were to revolve.

Only the young Gambetta in the Government stood out firmly and consistently against this defeatist policy. But even he in the last resort, as will be seen, when faced by the eventual capitulation of France, supported the position of his colleagues against the 'reds'. After all he had been sufficiently unnerved by his electoral campaign of 1869 in Belleville to opt for Marseille in preference to Paris. The fourth of September had made him, for a while, a 'revolutionary malgré lui',[1] at least to the extent of wanting the Government to throw its full energies into winning the war. This attitude to the war meant that Gambetta remained a party man, unlike the other republicans in the Government, who subordinated party interest to the overriding need to establish order. As Minister of the Interior, an important post to which Gambetta had just pipped the more cautious homme d'affaires Ernest Picard after 4 September, his first act had been to nominate good republicans as mayors for each of the twenty arrondissements in Paris. As Mayor of Paris Gambetta had Etienne Arago, a literary figure of the time of Balzac who had turned politician in the 1848 Revolution. Arago had been one of the radical republicans of that time and had been exiled in 1849 for his part in the left-wing republican uprising of June of that year. These first steps of Gambetta's in his republicanization of France were taken without consulting the other members of the Government, who certainly objected, though after it was too late, to some of his more radical choices. Picard was particularly bitter against this first act of his rival to the post, and said there was no reason why the old mayors should not have been left in office. Georges Clemenceau in the 18th arrondissement was much too radical for conservative opinion, as was Ranc in the 19th, Greppo, a working-class Republican of 1848, in the 4th, Corbon in the 15th and Henri Martin in the 16th. The rest of the Government did try to have some say in the new Prefects Gambetta insisted on appointing, but here again conservatives were

[1] J. P. T. Bury, Gambetta and the National Defence, London, 1936, p. 269.

shocked at seeing out-and-out republicans appointed to these vital
provincial posts. Picard and Favre did manage to ensure that hardly
any changes were made in their respective ministries of Finance and
Foreign Affairs, and Rouland was kept on as Governor of the Bank
of France, though again in his own Department of the Interior
Gambetta installed many of his own party men.

There was also something decidedly odd about the Government
of 4 September remaining in Paris, with only a delegation consisting
(until Gambetta joined them in October) of the oldest members in
the provinces. As Lord Lyons, the British Ambassador, said to
Favre's deputy at Tours, the seat of the Delegation, 'not only was
the origin of the government simply (so to speak) fortuitous, but it
was difficult to say what the Government of France was at this
moment, or even where it was to be found. A part of it was at Paris,
and a part of it was at Tours; the two parts had very scanty communication with each other, and it naturally followed that . . . they were
often at cross purposes.' Trochu was in favour of the Government
leaving Paris, as he would then have been free to concentrate on the
purely military issues of the siege. Gambetta too thought that this
was the most logical way to conduct the defence of France. But the
senior Republicans in the Government realized that if they left
Paris there was every likelihood that another revolution would lead
to the establishment of the Commune. It was to forestall this that
they had taken power on 4 September; it was for the same reason
that they remained in Paris.

At first the new Government received public declarations of
support from all sides. The Paris Council of the International published an address to the German people, recalling the German
Emperor's distinction at the outbreak of the war between the French
Empire and the French people. Since the Empire no longer existed,
the address argued, the *casus belli* had gone. If the Germans continued their invasion of France this would turn the war into one of
national survival. In such a case, the Internationalists warned, 'by
the voice of thirty-eight million people . . . inspired by the same
patriotic revolutionary feeling, we repeat to you what we declared
to the European coalition of 1793: "the French people do not make
peace with an enemy that is occupying its territory" . . . Return back
across the Rhine.'[1] The Marseille branch published a similar address,
calling on the Germans to retire across their frontiers, for otherwise

[1] *Le Rappel*, 6 September; M.P., I, p. 6.

'the French workers will be the first to fight against you and to shed their blood to defeat you'.[1] Marx in London was infuriated by this address, calling it an 'absurdity' in which Internationalist principles had given way to an outburst of French patriotism. He particularly picked on the remark calling on the Germans to retire across the Rhine. This he condemned as a 'chauvinistic phrase',[2] since to be clear of French soil the Germans had no need to withdraw to the eastern bank of the Rhine.

Seraillier, who had been sent over by the General Council to report on the situation in Paris, was also astonished by the French socialists' seeming enthusiasm for the war. As a part explanation he granted that the leaders of the International in Paris had no choice, as they would have lost their support amongst the working population if they had tried to take up any other attitude. When Seraillier remonstrated with the Paris Internationalists whom he met, they replied that 'if they had adopted any other tone they would be sent packing'. Thus, reported Seraillier, they could do nothing better than parody the revolution of '93.[3] And Marx concluded that it would be a good thing if this 'cult of the past' was broken once and for all, which might happen when Paris was forced to capitulate.

In using language borrowed from the first Revolution, the Internationalists were typical of the reaction of the Left, which claimed that the establishment of the Republic had given a new character to the war, especially as this had been done by adding yet another *journée* to the tradition of Paris revolutions. Now, it was felt, all thoughts and energies could be directed to victory, and Sarcey reports hearing a worker say to a comrade that the Prussians would not dare come, 'now that we have it' – that is, the Republic.[4] The Workers' Delegation, which had been formed out of the delegates elected to visit the 1867 Exhibition, for example, took the same position as their 'brothers' in the International. They assured the

[1] *Le Rappel*, 18 September.
[2] Marx to César de Paepe, 14 September: given in *L'Actualité de l'Histoire*, October–December 1958, p. 26. The phrase Marx was criticizing was not just a slip of the pen; *Le Rappel*, 8 September, reports a meeting of the Paris Federation of the International at which Briosne said, in the debate on this address, that the French should demand that the Germans 'return to the other side of the Rhine' before negotiations could be opened. See too Lefrançais, op. cit., p. 83.
[3] Quoted by Marx in his letter to de Paepe, ibid.
[4] Sarcey, op. cit., p. 29.

Provisional Government of their support in a proclamation calling on their members to devote all their energies to the defence of the nation, for 'from today all workers form simply one family whose members are ready to sacrifice their lives for the defence of the Republic'.[1] Several of the main Paris daily papers republished this declaration as a sign of the support for the Government from all classes of the population. Support also came from the Paris telegraph employees, who affirmed that 'today the only question is that of the security of the defence', and from the Paris iron-workers.[2] The *Marseillaise*, which had been the scourge of the Empire, published an article in which the future Communard Benoît Malon commended the Paris working class for its energetic attitude in the face of invasion. This showed, he wrote, that they had 'understood that all disagreements must be effaced before the danger to the country'.[3]

The older revolutionary republicans of the '48 generation committed themselves just as wholeheartedly as the working-class groups to supporting the Government in its task of defending the nation. Delescluze spoke of 'the old blood arising with its original character as soon as the country is in danger'.[4] Faced with the Prussian threat to Paris, Blanqui's Jacobin patriotism dominated over his dislike of the Deputies who composed the recently established Provisional Government. Together with nineteen of his followers, including Eudes and Tridon, Blanqui publicly declared that 'in face of the enemy, no more parties, no more differences ... the government that came out of the great movement of 4 September represents the republican idea and the national defence. That is sufficient. All opposition, all dissent must give way to the common safety. Henceforth there is only one enemy, the Prussian, and his accomplice, the supporters of the fallen dynasty.'[5] Vallès wanted Blanqui to add a revolutionary phrase to warn his followers to keep on the alert against the danger of a reaction, considering that otherwise the declaration was too much of a compromise. Vallès was to be proved

---

[1] *Les Délégations ouvrières du Département de la Seine au Gouvernement de la Défense Nationale*, Paris, 1870.

[2] *Le Soir*, 12 September (Telegraph workers); *La Gazette de France*, 11 September (Ironfounders). *Le Soir*, 10 September; *Le Petit Journal*, 12 September; *La Presse*, 13 September, were among the papers publishing the address of the Workers' Delegations.          [3] 7–9 September.

[4] *Le Réveil*, 7 September: cf. 15, 16 September.

[5] *La Patrie en danger*, No. 1, 7 September.

right when he remarked to Blanqui that within a month he and the Government would be 'at daggers drawn'. But Blanqui replied that if this were to occur it would be the Government's fault and not his.[1] So far as the Blanquists were concerned, 'when France fights for the Republic, she fights for the liberty of the world'.[2] Blanqui supported the Government because he considered that the defence of France had to override all other considerations, including the social and political policies of the new Republic, though he probably hoped that the populace would be able successfully to exert pressure on the Government through its clubs and demonstrations, as had happened during the great Revolution.

The strength of popular feeling was brought out when Cluseret, one of the future commanders-in-chief of the army of the Commune, attacked Gambetta in the *Marseillaise* for not arming the popular battalions of the National Guard, arguing that in effect Gambetta was helping the Prussians by his suspicions of the populace. Cluseret called his article '*La Réaction*', since this was his opinion of the nature of a government that had put the conservative Breton Kératry at the Prefecture of Police and Trochu in charge of the army.[3] The tone and title of this article were too strong for the excited state of popular feeling in Paris so soon after 4 September. A crowd from Belleville forced its way into the offices of the *Marseillaise* and burnt copies of the offending issue. Cluseret was astonished at the effect of his article, and he had to pacify the crowd by explaining that his attack on Gambetta was not meant as an attack on the Government as a whole. This modification of the purport of his article satisfied the crowd, and everyone hastened to shake him by the hand. That evening he toured the clubs in Belleville, Montmartre and Les Halles to explain his views. Cluseret also had to face an attack by Rochefort, who wrote a letter to the *Journal Officiel* dissociating himself from the paper and accusing Cluseret of having in his article incited the population to civil war at a time when all citizens had laid aside their political grievances to form a united front against the common enemy. This accusation was repeated by Blanqui, who condemned the whole affair as encouraging a 'civil war at a time of national war'.[4] To defend himself Cluseret wrote a letter to one of the leading

[1] *L'Insurgé*, Ch. 19.
[2] Gustave Tridon in *La Patrie en Danger*, 8 September.
[3] 7–9 September; see too G.-P. Cluseret, *Mémoires*, Paris, 1887, vol. 3, pp. 276–81.     [4] *La Patrie en Danger*, 9 September.

republican papers, *Le Rappel*, which concluded with an assurance that henceforth he would devote himself solely to the defence of Paris. But as a result of the whole affair the *Marseillaise* ceased publication.

This incident was noted by the Ministry of the Interior in its report on the daily Parisian Press to the Ministry of War, and attention was drawn to the protests this had caused, particularly that of Blanqui.[1] The moderate republican papers also seized on the occasion to emphasize the need for unity under the new Government. The *Cloche* published Blanqui's declaration of support of the Government, and the paper suggested that the other revolutionaries should follow his example, since Blanqui could not be called 'an Orleanist or a reactionary'.[2] Other leading papers also took the response of Blanqui and Rochefort to the offending article of Cluseret's as among 'the best signs of the situation'.[3]

The Republic of 4 September was accepted by the Left, and the example of Cluseret was sufficient to ensure that the revolutionaries and the socialists would hesitate to express publicly whatever doubts they might have had. The danger of any further political changes seemed averted by the common demand for unity in the face of invasion. The middle-class illustrated magazine, *L'Illustration*, therefore, could assure its readers on 10 September that there was no need to fear the political exiles who had returned to Paris after the fall of the Empire. 'Everyone has only a single thought, that of union, and everyone is patriotically rallying to the Government of National Defence! Listen to Blanqui ... to Louis Blanc ... to Victor Hugo: You see, from the arctic to the antarctic poles of democratic opinion there is only one cry, Union!'

This early enthusiasm for unity could not long survive the divergence in ends between the Government and the Paris population. Many on the Left had few illusions about a Government consisting of the 'men of '48' who had so strenuously opposed socialist reforms during that Revolution. On the evening of 4 September the Corderie, the home of the Paris Council of the International and of the Trade Union Federation, was full of 'revolutionary socialists', as Lefrançais,

<hr />

[1] A.H.G., Lo 21, 9 September.                                    [2] 10 September.
[3] *La France*, 10 September; cf. *Le Soir*, 11 September; *Le Petit Journal*, 13 September; *Le Figaro*, 10 September; *Le Gaulois*, 10 September; *La Gazette de France*, 9 September; *Le Pays*, 10 September; *Le Siècle*, 10 September, among others.

himself a future Communard, calls them,[1] discussing the situation. As a public act in tune with the mood of the day they drew up the address to the German people, whilst privately agreeing they could not attack the Government 'in view of the unpreparedness of the popular forces, still so unorganized', most of the workers having been called up for the army. The International sought to remedy this situation hoping to be able 'to organize a force sufficiently strong to compel the Hôtel de Ville to take both the defence of Paris and the Republic seriously'.[2] As a first step they sent off a delegation to the Government to back up their declaration of support by setting out their conditions. These were that elections would be called for a municipal council, the Prefecture of Police would be abolished, and that all judges should be submitted to the process of election. Additional demands were for the removal of all restrictions on the Press and on the right to form associations and hold meetings. An end was called for to the support the Church received from public funds. Gambetta, who received the delegation, as a good republican was able to assure them that the new Government was already enacting these latter demands. But on the vital issue of elections he would make no promises.

The next day the International called an open meeting which was attended by some 400–500 delegates from the local sections and from the Trade Unions. From this meeting came a call, published in Delescluze's paper, Le Réveil, on 7 September, for the formation of 'republican committees' in each of the twenty arrondissements of Paris, since these had been 'so useful in '93', and a provisional Central Committee was elected, headed by the bookbinder Eugène Varlin. During the next few days local 'committees of vigilance' were organized in the arrondissements of Paris. The International was not strong enough to organize these throughout the city, and to accredit it with this degree of power would be to repeat the mistake of the reaction after the Commune, which tried to blame the International for everything that had happened. Such a grand conspiracy was far beyond the means of the French branch of the International, let alone its London General Council. The International does seem to have been largely responsible for first organizing vigilance committees in seven of the arrondissements, and to have played a lesser role in a further five. These were mainly on the Left Bank, or were

---

[1] G. Lefrançais, Souvenirs, Brussels, 1902, p. 393.
[2] Lefrançais, op. cit., p. 394.

in the central arrondissements on the Right Bank. The role of the International was often simply to call a public meeting which then elected a local committee. In the 15th arrondissement, the local vigilance committee, composed mainly of Internationalists, presented themselves to Mayor Corbon with a letter of recommendation from Rochefort. The International also took the initiative in forming a military commission on 9 September, but this seems hardly to have functioned for any length of time. In the Eastern and Northern arrondissements on the Right Bank the Blanquists were generally dominant, especially in the 19th and 20th arrondissements where the two committees worked closely together. This whole committee movement was more or less spontaneous and sprang from the political activity that had already grown up as a result of the constant public meetings and agitation that had marked the last year of the Empire, giving the committees a wider base than just the Internationalists or Blanquists. But at the same time this meant the movement was primarily one of republican patriotism, which would only slowly move towards a position of open revolt in face of the Government's clear desire for peace and increasingly obvious incapacity and unwillingness to prosecute the war.

The Central Committee of the Twenty Arrondissements itself, having received no satisfaction from the Government over its demands, published these in its first *affiche rouge* that appeared on the walls of Paris on 15 September.[1] This poster demanded the replacement of the police by the National Guard, the arming of all citizens, election of officers in the *garde mobile* (they had always been elected in the sedentary National Guard), and the establishment of 'popular control over all measures regarding the defence'. With regard to the state of siege in Paris the demand was made that all the existing private stocks of food should be expropriated and committees chosen to see to its distribution. This was but the first time that the popular organizations pressed the Government to institute a complete system of rationing, a reasonable enough suggestion for a besieged city. The authorities, however, preferred to rely for most goods on what Molinari, a Liberal correspondent for the *Journal des Débats*, called 'rationing by high prices'. The poster concluded by calling for a *levée en masse* throughout France and the sending of delegates as in 1793 to organize the provinces. A further delegation was sent to the Government three days later from a meeting of

[1] M.P., I, pp. 90–1.

Internationalists, Trade Unionists and Blanquists chaired by Blanqui to demand once more that elections be held in Paris. But Ferry was able to ward them off with a few promises and assurances of the Government's devotion to the defence.

This of course was far from being the case. As a first step towards peace the Government of National Defence had persuaded Thiers to leave his 'retirement' and make the diplomatic round of the European capitals to see if he could win any allies for France, or, if not, at least to 'bring about an opportunity for an armistice'.[1] The British Foreign Office acted as intermediary in arranging a meeting between Favre, the acting secretary for Foreign Affairs, and Bismarck. On 18 September, whilst Ferry was pacifying the delegation at the Hôtel de Ville, Favre secretly left Paris and crossed the Seine to reach Prussian lines. The next day he joined Bismarck at the Rothschild's chateau at Ferrières. Bismarck immediately threw Favre off balance by opening with the remark that he was in touch with the Imperial Court. The Prussian demands for peace were severe – Alsace, Metz and part of Lorraine. But this was not the problem. The negotiations broke down at Moltke's and the German Emperor's insistence that they would only allow Paris to be re-provisioned if Prussia was given security in the form of the occupation of Strasbourg and Mont-Valérien, the biggest fort of the Parisian defence. This Favre realized the Government could not accept. Trochu, following the rules of war, would not surrender the capital without an agreement that supplies would be allowed to enter. But to hand over Mont-Valérien, together with the surrender of Strasbourg, would make it clear that this was not just an armistice but the prelude to peace. The Government would have been overthrown by a revolution in Paris. So with tears in his eyes, though Bismarck was convinced this was just court-room dramatics, the lawyer left and returned to Paris empty-handed, and secretly, for in Trochu's opinion 'he would not have got back into Paris alive' had his journey been known.[2]

Whilst Favre was negotiating, the Government on 19 September put on a 'military demonstration',[3] the sortie of Châtillon, in order to show that Paris had resisted before, as it was hoped, she surrendered. Trochu's instructions made clear that nothing serious was expected from this: the French commanders were 'to probe the [Prussian] flank, but with the greatest circumspection'. It was the

---

[1] *Dépositions*, I, p. 20.          [2] *Dépositions*, I, p. 290.

[3] As Guillemin calls it: op. cit., p. 105.

fiery Ducrot who had persuaded Trochu to try to defend the heights
at Châtillon so as to protect the forts to the south of Paris. Ducrot
had been raised by Trochu to commander of the XIV corps, a
position that should have gone to the elder Vinoy, and was eager for
a battle in which he could cut a good figure to go with his new
promotion. He attacked vigorously, and was surprised and then
furious when he found the other generals were sticking to the spirit
of Trochu's order of the day. Finally he had to be ordered to retreat
from his isolated position. He returned fuming and threatening to
court-martial General Caussade who, instead of backing him, had
retreated early in the day. Meeting Trochu, Caussade had told him
the battle was over and Trochu, not surprised, had gone off to
inspect the ramparts.

The withdrawal, or stampede as the retreat developed into, did
not help make credible the Government's claim to be energetically
pursuing the defence. And, on top of this, news leaked out of Favre's
supposedly secret attempt to negotiate a peace with the Prussians.
News that negotiations were under way had been published in the
conservative *Electeur Libre*, and Picard, who had leaked this information, was able to make a little out of the rise that this good news
caused on the Bourse. When Picard defended himself in the Council
by saying he was simply repeating what everyone knew, Gambetta
exploded, saying he for one had no idea that the Government was
already seeking for peace instead of preparing for a long defence.
The news came as an even greater surprise to the Paris population,
and the Government felt that it had to explain its action publicly.
This it did by an announcement that it had only wanted to find out
the enormity of the Prussian demands so as to stiffen the morale of
the population, which was hardly necessary in view of the patriotic
frenzy of the majority of the citizens of the capital. The proclamation
concluded with one of those bombastic phrases which the French
authorities were so free with during this war: 'Not an inch of our
territory, not a stone of our fortresses.'[1] This was hardly a realistic
negotiating position, as Favre well knew, but this was intended solely
for internal consumption as an attempt to placate popular opinion.
The Government nonetheless had to receive on 20 September yet
another delegation from the Central Committee of the Twenty
Arrondissements demanding an explanation. At a meeting earlier

[1] The expression had first been used by the Comte de la Tour in the Chambre on
24 August.

that day the Committee had voted in the revolutionary patriotic tradition that '1. The Republic cannot treat with an enemy that occupies its territory. 2. Paris is resolved to bury itself under its own ruins rather than surrender.' At the Hôtel de Ville Ferry, it was believed, gave his word of honour that the Government would not seek to negotiate. Arago, at this period acting as Mayor of Paris, promised that he would rather die on the steps of the building than surrender it to the Prussians. The issue of municipal elections was raised again, but on this point the delegation could not extract a definite date. The delegation was willing not to press this last point, however, because of 'the very precise and clear reply that they received with regard to the intention of the Government to pursue the war to the bitter end'.[1] During the next two days the Government was pressed by a series of delegations representing comparatively moderate opinion. They were all equally shocked by the duplicity the Government had shown in seeking to negotiate with the enemy, and questioned the Government as to when it would hold the promised elections. In each case the Ministers stalled with heroic talk of Paris 'resisting to the last extremity'; but no action was taken either militarily or politically.

This stalemate could not last for long. The local committees themselves were constantly crossing the border between active attempts to 'aid' the Government in conducting the defence and attempts to supplant the official administration because it was not vigorous enough. They had not been able to get their own nominees into the Mairies, Gambetta and Arago having forestalled them by quickly appointing new mayors. The committees had had one success in the 13th arrondissement where a local group had succeeded in establishing their own spokesman, Passedouet, a member of the International, immediately following 4 September. (The minority nature of his support was shown in the November mayoral elections when he was defeated by a moderate supporter of the Government.) The local committees were more successful in electing their own representatives as National Guard commanders. Blanqui, for example, was elected commander of the 169th battalion of Montmartre at a meeting presided over by Clemenceau. They were unable to get control over the police, but the old Bonapartist *sergents de ville* were so unpopular that the new Prefect of Police, Kératry, withdrew them, many having already in any case taken

[1] *Le Rappel*, 22 September.

cover for fear of their lives, and they were re-formed into a company in the regular army. Later they were slowly reintroduced into police duty in the city, having shaved off their Imperials, changed their bicorne for a republican kepi and their name to *gardiens de la paix*. But they still dared not enter the working-class districts, and throughout the siege the Government found itself unable to police all of the city.

On 2 October came the news of the surrender of Toul and Strasbourg. This was followed three days later by the first sign of armed revolt in the form of Gustave Flourens, acting entirely on his own, leading five battalions of armed National Guardsmen to the Hôtel de Ville. Flourens was the son of a celebrated Professor at the Collège de France, and had taught there for a while himself. He lost his post after publishing a short study depicting a future society in which 'men, freed from their chains, governed themselves'. In Byronic fashion he had then gone off to Crete to fight against the Turks. He was in Switzerland when the war broke out, and in August, deciding that the Empire was finished, he tried to return to France, but was arrested at the frontier as a Prussian spy. Rochefort secured his release after 4 September, and Flourens sped to Paris where he organized his Belleville battalions, equipping them with chassepots, the best French army rifles. Trochu had even given him the special title of 'major of the ramparts' in recognition of his enthusiasm for the defence. Unable to contain his impatience and anger at the inactivity of the Government, he was now, a month after the establishment of the new Republic, demanding to see Arago as Mayor of Paris and 'our friends in the Government of National Defence', because 'we want to have a very serious talk with them'.[1] Trochu, Garnier-Pagès, Dorian and Arago each in turn tried to convince Flourens that the Government was doing all that could possibly be done, but Flourens refused to be deceived. In an attempt to shame them he renounced the 'command' Trochu had given him, an act he was later to regret.

Flourens' precipitate action only frightened off many republicans. The Vigilance Committee movement was not united in seeking a confrontation with the Provisional Government. The moderates, amongst whom were both Proudhonists and neo-Jacobins, wanted a union of all republicans. The more revolutionary wing, to which the anti-Jacobin Lefrançais belonged as well as many Blanquists,

[1] Mayor Arago, *Dépositions*, I, p. 537.

took as their model the 'sections' of 1793. The 18th arrondissement declared that 'the *quartiers* are the fundamental base of the democratic Republic',[1] while the International in a circular described the committees as 'the first elements of the future revolutionary Commune'.[2] At the end of September Lefrançais had proposed that the Central Committee of the Twenty Arrondissements itself should hold an armed demonstration in support of a manifesto declaring that 'only the formation of the Paris Commune can put an end to the obstructions and irresolutions of the Provisional Government. The safety of the country and of the Republic, citizens of Paris, depends on your energy and your resolution.' But the moderates within the Central Committee were able to tone this down, and the final proclamation declared that 'far from wishing to provoke conflicts', they sought 'only to use their influence, their moral force, to arouse the people themselves, by means of their own regularly elected delegates, to take over the direction of the present and the responsibility for the future'. It called on the population to hold local assemblies on 9 October 'to prepare for yourselves the constitution of your municipality'.[3]

A few days later the Central Committee issued another 'Declaration of Principles' in which it said that it accepted the authority of the Government and of the Mayors, which did not prevent it continuing to announce the imminence of Communal elections.[4] In support of these the Central Committee staged its own demonstration on 8 October in front of the Hôtel de Ville, but neither the International nor the Trade Union Federation would join it. It had also failed to assure itself of the support of the National Guard, and rather than seeing the formation of election committees the Government was able to call out reliable National Guard battalions and

[1] *Le Combat*, 21 September.
[2] *Liberté. Egalité. Fraternité. République Française. Association Internationale des Travailleurs.* 'Dans l'impossibilité ou nous sommes de répondre à toutes les lettres particulières . . .', Paris, 1870: reprinted in J. Rougerie, '*Quelques documents nouveaux pour l'histoire du Comité central des vingt arrondissements*', *Le Mouvement Social*, October–December 1961, pp. 7–8. This article is one of the most important studies of the committee movement, as are J. Dautry and L. Scheler, *Le Comité Central Républicain des vingt arrondissements*, Paris, 1960; and R. D. Wolfe, '*The Origins of the Paris Commune: The Popular Organisations of 1868–71*', unpublished Ph.D. thesis, Harvard, 1966.
[3] *Le Combat*, 5 October: see Dautry and Scheler, op. cit., pp. 84–8; Rougerie, op. cit., p. 12.                [4] *Le Combat*, 9 October.

turn the occasion into an ovation for itself. Favre made a speech which concluded with a scarcely veiled threat against those who continued to trouble the Government's conduct of the defence. After this check of the Committee, Favre, Trochu and other members of the Provisional Government felt confident enough to beard Belleville itself during the next few days where, according to Ferry, they were generally enthusiastically received. The Government formally banned all further demonstrations, and bluntly declared that municipal elections would be postponed until after the siege was over. This firmness by the Government, however frustrating to the popular movement, caused 'great satisfaction' in other quarters, where it was taken as 'a sign of a rupture between those of the extremist party' and the Government itself, which clearly 'no longer intended to receive the law'[1] from the likes of Blanqui, Delescluze or Flourens. The Government tried to go even further and arrest the leading revolutionaries, particularly Blanqui and Flourens. But the Prefect of Police had to confess that his police dare not try to enter Belleville to effect this. Instead Kératry proposed that Trochu should invite Flourens to a conference so that he could be arrested when he left the security of the popular districts. Trochu, however, was not willing to compromise his honour in such Machiavellian schemes, nor would he allow the regular army to be used to effect any arrests. And so the Government had to abandon for the time being its hope of laying hands on its opponents. Its chief of police resigned instead, cursing Trochu's 'softness'. The wealthy, staunch republican Edmond Adam replaced Kératry at the Prefecture.

The difficulties the Provisional Government was facing in Paris were not appreciated by the Delegation at Tours, which decided independently to go ahead with the elections for an Assembly. This would have undermined the Government of National Defence's whole position, for if the provinces could have separate elections, so could Paris. The Government decided that the Delegation at Tours must be strengthened. The most obvious candidate, as the senior republican in the Government, was Jules Favre. This would have the additional advantage of freeing the Foreign Secretary from the difficulties of conducting his affairs from within a beleaguered city. But Favre refused, pleading patriotically that he could not leave the 'post of peril'. Favre also referred to the 'political difficul-

[1] D'Haussonville, op. cit., pp. 225-6.

ties' caused by the 'excited Paris population' that prevented him from leaving.[1] Jules Simon spelled this out when he wrote that 'in losing M. Jules Favre the Government would have lost its chief and principal force against the civil agitation',[2] for had not Favre once taken such revolutionaries as Louise Michel, Rigault and Ferré and hugged them in his big arms on the steps of the Hôtel de Ville.[3] There was too a question of age, since the journey out of Paris had to be made by the unsteerable and otherwise equally untrustworthy method of a balloon filled with highly inflammable coal-gas. It was upon the younger and fearless Gambetta that the honour fell on 7 October of being the first Minister of any government to make a balloon flight – with the additional danger of having to cross the fire of the enemy lines. His departure and eventual safe arrival to head the Delegation at Tours certainly roused up the provinces, but it was not completely cynical of Fidus to remark that 'his colleagues, regarding him as too inclined to side with the communists [over the conduct of the defence], persuaded him to go to the provinces under the pretext of hotting up the war, but in reality to free themselves of him'.[4]

The firmness of the Government against the pressure of the popular committees and the National Guard battalions led to a shift in outlook within the committee movement. The Central Committee of the Twenty Arrondissements tried to persuade the International and the Trade Union Federation to regain their leading role in the vigilance committees and give them a firm leadership. But both organizations of the Corderie refused to become officially involved in 'such uncertain events' which could 'compromise' them in their prime task of social and economic reform.[5] Instead it was left to the Blanquists and other revolutionaries to move away from the vigilance committees and found their own clubs, inherently a more revolutionary form of organization than the open public meeting on which the committees had been based. Thus when the Liberal majority at the Folies-Bergères meetings came out in support of the Government, the Blanquists left it and founded the Club des Montagnards. The revolutionary minority of the meeting in the rue du Château

---

[1] *Dépositions*, I, pp. 336–7 (Favre); p. 283 (Trochu); pp. 392–3 (Ferry); p. 548 (Gambetta).
[2] Simon, op. cit., p. 4.          [3] Michel, op. cit., p. 70.
[4] 11 October: Fidus, *Journal*, Paris, 1889, vol. 1, p. 102.
[5] Lefrançais, *Etude*, pp. 90–1; *Souvenirs*, p. 409.

d'Eau in the 10th arrondissement founded the Club de la Commune. The point about a club was, as the neo-Jacobin Andrieu said, that it could pass quickly 'from words to action'.[1] The clubs were usually doctrinally more intransigent, and in several cases they issued general statements of principle, though these mostly went no further than the French Revolution's Declaration of the Rights of Man. But when a member of the audience at the Club de la Revendication tried to defend the Government the President told him that 'the meeting was a club and not a public meeting where anyone could enter and speak as he liked; that in order to take part in the club, it would be necessary to inscribe oneself in favour of the principles sustained by the committee'.[2] Blanqui's own club, the Club de la Patrie en danger, declared that 'we have resumed the reasonable traditions of '48 and '93. We do not force anyone to take part in our assemblies; but we intend to retain control over them.'[3] Not all clubs were so radical, and some were run by Orleanists and liberal republicans – for example, the Club de la Porte Saint-Martin, where Lefrançais was shouted down when he tried to speak. As the counterpart of this movement towards more closely defined clubs the Central Committee ceased to exercise any wide influence, and by November it had become simply a federation of the clubs of the central arrondissements.

The test of their passing to action came at the end of October. On 27 October Félix Pyat's paper, Le Combat, announced that the 'glorious' Bazaine had treacherously surrendered Metz. Pyat was one of the most demagogic of the returned exiles of '48, and was soon to bedevil the debates of the Commune itself. Since Pyat later claimed he had received the news from Rochefort, who had told him to keep it quiet, it seems unlikely that the Government was in complete ignorance of the fact that Bazaine was indeed at that very moment negotiating the details of the surrender. The news of the surrender had already been published by the British Press the day after it had by Pyat. It was none too wise therefore to brashly declare that not only had Metz not surrendered, but that Bazaine was supposedly carrying out 'brilliant sorties' against the enemy, something he had always been too cautious to attempt at any time during the siege. But at least the denunciation of the paper as a 'Prussian

[1] A.H.G., quoted Wolfe, op. cit., p. 192.
[2] 8 October: see La Cloche, 13 October.
[3] La Patrie en danger, 5 October.

organ' turned the crowds against Pyat. Copies of the newspaper were burnt and its offices wrecked.

The next day vengeance turned to elation as Paris received the news of the first French victory since the beginning of the siege. An ambitious French commander, Carey de Bellemare, chafing at inaction, had on his own initiative seized the exposed plain of Le Bourget (where the airport is today). On the morning of this unexpected victory de Bellemare hastened back to Paris to deliver the good news personally to Trochu, expecting to be promoted to General on the spot. Trochu was less than pleased, and having pointed out the strategic uselessness of the captured position, suggested to the crestfallen commander that he return to his post before the Prussians recaptured it, which they did the following day. On 30 October, therefore, the Government had to announce that Le Bourget had been retaken (at the cost of 1,200 French soldiers, chiefly prisoners), and Trochu's explanation that it was unimportant as it was 'not part of our general system of defence' seriously failed to mollify an outraged public opinion. As Sarcey says: 'in itself the loss was nothing . . . but it came at a very unfortunate moment and in the most offensive manner possible'.[1]

Finally, on 31 October, the Government had to eat its words and officially admit that Metz had indeed fallen. Alongside this, as supposedly 'good news'[2] to match the bad, it also posted up the news that Thiers was negotiating with Bismarck and was likely to obtain an armistice. This latter news did indeed raise the hopes and confidence of the 'peaceful section of the well-off and business classes'.[3] But on the popular classes it had the reverse effect, compounding the news of Bazaine's surrender, which the populace immediately put down to treachery, by making it appear that the Government intended Paris to follow the example of Metz.[4] The workers, according to Fidus, made no secret of their intention to overthrow the Government if it tried to treat with the enemy.

These 'three blows to the chest', as Lissagaray calls them, were the

---

[1] Op. cit., p. 139.  [2] Ferry, *Dépositions*, I, p. 395.
[3] Fidus, 30 October, op. cit., pp. 188-9.
[4] At Tours Gambetta published a proclamation declaring Bazaine a traitor. After the war Bazaine was court-martialled and imprisoned. He was probably allowed to escape, and he lived out his exile in Spain. More recent explanations put his conduct down to incompetence along with a doubtful loyalty rather than to outright treachery: cf. Howard, op. cit., pp. 276-83.

Sedan of the Government of National Defence, though they survived their 4 September. Towards midday a delegation from the arrondissement Mayors demanded that the Government hold elections in Paris. Arago took refuge in repeating his grand phrase that he would rather die on the steps of the Hôtel de Ville than surrender it. Trochu and Jules Simon likewise were profuse in assurances of their devotion to the Republic and its defence. By now the popular battalions of the National Guard were massing on the square in front of the Hôtel de Ville carrying tricolors (though not red flags) with '*A bas l'armistice!*', '*Vive la Commune!*', '*La levée en masse!*' on them. The Government tried to counter this demonstration by repeating its tactic of 8 October and sounding the *rappel* in the districts of the 'good' battalions. But the National Guards of these districts did not respond, or else simply joined in with the demonstrators in the square. This is the important similarity with the events of 4 September, or, looking ahead to the Commune, with 18 March. It was clear that the battalions of the National Guard were not willing to be used to hold back the crowds. The crowd in front of the Hôtel de Ville, as Trochu said, 'was drawn from all ranks of society'.[1] Favre, in his account, said that the reason the Government could not get any support from the National Guard was that 'the whole city had been caught up unreflectingly by a feeling of irritation which, for an instant, made it instinctively look for the safety of the country in the replacement of the Government by more energetic men'. Similarly, before the Commission of Inquiry into the causes of the Commune, he insisted that 'the most reasonable of men, the most well-to-do, the property owners who were most interested in order, the most noted among the conservatives, were prey to extremist exaltation; the idea that the Government could request an armistice from the enemy was intolerable to them'.[2]

Early in the afternoon the rumour began to spread that Arago had agreed to elections and that Trochu would be replaced by Dorian. The latter was an industrialist who was Minister of Works, and very popular because of the energy and efficiency he had shown in his task of providing arms. He later boasted that none of his workers had ever joined any of the demonstrations, as they were all too busy at their labour. The rumour of an agreement between the demon-

---

[1] *Dépositions*, I, p. 293.

[2] J. Favre, *Le Gouvernement de la défense nationale. Simple récit*, Paris, 1873, vol. 1, p. 324; *Dépositions*, I, p. 337.

strators and the Government seemed sufficiently certain for the
national printing press to begin to roll off a poster announcing
elections, which was signed by Arago and Dorian. With elections
assured, as it was thought, some of the popular battalions began to
withdraw.

Until now neither the Blanquists nor the Central Vigilance
Committee had taken any part in the action. But towards the middle
of the afternoon a 300 to 400-strong demonstration led by several
members of the Central Committee, according to Lefrançais,[1]
marched off towards the Hôtel de Ville, and on the way met some of
the returning Guardsmen, who told them it was all over as elections
had been guaranteed. As Fidus said, some of the Belleville battalions
returned that afternoon because with the 'naivety of common people
and of children they believed everything was safely over'.[2] Already
the National Guards supposedly guarding the Hôtel de Ville were
themselves entering the building, and Lefrançais had little difficulty
in forcing his way into the Hôtel de Ville itself. He came across
Trochu, who was explaining to a group of Mayors how Le Bourget
had not been strategically important. Trochu and the rest of the
Government disappeared, and locked themselves in the Salon Jaune
on the south-west corner. Rochefort put in a brief appearance, and,
having failed to appease the crowd, he too disappeared. Lefrançais
claims that he read out a list of names to form a Commune, which
would have been headed by the ever-popular Dorian. (Trochu afterwards compared Dorian's popularity and role on this day to his own
on 4 September.)[3] The crowd seems then, by breaking open a door,
to have finally discovered the members of the Government. Lefrançais and others now tried to persuade Dorian to accept the new
honour of being President of the Commune, whilst trying to force
the others to resign. But Dorian preferred to stick to his guns, and
it looked as if the proclamation of the Commune was no nearer.
Then into what was already a confused, noisy, though surprisingly
non-violent situation, Flourens burst in, leading his Belleville sharp-
shooters, who were carrying their famed chassepots which, according
to Flourens, were loaded. In general very few National Guards
actually had any ammunition for their rifles. Brandishing his sword,
he jumped onto the table and proceeded to march up and down it,
tearing the green baize with his spurs, before the noses of the

[1] *Souvenirs*, pp. 416–17.                    [2] Op. cit., p. 234.
[3] *Dépositions*, I, p. 299.

ministers. Most of the latter remained comparatively calm. Trochu's philosophical disposition was able to ride above this breakdown of 'moral force', and with his back to the rest of the Government he sat immobile, puffing a cigar – and, adds Flourens, probably praying. Favre concentrated his attention on drawing geometrical doodles. Only Garnier-Pagès seems to have been attacked by a sudden sense of panic, and was rushed to the windows for air. Inevitably Flourens had his list for a Commune, or, as he seems to have preferred to call it, Committee of Public Safety. This, apart from the addition of his own name, was similar to earlier lists of the day, and consisted of Dorian, Blanqui, Millière, Ranvier, Félix Pyat, together with more moderate republican figures such as Louis-Blanc, who the next day was furious that he should have been considered for such an *équipe*, Ledru-Rollin, Raspail, Delescluze, the militant Internationalist Avrial, and Mottu, the Mayor of the eleventh arrondissement. This unhomogeneous group was to be rounded off by the addition of Victor Hugo.

Other Blanquists, including Blanqui himself, now arrived. Blanqui did not come until around 6.30 p.m., after he had heard that he had been made a member of the new government, for neither the Old One nor some of his younger followers had been very enthusiastic about getting involved with this demonstration. Outside, the crowd was fading away, tired and wet, and satisfied that there were going to be elections. Blanqui set to work in an adjoining room, issuing orders for the gates of Paris to be shut in case the Prussians decided to seize this opportunity to enter the city. He issued decrees for the requisitioning of food, and appointed Rigault to the post of Chief of Police. The latter set off to establish his claim at the Prefecture with 400 men, but was met by an armed deputy-prefect who informed him that Flourens had already appointed someone else. Calling Flourens 'an idiot, blunderer and imbecile' he went off to get reinforcements. A further message came from Flourens requesting his horse, which had somehow got lost in the general melée.[1]

By six in the afternoon it looked to many observers that in the American ambassador's words 'the revolution had been practically accomplished, and that we should have a genuine Red Republic'.[2]

[1] Lamber, op. cit., pp. 220–1; Da Costa, op. cit., pp. 340–1, says Rigault did prepare to take the Prefecture by force, but the collapse of the revolt prevented this.

[2] Washburne, op. cit., p. 210.

Lefrançais had already left the Hôtel de Ville to attend a crowded meeting of delegates from the arrondissement committees in the Ecole de Médecine in order to prepare lists of candidates for the expected elections. This meeting, confident that all was safely over, discussed names until four in the next morning.[1] But already the revolutionaries' hold over the Hôtel de Ville was beginning to slip. Picard had left as soon as the crowd had first entered and Adam was marched out by some of his own men pretending to 'arrest' him about the time of Flourens' arrival. As the news spread that the Government was a prisoner officials and leading citizens such as the Orleanist Comte D'Haussonville gathered in the Louvre to try to find someone who would call out the army against the insurgents. A few of the 'good' battalions of the National Guard had now somewhat tardily begun to assemble on the news that the Blanquists were in control at the Hôtel de Ville. Colonel Ibos, commander of the 106th battalion of the quartier Saint Germain, had managed with great difficulty to persuade about half his battalion to make an attempt to enter the Hôtel de Ville to rescue the Government. The next day some of his battalion published a protest against his action, saying they had not meant to overthrow the Commune, whilst another section published a counter-proclamation to this defending Ibos' action. 'Jesuistically', as Flourens puts it, crying '*Vive la Commune*', this battalion forced its way into the Salon Jaune. Ibos joined Flourens on the commanding position of the table, which collapsed under their combined weight. This incident seems to have diverted the eagle eye of Flourens, for when he got up neither Trochu nor Jules Ferry were any longer there. Ibos' men managed to smuggle out Trochu, who had removed his epaulettes and put a National Guard kepi on his head, with Jules Ferry clinging to his coat tail.

Trochu's appearance at the Louvre around 8.30 p.m. raised the hopes of those there. But then, instead of ordering the use of force, he actually checked Ducrot, who, when he heard late in the day that Trochu was a prisoner, had called for his horse and was half-way down the Champs-Elysées with a whole infantry division and a battery of cannons and machine guns, on his way to take the Hôtel de Ville by force. Trochu insisted that only the National Guard should be used, and proceeded to astonish his listeners by excusing the rebels, saying that their passions had been exasperated by the

[1] Lefrançais, op. cit., p. 421.

D

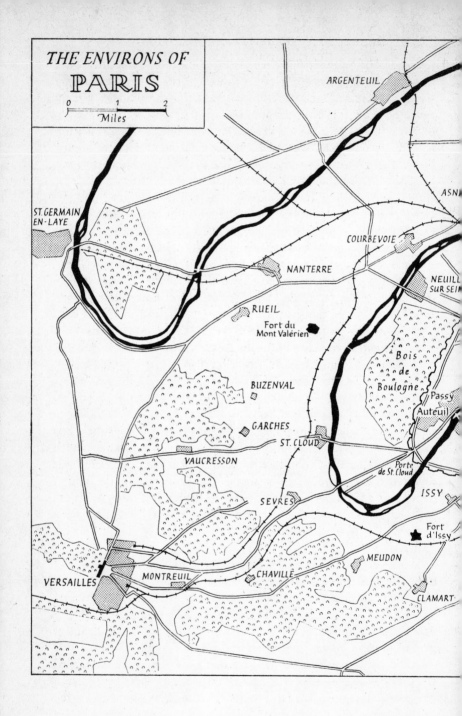

# THE ENVIRONS OF
# PARIS

0  1  2
Miles

ARGENTEUIL

ASN

ST.GERMAIN
EN-LAYE

COURBEVOIE

NANTERRE

NEUILL
SUR SEI

RUEIL

Fort du
Mont Valérien

Bois
de
Boulogne

Passy

Auteuil

BUZENVAL

GARCHES

ST. CLOUD

VAUCRESSON

Porte
de St.Cloud

SÈVRES

ISSY

Fort
d'Issy

MEUDON

VERSAILLES

MONTREUIL

CHAVILLE

CLAMART

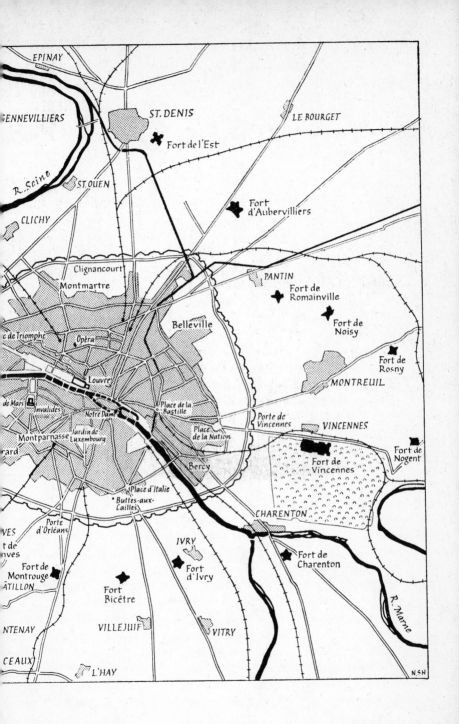

news of the fall of Metz.[1] Accordingly, Jules Ferry and Adam set out at the head of the assembled National Guards. Some shots were fired in front of the Hôtel de Ville, though no one was hit, and Delescluze then came out to parley. It was agreed, according to Adam, that the Hôtel de Ville would be evacuated on the understanding that the Government should hold to its promise over elections. Two more hours passed, and Delescluze was clearly having difficulty enforcing his role of mediator. Then someone remembered the secret underground passageway dating from the time of Napoleon I linking the Hôtel de Ville to the nearby barracks. Adam, since Ferry thought it below his ministerial dignity, led a group of *mobiles* into the midst of the insurgents by this subterranean entrance. Ferry too managed finally to get in and join up with Adam. The revolutionaries now realized that both inside and certainly outside they were outnumbered. After further negotiations they agreed to leave, on the understanding once again that municipal elections would be held the next day, that the Government would put itself to the test of universal suffrage, and that there would be no reprisals. As a sign of this latter agreement, General Tamasier, the official Commander of the National Guard, in person escorted Blanqui down the main staircase, out into the deserted place, where they shook hands and separated. It was around 4.0 a.m. and after a last look round to make sure the Hôtel de Ville was indeed empty, Ferry and Adam went home too.

The next day when the Government met there was a stormy session. Adam, who had been awoken by a cheerful Picard asking if he had already arrested Blanqui, Pyat, Flourens, Millière, Delescluze and the other insurgents, stood firm that a contract had been made with the revolutionaries the previous day. On his honour he refused to sign a decree for their arrest, and he and Ferry exchanged sharp words over this. Dorian, with Adam's encouragement, was more compliant, and since he did not actually have to sign anything he agreed to 'sacrifice' his 'dignity' in the interests of his country, and he remained to direct the armaments production. Rochefort also resigned, though his reason was that the Government insisted on staying in Paris. Adam was replaced by Cresson, and General Clément Thomas took over as head of the National Guard in place of Tamasier, who felt his honour would not let him remain at his post if the Government decided to arrest Blanqui. Lefrançais, Vallès, Jaclard, Vésinier, Vermorel, Eudes (of La Villette fame) and others

[1] D'Haussonville, op. cit., p. 264.

were arrested during the next few days. But the Government had
no way of getting hold of Flourens or Blanqui at the beginning of
December, whilst they remained in Belleville. Flourens was later
caught at the front line with his battalion at the battle of Champigny,
but was then released in the last revolt of the siege. When they were
eventually all brought to trial in February, only Vallès was given a
sentence, and even he managed to escape from the courtroom with
the help of a sympathetic guard, 'an old moustached long-service
sergeant'. Blanqui and Flourens in their absence were condemned
to death. Blanqui was apprehended in the provinces, to the great
satisfaction of Thiers, on the eve of the Commune.

Clearly something had to be done to satisfy the constant demand
for elections, and so the Government reversed the order and decided
to submit itself not to the test of elections but to the Bonapartist
system of a plebiscite, which amounted simply to asking for a vote
of confidence. This was to be followed by elections for Mayors only,
not for a full municipal council. Arago's poster of 31 October was
torn down, which did not prevent the Mayor of the 6th arrondissement from publishing a declaration calling for the Government to
get rid of all the 'generals, who are the cause of our disasters', and
Clemenceau from declaring himself on the side of the agreement of
31 October. Ferry replaced the too-compliant Arago as Mayor at
the Hôtel de Ville. The arrests soured opinion, leading many moderate papers to attack the Government because of them, and Ferry
later admitted that to have tried to execute any of the insurgents at
this stage would only have produced another revolt.[1] The plebiscite
of 3 November gave the Government a big majority with 322,900
civil and 237,000 military 'yea' votes against 54,000 civil and 9,000
military 'noes'. This victory, said Ferry, opened up a long credit to
the Government of National Defence. The mayoral elections were
less satisfactory, though there was a forty per cent drop in turnout
which may well have been due to abstentions by bourgeois voters,
and the elections for the mayoral deputies, the adjoints, were for the
same reason still more distasteful to conservatives. Particular exception was taken to the election of Mottu in the 11th arrondissement,
Delescluze in the 19th, and Ranvier, with Millière and Lefrançais as
adjoints, in the 20th. In this latter case those elected had just been
arrested for their part in the events of 31 October, and so the Government had to declare the election null and appoint a provisional

[1] *Dépositions*, I, pp. 402-4.

council. But on the whole Ferry was able to declare himself satisfied with the results.

The Mayors, now that they were elected, in many cases administered their arrondissements with considerable autonomy. There was a regular meeting of about half the Mayors once or twice a week in the Mairie of the 8th arrondissement. According to Mayor Corbon, who later opposed the Commune, this was because many of them had little confidence in the Government's conduct of the siege. At one of these meetings, for example, a project was drawn up to settle the question of a moratorium on rents without any consultation with the Government at the Hôtel de Ville. Choppin, the deputy-Prefect of Police, afterwards complained of this independence of many Mayors, saying that they tried to 'carry out an entire legislation' of their own.[1] Bonavalet was singled out by Choppin for having decreed and tried to enforce compulsory primary education in the 3rd arrondissement. Bonavalet also organized the policing of his arrondissement by the National Guard and forbade entry to any of the regular police agents. In the 11th arrondissement the Mayor, Mottu, carried out a full secularization programme. He forbade all religious teaching in the schools, and removed the crucifixes from the municipal ambulances. Ferry had earlier tried to get him dismissed for such an abuse of his authority, but he had been triumphantly returned in the November elections. Mottu had also classified an unmarried father along with the married men to prevent him being sent to the front along with the bachelors. The report of this action gained applause at the club de Faubourg Saint-Antoine, where Tartaret of the 1867 Workers' Delegation had raised the important class issue of those workers who, because they had not become married, were therefore ineligible for a Guardsman's marriage allowance.[2]

This *de facto* decentralization was most marked in the outer arrondissements. In the 17th the Internationalists led by Malon, the adjoint, with the help of Varlin gradually took over the administration of the municipality from the aged Mayor, François Favre (no relation to the Minister, Jules). Favre afterwards had to confess that 'I would throw the Internationalists out by one door and they would come back in by another'.[3] Malon helped set up a new branch of the

---

[1] Choppin, *Enquête*, II, p. 119.

[2] M. G. de Molinari, *Les Clubs rouges pendant le siège*, Paris, 1871, p. 75.

[3] *Enquête*, II, p. 381.

International in the western part of the arrondissement, the section Ternes, and its members were given posts in the municipal administration.[1] There were many refugees from the Prussian advance as well as unemployed, and efforts were made to provide food and lodging. André Léo, the feminist novelist and future wife of Malon, used the mutual aid society she had started, La Solidarité, to draw up a list of those in need in the arrondissement and distribute a daily allowance. A municipal restaurant was established, inevitably called La Marmite. Malon instituted a voucher system to guarantee a week's lodging in empty apartments. But the angry owners evicted their unwelcome tenants, knowing they could rely on the central government to back them up against the Mairie.[2] Attempts were made to secularize education, and Ferdinand Buisson, later a Radical-Socialist Deputy in the Third Republic and active in educational reform, was asked by Malon to take charge of the 'secular municipal orphanage' for the 'children of Free-Thinkers' that had been started by the end of January.[3] Workshops were established to make uniforms, and these gave work to some five hundred women.[4] By the end of the siege Mayor Favre was receiving letters complaining that the middle classes were being discriminated against in favour of the poor.[5] The advent of the Commune simply removed a hostile central authority, giving the arrondissement complete freedom to develop its measures of social self-help.

The failure from the revolutionary point of view of 31 October, the only serious uprising in Paris during the siege, showed up the revolutionaries' lack of organization. When they had the Government of the day in captivity, as it were, they did not know what to do with the opportunity that had fallen into their hands. Then, as the plebiscite and elections showed, they were still a small minority in Paris. The Central Committee, the *Réveil* (of Delescluze), the *Patrie en Danger* (of Blanqui), the *Combat* (of Pyat) campaigned against the Government over the plebiscite, but they were only followed in the polls by the northern and eastern suburbs, which had been

[1] *Le Rappel*, 9 November.
[2] André Léo, '*Mémoires*', I.I.S.H., 'Descaves Collection', pp. 75–6.
[3] *La République des Travailleurs*, 5 February 1871; Minutes of General Council of International, London, 21 March: *Documents of the First International*, London, 1967, vol. IV, p. 160.          [4] Léo, op. cit., pp. 73–4.
[5] See letter of E. Joly, February 1871: I.I.S.H., 'Descaves Collection', papers on 17th arrondissement.

solidly against the Empire in the plebiscite of May 1870. It has been
suggested that the plebiscite and mayoral elections, taken together,
show that about fifteen to twenty per cent of the Paris population,
heavily concentrated in the four north-eastern arrondissements
(11th, 18th, 19th and 20th), was 'revolutionary socialist' as the term
was used then.[1] But for the rest of the population, as the events of
31 October had shown, the name of Blanqui was sufficient to chase
them into the arms of the Government. General Tamasier, in his
account,[2] rightly divided 31 October into two parts, before and after
the freeing of Trochu. It was the arrival of Flourens and then of
Blanqui that finally decided the bourgeois battalions to intervene.
The Revolutionaries were not a coordinated group: the Blanquists
were divided amongst themselves as to what to do, and the Belleville
battalions did not appear in full strength. But even had the revolutionaries overthrown the Government of National Defence, there
would have been no direct threat of a revolutionary government.
The lists of the proposed Commune, each headed by Dorian, show
that, far from wishing to impose a dictatorship, the desire was to
appeal to a wide range of opinion. The prime task was the winning
of the war; it was the Government's failure to set a lead in this that
had given the revolutionaries their opportunity, whilst at the same
time limiting both what was desired or could be accomplished.

One effect, however, was to make an armistice impossible at this
time, and the men of affairs had to postpone the 'projects' they had
been planning. Bismarck still insisted on the occupation of a fort
as a *quid pro quo* for allowing Paris to be reprovisioned, and Trochu
would not agree any more now than in September to surrendering
Paris without revictualling. Bismarck's insistence on a fort made it
impossible for the Government to put the idea of an armistice across
to the Paris population. Then when Bismarck heard of the revolt of
31 October, the very day Thiers was hoping finally to complete the
negotiations, he declared that the Prussians could not treat with a
government that might be reversed at any moment. According to
Thiers, he and Bismarck wondered whether it would not be better
to proceed to 'volume two', as Bismarck put it, and conclude a
peace treaty then and there. But this idea was even more impractic-

---

[1] By Wolfe, op. cit., p. 249.

[2] *Dépositions*, II, p. 333 (Tamasier); Ferry says that 'if the name of Blanqui
had not been mentioned the elections announced by the poster of Arago and
Dorian would have taken place' (I, p. 431).

able, and Thiers could not even return into Paris because of the state
of popular indignation. So Thiers and Favre had to meet on 5
November in a depressing half-destroyed house in no-man's-land
at Sèvres. Favre knew that the Provisional Government dare not
accept Bismarck's terms and surrender a fort as part of an armistice
agreement, and so for a second time negotiations had to be broken off.

After the check of 31 October and the November elections, there
was a second burst of activity in the forming of new clubs and
leagues. One of these leagues was the former railway worker's,
Antoine Rocher's, Légion Garibaldienne, which attracted both
Internationalists and Blanquists. This was primarily a military
organization and the intention was to form a corps of volunteers
under the red flag to break through and join Garibaldi in the south.
More explicitly socialist was the Ligue républicaine de la défense à
outrance, which linked defeat of the Prussians to the need for social
and democratic reforms. It grew out of a proposal by Chatelain, the
secretary of the Central Committee of the Twenty Arrondissements,
and by December about half of all the local vigilance committees had
joined it, particularly those of a Blanquist orientation. The Legion
and the League at the end of November joined forces with the help
of the Central Committee and formed the Club Central. The Blanquists were dominant in this also, seeking to organize the overthrow
of the Government by a revolutionary *coup*. The International still
pursued its policy of keeping clear as a body of such political groups,
especially any dominated by the Blanquists. But together with the
Workers' Trade Union Federation it did publish a protest against
Thiers' negotiations at a time when 'the soil of France is invaded',
declaring that the working class was more than ever determined to
'sustain the war *à outrance*'.[1] Individual members of the International,
in contrast to the official aloofness, played a full role in the clubs and
committees, and by mid-December there was a whole series of
interlocking popular organizations throughout Paris, particularly so
in the predominantly working-class and petit-bourgeois districts.
In the 5th arrondissement, for example, the public meeting of the
rue d'Arras was affiliated to the Légion Garibaldienne; the Club de la
Révolution to the Ligue républicaine; the Club du Collège de France
to the Club Central; and the Club démocratique socialiste de l'Ecole
de Droit to the local vigilance committee and to the Central

[1] *République Française. Liberté, Egalité, Fraternité.* 'Citoyens, *Au moment ou le sol de
la France est envahi . . .', Paris, 1870.

Committee of the Twenty Arrondissements. In addition the president of the Club de la Révolution, Edouard Rouillier, also belonged to the vigilance committee of the 5th arrondissement, and the leader of the rue d'Arras meeting, Rocher, was a member of the Central Vigilance Committee.[1]

Many of these clubs, like those before October, sought to limit membership in order to maintain a militant posture. This was true for example of the Democratic and Socialist Club of the 13th Arrondissement, founded in mid-November by the young lawyer and future Communard, Léo Melliet. The aim of the club, according to its rules, was 'to study all the political and social problems concerning the freeing of labour and the emancipation of workers, and to pursue the solution by revolutionary means'. It intended 'to use its influence to provoke the insurrection of labour against any attempt at a monarchist restoration or against the action of any government that tried to check or defer the arrival of the democratic and social Republic'. Members had to be ready at any time to respond to the call to turn out in the streets. On 25 November the club voted to join the International en bloc.[2] Its membership included several Blanquists and radical republicans who were to play major roles in the Commune; Duval and Rigault in particular. Such clubs still held open meetings from time to time, and a few successful attempts were actually made to start newspapers. One of the local branches of the International, that of Batignolles and Ternes in the 17th arrondissement, had its own paper, *La République des Travailleurs*. The strongly Internationalist Club de l'Ecole de Médecine in the 6th arrondissement published the *Lutte à outrance*, with which the central Council of the International considered officially associating itself just before the end of the siege. But by this time the paper was on the verge of folding up; at least said Lacord, at the Council meeting of the International of 26 January, the paper should go down in 'a worthy manner by getting itself suppressed for publishing an appeal to the army', as would have befitted its patriotic title. The Blanquist club had *La Résistance* and the appropriately named *Oeil de Marat*.

In the 18th arrondissement the Blanquist vigilance committee, whose membership was about sixty per cent working-class by profession, decided to form the Club de la Révolution following the

[1] Wolfe, op. cit., p. 361.
[2] A.H.G., Ly 22 *bis*, 'Clubs'; their declaration of adherence was published in *La Patrie en Danger*, 28 November.

events of 31 October. This consisted on the one hand of a loose federation of the local clubs in the various districts of the arrondissement, whilst at the same time, anyone who regularly attended the meetings of a local club could become an 'active' member if he subscribed to their declaration of principles. This Declaration combined Jacobin republican virtues with a somewhat Proudhonist definition of socialist equality. 'Revolutionary' it defined as 'to place force at the service of right in order to establish justice'. But the real uniting element was the cry for a 'revolutionary Commune'. The 'active' members held meetings of their own. The executive body of this federation was the vigilance committee of the arrondissement, which was now responsible only to the 'active' members of the Club de la Révolution. By the end of the siege its 'active' membership was probably close to 1,000, and the total membership was a significant proportion of the nearly 6,000 voters who had voted against the Government in the November plebiscite.[1]

The clubs were in effect the only form of entertainment for the populace in the city, theatres and other places of amusement having closed down at the start of the siege. As the winter became worse the clubs were at least warmer and lighter than most dwellings – places where one could rekindle body and spirit. The debates were usually very disorderly and covered all the immediate problems of the city's defence. Constant demands were made for rationing and for the seizure of food stocks in shops so that they could be equally distributed. Right at the beginning of the siege, on 26 September, at the Club Belleville, Vésinier, who had been Eugène Sue's secretary and valet-de-Chambre, had proposed the arrest of Godillot and the expropriation of his shoe factory to the profit of the nation because he treated his workers in a fashion 'incompatible with republican institutions'. Fidus, who noted this proposal with horror, said the workers intended to apply this to other industries too.[2] Ingenious methods for defeating the Prussians were proposed, of which the use of Greek Fire was the most canvassed, but that of poisoning the Seine the most comprehensive – as was pointed out to its protagonist by another speaker at the Folies-Bergère club on this occasion, who was understandably concerned about what would be left for the Parisians to drink.[3] Jules Allix, a socialist theorist of the Fourierist

[1] R. D. Wolfe, 'The Parisian *Club de la Révolution* of the 18th Arrondissement, 1870–1871', *Past and Present*, April 1968, pp. 94–8.    [2] Op. cit., p. 114.
[3] Molinari, op. cit., pp. 45–7: Folies-Bergère club, 2 October.

school, who had organized the formation of the vigilance committee in the 8th arrondissement, proposed to the feminist club at the Gymnase Triat his idea of 'prussic acid fingers'. Allix, in 1850, had already shown his inventive skills by his telegraphic system of 'sympathetic snails'. His new idea was for indiarubber thimbles tipped with a small pointed tube full of prussic acid, which he claimed would be an ideal weapon for the women's brigade that Félix Belly had proposed creating. These were to be called 'the Amazons of the Seine', and were to be dressed in a uniform of black and orange, with a crossbelted ammunition pouch, and were 'to defend the ramparts and the barricades, and to afford to the troops in the ranks of which they will be distributed all the domestic and fraternal services compatible with moral order and military discipline'. Armed with Allix's prussic acid pins the Amazons would be able to kill every Prussian who tried to attack them, until they would end up 'still standing, still pure and holy, in a circle of corpses!' Belly claimed 1,500 women signed up, but Trochu would have none of it.[1]

A more practical activity of Allix's was the Comité des femmes in the rue d'Arras, which he founded. Allix advocated the establishment of communal workrooms for women. Mme Poirier (Sophie Doctrinal), whose husband was prominent in the vigilance committee of the 18th arrondissement, set up a workshop which employed some 70–80 women making clothing for the National Guard. This was a truly socialistic enterprise, for profits were shared in place of a salary. Louise Michel, the most famous of the women Communards, was active at this time in the vigilance committee of the 18th arrondissement, where were found 'enthusiasts and sceptics equally fanatical for the revolution, wanting it beautiful and ideally great'. Her favourite club was that of Blanqui's La Patrie en Danger, and she wrote that both there and in the Montmartre vigilance committee she spent 'the finest hours of the siege. One was a little more fully alive there, with the joy of feeling oneself in one's element, in the midst of the intense struggle for liberty.'[2]

Some of the new clubs formed in November and December were strongly working class in membership. In these the revolutionary slogans of 1792 and 1848 were combined with demands for specific

[1] E. Thomas, *The Women Incendiaries*, Eng. trans. London, 1967, pp. 34–5.
[2] Michel, op. cit., pp. 91–2.

improvements in the lot of the working class. One such workers' group in the 20th arrondissement published an appeal which began:

> In the name of the fatherland in danger, in the name of France – deceived, divided, despoiled and upon the brink of the abyss – the citizens comprising the *groupe de Charonne* call upon the republican socialists of the various schools to unite and to cooperate better than they have done up to now with the men who, by their experience, courage and ability have given obvious proofs of their devotion to the republican cause, and to spontaneously institute the Commune. The revolutionary Commune, the majority of whose members, to be fair, should consist of workers; of true workers, of workers who are not property owners, but workers labouring with their hands in order to attend to their needs; of workers, finally, supporting the full weight of life's difficulties and understanding all of the aspiration of our republican slogan, all of the importance of association and solidarity.

They went on to demand the overthrow of the men of the Hôtel de Ville, 'the debris and echo of all the monarchies, permanent and pitiless line of the exploitation of the proletariat', and the establishment of a 'Committee of Public Safety' as well as the Commune.[1] The revolutionary programmes of other clubs were often less explicit, having a more varied membership and a less *ouvriériste* outlook, but all alike called for a revolution in the interests of the working classes. 'It is necessary,' said the Internationalist Armond Lévy at the Club de l'Ecole de Médecine, 'that new forces emerge from the masses. We were defeated in 1792 so long as we were led by men of the old regime; it is with the men of the rising class that the decisive victory, with new tactics, will be ours.'[2]

Confronted by the public demand for action, and with no immediate prospect of attaining an armistice, the Government had to bestir itself to military action. Trochu, it was said, had a plan, and soon all Paris was talking, though usually with considerable scepticism, of '*le plan Trochu*'. At the beginning of the siege, Trochu seems to have hoped that the Prussians would try to mount an attack on Paris, which would enable the Parisians to repeat the story of Saragossa in reverse – where Trochu's idol Bugeaud in 1808–9 had taken the city house by house – and in line with this Trochu had

[1] *Le Combat*, 17 January.
[2] *La Lutte à outrance*, 12 nivôse, an 79 (1 January 1871).

appointed Rochefort Minister of barricades. Moltke, however, realized that he would meet with fierce resistance and had settled down to starve the French out. Bismarck, as he wrote to his wife, was quite content to let the Parisians 'stew in their own juice for a while'. Since the Prussians did not attack, the few sorties that did occur depended, so far as Trochu was concerned, simply on chance circumstances. The restless Ducrot, however, persuaded Trochu to agree to attempt to break through at what was thought to be one of the weakest points in the Prussian lines, that of the north-west across the Gennevilliers peninsula on the Seine. If they could break out past Argenteuil, the way would be open through unoccupied country towards Rouen and the port of Le Havre. Preparations were begun and a build-up started, which was not unnoticed by the Germans, so as to be ready some time towards the middle of November.

Then came news from the south. Gambetta, in Tours, had set to work with vigour to build up a third French army, the army of the Loire, and by carefully massing his troops to gain a three-to-one numerical superiority. This army of 100,000, under its commander d'Aurelle de Paladines, no less cautious than the majority of Bonapartist Generals, had forced the Bavarians to retreat from the battlefield of Coulmiers on 9 November. The next day the French reentered Orleans, amongst great rejoicing at this signal victory. But this attack on Orleans had been delayed for ten days, on Thiers' insistence that there be no fighting whilst he was negotiating with Bismarck. As a result, instead of the French army's starting its move north whilst the army of Prince Frederick-Charles was still tied down before Metz, this second Prussian army had time to move south to strengthen the forces between d'Aurelle and Paris. 'We have had the misfortune,' Gambetta wrote to his deputy Freycinet, 'to see our cleverly conceived plan of offensive endangered ... by the intervention of M. Thiers,' who was of course more interested in concluding peace than waging a war.

Even now, had d'Aurelle pursued his advantage, he might still have outdistanced Prince Frederick-Charles, who wrote in his *Memoirs* of this time that nothing could have stopped the French advancing on Paris. And certainly at the German headquarters in Versailles the news of Coulmiers was considered very disconcerting. Engels, acting as a commentator on the war for the *Pall Mall Gazette*, wrote on 26 November, that 'before the 9th November, there appeared to be no serious obstacle to prevent this mass of men [i.e. the German armies] from overrunning the greater part of central and even southern France. But since then things have changed considerably, and it is not so much the fact of Van der Tann having been beaten and compelled to retreat [after Coulmiers], or that of d'Aurelle having shown his ability to handle his troops well, which has inspired us with a greater respect for the Army of the Loire than we confess we had up to that day; it is chiefly the energetic measures which Moltke took to meet its expected march on Paris which have made that army appear in quite a different light.' But d'Aurelle's raw troops were exhausted after their first experience of action, though their morale was naturally high. Instead, therefore, of preparing to push forward as soon as he could, d'Aurelle proceeded to establish himself in Orleans as if he himself was about to be besieged, rather than advancing to relieve one. False news that an army of 80,000 German troops were close at hand encouraged d'Aurelle in his dilatoriness, though at this time there were not more than half that number before them. Thiers seemed to have passed on this unencouraging piece of exaggerated information, and his advice to Gambetta after Coulmiers was that negotiations should be reopened, as this military victory had saved the 'honour' of France and so peace could now be made.

Gambetta's position in the provinces was the reverse of the Provisional Government's in Paris. In the latter case a government seeking to obtain peace was being constantly harried by a population feverish for war. In the provinces the peasantry and local notables wanted peace, whereas Gambetta was trying to create a mass movement for a protracted war.[1] After the war the rural right in the Assembly at Bordeaux attacked him viciously as a tyrant. The generals in the provinces intensely disliked being under Gambetta, with his constant talk of fighting to save the Republic. Bourbaki had refused to take command of the Loire army, and after Coulmiers d'Aurelle in effect retired, and failed to come up with any further plans. 'The French generals,' said the German Colonel Lecomte, seemed to be fighting 'against their own wishes,' and Von Stosch wrote on 14 November that 'had the French a notion of generalship, things might turn out very badly for us'.[2] Confronted by d'Aurelle's

---

[1] J. Simon, *Le Gouvernement de M. Thiers*, Paris, 1878, p. 101: 'The Delegation at Tours was for the war *à outrance*, while at Paris the Government was constantly seeking peace.'

[2] Guillemin, op. cit., vol. 2, p. 21; Bury, op. cit., p. 182.

inaction, and unable to sack his only victorious general (Chanzy would have been an excellent replacement), Gambetta and his engineer deputy Freycinet decided to make a two-pronged advance. But by now German reinforcements had arrived, and Prince Frederick-Charles was firmly astride the route to Paris.

The only real support for the war in the provinces came from the big cities. In August there had been demonstrations in Lyon, Marseille – where the demonstrators seized the Hôtel de Ville for a time – and Le Creusot, where the red flag was paraded through the streets. On 4 September Lyon had anticipated Paris by a few hours in declaring the Republic, and a Committee of Public Safety had been proclaimed. Radical municipal councils were established in Toulouse, Grenoble and Marseille, and in Le Creusot, though the council was not changed, the worker Dumay was nominated as Mayor. On 28 September, Bakunin arrived in Lyon and tried, together with the Internationalists Albert Richard and Bastelica, from Marseille, to carry out an anarchist revolution. Having declared the abolition of the State from the Hôtel de Ville, 'the State, in the form and shape of two companies of bourgeois National Guard battalions, entered by a door that had been left unguarded and caused Bakunin to rapidly take the road back to Geneva'.[1] There were further disturbances in Lyon at the beginning of November, on the news of the fall of Metz, and in December a *canut* was killed by the crowd when he refused to lead his National Guard battalion against the Hôtel de Ville. Gambetta went to his funeral and there was a wave of arrests. Further south, the Ligue du Midi, a patriotic local republican organization, was centred on Marseille where the radicals Esquiros and Gaston Crémieux practically organized an independent government, with support from Bastelica and the local International. The programme of this League was mainly political and anti-clerical, though it did' call for a tax on wealth. The news of Metz caused a further uprising in Marseille, but this was to the disadvantage of the radicals, and Gambetta's delegate was able to establish some sort of control and put an end to the 'revolutionary Commune'. Saint-Etienne, on 31 October, had 'one hour of the Commune', as Lissagaray called it, and had hoisted the red flag and joined the Ligue du Midi. Toulouse on

---

[1] As Marx sarcastically put it in his 1873 pamphlet against Bakunin, 'L'*Alliance de la démocratie socialiste et l'Association Internationale des travailleurs*', given in J. Freymond, *La Première Internationale. Recueil de documents*, Geneva, 1962, vol. 2, p. 397.

the same day forced the commander of the local garrison to resign. And there was always the symbol of Garibaldi, who had raised a volunteer corps in Italy on the news of the fall of the Empire, and to the embarrassment of the Government in Paris and the military's distaste was fighting vigorously in the French Alps.

The only possible strategy for Gambetta would have been to have prepared and engaged in a partisan war across France.[1] The Germans

---

[1] This was the suggestion of Garcia Benito Juarez, the President of Mexico, who had driven the French out in 1867. Bazaine had been the French commander of the disastrous French expeditionary forces in Mexico, and thus, as Juarez said, he at least should have learnt the value of 'a partisan struggle, the truly defensive war against a victorious invader': letter of 18 December 1870, to a French friend, given in E. Lepelletier, *Histoire de la Commune de 1871*, Paris, 1901–13, vol. 1, pp. 536–8. Engels in his 'Notes on the War' for the *Pall Mall Gazette*, 11 October 1870, had made a similar point. He argued that, even after the fall of Strasbourg, the siege of the two fortresses of Metz and Paris was sufficient to tie down practically the whole German army. Thus 'it must be evident that if there was a real national enthusiasm alive among the French, everything might still be gained. While the whole forces of the invader, all but 60,000 men and the cavalry which can raid but not subdue, are laid fast in the conquered territory, the remaining five-sixths of France might raise armed bands enough to harass the Germans on every point, to intercept their communications, destroy bridges and railways, provisions and ammunition in their rear, and compel them to detach from their two great armies such numbers of troops that Bazaine might find means to break out of Metz, and that the investment of Paris would become illusory ... What would be the fate of the Germans if the French people had been stirred up by national fanaticism is not nowadays within the habits of civilized nations. It might be found among Mexicans and Turks; its sources have dried up in the money-making West of Europe, and the twenty years during which the incubus of the Second Empire has weighed upon France have anything but steeled the national character.' Engels' ironical reference to 'the habits of civilized nations', i.e. the 'money-making West of Europe', with regard to war was an issue the *Pall Mall Gazette* itself discussed in subsequent numbers. The next issue after Engels' article, 12 October, carried a leader on the subject of 'The Guerrilla Warfare of the Future', which discussed whether ordinary citizens had the 'right' to take up arms to defend their country against the forces of a regular invading army. Such partisan warfare, it was argued, was outside the 'recognized code' regarding war 'in civilized countries'. The problem was that 'acts done within the limits of that code are sanctioned by it. Outside the limits of that code all is vague. There is neither law nor recognized morality.' As this and subsequent issues (21, 23, 30 November and 24 December) makes clear, the Franco-Prussian war was seen as introducing into the conduct of 'civilized' Europe practices in war which until then had been used only against native populations in wars of colonial conquest. The

were in a fog about the French armies. The appearance, for example, of a French detachment of 35,000 men at Houden (two marches from Versailles) had caused the Germans to contemplate removing their headquarters, as they feared this was an advance of a large French army. But a partisan war would have implied a spirit of resistance throughout France that on the whole was lacking. It would also have meant, as it would have meant in Paris too, the revolutionizing of the war. The victories of the famous volunteer battalions of 1792–3 had been won because a revolutionary government, culminating in Robespierre's Committee of Public Safety, had exercised its will through its *représentants en mission*. New tactics and new commanders were found to replace the generals (most of whom had quickly emigrated) and parade ground formations of the Old Regime. The revolutionary armies in the end became agents of the Terror.[1] It was precisely this that the Government of National Defence wanted to avoid in Paris, whilst in the provinces, for all his republican patriotism, Gambetta was not willing to go that far. Nor was there in 1870–1 the peasant revolts, a *jacquerie*, which had contributed so greatly to the establishment of the first French Revolution.

The news of the French victory of Coulmiers in the south reached Paris on 14 November by a pigeon like a 'dove returning to the ark', and the Government placarded the news. 'The hour of deliverance has sounded,' wrote Sarcey,[2] and the *Figaro* naturally had to proclaim d'Aurelle a latter-day Maid of Orleans. Wiser spirits, such as D'Haussonville, hoped that Favre's public jubilation would be balanced by the 'good sense' of the military.[3] Trochu had earlier sent Ranc by balloon with only a very general message to Gambetta about

paper condemned both sides: the French because of 'the terrible consequences to civilization of doctrines sanctioning a *guerre à outrance*', i.e. by 'rousing up an unorganized nation to meet violence with violence'; the Prussians because 'of the novel organizing of military nations which suggest such doctrines', i.e. by using a conscripted army. In fact, of course, there were precedents for both forms of warfare in the French Revolution. But the sense of novelty expressed by these articles in the Press does emphasize the point that for France to have engaged in a real *guerre à outrance* in 1870 would have had revolutionary social implications.

[1] R. Cobb, *Les Armées révolutionnaires*, Paris, 1961–3, vol. 2, pp. 738–40; A. Soboul, *Les Soldats de l'An II*, Paris, 1959, pp. 79–209.
[2] Op. cit., p. 206.
[3] D'Haussonville, op. cit., p. 289.

the proposed sortie towards Rouen. In Tours, according to Gambetta, he and his military advisers studied the possibility of an advance on Paris from the north-west, but decided it would take far too long to build up sufficient forces, and so went ahead with their plans of an advance from the south. After Coulmiers, Gambetta sent a message that arrived in Paris on 18 November, suggesting that the Government there try to make a sortie, even if it was towards Normandy, as any direction would compel the Germans to relieve the forces opposing d'Aurelle. But by this time Trochu had already decided to change the direction towards the south, probably because he felt that this was what public opinion was clamouring for. On 29 November Ducrot's troops began to cross the Marne at Champigny. They had lost any advantage of surprise because at the last moment the attack had to be delayed twenty-four hours as the river was too swollen to get the pontoon bridges in place. Ducrot had refused to allow the National Guard to be used, which meant the clubs remained unsatisfied. At the end of three days the French were defeated at all points, and were half frozen from bivouacking in the bitter winter cold.[1] Ducrot, who had vaingloriously proclaimed that he would only 're-enter Paris dead or victorious', had to return alive and defeated.

Trochu had entrusted the vital message about the proposed sortie to a single balloon only five days earlier. This reached Gambetta the day after Ducrot had begun his sortie, since the message had been relayed on from the French consul in Norway, where the Ville d'Orléans had landed after unexpectedly making what was probably until then the longest manned balloon flight. The next day, 1 December, there came a dispatch to Tours from Favre, sent this time by two balloons, announcing the early French successes, including the capture of Epinay. Gambetta optimistically concluded that this must be the Epinay to the south of Orly, whereas in fact it was simply the diversionary attack to the north on Epinay-sur-Seine, and thus it seemed as if the sortie had indeed managed to break through the German lines. So Gambetta ordered his divided forces forward towards Paris. This was by now a hopeless move, and the French were driven back, until finally, on 4 December, Orleans had to be evacuated, the same day as Ducrot's withdrawal to Paris.

---

[1] The French treated their campaigns as if they were still an expeditionary force in the Sahara rather than an army that could have its own baggage train and find billets – as the Prussians did.

Gambetta and the Delegation had to move for safety's sake to distant Bordeaux.

With this double defeat the surrender of Paris was simply a matter of time. Winter had also set in, the coldest in living memory. Before the Prussians had completed their investment of Paris, the Government had tried to build up stocks of provisions. Early in September sheep, oxen, though through an oversight no milch cows, were grazing in the Bois de Boulogne and on many of the city's squares. The peasant farmers retreating to Paris before the advancing Prussians came loaded with produce, 'carts of cabbages, carts of pumpkins, carts of leeks',[1] and the Granaries were bursting. The Government was hopeful in a *laissez-faire* manner that these preparations would be sufficient. The liberal economic principles of the lawyers and financiers of the Provisional Government made them very unwilling to exercise any restraints on the operation of the free market in the besieged city. There were a few exceptions; meat was rationed by the end of September, though it was seldom available. Bread was in a sense rationed in that the Government owned nearly all the stocks of grain and so could control the daily distribution. But on 12 December an official poster was published to assure those who feared that their private supplies might be requisitioned that the Government had no intention of proceeding with the actual rationing of bread. By the end of the siege in January, however, the Government feared that lack of food might easily lead to agitation in the popular quarters. Reluctantly the Government accepted that they would have to 'transgress economic principles' and 'subscribe to a kind of socialism' by formally rationing bread.[2] This was a measure that the popular Press and the clubs had advocated right from the start of the siege, as had moderates such as Mayor Vacherot of the 5th arrondissement, only to be told that these were 'revolutionary measures that had no economic sense'.[3] Municipal canteens had been set up, and there were occasional distributions of rice, beans, dried peas, herrings and salted meat, chocolate even, but these were never sufficient to go round and often were sold off to

[1] Goncourt, 13 September.
[2] *Dépositions*, V, p. 454; see too Simon, *Histoire du G.N.D.*, pp. 239–62; E. L. Katzenbach, 'Liberals at War: The Economic Policies of the Government of National Defence', *American Historical Review*, July 1951, pp. 818–20.
[3] Vacherot, *Enquête*, II, pp. 390–1; Blanqui had been one of the first to demand rationing; see *La Patrie en Danger*, e.g. 7, 28 September, 22 October.

the highest bidders. If in December Edmond de Goncourt could write that 'hunger begins and famine is on the horizon',[1] noting that even his circle of privileged friends were complaining about monotonous and inadequate food, it can be imagined how grievously the system of 'rationing by dearness' was affecting the majority of the population. Horsemeat, first introduced a few years previously for the poor, now became fashionable for all classes. But the more exotic foods, such as the fabled rat, or the inmates of the zoo, including the two much-beloved young elephants, Castor and Pollux, did not really solve the food problem on anything like the large scale needed. Such unaccustomed meats, especially rats, needed lavish and expensive sauces to make them edible. So it was at the Jockey Club that menus appeared with *salmis de rat* and 'rat pie'. After the siege was over Goncourt and his friends presented to *Chez Brébant* a medallion inscribed: 'During the Siege of Paris a few people accustomed to foregathering at Monsieur Brébant's once a fortnight never on one single occasion perceived that they were dining in a city of two million besieged souls.' Just before the end, Goncourt felt the need to note that 'one must truly render justice to the Paris population and admire it. It is astonishing that this population, confronted by the insolent display in the food shops, heedlessly reminding a population *dying of hunger* that the rich with their money could always, yes always, obtain for themselves poultry, game, and other delicacies of the table, did not break the shopwindows nor attack the shopkeepers and their goods.' Faced by such effrontery, Goncourt went on, it was easy to sympathize with Marat's attacks on hoarders, and in a final burst of sympathetic anger Goncourt added that the Government should have 'hung a few of the hoarders from the fronts of their own shops' as an example to the rest.[2]

It was the women and children, milk being particularly scarce, who suffered most. The women had to go from queue to queue in the rain, cold, and finally snow. During the bombardment in the New Year several women were blown to bits waiting at night outside the shops so as to be first in the queue in the morning. Their men were comparatively better off, having as National Guards their army rations. Wine was about the one thing that was never scarce, and either in cafés, boasting how they would effect a great sortie that would once and for all finish the Prussians, or on the ramparts there was always company and usually some warmth from a fire. Inside the city fuel too was becoming scarce. On 25 November oil was requisitioned, which apart from removing a common source of heat, 'plunged the *ville lumière* into darkness'.[1] Coal ran out, leaving only wood. Soon trees throughout the city were being cut down by bands of workers, who did not spare the wooden fences in the more fashionable quarters. During the last week of the siege one thousand deaths were attributed to respiratory ailments. What is surprising is that there was no serious outbreak of plague, though by the end of the siege smallpox and typhoid deaths had risen from 203 a week to 755.[2]

After Champigny no more was heard of any 'plan' from the Government. The popular organizations were now converging on the idea of installing a revolutionary Commune, as clearly the Government was determined to avoid elections. Flourens' attempt to proclaim a Committee of Public Safety on 31 October had not been at all popular with the Corderie workers or with the members of the Central Vigilance Committee. But the idea of the Commune had a wide appeal, as many who did not admire the Hébertist notion of a dictatorship did support the assertion by Paris of its municipal rights. At the Blanquist Club de la Révolution in the 18th arrondissement on 16 December the future Communard Théophile Ferré proposed a list of ten delegates for the future Commune in order to prevent 'our party being reproached with not being organized, and thus to put us in a position to confront the events which cannot fail soon to occur'.[3] The list that was passed around the local clubs in this arrondissement for their approval included five of its own militants – the Blanquists Ferré and Jaclard, the Internationalists Schneider, Dereure and Dupas. These were to be joined by Emile Dereux, the socialist president of the Club Montmartre, Theisz, a local Trade Union leader and member of the International, Clemenceau, Lafond, and course Blanqui. In the Communal elections in March four of these – Blanqui, Ferré, Dereure and Theisz – were chosen by the 18th arrondissement. About this time the Club Montmartre, under Dereux's presidency, after the departure of Delescluze, joined forces with the Blanquist Club de la Révolution, which thereby became the Club de la Révolution de Montmartre. Dupas, who had drawn up the original programme of the Club de la Révolution, then proposed to the Central Vigilance Committee at

---

[1] Horne, op. cit., p. 219.    [2] Horne, op. cit., p. 221.
[3] *Le Combat*, 12 December.

its meeting of 23 December that the other local vigilance committees follow the example of the 18th arrondissement and form 'sub-committees in each arrondissement for the purpose of creating an individual club in each quarter in order to unite as much as possible the living forces of the Republic'. This proposal was accepted and a commission was formed from each of the other arrondissements 'to study the best form of organization in each arrondissement from the revolutionary point of view'. The Central Committee of the Twenty Arrondissements had now regained its position as the leading popular organization, and it held a series of sessions at the end of December to discuss 'the Revolutionary Commune and the practical means of its revolutionary installation'.[1] This movement was stimulated by the failure of Trochu's effort on 21 December to retake Le Bourget (in spite of his earlier declaration of its uselessness) as part of an attempt to break through the Prussian lines towards the French army in the north, which was threatening the Germans at Amiens.

On New Year's day, 1871, there was a special meeting in the rue d'Arras in the 5th arrondissement of delegates from most of the clubs and vigilance committees. This announced that 'the republican Central Committee has dissolved itself and delegates have been named by the twenty arrondissements with a view to establishing the Paris Commune'. The delegates took the title of 'Delegation of the Twenty Arrondissements of Paris', and at their first session on the next day Ferré, who presided over the meeting, declared that by the meeting of the previous day 'the Commune has been con-stituted', and it was now a matter of deciding 'upon the measures to be taken in order that it may carry out in a revolutionary way the mis-sion with which it has been entrusted'. The others present from the 18th arrondissement announced that 'their men were on permanent duty, with arms and munitions, the clubs also', but the majority were not willing to follow the Blanquists and Hébertists in attempting to take the Hôtel de Ville by a *coup de main*. Instead the majority pre-ferred to hope for a mass uprising to bring about the Commune, and a poster was drawn up as an appeal to the Paris population at large. On 6 January, the morning after the first shells of the German bombardment had fallen on the Left Bank, Paris woke up to read the famous second *Affiche rouge*: 'The policy, strategy, administration of the Government of 4 September, continuations of the Empire,

[1] See Wolfe, *Past and Present*, pp. 99–101; Rougerie, op. cit., pp. 23–5.

are condemned. Make way for the people! Make way for the Commune!' At the foot were 140 signatures of members of the local vigilance committees and clubs, the majority of whom were unknown workers who had not previously played any public role.[1] Thirty of the signatories were later members of the Commune. But the hoped-for mass uprising did not occur and the Blanquists and Hébertists decided to seek an opportunity to carry out their own revolutionary *coup*.

Jules Favre, who ever since the beginning of December had been regularly telling the Council that food supplies were on the verge of running out, was by now determined that the siege must finally be ended. It was decided by the inner group that Trochu must go. His religious fervour was irritating to the republican Deputies, and Favre exploded when Trochu suggested at one meeting that it should be officially announced that he had invoked the intercession of Saint Geneviève, the patron saint of Paris. Equally foolishly Trochu had responded to the challenge of the *Affiche rouge* by declaring that 'the Governor of Paris will never capitulate'. But since by this, as he explained privately to the other members of the Government, he only meant himself personally, though publicly the implication was not corrected that the whole Government was so committed, it was simply a matter of a little casuistry to abolish the post of Governor, thus leaving the way open for a capitulation. To avoid a repetition of the events of 31 October it was agreed that the fevered patient needed a touch of the medieval remedy of bleeding.[2] The National Guard would at last be given their chance to fight the Prussians. It was hoped that the experience would prove salutary, giving the Government a respite from the popular clamour in which to conclude an armistice. Ducrot, who had never hidden his contempt of the National Guard and the revolutionary faubourgs, wrote in his history of the Defence that this sortie of Buzenval was undertaken more 'to appease public opinion' than from any hope of victory, and he quoted a member of the Government who said 'that all the same there must be a big sortie of the National Guard because

---

[1] M.P., I, pp. 490–91; Wolfe, 'Origins of the Paris Commune', p. 378, checked the occupation of seventy-seven of these names and found that forty-five (sixty per cent) were workers; the overall percentage probably would be higher because the worker signatories were most likely to remain unknown.

[2] Comte M. d'Hérisson, *Journal d'un officier*, Paris, 1885, p. 309: 'To cure Paris of its fever a few pints of blood must be drawn.'

opinion will only be appeased when there are 10,000 National Guards dead on the ground'.[1]

Since the purpose was to 'incline the Parisians to the idea of a capitulation', as Sarcey described it,[2] the military organization was even more lacking than usual. In his impatience to get started on negotiations, Favre made matters worse by insisting the date be advanced two days. The National Guard battalions were divided equally between the three regular army columns, and on the morning of 19 January many Guardsmen were wandering around, lost and looking for their units. Some 100,000 men had to cross to their positions by one of two bridges and move forward along roads blocked by barricades (as part of Paris's defences) and encumbered by private ambulances. Trochu himself was late in reaching Mont-Valérien, the command point, and failed to keep his promise to delay the start until Ducrot's column on the right had had time to move into position. With such a disastrous beginning, and against strong German defences, the humane Trochu was soon able to decide that the National Guard must have learnt its lesson, and he ordered the retreat, which degenerated into the usual scramble and flight.

It was hardly a massacre, the French losing only six hundred men, mainly National Guardsmen, but Trochu sent back a call for all possible transport and ambulances, frightening Paris, where it was quickly believed that at least seven or eight thousand men must have been killed. Nor did it appease Paris opinion. It had hardly been the long awaited *sortie torrentielle*, and either out of fear or military prudence (and class prejudice) the popular battalions had not been used in the first attack, so it was only the bourgeois battalions that had seen any action.[3] This afterwards enabled criticisms to be made of the popular battalions for cowardice in contrast to the 'heroism' of the bourgeois battalions, which had provided most of the dead. But it was less a matter of courage, as was shown during the ensuing civil war, as of two different conceptions of warfare. As General Le Flô, the Minister of War, said, the National Guard was never employed in a serious manner, 'almost derisively' rather.[4] For most of the siege there had been very little for it to do, except mount guard

[1] Ducrot, op. cit., vol. 4, p. 163.                    [2] Sarcey, op. cit., p. 323.

[3] Lepelletier, op. cit., vol. 1, pp. 83–92.

[4] *Enquête*, II, p. 82; cf. *Histoire critique du siège de Paris par un officier de marine*, Paris, 1871, p. 201.

on the ramparts, and even then there was three times the number needed. It could hardly be expected that the sedentary National Guard could immediately develop into a force capable of beating a professional army. Clearly panic and desertion would occur, as indeed happened at Buzenval; but had not the famed zouaves fled at Châtillon when a few Prussian shells fell on their position? In 1792 the French volunteer battalions had at first panicked and been defeated before they won at Valmy.

There was also animosity between the popular battalions and the army. The army had been used to put down the June 1848 revolt and to establish Napoleon III, as well as frequently being used against strikers. As a result of this role the army had begun to attract officer recruits from the upper ranks of the bourgeoisie during the Second Empire and to slough off the revolutionary traditions constantly evoked by the popular orators of 1870–1. The contingent was chiefly made up of peasants, and particular scorn was felt in Paris for the Bretons, with their religious amulets, who were led by their priests into battle. The *ruraux*, especially again the Bretons who did not speak French, had no sympathy for the constant discussion, pamphleteering, café bravado, as it seemed, of the *à outrance*, as they called the Parisians. The attempt to reorganize the army in 1868 led to the division of the National Guard into active units, which were part of the army reserve, the *Gardes Nationales mobilisés*, and the sedentary National Guard. Some 100,000 *mobiles* had been called into Paris from the provinces at the start of the war. These were men who had avoided the army call-up either by the luck of the draw in the selective service system or by buying their way out through selling their 'bad number' to a replacement, usually a poor peasant, whom the Parisians called the *vendus*. Accordingly, many *mobiles* were of good social origin and had left their farm or business in the provinces with great reluctance. When the Government extended the electoral system for officers, which had always been the rule in the National Guard, to these *mobiles*, in most cases they simply elected their original commanders, the division between *château* and cottage being still maintained in the countryside. There was, therefore, a sharp social distinction between most of the Parisian National Guard battalions and the *mobiles* from the provinces. The Paris National Guardsmen in any case did not want to join Trochu's volunteer companies of *mobilisés*, because this would have been an individual act, and meant leaving his friends snug in their cafés, playing dominoes, eyeing the girls. Rather than getting themselves killed for the 'former Bonapartist policemen, coast-guards, aristocrats and seminarists', as a speaker at the Club Favié in Belleville put it, 'they wanted to go out *en masse*'[1] – or not at all. Such an idea was far from the intentions of the Provisional Government and its military commanders. Instead at Buzenval they sought as far as possible to absorb the National Guard into the regular army units by dividing the National Guard between the three regular columns. In 1793, on the other hand, the opposite had occurred, and it had been the explicit policy of the Convention to absorb the regular troops into the volunteer battalions so that the civic spirit of the Revolutionaries would prevail over the military traditions of the troops of the ancien regime.

With the military side of the war completed after Buzenval the way seemed clear for concluding an Armistice. But almost all sections of the population were seething with anger at the way the National Guard had been thrown away at the battle. Vacherot, the far from revolutionary Mayor of the 5th arrondissement, remarked on the 'patriotic excitement' of the population; Héligon, a member of the International and deputy Mayor in the 14th arrondissement, who was strongly against the revolutionaries, said 'the bourgeoisie realized that Buzenval was a comedy'; Fribourg, one of the Proudhonist founders of the International, said he returned from the battle 'fuming with anger'. When the Government, therefore, summoned the Mayors to try to win them over to the necessity of capitulating, they replied that far from being chastened the National Guard wanted to make yet another 'supreme heroic effort'.[2] The patriotic republican leagues were completely disillusioned with Trochu's conduct of the siege, and one group, before Trochu had time to resign, canvassed some of the other Generals to see if any of them were willing to take over the conduct of the siege from Trochu.[3] Finding no support in the army this same group, the Alliance républicaine, which was led by Jacobin radical republicans of the '48 generation such as Delescluze and Ledru-Rollin, considered entering into negotiations with the revolutionaries of Montmartre and Belleville.

[1] Molinari, op. cit., p. 94: 19 November.
[2] *Enquête*, II, p. 394 (Vacherot); p. 546 (Héligon); p. 570 (Fribourg); pp. 352–3 (Dubail).
[3] Arnould, op. cit., vol. 1, pp. 67–8.

The two days following the withdrawal from Buzenval saw considerable activity in the popular eastern districts, with secret meetings being held to discuss what action should be taken to get rid of the Government. On the night of 21 January at a general meeting of the Club de la Révolution in Montmartre a solemn oath was taken to appear armed on the Place de Grève in front of the Hôtel de Ville the next day at noon.[1] The Government, after its experiences on 31 October, had moved itself to the Louvre, but no one, however, could imagine proclaiming the Commune from anywhere but the Hôtel de Ville. A group of Blanquists then descended towards the 4th arrondissement, where they joined up with a group who had been holding similar meetings in the Salle Bourdon. These combined forces went off to the Mazas prison where they managed to surprise the guard, and holding a pistol to the Governor's head obtained the release of Flourens and the other political prisoners held there. Flourens took his men back to Belleville where he immediately claimed his electorial position at the Mairie and summoned the commanders of the National Guard battalions. But only a few turned up, not enough even to hold the Mairie. At the Louvre, the news of Flourens' release caused a great flurry, and Vinoy, an ex-Bonapartist General who had helped in the repression after Napoleon III's *coup d'état*, was appointed to Trochu's vacant place, taking the title of Commander-in-Chief of the Army in Paris. He at once issued a proclamation appealing to the 'good citizens' to support him in maintaining order against 'the party of disorder'.

On the morning of 22 January, alongside the poster of the Alliance républicaine calling for the holding of elections under the presidency of Dorian, there was General Clément Thomas's appeal to the National Guard to come out against the 'seditionaries' who were 'perturbing' the city. Neither appeal had much effect on the National Guard. The bourgeois battalions failed to respond when the Government beat the *rappel*. The naval officer Francisque Garnier reports that 'the National Guards of all shade of opinion almost unanimously declared that at no price would they uphold a Government whose feebleness and incompetence [against the Prussians] inspired them only with feelings of disgust'.[2] The battalions who were sent off from his sector, having been chosen as the most reliable, disbanded

---

[1] Da Costa, op. cit., pp. 348–9; Wolfe, *Past and Present*, pp. 103–4; M. Choury, *La Commune au cœur de Paris*, Paris, 1967, pp. 121–3.

[2] F. Garnier, *Le Siège de Paris. Journal d'un officier de marine*, Paris, 1871, p. 154.

en route and drifted back to their rampart duty or went home. Though on this occasion they did not go and join in the demonstration. The Alliance républicaine had been almost as alarmed as the Government when they heard of Flourens' release, as they wanted to have nothing to do with a 'socialist revolution'. They sent a small delegation into the Hôtel de Ville itself to present their demand for elections, but were instead warned that the building was well guarded.[1] Ferry was not on duty, leaving one of his deputies, Gustave Chaudey, in his stead, a peppery anti-revolutionary Proudhonian journalist, who lacked any authority over the military commanders. It is doubtful if the Delegation of the Twenty Arrondissements, the ex-Central Vigilance Committee, supported the idea of a demonstration considering how its moderate majority had overridden similar proposals in the past. Nor in the end did Flourens descend with his battalions, having been warned by his own men that any attempt at action would be useless and Blanqui had not countenanced this scheme of his more impetuous juniors.

By noon only a few National Guard battalions had turned up, mainly from the 17th and 18th arrondissements, led by several future Communards, namely Ferré, Benoît Malon and Vaillant. But these became lost in the Sunday crowd. Then Sapia arrived with some battalions from the 13th and 14th arrondissements which he lined up against the closed gates of the Hôtel de Ville, behind whose windows Breton *mobiles* could be seen, rifles in position. Shots rang out, and suddenly the windows opened and a fusillade poured down on to the crowd. In an instant the square was clear except for Sapia, cane in hand, lying shot dead beside a few of his Guards. Sapia, of a good bourgeois family, had been an army officer in French expeditions to China and Mexico, before he had had to resign and have a stay in hospital for mental treatment. In all some thirty or so Guards and civilians were killed, and Louise Michel, dressed in a National Guard uniform, later wrote that she could not take her eyes off 'those pale, savage figures who were emotionlessly and mechanically firing upon us, as they would have fired on a pack of wolves'.[2] Blanqui, too, was there, watching from a café on the square, as was Delescluze who had to be led away by his friends in a state of collapse, so great was this old revolutionary's distress. For about half an hour there was intermittent firing on the Hôtel de Ville from

[1] Arnould, op. cit., pp. 73–5.
[2] Michel, op. cit., p. 102.

the National Guards who had taken refuge in adjoining houses. But Vinoy sent in troops to clear the surrounding areas, thus completing his 'little Second of December'.[1] The *Illustration* called it the 'Waterloo of the anarchists'.[2] As a final measure the clubs were closed down, some eighty arrests were made and Delescluze's *Réveil* and Félix Pyat's *Combat* were suspended.

This was the first and only time during the siege that blood was shed within Paris, and Trochu's departure had evidently marked the end of rule by 'moral force'. When afterwards Jules Favre was asked by the Commission of Inquiry why the Provisional Government had not acted earlier with such firmness against the popular papers and the clubs, he replied that 'to have closed up such a safety valve would have run the risk of blowing up the whole machine'.[3] Evidently after Buzenval and 22 January, and with a whole army division occupying Belleville, it was thought the chance could be safely taken. In any case it was now almost all over. On 23 January Favre set off to see Bismarck at Versailles, though he still thought it prudent to take a circuitous route to throw off suspicion. After several more days of comings and goings between Paris and Versailles the capitulation was signed by Favre on 28 January. The four-month siege of Paris was over.

Favre had been given full rights to conclude an armistice for the whole of France, although the Provisional Government had only recently assured Gambetta that any armistice would apply only to Paris and its re-provisioning. The news of a general armistice came as a complete surprise to Gambetta, whose first reaction was to refuse it and continue waging the war from Bordeaux. In the end he decided that at least the armistice should be used to build up French forces ready to take the offensive again. Gambetta also wanted, quite unnecessarily as it turned out for in reality there was no danger of a Bonapartist revival, to exclude all ex-Bonapartists from standing as candidates in the coming elections so as to ensure, as he thought, a republican anti-peace majority in the Assembly. Bismarck, already considerably angered by the vehemence Gambetta had shown against the Germans during the war in contrast to the compliant attitude of Paris, threatened to break the armistice unless the Provisional Government brought Gambetta to heel. Bismarck even telegrammed Gambetta, directly telling him to comply with the

[1] Lamber, op. cit., p. 403.
[2] 28 January.
[3] *Dépositions*, I, 350.

terms agreed upon with Favre and the ministers in Paris. Gambetta proclaimed this intervention by Prussia in the internal affairs of France and posted up the telegram, branding the ministers in Paris as 'the allies of Monsieur de Bismarck'. Jules Favre and three other members of the Government had to make a special journey from Paris to force Gambetta to drop his opposition to the armistice terms, which he did by resigning out of disgust. He had no choice, for in the last count he could not break with his republican allies in Paris and turn for support to the crowds demonstrating in his favour in Bordeaux, nor accept the offers from Lyon and other large cities, as more avowedly republican bases for continuing the national resistance. His experiences in the north-east of Paris in the 1869 election campaign had been sufficient warning for his political, non-socialist republicanism.[1]

The terms of the armistice were basically the same as those which earlier both Favre and Thiers had felt it inexpedient to accept. In return for being re-provisioned, the forts surrounding Paris were to be surrendered and the guns spiked. This meant, as was immediately realized, that the armistice was in fact a capitulation since without the forts there was no chance of Paris taking up the war again. An indemnity of 200 million francs was to be paid, being the lowest price Bismarck was prepared to put on the city of Paris. But most important for the immediate future were the detailed questions of the disarming of the French troops and the line of the armistice. Moltke insisted that the National Guard should be disarmed and the Paris Government allowed to keep only two divisions to maintain order in the city. Bismarck modified this to ten battalions of the National Guard. But Favre had to admit despairingly that the Provisional Government could not possibly do this, as any attempt would lead to its overthrow. Bismarck coldly suggested to Favre that if that was indeed so he should 'provoke an uprising, while you still have an army to suppress it with'.[2] Favre's reply was to threaten to hand over this latter task to the German army, and there were those in Paris who would have been relieved if the Prussians had been willing to undertake it.[3] But Bismarck wished to avoid so far as possible

[1] Cf. above, p. 34.
[2] M. Busch, *Bismarck in the Franco-German War*, Eng. trans. London, 1879, vol. 2, p. 265.
[3] Sarcey, op. cit., p. 87, posed the question of what would have happened if civil war had broken out after 4 September on the assumption that Belleville

becoming involved militarily in France's internal struggles, so it was agreed to let the National Guard keep its arms, humiliating as this was for the regular army, which Moltke now insisted should be completely disarmed except for one division. For the same reason – fear that it might provoke an uprising – the Prussians agreed to reserve their demand for a ceremonial entry into Paris until the final stage of the peace negotiations.

Bismarck gained ample recompense for these concessions when it came to drawing up the lines of the cease-fire. Favre had no information on the position of the armies in the south, west or east of France, and could not wait to consult the Delegation at Bordeaux. So he had to accept the information provided by the Prussians, who took advantage of Favre's ignorance to include on their side of the cease-fire line territory that it would have taken them at least a week of campaigning to win. Most disastrous was Favre's willingness to exclude Bourbaki's army of the East from the armistice at all. The Prussians wanted to make sure that the 100,000 troops in this region ceased to be a threat to Alsace and Lorraine, and being confident of imminent victory they made it clear to Favre that the armistice would be delayed if he insisted on a cease-fire in that region. Favre's military adviser, General Beaufort, overcome by the rich repast at the negotiations after months on siege rations, disgraced himself by making clear over the table what he thought of such a cavalier disposal of France's remaining army. Favre replaced him by the more compliant General Valdan, and the terms of the armistice were quickly completed. Then to compound matters Favre forgot, probably because he dared not, to inform either the military in Paris or the Delegation at Bordeaux that Bourbaki's army had been

---

would have won: 'Who knows? Perhaps it would have been the vanquished who would have opened the gates to the Prussians and thrown itself into their arms begging them to restore order in the city.' A school-teacher friend of Sarcey's, Arthur Bary, wrote to his sister, the wife of the architect Garnier, on 26 March, that some of those who opposed the elections for the Commune 'were waiting for and even *hoping* for . . . the intervention of the Prussians' ('*Lettres écrites pendant la Commune de Paris, 1871*', *Revue hebdomidaire*, vol. 9, August 1904, p. 16). *The Times* correspondent noted that there was a feeling of sympathy for the Germans and rumours that Versailles had asked them to put down the revolt (which was not quite the case): 'The Germans will find a good deal more sympathy in some quarters the next time they enter Paris than they did the last, and men are beginning in muttered curses to pray for them' (21 March).

(a) General Louis Trochu

(b) Léon Gambetta

1(a) and (b) Leaders of the Government of National Defence

1(c) Adolphe Thiers – Chief Executive of the Government at Versailles

1(d) The Marquis de Gallifet – one of the Generals in charge of the repression of the Commune

2(*a*) A cannon on the Butte Montmartre

2(*b*) The artillery park on the Butte Montmartre in March, dominating Paris

specifically excluded. Hence on the French side fighting stopped in the East, while the Prussians, properly informed from Versailles, carried out their final movements to force Bourbaki's retreating army back into Switzerland. The defeated general tried to shoot himself, but was a failure even in this final gesture. French military honour in the end was salvaged, for the only signature on the armistice was that of the civilian Favre.

The members of the Government of National Defence were now about to be relieved of their great burden; revolution had been avoided and the war brought to an end. But, as was widely recognized, the issues raised by 4 September had only been postponed. The effect of the double policy pursued by the Provisional Government had been to divide the moderate, parliamentary republicans completely from the radical and revolutionary republicans and socialists. These latter groups had had four months in which to organize themselves, as had occurred in the clubs and vigilance committees. By the end of the siege these presented a formidable and avowedly revolutionary opposition, which had been able to so develop because the Government lacked both the means and the authority to police and control the city. As a result a considerable degree of autonomy had been gained at the local, arrondissement level, and the popular districts, comprising a big majority of the total population, had come close to being self-governing. The war, particularly the special circumstances of the siege, had broken up the political forces of repression so greatly relied on by the highly centralized system of government in France. Instead the Paris population had begun to assert itself. It was also a population that was armed, and the National Guard did not feel it had been defeated. On the contrary, it was spoiling for a fight and needed little to turn it completely against a Government that was held to have betrayed the nation. This frustrated patriotism was important in providing a general animosity which extended to a wider section of the population than just the regular revolutionaries. And, finally, the siege had had a disastrous effect on the economy of Paris, for it had brought the economic life of the capital to a standstill. There was large-scale unemployment, except so far as the National Guard pay was a form of public assistance, and a grave shortage of food and fuel. All these factors converged to make Paris on the morn of the capitulation highly inflammable, for it was a situation that affected all but the very prosperous. But nonetheless it was a crisis that could

possibly have been surmounted without too great a disaster had
Paris been treated with understanding, and some concessions made.
But instead, as will now be seen, the central Government only
exacerbated matters until finally the long-feared revolution did
break out.

Chapter 4

# PARIS PREPARES

In Paris the news of the armistice, the details of which were only slowly let out, caused an 'explosion of joy' amongst the upper bourgeoisie.[1] The rest of the population greeted it with a stunned silence, but there was no movement of revolt. The fact that an armistice had really been concluded came as a numbing shock, for many had never fully accepted that the Government would actually betray, as it was regarded, the resistance of Paris. The miseries of the siege, the losses suffered during the bombardment and in useless excursions against the enemy, had been to no avail. The Republic that had been born on that bright Sunday, in what must now have seemed like a distant past, had come to this point of humiliation. It was rumoured, hoped, that Admiral Saisset would not surrender the forts, which he had ordered his men to guard as if they were ships, and the ever-anxious Trochu had been a little concerned on this regard. But only one naval captain and a gunner blew their brains out. The ex-cavalry officer and National Guardsman Brunel tried to rouse the National Guard in order to go and take over one of the forts to continue the struggle, but only a few hundred men replied to his sounding of the tocsin and Brunel and his second-in-command, Piazza, were arrested the next day.

The most immediate problem was that of food, though supplies were being rushed into the city as fast as could be managed in a country disorganized by war. Prices remained high, though suddenly stocks appeared of goods brought out of hiding now the siege was over. On the opening day of one of the markets in Les Halles a crowd pillaged the store, much to the horror of the better off. Molinari in the *Revue des Deux Mondes* criticized the Government for doing nothing to stop the crowds looting 'from those

[1] Fidus, op. cit., vol. 2, p. 276; not Flaubert, however, who wrote on 1 February, 'I refuse to wear my red [Legion of Honour] ribbon . . . For the words "honour" and "French" are incompatible.'

whose perseverance and ingenuity entitled them to profit from their monopoly'.[1] Fidus tells of a man he saw in the rue de Rivoli one afternoon transporting a barrel of butter in a cart. A crowd of passers-by suddenly seized his booty, and in the ensuing scramble someone fell into the barrel to emerge covered in enough butter to meet his immediate needs. After the barrel had been scraped to the bottom, women tore the planks apart for firewood.[2] The police confronted by such daily occurrences, dared not try to intervene, and the Prefect of Police, Cresson, had resigned as soon as the armistice was concluded to attend to his own affairs, leaving a reluctant Choppin in charge. The National Guard would of course do nothing to help the Government, which because of the armistice terms had no more than 12,000 troops left with arms, the rest, some 220,000, simply wandering loose in Paris joining the general hunt for food, shelter and warmth. The Ministers themselves had in effect abdicated their responsibilities, the Government dissolving itself into the election campaign for the National Assembly.

The national elections were to be held on 8 February, and the clubs, officially closed since the demonstration of 22 January, soon resumed their activities under the form of 'electoral meetings', and published lists of candidates. The most important of these, representing most likely the agreed combination of the revolutionary clubs and committees, was the 'revolutionary socialist' list issued by the Delegation of the Twenty Arrondissements, the International and the Trade Union Federation. But when it came to the test of the elections this slate won only 50,000 votes through Paris, which was about the same as the civilian votes against the Government of National Defence in the November plebiscite following the events of 31 October. Paris as a whole voted in the republican opposition manner of 1869, putting Louis Blanc at the top of its poll, followed by Victor Hugo, Garibaldi, Edgar Quinet, Gambetta and Rochefort. A few neo-Jacobins were elected such as Delescluze and Ledru-Rollin, as were the socialist figures of Millière and Proudhon's old friend and executor, Jérôme Langlois. But only the most widely known figures of the 'revolutionary socialist' slate who had also appeared on other lists were elected – Garibaldi, Gambon, Félix Pyat, Tolain and Benoît Malon. Blanqui, for example, received only

---

[1] 1 February 1871, p. 746.
[2] Op. cit., vol. 2, pp. 287–8, 30 January; cf. Martial Senisse, *Les Carnets d'un fédéré 1871*, ed. J. A. Faucher, Paris, 1965, p. 22.

50,000 votes, and would have needed half as many again to make even the bottom of the Paris representation. Admiral Saisset was elected as one of the few popular commanders of the siege, whereas Trochu in contrast did not even stand for the city of which he had so lately been Governor. Towards the bottom of the list came Thiers and Jules Favre, the only member of the late Paris Government to be elected by the capital. The other large cities voted similarly to Paris. The countryside did not, and in the absence of any Government direction elected local notables, with their conservative, Catholic and monarchist preferences, which gave a divided Monarchist majority to the new Assembly when it met at Bordeaux. This was to prove disastrous, for the peasants and small towns were voting for an end to the war but not for a monarchy, as subsequent elections giving republican majorities were to make abundantly clear. But the effect of the elections, apart from giving a clear majority for peace, was to produce a reactionary National Assembly, which at once showed its true colours by howling down Garibaldi on the only occasion he tried to speak. A voice from the galleries shouted, 'It's a disgrace! You are nothing but a rural majority!', and the denomination stuck.

Thiers, in contrast to his poor showing in Paris, had come head of the list in twenty-six Departments, and he now formed a Government of moderate conservatives. He kept on from the previous Government Favre, Minister of Foreign Affairs; Picard, now finally at the Ministry of the Interior; the free-thinker Jules Simon, at the sensitive, in view of the Catholic majority in the Assembly, Ministry of Education; and General Le Flô at the Ministry of War. To these Thiers added four monarchists and a former Bonapartist. The first task was to conclude peace, and Thiers for a second time went to see Bismarck. On 26 January the details were agreed, which were essentially the same as those of the previous November. France was to lose all of Alsace and Lorraine, and pay as a war indemnity the unprecedented sum of 5,000 million gold francs. Until this was paid off Prussian troops would remain in Northern France.[1] Most important in its effect on Paris was the German insistence on a triumphal entry into the capital to which Thiers acceded in return

[1] The indemnity was later reduced to 4,675 million gold francs in recognition of the value of the railway concessions lost in Alsace-Lorraine. Bismarck had expected a long occupation, considering the size of the indemnity, but it was paid off in two years and the occupation ended in September 1873.

for keeping the fortress city of Belfort. The rural majority did not need Thiers' threat of resignation to speed through ratification of the treaty on 1 March by 546 votes to 107. Most of the Paris Deputies spoke and voted against the treaty, including Clemenceau. Edgar Quinet warned that to cede Alsace-Lorraine was to perpetuate 'war under the guise of peace'; Victor Hugo in magniloquent phrases (he read his speeches) said that a regenerated France would, in the tradition of 1792, seize back not simply Alsace and Lorraine, but the natural frontier of the Rhine. Louis Blanc spoke of the danger to the whole of Europe of such a change in the balance of power brought about by the rise of a 'German Caesar'. Gambetta and the other Deputies from Alsace-Lorraine resigned, as did Tridon and Rochefort, Félix Pyat and Malon from Paris, soon to be joined by Victor Hugo.

With the peace ratified the Assembly turned to restoring order and business inside France, which essentially meant dealing with Paris. The economic difficulties of the last years of the Empire had only been intensified by the defeat in war and the siege of the capital. Paris by 1871 was in a state of economic 'catastrophe' and political turmoil that neither Thiers' ministry nor the rural majority in the Assembly showed any signs of even seeking to comprehend. 'We provincials were unable to come to an understanding with the Parisians,' admitted the Vicomte de Meaux, elected by the legitimist Right as one of the Secretaries of the Assembly; 'it seemed as if we did not even speak the same language, and that they were prey to a kind of sickness'.[1] This 'pack of peasants', as Rochefort called them in his *Mot d'Ordre*,[2] proceeded to enact a series of measures each one of which exacerbated different sections of the population in Paris until practically the whole city was united against the National Assembly. On 7 March the moratorium on goods deposited at the Mont de Piété, the State-run pawnshop, was lifted, and objects would be put up for sale if they were not reclaimed. *The Times* correspondent visited it a few days later and noted that '2,300 poor wretches had pawned their mattresses, and starving seamstresses had pawned 1,500 pairs of scissors . . . How many necessaries to existence were stored away in these cruel galleries . . . the gaunt secret frowning on us from every loaded shelf . . . starvation!'[3] Some relief was gained through the English 'patriotic gift', which was used

[1] Vicomte de Meaux, *Souvenirs politiques*, Paris, 1905, p. 46: 6 March.
[2] 6 March.                                                          [3] 15 March.

to redeem tools pledged during the war. A similar measure declared that landlords could demand immediate payment of all back-rent owing from the beginning of the siege – this in a city where all work had been completely disorganized and there was large-scale unemployment. And thirdly the new Government abolished what in effect had become a form of unemployment pay, the daily thirty sous allowance to the National Guard, in an attempt to eliminate 'those plebs', as Fidus called them, 'by now accustomed, as in Imperial Rome, to receiving pay for doing nothing'.[1] After 15 February this allowance could only be obtained on proof of need, and thus what had been regarded as a patriotic due became something to be begged for. The effect of this measure was similar to the closing of the National Workshops in June 1848. With the working classes thoroughly alienated, the Assembly equally roused the hostility of the petty bourgeoisie, forcing them towards a common alliance with the poor by passing a law on *échéances*, or overdue bills.[2] A great deal of Paris business in normal times depended on promissory notes. The siege had naturally made repayment impossible and the Government of National Defence had declared a moratorium on all such paper notes. On 10 March the Bordeaux Assembly decreed that these would become payable with the interest due within the next four months, those dating from August last becoming due at once. As Tolain warned the Government in the debate, the effect of this law would be 'to aggravate the situation of the small-manufacturers and the small-traders'. It was hardly realistic of the Minister to defend himself by giving the Rothschilds as an example of those who had already been able to pay off their creditors. In short, the majority of Parisian traders and shop-keepers were being handed over to the mercy of a few big financiers, particularly the Bank of France, in order that confidence could be restored to raise the loans needed to pay off the first instalments of the indemnity.

Apart from its ill-judged economic measures, the existence of a Monarchist majority in the Assembly was a cause of extreme

[1] Fidus, op. cit., p. 331, 22 February.
[2] Cf. *Enquête*, II, pp. 120–1. Police chief Choppin remarked of this measure that as a result 'if the small manufacturers did not throw themselves into the revolutionary movement, at least they said to themselves that it was not worth the trouble to defend the Government'. And *The Times*, 11 March, similarly with regard to the decree on rents: 'One thing seemed certain, that the tenants either could not or would not pay, and that under the circumstances it would be dangerous to force them.'

concern to most Parisians, who considered that the constitutional issue of the Republic had been definitely settled by the Revolution of 4 September. The Assembly did not allay the fears of Paris and lost no occasion to make it clear that it regarded the existence of the Republic as only provisional. The appointment of General d'Aurelle de Paladines, who had both won and lost Orleans, to replace Clément Thomas as head of the National Guard was seen as a royalist insult to the republican *à outrance* of Paris. The last insult came when the Assembly had to fix its next place of meeting. Thiers insisted this be nearer to Paris as it was difficult to see to the execution of the peace treaty from the far west of France, and Rouland, the Governor of the Bank of France, was complaining emphatically that at such a distance *'we cannot yet feel the directing hand, the rallying unity, the decision which sets uncertainty at rest'*.[1] Putting any traces of pride aside, the Assembly grudgingly agreed to Thiers' suggestion of Versailles, which the German High Command was on the point of leaving. It was precisely the same reason as had led the Prussians to choose Versailles that recommended it to Thiers;[2] militarily it was the best position from which to conduct an army against Paris in the case of an uprising. The debate on this issue brought out the full antagonism of the rural Right against Paris. Several petitions were placed before the Assembly from rural electors proposing that in 'the future the political Assemblies of France be held outside of Paris'.[3] Privately Thiers saw Versailles as a move towards the ultimate stage of Paris, but to the population it seemed as if Paris was to be 'decapitalized' as a step towards a monarchist restoration. *The Times* could not be accused of exaggeration when it commented that 'the conduct of the Chambre at Bordeaux has not been such as to inspire the country with confidence'.[4] The Assembly then dissolved itself. When it next met, Paris was in revolution and the Government in flight.

In the capital itself the popular organizations had become increasingly active, following the election campaign and the transfer of the Government to Bordeaux. The Council of the International held a number of meetings at the end of January and throughout February and March to discuss whether it was possible to start up the

[1] D. Halévy, *Le Courrier de M. Thiers*, Paris, 1921, p. 434.

[2] Thiers, *Notes et souvenirs (1870–1873)*, Paris, 1903, p. 136; *Enquête*, II, p. 9.

[3] *Annales de l'Assemblée Nationale. Compte rendu*, Paris, 1871, vol. 1, pp. 165, 231 (6 and 9 March).      [4] 15 March.

local sections again and what should be its relations to the clubs and
committees that had developed during the siege. The underlying
issue was whether or not the International should concentrate solely
on workers' trade organizations. This was not a matter of Proudhonian ideology but of trying to best interpret a very confused
situation; as Goullé wrote on 17 March, the International was 'very
embarrassed by the obscurity of the political situation; what should
be done?'[1] It was Marx's only personal friend on the council, the
Hungarian Léo Frankel, who on 22 February proposed that they
should set up a study group to produce a report on the unemployment and accommodation situation in Paris, which could then be
communicated to Malon and Tolain for discussion in the National
Assembly. A number of local sections and 'study circles' started up
again in early March, and in the 13th arrondissement the Democratic and Socialist Club fused with the local branch of the Légion
Garibaldienne and the International to form a new branch of the
International.[2] The triumvirate of the Corderie – the International,
the Trade Union Federation and the Delegation of the Twenty
Arrondissements – followed the election campaign by drawing up
a declaration of principles and statutes, which were adopted at a
general meeting of delegates from the various local committees on
20 and 23 February. This meeting formalized the committee movement into what was called 'the revolutionary socialist party'. Only
those who subscribed to its declaration of principles could henceforth belong to a local vigilance committee. In so subscribing, each
member declared that he would 'seek to obtain by all possible
means the suppression of the privileges of the bourgeoisie, its overthrow as a controlling class and the political accession of the workers.
In a word, social equality. No more employers, no more proletarians,
no more classes.' Whilst awaiting this 'political and social revolutionary liquidation' he would recognize as the Government of Paris
only 'the revolutionary Commune arising from the delegation of the
revolutionary socialist groups of the city', and would defend the Republic, by force if necessary, against any 'so-called National Assembly'.
Each local committee was to seek to incorporate representatives from
all the various groups in any one arrondissement, so long as these
additional members were of a 'revolutionary socialist' character.[3] This

[1] *Enquête*, III, p. 241.          [2] *Le Cri du Peuple*, 1, 4, 6, 7, 9 March.
[3] A.N.: given in G. Bourgin, *La Guerre de 1870–1871 et la Commune*, Paris,
1939, p. 182.

was the organizational and ideological culmination of the vigilance committees and clubs, which themselves had developed out of the public meetings of the last year of the Empire. But its base was very narrow, as the February elections showed. It was not this party that was causing the Government and the bourgeoisie so much alarm, but the 'revolution armed' in the form of the Paris National Guard and the autonomous federation it had formed.

The composition of the National Guard had taken a further shift towards the popular classes at the conclusion of the armistice. As at the beginning of the investment of Paris, as many as could left the city as soon as the siege was lifted to see their families, for business reasons, or simply for food and rest. This emigration of something like 100,000–140,000 was overwhelmingly drawn from the bourgeoisie, with the result that the strength of the National Guard battalions that might have been expected to defend order was gravely depleted, so much so that General Clément Thomas and his chief-of-staff Colonel Montaigu resigned on 12 February in face of such a 'mass emigration'. Several days earlier a number of National Guard battalions, notably in the 3rd, 4th, 9th and 11th arrondissements, had sought to concert their action for the coming national elections. A general meeting was held of delegates from a larger number of battalions at the National Circus (now the Cirque d'Hiver) on 6 February. This meeting decided to support the slate proposed by the republican groups of the Alliance républicaine, the Union républicaine and the committee of the Défenseurs de la République, a slate also supported by the International. The meeting closed by electing a committee responsible for calling another meeting if there was a second round of elections.[1]

This second meeting took place on 15 February in the Tivoli-Vauxhall in the 10th arrondissement. The first electoral results showing the marked swing to the monarchist Right had shocked republican opinion in Paris, and so this meeting established a working party of twenty members, hardly any of whom were at all known for any previous political activity, to draw up statutes for a federation of the Paris National Guard. These were presented just over a week later at a general meeting attended by some 2,000 delegates representing most, though not all, of the National Guard battalions. This meeting voted that the proposed statutes should be printed and circulated throughout Paris for discussion, and then passed three

[1] M. Choury, *Les Origines de la Commune: Paris livré*, Paris, 1960, pp. 163–6.

additional resolutions to be posted up on the walls of Paris. Firstly, they declared that any attempt to disarm the National Guard would be resisted. Secondly, if the Prussians entered Paris, they would be met by force. Thirdly, the National Guard refused to recognize any commander-in-chief not chosen by itself. Garibaldi was its first choice, but he declined, whilst the Government's new replacement, d'Aurelle de Paladines, was far too royalist for the republican allegiance of most of the Parisian officers. The meeting, having fixed the date of its next assembly, then adjourned by processing to the Place de la Bastille to 'pay homage to the martyrs of 1830 and 1848',[1] it being 24 February, the anniversary of the 1848 Revolution.

The next three weeks, which led up to the revolution of 18 March, witnessed the complete breakdown of all form of official government in Paris. This was partly festive, partly violent. As in 1830 and 1848 the street vendors, the *camelots*, appeared along several of the main streets, producing what the acting-Prefect of Police, Choppin, called 'a permanent fair'.[2] The police were helpless, and were hounded by any National Guardsmen they had the misfortune to meet. On one occasion when Choppin intervened personally to try to release two of his agents who had been searched and disarmed he too was temporarily arrested by the National Guard. At the Bastille the demonstration of 24 February continued for succeeding days. Speeches were made and National Guard battalions with their bands playing lowered their banners as they marched past the monument to the Revolution, decorated for the occasion with wreaths and crowned by the red flag. Regular soldiers joined in, as did some 3,000 Parisian *mobiles*, who then broke into the naval barracks at Pépinère in an effort to persuade the sailors to rally to the side of the people.

This was not, however, simply a festive crowd such as that which had invaded the Chambre on 4 September. The elements of terror were there too. A police spy called Vicenzini was recognized, seemingly taking down the battalion numbers. The cry of *mouchard*, informer, immediately angered the crowd and he was dragged off towards the canal. He was temporarily saved by a National Guard officer who shut him away in a nearby guard-house. But a mob of 400 or 500 overran the guard-house and Vicenzini was dragged half senseless along the quay. He was tied up, thrown into the Seine

---

[1] *Enquête*, III, p. 14.                    [2] *Enquête*, II, p. 110.

under a hail of stones and was swept off out of the sight of several thousand spectators to his death. The newspapers on the next day widely reported this incident in gruesome detail. It was but a fore-taste of the greater violence to come.

As each day passed the Government received reports of the pil-laging of the arms depots, which had been dispersed throughout Paris to minimize the danger of explosions during the Prussian bombardment. The Government had insufficient troops to guard these properly and had therefore to rely on the National Guard, which as often as not made no attempt to stop the ransacking. The Govern-ment likewise lacked enough horse-teams to collect into a few central depots all the cannons that were scattered throughout the city. What horses had not been eaten during the siege were now needed to bring in food to the near-starving capital. One of Vinoy's biggest fears was that bread supplies would run out, which would have precipitated an immediate riot, if not a revolution.

The local National Guard committees, ever since the meeting of 24 February, were on permanent watch, ready to resist any attempted *coup de force*, and the exalted Guardsmen often passed days with no sleep.[1] On the night of 26 February the *rappel* was beaten, and a huge crowd paraded up and down the Champs-Elysées ready to resist the rumoured Prussian entry. In the extremely respectable districts of Passy and Auteuil, which lay in the path of the forthcoming Prussian ceremonial entry, the local National Guard in agreement with the municipality went and transported a number of cannons left behind by the army to the park Monceau in the area out-side of the Prussian occupation. In this way began the affair of the cannons, which was to be so important by 18 March. It was a popular action, as Jules Ferry said, by the 'good' bourgeois battalions consisting of citizens who were 'strong supporters of order'.[2]

The popular quarters too were equally concerned over the Government's neglectfulness regarding the Prussian entry into Paris. To Thiers and his ministers the war was over and this was merely a ceremonial occasion. But most Parisians had not yet accepted that peace was in fact made, and hence they were determined that the Prussians should not be able to use the occasion to their military

[1] Cf. J. Allemane, *Mémoires d'un Communard*, Paris, 1910, p. 14.
[2] *Enquête*, II, p. 63; cf. p. 466 (Colonel Lavigne); pp. 453–4 (De Mortemart); p. 514 (Langlois).

advantage. The National Guard in its Federation had sworn to oppose the Prussian entry, which was an additional reason for getting back its own cannons, many of which had been bought by public subscription and were considered therefore as belonging to the National Guard; the guns, for example, had their National Guard battalion numbers engraved on their barrels. The Government had collected together what guns it could into an artillery park on the Place Wagram. But Wagram, in the bourgeois section of the 17th arrondissement, seemed too close to the Prussians for the populace of the eastern districts, and the Government itself seems to have had fears that they were not safe.[1] The cry of 'What about our cannons! the Prussians are going to get them!' led a crowd of National Guards, women and children to surge up to the Place Wagram. During the two days of 26–27 February the cannons were dragged across Paris to the security of the popular districts, where they were formed into various artillery parks most notably in the Place de Vosges and on the heights of Montmartre and Belleville.

In the event the Prussian entry passed off peacefully. Although the Montmartre National Guard committee pressed for the implementation of the resolution of the 24th calling for resistance to the Prussians, the newly reformed Delegation of the Twenty Arrondissements together with the International and the Trade Union Federation considered that 'a struggle undertaken in such circumstances would be the death of the Republic and the ruin of the future of socialism'.[2] The Corderie, as Lissagaray later put it, 'looked with a jealous reserve upon this embryon of a Committee [of the National Guard], composed of unknown men, who had never taken part in any revolutionary campaign',[3] and delegates were sent to the evening meeting of 27 February of the National Guard Federation in the Tivoli-Vauxhall. Here they helped to persuade a somewhat differently composed National Guard Central Committee to back down on its earlier war-like resolutions. The next day the Corderie published a poster warning the workers to abstain: 'Any attack would serve to expose the people to the blows of the enemies of the Revolution, who would drown all social demands in a sea of blood. Let us

---

[1] De Mortemart, *Dépositions*, II, pp. 344–5, says National Guards had been put on guard so that if the Prussians seized them the army would not be blamed. But in *Enquête*, II, p. 453, he denies there was any danger.
[2] 27 February; Dautry and Scheler, op. cit., p. 202; *Le Cri du Peuple*, 1 March.
[3] Lissagaray, op. cit., p. 65.

remember the dark days of June.'[1] And later that same 28 February, the National Guard Central Committee published its decision, edged in black, that since the 'general feeling of the population seemed to be not to resist the Prussian entry into Paris', the National Guard would simply join the army in establishing a cordon around the occupied area.[2] It was largely a silent population that watched the Prussians glitteringly parade down the Champs-Elysées on 1 March. But passers-by who were too openly friendly towards France's conquerors were roughly treated by the crowd and a café was sacked because it had unpatriotically stayed open. During the next couple of days groups of Prussian officers tried to visit the Louvre, but, as Vinoy had pleasure in informing them, the paintings and treasures had been removed because of the German bombardment during the siege, and so they had to be content to stroll in the deserted courtyards. They did not insist on visiting the Invalides after Vinoy had said he could not guarantee their safety from the Paris crowds. Then, with the first instalment of the indemnity having been quickly raised, the Germans withdrew, much to the disappointment of the Emperor Frederick William, who had expected to have had time to march his whole army in triumph into Paris.

That order was maintained was less a tribute to the Government than to the new 'occult' body, as the conservative Press called the National Guard Central Committee. The International was also forced to realize that this was quickly becoming the major popular organization in Paris. After some debate the International accepted the invitation to send four delegates to the next meeting of the Federation on 3 March. These were not the only Internationalists there, as others had followed the bookbinder Varlin's suggestion to attend 'not as members of the International but as National Guards working to win over the spirit of that assembly'. For, Varlin warned his colleagues, 'if we remain isolated from such a force our influence will disappear, while if we unite with this committee it will be a big step towards the future of socialism'.[3] This meeting

---

[1] Op. cit., p. 65; cf. Senisse, op. cit., p. 31, who reports how his patriotic Blanquist friend, Thoumieux, blamed Frankel and Varlin of the International for checking the patriotic movement, which, according to Thoumieux, they had done because the 'Prussian Karl Marx is flying to the aid of the Prussian Bismarck'.

[2] M.P., I, p. 971.

[3] *Les Séances officielles de l'Internationale à Paris pendant le siège et pendant la Commune*, Paris, 1872, pp. 82, 84, 1 March.

provisionally adopted the statutes of the federation. The preamble to these consisted of purely republican sentiments, which represented the dominant mood of the meeting, though it concluded with the devise 'All for each, and each for all', showing that the Internationalists had been able to make their presence felt. The Central Committee was to consist of the delegates from local battalion 'circles' in each arrondissement, together with the battalion commanders. The Central Committee would have its own 'vigilance committee' of five to be permanently ready to give the alarm.[1] Posters were put up calling on the local Guardsmen to organize themselves for the coming election of delegates.

In so organizing itself the National Guard adopted the same form of federation as that of the other popular organizations in Paris, for the effect of the war had been to substitute the National Guard companies for the workshops as the natural group basis. During the siege the *conseils de famille*, which were authorized bodies supposedly concerned solely with the administrative affairs of each regiment, had already shown signs of becoming political groups. In December, the Government had tried to restrain them, but instead they had simply gone underground, reducing still further the Government's hold over the popular battalions. During the siege over three hundred sergeants had lost their stripes and more than four hundred officers had been dismissed for 'indiscipline' – that is, probably in most cases for political agitation.[2] The idea in itself of a federation of the National Guard went back to the federation movement of the first year of the French Revolution, which had culminated in the 14 July anniversary of 1790 on the Champs de Mars in the presence of the King. This organization was now revived in order 'to protect the country better than the permanent armies had done, and to defend the threatened Republic by all possible means'.[3]

In the face of this direct challenge to its authority all the Government could do was to appeal to the good citizens against what it called 'an anonymous central committee' that was preparing 'for civil war'. Troops had to be withdrawn from the popular quarters, where the officers no longer dared appear in public in uniform. The crowd overran the Gobelins police barracks, capturing a stock of

---

[1] *Enquête*, III, pp. 22–6.
[2] *Enquête*, II, pp. 447–50 (Mortemart); p. 353 (Dubail); Report of Col. Chaper to Inquiry Commission into the *Actes du Gouvernement de la défense nationale*.
[3] Poster of 4 March: *Enquête*, III, p. 24.

chassepot rifles, and the *gardes républicaines* sent to the rescue were in turn mobbed by the crowd. As a result the next day, 4 March, this arrondissement was evacuated of troops and police, who were withdrawn to the barracks in the rue Tournon by the Luxembourg Palace. That night the Sainte-Pélagie prison was forced by threat of being invaded to give up those arrested for the 22 January demonstration. Faced by such a series of affronts Vinoy sent off an urgent request to Bordeaux for more troops, saying that 'a serious insurrection was being organized'. In the provinces, so inflamed was the feeling about Paris, Vinoy's foreboding was taken as an accomplished fact and rumour soon had it that Paris was already in the throes of an insurrection, and whole districts were believed to be in flames with Vinoy in full retreat. In turn the Paris paper, *Le Temps*, sardonically commentated that 'its readers would be somewhat surprised by these singular revelations', and it suggested that the Assembly should return to Paris and see the true situation for itself.[1] But the situation was more serious than the moderates allowed – as Arnould wrote afterwards, 'in effect the Commune was already in existence' in that Paris had been 'left to itself' and accordingly 'enjoyed complete and absolute independence'.[2]

The Government was squarely caught between the Prussians and the Paris National Guard. By the terms of the armistice, which had to be strictly adhered to on Moltke's insistence, more than 200,000 disarmed troops had to be turned loose in the capital. These were practically in a state of mutiny against the Government. The Parisian *mobiles* could have been discharged at once, but, as Vinoy said, this would only have added to the number of the insurgents, for there was no likelihood that they could find any employment.[3] But the Government's indecision was ended when, on 7 March, three battalions arrested their officers and marched them off to the National Guard Central Committee. The officers were not held, but the Government decided that it had no choice but to release the *mobiles*, giving them ten days pay in the hope that this might keep them out of trouble. The next to go were 26,000 *mobiles* of the Seine region, who lived within four days walking distance. They were simply sent off on foot. The remaining 54,000 *mobiles*, who could not be got rid

---

[1] F. Damé, *La Résistance: Les Maires, Les Deputés de Paris et le Comité Central du 18 au 26 mars*, Paris, 1871, pp. 261–2.

[2] Arnould, op. cit., vol. 1, p. 92.

[3] Vinoy, *L'Armistice et la Commune*, Paris, 1872, p. 173.

of so easily, had to be despatched as fast as an overburdened train service could transport them. By 15 March the last of the provincial *mobiles* left Paris, in one case having set fire to their barracks as they left. On the same day the Government decided on the 'radical measure' of forming the remaining 120,000 regular troops into three columns, each with a general in charge, and marching them away from the capital in the directions of Orleans, Chartres and Evreux. As the unreliable troops were disbanded and cleared out of Paris so the Government set about reconstituting its forces by obtaining permission from Bismarck, though Moltke tried to obstruct this, to bring men from 'the élite' of the provincial army across the Prussian lines and into camps in Paris. It was planned to form three divisions, as well as one of cavalry, but transportation was slow, and the morale of these troops turned out to be little better than those the Government had so hastily got rid of. Time would be needed to discipline them into their new regiments; but time the Government did not have.

Ever since the seizure of the cannons prior to the Prussian entry into Paris, conservative opinion had been demanding that the Government restore order in the nation's capital. How, it was being asked, could business be resumed, shops opened up, credit restored in a city ruled by a Committee in declared opposition to the National Assembly and with a population that was daily arming itself, most noticeably by the 'guns levelled on the city' from the heights of Montmartre? As Thiers said afterwards, 'businessmen were going around constantly repeating that the financial operations would never be started until all those wretches were finished off and their cannons taken away. An end had to be put to all this, and then one could get back to business.'[1] In Paris itself, in contrast to the Government at Bordeaux, there was considerably less concern over the cannons amongst the population at large. The Parisian Ministers in the Government, most notably the financier Picard, Minister of the Interior, seem not to have regarded the situation as all that critical. At their sessions in Paris, during the interregnum after the Assembly had left Bordeaux and before it met at Versailles, little serious action was taken, at least until the arrival of Thiers, Picard good-humouredly telling jokes and assuring the worried d'Aurelle de Paladines that 'it's nothing, one gets used to all that; you know what the Paris population is like.'[2] Rather than resort to force Picard had appealed

[1] *Enquête*, II, p. 11.                    [2] De Paladines, *Enquête*, II, p. 433.

to the Mayors to use their influence to persuade the National Guard to surrender their cannons. On 8 March the National Guard intercepted an infantry battalion heading towards Montmartre. But other National Guards were growing tired of the continual sentry duty, and often left their post without bothering to await replacements.[1] Clemenceau was optimistic that he could get the National Guards of Montmartre to hand over the cannons, especially as the 61st battalion published a letter saying the cannons had only been taken to keep them from the Prussians. On the eve of 18 March, the Paris Deputy, Schoelcher, was confident that he had persuaded the Guards to hand over the cannons in Montmartre to the Government.[2]

The optimism of some of the Mayors and Paris Deputies was not shared by the military or by Thiers. The tenth of March was the day Clemenceau had agreed with the Guards in Montmartre to hand over the cannons, but he had warned Vinoy not 'to rush matters'. Instead, Vinoy chose that day to issue a decree suppressing six of the revolutionary papers 'for preaching sedition and disobedience of the law'. This was an extremely ill-judged measure, and was criticized by the conservative Press as well as by the revolutionaries. It angered the local National Guard Committee, which now broke its agreement and refused to hand over the cannons when Vinoy sent a detachment to collect them.[3] Opinion became more hostile to the Government when the news reached Paris that a court martial had sentenced in their absence Blanqui and Flourens to death for the events of 31 October. Even Trochu at the time had been willing to excuse them. This was also the day of the Assembly's law on the overdue bills, which led the moderate L'Opinion Nationale to comment that 'there is a public danger, a serious and imminent peril, if this incredible law is not repealed'.[4] Within a week there were 150,000 declarations of bankruptcy in Paris. That day there was another assembly of the National Guard during which the President, Arnold, emphasized that the National Guard had as a result of the peace treaty, the monarchist Assembly of Bordeaux, and the Prussian entry lost all its 'illusions'. There could be no compromise with those who threatened the Republic.[5] That evening Favre wrote to Thiers say-

---

[1] De Paladines, *Enquête*, II, p. 434; *The Times*, 12 March.
[2] *Enquête*, II, pp. 320-1; Damé, op. cit., p. 32.
[3] Damé, op. cit., pp. 28-33; *The Times*, 15 March.
[4] Lepelletier, op. cit., vol. 1, p. 284.
[5] *Enquête*, III, pp. 29-30.

ing his presence in Paris was needed because it had been decided 'to finish with the redoubts of Montmartre and Belleville'.[1]

There were a couple more efforts to regain the cannons, aimed at the park in the Place de Vosges, which it was hoped might prove less militant than Montmartre or Belleville. On 11 March a National Guard battalion from the 5th arrondissement went to the Place de Vosges to claim its cannon, named 'Alsace-Lorraine', which was then paraded back to the Mairie on the Place du Panthéon, where Mayor Vacherot, on the side of the hawks amongst the Mayors, made a speech suggesting other battalions should follow suit. But no sooner was the 'Alsace-Lorraine' seemingly safe behind the walls of the nearby Ecole Polytechnic than the young revolutionary Guardsman, Jean Allemane, seized it 'in the name of the people', calling on others in the battalion to support him. A crowd of 200 then triumphantly took it back through the Latin Quarter and returned it to the Place de Vosges.[2] A more direct attempt was made a few days later, just after Thiers' arrival in the capital. This time an attack was to be made late at night, but word had leaked out beforehand and when the small detatchment Vinoy had sent arrived at the Place de Vosges it found that the National Guard was ready. The *rappel* was beaten, and the troops were enveloped by the crowd and had to withdraw.[3] The next day the cannons were transferred further east into the greater security of the Faubourg Saint-Antoine.

The National Guard elections were held on 15 March in 215 of the 254 battalions, establishing a Central Committee representing just over half of the arrondissements.[4] This was the Committee that was to be carried to power by the uprising of 18 March, not the 'revolutionary socialist' vigilance committee which had played the most active role during the siege. The central office of the International was not thinking of a revolution at this stage, and other leaders of the popular forces had given up all hope of a revolution now the peace was made. Lefrançais, for example, was preparing to join Vaillant, Blanqui and Tridon in the country near Bordeaux when he was surprised by the events of 18 March, and Vermorel was planning to emigrate to the United States.[5] Not all, of course, were so pessimistic. In the 5th and 13th arrondissements, after the failure of the

[1] Favre, op. cit., vol. 3, p. 208.    [2] Allemane, op. cit., pp. 7–11.
[3] *Enquête*, II, p. 454 (Mortemart); p. 373 (Vautrain); Lepelletier, op. cit., pp. 296–7.    [4] *Enquête*, III, p. 37.
[5] Lefrançais, *Souvenirs*, p. 460; *Etude*, p. 322.

attempt of Mayor Vacherot to win over the National Guard into surrendering its cannons, the local National Guard committees had united under the command of Duval in the expectation of further attacks. A cannon shot would alert the population should the Government resort to force. Nor were all the members of the newly elected National Guard Central Committee completely obscure. Duval and Eudes represented the 13th arrondissement, Duval having played an active part for several years in the strike movement as a Blanquist member of the International. The representatives of the 18th arrondissement were a member of the Club de la Révolution, Josselin, and the militant stonecutter Grolard, though neither of these had belonged to the local vigilance committee. Varlin, Mortier, Arnaud and Assi were working-class members of the International, Varlin and Assi being particularly well known for the part they had played in the 1870 strike of the iron and steel workers at Le Creusot. Ranvier and Allemane were locally known revolutionaries. Of the remaining twenty or so members, the professions of a few are known: Lisbonne, who had been a soldier, theatre director of the Folies Saint-Antoine and insurance broker; Blanchet, who had been a Capucin Monk before working for the Imperial police (the Commune later arrested him but then released him and he was condemned to death by Versailles); Billioray, a painter; Babick, of Polish origin, who had been a chemist and perfumer; Arnold, an architect; Jourde, a bank clerk and one of the few members of the Committee later elected to the Commune. But for the most part, both to the 'revolutionary socialists' and the Internationalists and even more so to the public at large the National Guard Central Committee consisted of 'unknowns' chosen by the local battalions from among the artisans, workers, petty-bourgeois and bohemians typical of the Paris population.

The arrival of Thiers in Paris on 15 March brought matters to a head, giving to the 'government a more decided complexion than it had hitherto had', as *The Times* assured its English readers.[1] He was an astute, hard, unscrupulous, shrivelled-up old man, sure of his own superiority over everyone else around him, with no love for the populace out of which he had long ago assiduously raised himself. As a minister under Louis-Philippe he had seen to the savage repression of the workers' revolts in Lyon and Paris in 1834, the latter going down in Paris working-class history as the massacre of

[1] 14 March; cf. De Paladines, *Enquête*, II, p. 433.

the rue Transnonain. He had been vituperative against the workers in June 1848, and two years later had supported penal and residency requirements in the electoral law that excluded about a third of the voters, chiefly the militant Left and the workers, the 'vile multitude' as Thiers called them in a phrase that was not forgotten by the popular imagination. It was Thiers who had been responsible for the plans to fortify Paris, during the 1840 crisis between England and France. It fell to his successor, Guizot, to see the scheme through, though the danger of war by then had faded. Thiers' continued support was important in getting the measure through Parliament and to his republican critics' charge of preparing the means to put down any further revolutions in Paris under the cover of providing for the national defence Thiers replied that they were 'calumniating any possible Government in supposing that it could some day attempt to maintain itself by bombarding the capital'. When the crowds saw Thiers in the streets in February 1848 they shouted at him 'Down with the bastilles'.[1]

Thiers was not prepared to enter into long-drawn-out negotiations in an attempt to mollify Paris opinion, some of which was expressing the hope that 'the Government will understand that the hour for action has at last struck . . . to restore order'.[2] The Assembly was to meet at Versailles on 20 March, and Thiers knew that the provincial reactionary majority would expect firm measures to be taken to restore order in Paris. He had therefore to force a decision one way or the other. The failure of the midnight attack on the Place de Vosges he took as a rebuff that left him no choice but to make one last full-scale attempt on the guns in the hands of the National Guard. If this failed then this historian chief executive was determined to apply the lessons of France's past history, as he interpreted them, and retreat from Paris so as to be able better to mate it. If the capital wanted another blood letting, another June 1848, the authoritarian Thiers was not one to disappoint it. Had he not insisted on Versailles because of its military strategic position?[3] On

[1] Thiers, *Notes et Souvenirs – 1848*, Paris, 1902, p. 50; *Discours parlementaires*, Paris, 1882, vol. 5, p. 360, 13 January 1841.
[2] *Journal des Débats*, 10 March.
[3] Thiers in his *Souvenirs – 1848*, p. 26, had criticized the indecision of Louis-Philippe in staying in Paris while the revolution grew around him. At the *Enquête*, II, p. 11, Thiers said of his attempt on 18 March that 'one could already say that if it was not a success then it would be necessary to leave Paris, but

17 March there was a full Council meeting at which it was resolved to use the combined strength of the army and the police to establish the authority of the Government throughout the popular districts. Vinoy demurred, knowing that the army needed several days more to be fully prepared, and suggested that the National Guard might be brought to reason if its pay was stopped.[1] But Thiers would brook no further delay; 'It was,' he said afterwards, 'one of those times when everything had to be risked, when we had to go forward, whatever the cost.'[2] With faint hope of success Vinoy obediently prepared to make the attempt on the Butte de Montmartre.

---

before doing so it was necessary to have a try at a fight'. So unlikely was success that Thiers has often been accused of deliberately seeking to provoke a civil war in order to improve his standing with the Right by getting rid of the revolutionary Left: e.g. Lepelletier, op. cit., p. 274. More likely, since a civil war would seem too uncertain an event to be deliberately embarked on, the Government underestimated the strength of the Paris resistance. If the attempt failed it probably expected something more like the three-day uprising of 1848 than the eight-week campaign they brought on themselves.

[1] Favre, op. cit., vol. 3, p. 209; Vinoy, op. cit., pp. 207–8; *The Times*, 12 March, reported that a police agent had toured the National Guard companies warning them that their pay would be stopped if they did not surrender the cannons.

[2] *Enquête*, II, p. 11.

# Chapter 5

# SATURDAY, 18 MARCH

Thiers' 'burglarious' attempt on the cannons of Montmartre, as Marx called it, was a coordinated plan of the military and police to reduce revolutionary Paris. Strategic points throughout the eastern popular quarters were to be occupied by the army. On the Right Bank regiments were to be sent to the Place de la Bastille, the Tuileries, the Hôtel de Ville and the railway stations. The bridges and the Ile de la Cité were to be guarded. Brigades at the Panthéon and the Luxembourg were to stand in reserve in the heart of the Latin Quarter. General Vinoy established his headquarters at the Ecole Militaire close to the Invalides, where troops were standing by to receive the captured cannons. The main attack under Generals Lecomte and Paturel was to be from the north against the heights of the Butte Montmartre, where today stands the Sacré Cœur Church erected in 'expiation' of the Commune, and the Buttes-Chaumont in Belleville. On these two cliff-like hills, accessible only by the steep, narrow and winding streets and stairs of this un-Haussmannized area of Paris, the populace had established the two biggest artillery parks for the guns seized during the previous weeks. Earthworks of 'formidable proportions',[1] with loopholes for riflemen, gave the appearance that these would be stoutly defended. In all there were 417 guns held by the National Guard throughout Paris, Montmartre accounting for 171, Belleville for 74.

This military attack was to be supplemented by a police operation. The Prefect of Police had finally agreed to send in his police agents under the cover of the army to arrest the leading revolutionary figures. A list had been drawn up a few days previously of thirty members of the Central Committee of the National Guard who should be arrested.[2] Armed police and *gardes républicains* also made up the first column of the attack on Montmartre. This was a last-

---

[1] *The Times*, 11 March.  [2] Mortemart, *Enquête*, II, p. 449.

minute change by General Lecomte because of the unreliability of his own troops. An attempt was also made to get the support of the 'good' battalions of the National Guard.

On the evening of the attack General d'Aurelle de Paladines, the official Commander-in-Chief of the National Guard, summoned the commanders of thirty or forty battalions from the bourgeois districts on whom the Government thought it could rely. De Paladines could not be very explicit before even this selected group since surprise was the Government's main advantage. All he could do was to ask them to be ready to assemble their men early the next morning if the *rappel* were beaten. To the obvious question of whether an attack was being planned on the cannons of Montmartre, d'Aurelle could only reply 'prudently' that he was not authorized to say. Nevertheless, Jérôme Langlois, a long-standing friend of the labour movement but a firm supporter of order at this time, speaking for the other commanders told de Paladines that the National Guard would not fire on fellow-Guardsmen defending their cannons. The most that could be expected, said Langlois, of the 'good' battalions would be to defend their own *quartiers* against the Bellevillois.[1] Thiers afterwards put much of the blame for the defeat of his plan on the bourgoisie for failing to come out and support the Government in the streets. But there was sufficient evidence available in advance to show that such a hope was likely to prove unfounded.

As a final measure a proclamation was drawn up by the national government addressed to the 'Inhabitants of Paris' appealing to the 'good sense, wisdom and patriotism' of the 'good citizens . . . to separate themselves from the bad in order to help rather than resist the public authorities'. The 'warning' was given that they should 'approve this recourse to force, because, at all costs and without a day's delay, there must be the complete, immediate and unalterable restoration of order, the condition of their welfare'. Such crude propaganda was too reminiscent of Louis-Napoleon's placard on the morning of his *coup d'état* that 'the bad should tremble, the good should feel reassured'. It only alienated opinion further from 'little Thiers', as the market crowd in the rue Saint-Antoine called him when they read of his 'projects'.[2]

At first all passed off quietly. The troops were woken up in the

[1] *Enquête*, II, p. 435 (De Paladines); p. 456 (De Mortemart); p. 431 (Colone Ibos).
[2] *The Times*, 20 March.

middle of the night, towards 3.0 a.m., and set off across Paris, the fog hiding their movements. Many had not even had time to get a cup of coffee and they were carrying no provisions with them, as Vinoy had insisted on leaving the knapsacks behind. Except for the bill-posters the streets were deserted, and the members of the National Guard Central Committee walking home after a late meeting were at the other end of Paris to the troops at this early hour. General Lecomte descended from the north via the boulevard Ornano, the chausée de Clignancourt and up the rue Muller to take Montmartre from behind. To the left General Paturel's brigade skirted the heights of Montmartre to establish itself at the foot of the Butte and cordonned off the boulevard from the Place Clichy to the Place Pigalle, where General Susbielle set up his divisional command. The only alarm came from the National Guard post at the Tour Solferino restaurant on the Butte itself, but the sentry on duty, Turpin, was immediately shot down by the gendarmes. The rest were easily overrun and locked up. A few did get away and began to spread the alert. But in the grey dawn over Montmartre the attack seemed to have succeeded. Already the engineers who had accompanied the troops had cleared the way and a number of cannons had been carried down to the Place du Tertre. *The Times* correspondent had been on the scene early at Montmartre and he now hurried off towards Belleville convinced that there would be nothing further of interest happening at Montmartre.

Nearly two hours later, around 8.0 a.m., Lecomte's men were still there waiting for the arrival of the horses to draw away the captured guns. This delay, yet one more example of the inability of the French High Command, was fatal for the success of the attack on Montmartre. After the Civil War Vinoy tried to defend himself against his many critics by arguing a shortage of horses because they had been killed off for food during the siege. In any case, he argued, the horses could not be sent along until it was certain that the heights had been taken, as they would have been a serious hindrance in case the troops had been forced to retreat. This had not been the young Bonaparte's tactic in 1795 when his 'whiff of grapeshot' had saved the Convention from being stormed by the crowd.[1]

[1] Cf. General A. Zeller, *Les Hommes de la Commune*, Paris, 1969, p. 183. Vinoy before the Commission of Inquiry and in his account, *Enquête*, III, pp. 98, 103, *L'Armistice*, p. 219, made the curious excuse that it would have taken two or three days, not hours, to clear the guns from Montmartre and the rest of Paris. If

Slowly the village awakened. Women came out to fetch milk and saw the troops everywhere. Astonished, they were joined by their children and menfolk. Shops and cafés opened up their shutters. The troops were now famished and cold, having been up some five hours. Not having their packs with them, many laid down their rifles and went off to buy some food from nearby. It was the women most noticeably who began to remonstrate with the soldiers, asking where they thought they were going to take the cannons: 'To Berlin?' At the same time the local women offered the troops wine and bread, though not to the despised gendarmes. In the streets below the drums were now beating out the *rappel* and the local committee of the 18th arrondissement was beginning to assemble the National Guard battalions.

The Mayor, Georges Clemenceau, had been woken up at 6.0 a.m. with the news that the army had occupied Montmartre. Cursing the stupidity of such a precipitate action he hurried off to the Butte. He expressed his 'extreme surprise and disappointment' to General Lecomte that the Government had acted without informing the Mayors, who after all had been trying to negotiate the return of the cannons.[1] Then he went to the headquarters of the local National Guard in the rue des Rosiers, where he found Louise Michel, whom he knew and respected, tending the mortally wounded Turpin. A few days later Turpin died, glad, so he said, to have lived to see the Revolution. As a doctor, Clemenceau wanted to get him carried away, but Lecomte refused to allow a 'promenade of a corpse' that might easily rouse up the crowd. Instead Lecomte offered the services of a military doctor.

Louise Michel, revolutionary, feminist, school-teacher and poet left Turpin when Clemenceau arrived and ran off down the streets crying 'treason'. In the square below the teams had finally arrived to take away the cannons, but the crowd cut the traces of the horses. Instead of trying to disperse the crowd and advance to support Lecomte, Paturel retired to join his divisional commander at the Place Clichy. Columns of National Guards were now assembling throughout Montmartre and each time they came across detach-

---

this were really so, than it is hard to see how it could be expected Paris could be held down with so few troops against a hostile National Guard. Nor in this case is it clear why such an early start was made and why the troops left their packs behind as if the whole operation would be over in a few hours.
[1] J. Martet, *Clemenceau*, Eng. trans. London, 1930, p. 167.

ments of the army the troops fraternized, their officers and the gendarmes being made prisoners if they did not escape quickly enough. *The Times* correspondent in his journey across the north of Paris was greatly astonished by 'the extreme demonstration of fraternization' that he witnessed in the boulevard Ornano.[1]

At the top of the Butte Lecomte's small army was by now surrounded by the crowd, still predominantly women, and Louise Michel was surprised on her return to find her old mother out because she 'was worried for us'.[2] By the time a column of National Guards arrived the essential distance between troops and citizens had become gravely compromised. Two National Guard officers stepped forward to parley with the line. The rest of the Guards and the soldiers who had already joined with them raised the butts of their rifles in the air. Lecomte, seeing the danger, rode over to personally take command. Women from the crowd thrust themselves between the two groups shouting to the troops, 'Will you fire on us? On your brothers? Our husbands? Our children?' Four times Lecomte vainly ordered his men to fire. In this expectant silence warrant officer Verdaguer called on his fellow soldiers to ground their arms and the crowd surged forward to embrace the troops crying 'Long live the line'. The gendarmes were overrun and disarmed before they could fire, the officers were pulled off their horses and Lecomte himself was seized. By nine in the morning it was all over. Everyone was drinking to the victory of the people. The gendarmes were marched away to the Mairie where Clemenceau locked them away for their own safety. Lecomte and several of his officers were far less fortunate, many in the crowd thinking they had captured Vinoy, and he had to be rescued by the National Guard, who took this group off to the Château-Rouge music-hall in the rue de Clignancourt, which had been converted into a National Guard post. The captain in charge, Simon-Mayer, properly went off to inform Clemenceau of the capture of such important prisoners. There was nothing Clemenceau could do but trust Mayer, since he himself was popularly suspected of having collaborated with the Government in the attack on the cannons. Having assured Clemenceau the officers were safe, Mayer went back, taking with him six luncheon rations.

The attack on Montmartre had failed, with barely a shot being fired. The only serious clash of this operation occurred when General

[1] *The Times*, 20 March.
[2] Michel, op. cit., p. 140.

Susbielle finally showed some consciousness of what was happening and gave the order to clear the Place Pigalle. The cavalry tried to do this by gently backing their horses into the crowd. But they were hissed and whistled at, and the furious captain turned his squadron round and ordered a charge. His men hesitated, so he rode down onto the crowd, sabre drawn. Two shots from a National Guard felled him. The gendarmes replied and there was a short combat. But Susbielle did not give the order to pursue the action and his men began to fraternize with the population. Vinoy, who had just arrived on the scene, gave the order to withdraw completely to the Left Bank, and then galloped off leaving, so it was said, his General's cap lying in the square. Lecomte and the other imprisoned officers were thus abandoned to their fate.

The crowd in the Place Pigalle included a new element not previously apparent among the good women of Montmartre. This was those who plied their trade in the cafés and hotels of the exterior boulevards, 'sad scum of prostitution on the revolutionary wave', as da Costa calls them.[1] They had reasons of their own to hate the police. So did many of the soldiers who had joined in the revolt, for it was darkly rumoured that gendarmes had arrested recalcitrant soldiers the night before. The slain officer's horse was torn to pieces where it lay in the square, a common enough practice dating from the siege. The disbanded soldiers were ready to kill any of their officers they could get hold of.

In these circumstances it was a mistake on the part of the local National Guard committee to order Simon-Mayer in the early afternoon to transfer his prisoners back to the Committee's headquarters in the rue des Rosiers. For the latter was a simple house and garden, not easily defensible, and the sight of the officers again only further excited the crowd, turning the journey into 'our real agony, our stations of the cross', as one of the survivors afterwards piously described it.[2] It was only with the greatest difficulty that the National Guards prevented them from being massacred on the way. Once they reached the rue des Rosiers, they were locked away on the ground floor whilst someone set off to try to find the members of the National Guard Committee. But these had dispersed, some to the Mairie, others to the arrondissement Vigilance Committee, satisfied

[1] Da Costa, op. cit., vol. 1, p. 22.
[2] Comte de Beaugnot, Le Soir, of Versailles, 24, 25 March: given in D'Hérisson, op. cit., pp. 46–58. The rue des Rosiers is today the rue des Roses.

that they had the hostages safely in their charge and away from Clemenceau's control. What they failed to take into account was the fury of the crowd, which was smashing the windows of the house trying to break in.

This difficult situation became impossible when around 5.0 p.m. a huge shout went up and a new group of prisoners arrived. A section of the crowd outside seized this opportunity to burst into the house itself. The centre of their hate was an old white-bearded figure in civilian clothes, General Clément Thomas who had been d'Aurelle de Paladine's immediate predecessor as Commander-in-Chief of the National Guard. Although a self-declared republican, he was detested because of the part he had played in the repression after the Blanquist revolt of May 1848. More recently he had expressed his contempt of the National Guard for their conduct at Buzenval, taunting them with cowardice. Curiosity had drawn him to the boulevard Clichy, where he was recognized by a National Guardsman. The artist André Gill and a friend were passing by and heard the Guard ask Clément Thomas if he was on their side. Clément Thomas tried to avoid the question, but an old Guard cut him short by telling the crowd that had quickly gathered round that Clément Thomas was 'one of the assassins of '48 and should be given his deserts'.[1] On such a day the crowd felt confident and successful enough to exact its justice on those whom popular tradition called 'murderers of the people'. Clément Thomas was dragged off to join the others in the rue des Rosiers.

The small National Guard contingent was completely overwhelmed. They did their best to hold back the crowd inside the house. One, Herpin-Lacroix, who had served with Garibaldi during the war, having failed to block the doorway with his huge body, gained a moment's respite by shouting out that there would be a court martial. But Clément Thomas was driven into the garden where he was finally done to death. General Lecomte handed over 1,000 francs to be delivered to his wife and family, stepped into the garden sword in hand, and was at once shot down from behind by one of his own soldiers. Others from the 88th regiment finished him off. The doctor who carried out the autopsy took forty bullets out of the body of Clément Thomas; nine from Lecomte's body. Most of them had been fired from army chassepot rifles.

[1] André Gill, *Vingt années de Paris*, Paris, 1883, pp. 109-11; Lepelletier, op. cit., vol. 1, pp. 453-4.

A few minutes later a breathless Clemenceau arrived, hopefully wearing his sash of office, having just heard the news of Clément Thomas's arrest. But Clemenceau had little enough authority left over the National Guard of his arrondissement, let alone with a mob such as he now faced. For his own safety he had to hurry away. 'Everyone,' he afterwards used to recount, 'was shrieking like wild beasts, without realizing what they were doing. I observed then that pathological phenomenon which might be called blood lust.'[1] The crowd now seemed appeased and did not prevent Simon-Mayer marching his National Guardsmen and their prisoners back again to the Château-Rouge. The next day a well-dressed man was haranguing a crowd near the Bourse from his coach on the murder of the two Generals. Arthur Arnould, soon to be elected to the Commune and far from being a supporter of terror, passed by. His anger was aroused and he shouted back at the speaker, 'There were only two; if what you call the supporters of order had won there would have been 10,000.'[2] It was to prove an underestimation.

These two deaths in the afternoon were the result of the popular hostility against the army, stemming from the role it had played in repressing working-class movements, a feeling that had been turned to fever pitch by the events of the siege. Though this bloodshed had not been desired by the National Guard committees, the revolutionaries did encourage the arrest of any army officers that could be found to be used as hostages, the Blanquists in particular thinking of an exchange against Blanqui himself, arrested the day before. Duval, for example, had posted guards at the railway stations. Hence, when General Chanzy arrived that afternoon at the Gare d'Orléans (Gare D'Austerlitz today) from Tours on his way to take up his seat as a Deputy in Versailles, he found himself seized and roughly conducted to the Mairie of the 13th arrondissement, the crowd mistaking him for the unpopular Ducrot or even Vinoy. In fact, Chanzy had been the staunchest military supporter of Gambetta during the resistance in the provinces, but this was hardly known in Paris, where in any case Gambetta's name had lost the popularity it had had in the revolutionary districts two years previously. As in Montmartre, the National Guard had a hard struggle preventing the crowd from killing their prisoner in the streets. He was finally conducted to the safety of the Santé prison. General Cremer, on the other hand, was fêted by the crowd and conducted in triumph to the Hôtel de Ville.

[1] Martet, op. cit., p. 184.        [2] Arnould, op. cit., vol. 2, p. 25.

He was popular because he together with a few other officers had escaped from Metz rather than surrender with Bazaine. There is some question whether he might not have joined the revolutionaries out of patriotism. But instead he used his popularity to set Chanzy free a few days later. The moderates on the Central Committee of the National Guard were in favour of this[1] on condition that Chanzy gave his word of honour not to fight against the Commune. He was true to his word.

The other operations in the rest of Paris followed the same pattern as in Montmartre of early success followed by the breakdown of all command as the troops fraternized with the crowd. At the Buttes-Chaumont General Faron had also had to await the arrival of the horses to take away the cannons. The National Guard turned out, barricades were raised right under the noses of the troops, and when an astonished *Times* correspondent asked why this was not prevented a 'gentlemanly-looking officer' gave him the curt reply that it was a 'dangerous place to be in, and still more dangerous to ask questions'. It all had 'a most strange and incomprehensible aspect to one not brought up to make barricades'.[2] Realizing the danger of the situation Faron wisely negotiated the withdrawal of his men. At the Place de la Bastille the red flag was pulled down by 9.0 a.m., but General le Flô had to call the *garde républicain* to his rescue when over-confidently he tried to persuade a group at the edge of the square of the justness of the Government's cause. Before noon the red flag was flying again over this symbolic spot of revolutionary Paris, across which there slowly passed a solemn procession. The crowd opened up the barricades and the National Guard presented arms and rolled their drums as they recognized the cloaked white-haired figure behind the coffin. It was Victor Hugo on his way to his son's burial in the Père-Lachaise cemetery, soon to mark the last stand of the victors of this day. The crowd then marched off to demonstrate in front of the Hôtel de Ville.

Further east, in the Faubourg Saint-Antoine, the Central Committee of the National Guard had left three of its members on duty in its newly established office in the rue Basfroi in case of an alert. At 5.0 a.m. they received the news of troop movements towards the Place de la Bastille, and an hour later it was confirmed that the

---

[1] *Le Procès de la Commune. Compte rendu des débats du Conseil de Guerre*, Paris, 1871, p. 51, for Chanzy's evidence to this effect in favour of Billioray and Lullier. [2] *The Times*, 20 March.

district was encircled. They beat the *rappel*, but it was not until after 9.0 a.m. that any other members of the Central Committee arrived. Barricades, however, were springing up everywhere and at 1.0 p.m. Ferry telegraphed from the Hôtel de Ville that all was lost in the 11th arrondissement. Yet at two in the afternoon the Central Committee had still not learnt of the news from Montmartre and Belleville.[1] The embryonic National Guard federation functioned only on the local level; it was not able, and hardly tried, to organize the battalions throughout the city.

On the Left Bank, the cannon of Duval's legion in the 13th arrondissement had not sounded to give the alarm until after 8.0 a.m. Allemane, however, had been woken by noise from the streets around 5.0 a.m., and had forced the sexton of Saint-Nicolas-du-Chardonnet (by the Place Maubert on the boulevard St Germain) to ring out the tocsin. The local National Guard assembled in the rue Geoffroy-Saint-Hilaire behind the Jardin des Plantes, and guardposts were established along the rue Mouffetard and on the Place Monge. From troops they arrested they soon discovered that this was indeed the expected attack. The public buildings around the Panthéon, including the Mairie, were occupied, and by mid-morning the troops in the Luxembourg had surrendered their arms amidst the usual scenes of fraternization. The enterprising Allemane was even able to capture the staff officers in the Palace itself. They joined the other prisoners in the Mairie. Throughout the eastern arrondissements on the Left Bank, the 5th, 13th and 14th, there were National Guards on all the streets, and an English correspondent passed 'scarcely a man or a boy without arms'. In the rue de Maine, behind the cemetery of Montparnasse, he was told by one boy, armed with a pair of pistols and a chassepot rifle twice as big as himself, that it was France that was in danger.[2]

In contrast to this uncoordinated animation in the popular districts the west of Paris was quiet, too quiet for the good of the Government. The *rappel* had been beaten for the bourgeois battalion of the National Guard at 5.0 a.m. But, as d'Aurelle had been warned the evening before, this was to no avail. By 7.0 a.m. there were only a few Guardsmen at the street corners. When an attempt was made to send off the few hundred Guards that had appeared to defend the

---

[1] Ferry, *Enquête*, II, p. 67; Rougerie, *Procès*, pp. 48-9, account of Nestor Rousseau, who was at the rue Basfroi: A.H.G., Ly 20.
[2] *The Times*, 20 March.

(*a*) Avenue Jean-Jaurès (19ᵉ)

3. The barricades of 18 March: the victors of the day

(*b*) Rue Basfroi (11ᵉ)

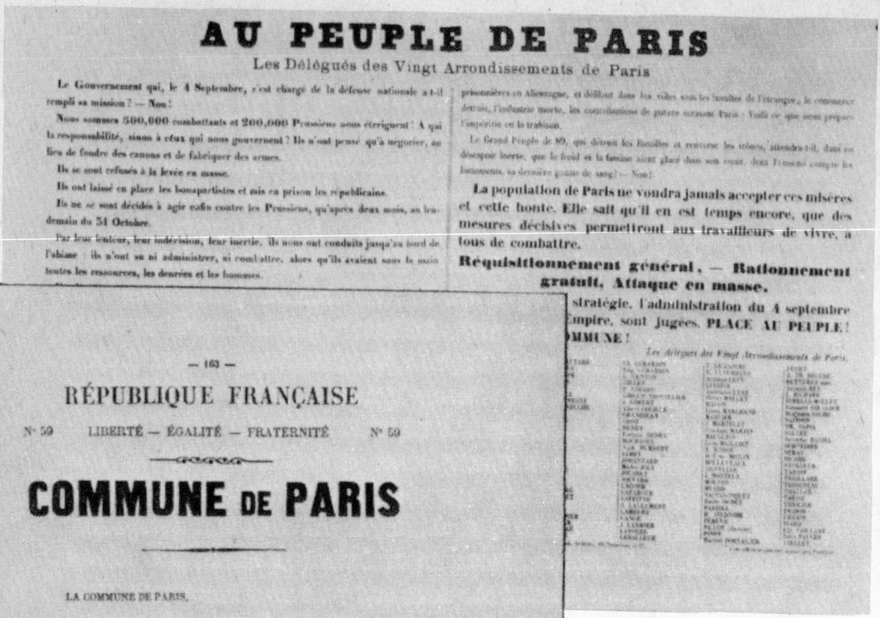

**AU PEUPLE DE PARIS**

Les Délégués des Vingt Arrondissements de Paris

[text in two columns, largely illegible]

**La population de Paris ne voudra jamais accepter ces misères et cette honte.** Elle sait qu'il en est temps encore, que des mesures décisives permettront aux travailleurs de vivre, à tous de combattre.

**Réquisitionnement général. — Rationnement gratuit, Attaque en masse.**

... stratégie, l'administration du 4 septembre ... Empire, sont jugées. PLACE AU PEUPLE! COMMUNE!

Les délégués des Vingt Arrondissements de Paris.

---

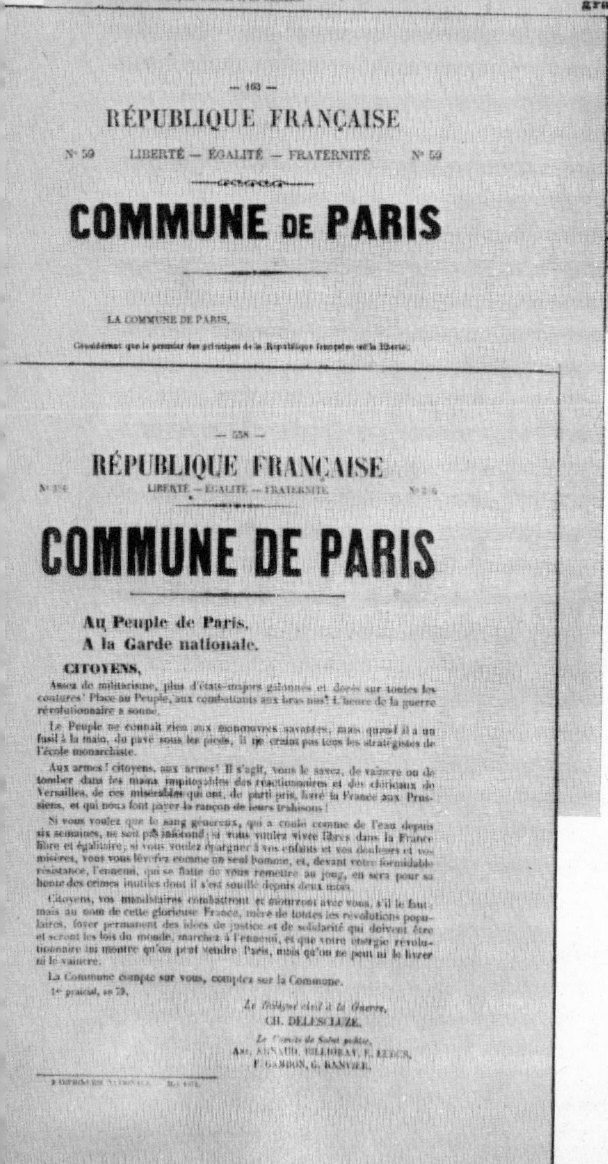

— 163 —

**RÉPUBLIQUE FRANÇAISE**

N° 59     LIBERTÉ — ÉGALITÉ — FRATERNITÉ     N° 59

# COMMUNE DE PARIS

LA COMMUNE DE PARIS.

Considérant que le premier des principes de la République française est la liberté;

---

— 558 —

**RÉPUBLIQUE FRANÇAISE**

N° 256     LIBERTÉ — EGALITÉ — FRATERNITÉ     N° 256

# COMMUNE DE PARIS

Au Peuple de Paris,
A la Garde nationale.

**CITOYENS,**

Assez de militarisme, plus d'états-majors galonnés et dorés sur toutes les coutures! Place au Peuple, aux combattants aux bras nus! l'heure de la guerre révolutionnaire a sonné.

Le Peuple ne connaît rien aux manœuvres savantes, mais quand il a un fusil à la main, du pavé sous les pieds, il ne craint pas tous les stratégistes de l'école monarchique.

Aux armes! citoyens, aux armes! Il s'agit, vous le savez, de vaincre ou de tomber dans les mains impitoyables des réactionnaires et des cléricaux de Versailles, de ces misérables qui ont, de parti pris, livré la France aux Prussiens, et qui nous font payer la rançon de leurs trahisons!

Si vous voulez que le sang généreux, qui a coulé comme de l'eau depuis six semaines, ne soit pas infécond; si vous voulez vivre libres dans la France libre et égalitaire, si vous voulez épargner à vos enfants et vos douleurs et vos misères, vous vous lèverez comme un seul homme, et, devant votre formidable résistance, l'ennemi, qui se flatte de vous remettre au joug, en sera pour sa honte des crimes inutiles dont il s'est souillé depuis deux mois.

Citoyens, vos mandataires combattront et mourront avec vous, s'il le faut; mais au nom de cette glorieuse France, mère de toutes les révolutions populaires, foyer permanent des idées de justice et de solidarité qui doivent être et seront les lois du monde, marchez à l'ennemi, et que votre énergie révolutionnaire lui montre qu'on peut vendre Paris, mais qu'on ne peut ni le livrer ni le vaincre.

La Commune compte sur vous, comptez sur la Commune.

Le 1er prairial, an 79.

Le Délégué civil à la Guerre,
CH. DELESCLUZE.

Le Comité de Salut public,
ANT. ARNAUD, BILLIORAY, E. EUDES,
F. GAMBON, G. RANVIER.

---

4. Three crucial posters: (*a*) 6 January: The *Affiche Rouge* of the Delegation of the Twenty Arrondissements; (*b*) 3 April: The first decrees of the Commune; (*c*) 21 May: The Call to the Barricades

Mairies they refused, being 'more disposed to do the opposite of what they were commanded'.[1] Colonel Ibos, who had rescued the Government trapped in the Hôtel de Ville on 31 October, found that only one or two hundred of the more unreliable members of his battalion turned out. As instructed, he read them the Government's victory proclamation announcing the capture of the cannons, but his men only smiled and said the reverse was true. Disconcerted, Ibos dismissed them.[2] Shopkeepers had not ventured to take down their shutters in the streets off the Place Vendôme, and along the rue de Rivoli Guards who had turned out thinking it was the Prussians they were going to fight were returning home when they found it was against 'citizens'.[3] On the other side of the Seine the solidly bourgeois 20th battalion of teachers, lawyers and traders had already two days previously let itself be disarmed by the plebeian 134th battalion.[4] Thiers' attempt to separate Paris into 'good' and 'bad' citizens had clearly failed.

By 1.0 p.m. Thiers, having visited Vinoy's headquarters and heard the reports, was already beginning to think of abandoning Paris. At 3.0 p.m. there was a full meeting of the Government at the Foreign Affairs Ministry on the Quai d'Orsay. The debate was cut short when three battalions of National Guards suddenly appeared marching along the quay, playing their drums and bugles. There were only a few troops on guard in front of the Ministry, and General le Flô, the Minister of War, caused panic by announcing that he thought they were all 'done for'. Thiers made a quick exit by a back staircase, giving out the order to evacuate Paris, and was driven away at full gallop for Versailles in a coach with an escort Vinoy had had waiting. Thiers just had time to pause and pencil out the evacuation order again, which he despatched via the lieutenant in charge of his escort. The National Guard battalions, oblivious that such a *coup* could have been theirs, continued on their way to demonstrate in front of the Hôtel de Ville, even marching back again equally unconcernedly half an hour later.[5]

By the afternoon, the National Guard Central Committee began to

---

[1] *Enquête*, II, p. 435 (De Paladines); p. 457 (Mortemart).

[2] *Enquête*, II, p. 431 (Ibos).              [3] Cf. *The Times*, 20 March.

[4] H. Dabot, *Griffonages quotidiens d'un bourgeois du Quartier Latin*, Paris, 1895, pp. 172, 179.

[5] *Enquête*, II, p. 97 (Vinoy); pp. 80–1 (Le Flô); p. 511 (Admiral Pothau); Allemane, op. cit., p. 20, also refers to this lost opportunity.

try to exercise some influence outside of the immediate district around its own headquarters. But it had no idea that Paris was open for the taking. At 2.0 p.m. it cautiously ordered the National Guard 'to stand by on the defensive in view of the troop movements'. In case of attack they were 'to barricade the side streets and be prepared to withdraw if the attack was too fierce'. At 2.30 p.m. the order was given 'to those battalions of the 17th arrondissement that were available to descend on Paris and capture the Place Vendôme in concert with all battalions available from the 18th'. A similar order was given to the 18th arrondissement.[1] But for a long time the local commanders hesitated to lead their men into the centre of Paris away from the safety of their own districts. It was not until the evening, around 8.0 p.m., that three or four battalions from the 17th and 18th arrondissements together with disbanded soldiers finally descended towards the Place Vendôme, where the Ministry of Justice housed the official headquarters of the National Guard. They were led by Georges Arnold and Eugène Varlin, both representatives from these two arrondissements on the Central Committee. The descent was checked before the square by a detachment of local National Guards of this bourgeois district and some regular troops. A deputation was sent to try to effect a peaceful entry. The officer-in-charge of the Place sent to d'Aurelle de Paladines for instructions, and back came the order that all resistance had been abandoned. The Internationalist Varlin and his men were able therefore simply to walk in and establish themselves in the Ministry, empty except for the steward who took the precaution of hiding away all the silver plate.[2]

The Panthéon, which had only recently been turned into a big munitions store as a place of safety from the Central Committee, finally surrendered to Duval's men at the end of the afternoon. With the Latin Quarter fully in his control, Duval was free to comply with the Central Committee's order and make for the main object of all Paris revolutions, the Hôtel de Ville. On his way he captured the Prefecture of Police on the Ile de la Cité, always a special object of concern to the Blanquists. He did this by sending a small detachment ahead across the pont Neuf, which then edged its way in single line to the main entrance where they knocked on the door with a pistol-butt. To their surprise it was opened by the caretaker, hat in hand,

---

[1] A.H.G., Ly 20, G. Laronze, *Histoire de la Commune de 1871. La Justice*, Paris, 1928, p. 10; Maxime du Camp, *Les Convulsions de Paris*, Paris, 1878–9, vol. 4, p. 5.
[2] *Enquête*, II, p. 458 (Mortemart); Laronze, op. cit., pp. 12–15.

who told them the place was deserted and invited them to 'make themselves at home'.[1]

No one had resisted Thiers' evacuations order more strongly than Mayor Jules Ferry at the Hôtel de Ville. It had been turned into a veritable 'fortress', with barricades at each window manned by marines ready to fire on any attacker. There were rations and ammunition for at least two days. In addition there were troops and gendarmes in the adjoining Lobau and Napoleon barracks. Colonel Vabre was convinced it would have needed a full-scale army attack to reduce the defence.[2] There had been several demonstrations in the Place de Grève since late morning, but they had all peacefully withdrawn, having learnt the lesson of 22 January. The Blanquists had already suffered some losses when they tried to attack it from behind. An attempt to do a reverse of 31 October and surprise the building by means of the underground passageway linking it to the Napoleon barracks was repulsed by the gendarmes. Hence Ferry's utter surprise when, at 2.50 p.m., he heard that the order had come to evacuate the barracks. He replied at once that rather they should be reinforced, adding caustically that it seemed as if 'someone had taken leave of their senses'.[3] Ferry continued to stall for the rest of the afternoon, with the support of Picard at the Ministry of the Interior, until in the end the military Commander-in-Chief, General Derroja, had to send an officer to get a written order from Vinoy. At 9.55 p.m. Ferry sent off his last telegram announcing the completion of the evacuation of the Hôtel de Ville and its barracks. He then went off to the Mairie of the Louvre (1st arrondissement). But he had to escape from there to a friend's house when the crowd learnt of his presence and surrounded the building, demanding his death. After an uneasy night in Paris Ferry caught the first train for Versailles.

The Mayors and a number of the Paris Deputies had held a meeting around 6.0 p.m. in the Louvre Mairie under the chairmanship of Tirard, a supporter of Thiers and Mayor of the 2nd arrondissement as well as being a Deputy for Paris. They had not yet heard of the decision to abandon Paris and sent off a delegation to the Ministry of Foreign Affairs. The Mayors hoped that if the Government promised municipal elections and appointed popular republicans to the posts of Mayor of Paris, Prefect of Police and Commander-in-Chief of the

[1] Da Costa, op. cit., p. 120.
[2] *Enquête*, II, p. 537 (Vabre); cf. p. 70 (Ferry).
[3] *Enquête*, II, p. 68 (Telegram of Ferry).

National Guard then the movement would be checked. Their idea was a compromise along the lines of that agreed to, and then broken, with the revolutionaries in the Hôtel de Ville at that earlier occasion of 31 October. At first Favre refused to receive them because his personal enemy Millière was part of the delegation. The first question he asked was whether it was indeed true that Clément Thomas and Lecomte had been assassinated. On the assurance that this was so, he flew into a rage and striking a theatrical pose declared, 'Gentlemen, what have you come here for? . . . One cannot discuss, one cannot treat with assassins.' Instead of concessions, he promised force.[1] The Mayors retired to form a centre of resistance to the National Guard Central Committee at Tirard's Mairie near the Bourse, and sent off a message to Thiers assuring him of their support.

There was a last evening meeting of the Ministers still in Paris held 'clandestinely' in the private house of Picard's secretary. So fearful were some of those present that they wanted to disperse the coaches from before the house lest they attracted attention.[2] There were still those who contested the complete abandonment of Paris, but Vinoy and the other generals insisted they had to obey Thiers' orders. This rump of the Government was now sufficiently chastened to take up the proposals put forward earlier by the Paris Mayors and Deputies. D'Aurelle de Paladines was to be replaced by Langlois, with Thiers' acquiescence. The council then broke up to leave for Versailles early the next morning after a final uneasy night in revolutionary Paris. As a last act Picard delegated the 'provisional administration' of the city to the Mayors. But neither this nor the nomination of Langlois could be expected to carry much authority either in Paris or in Versailles.

Thiers afterwards justified his retreat from Paris by reference to historical precedents. He recalled the example of Windischgratz, who in 1848 had withdrawn from Vienna and then returned to crush the revolution. Thiers himself had advised Louis-Philippe to leave Paris at the outbreak of the February 1848 Revolution and return with Marshal Bugeaud and 50,000 men. On that occasion he had been overruled, the King fearing the counter-example of Napoleon, but

[1] Favre, op. cit., vol. 3, p. 226; L. Rossel, Mémoires, Procès et Correspondance, Paris, 1960, p. 219, said such events are 'almost inseparable from revolutions', and he was not prevented from joining the revolutionaries by the two murders.
[2] Enquête, II, pp. 435–6 (Le Flô).

this time Thiers was able to 'triumph over the objections of my colleagues'.[1] Chief among these were Jules Favre, Jules Simon and Picard, who on political grounds were all against the complete abandonment of the capital to the revolutionaries. At least, it was argued, a military foothold should be kept in the west of Paris at the Ecole Militaire, the Trocadero or the Bois de Boulogne. The Minister of War was adamant on military grounds that there should be a complete withdrawal in order to preserve what was left of his army.[2] But the decision was essentially political and indicated there could be no compromise: Paris was to be crushed. Since the bourgeoisie had not come out in their National Guard battalions in response to the Government's appeals[3] they were to be 'abandoned'. Thiers alone of the politicians was prepared to be so relentlessly and coldly logical. Once safely at Versailles, he regained his composure, confident that clear of Paris he would be able to build up a reliable army.

To many others it did not seem obvious that the National Assembly at Versailles and the Government could alone claim that they were right against the capital and its population, which had suffered so greatly during the siege and been provoked ever since. Several years afterwards Clemenceau pleaded in the National Assembly for an amnesty for the Communards, implying it was little short of criminal for a government to have fled before an insurrection that had not even attacked any of the public buildings.[4] Another who shared this view was Louis-Nathaniel Rossel, a colonel in the Engineers, who had shown his patriotism and independence by being one of those who had escaped from Metz, denouncing Bazaine as a traitor. The condemnation to death of Blanqui and Flourens had already roused his sense of injustice because Rossel considered they had acted solely out of patriotism. Thiers' announcement of

---

[1] *Enquête*, II, p. 12; cf. Thiers, *Souvenirs – 1848*, p. 54. Thiers had also suggested the idea of withdrawal during the June days of 1848 and had proposed moving the Assembly to Bourges. Cavaignac, the General in charge of Paris at the time, had said he would 'shoot M. Thiers if he continued to make such suggestions': quoted in R. Dreyfus, *Monsieur Thiers contre l'Empire, la Guerre et la Commune. 1869-1871*, Paris, 1928, p. 293.

[2] *Enquête*, II, pp. 80-1 (Le Flô); p. 511 (Admiral Pothau).

[3] Two posters had been posted up by the Government during the day calling on the National Guard to take up arms against 'an insurrectional committee': Lepelletier, op. cit., pp. 481, 484.

[4] 16 March 1876; Vautrain and Tirard spoke of Paris as having been 'abandoned': *Enquête*, II, pp. 375, 338.

the evacuation of Paris finally decided Rossel to join the side of the insurrection. After the Commune was over, awaiting his execution in prison, he thus described the withdrawal: 'As if the army had not already disgraced itself sufficiently in this war, 40,000 men had to quit Paris without a battle, without even putting up a fight for one day, in face of such a contemptible enemy as is always an insurrection, and after even having had the advantage of being on the offensive.'[1]

The retreat of the army to Versailles was chaotic. The troops were insubordinate to their officers and it was only the gendarmes who could keep some sort of order. So hasty was the withdrawal that several regiments were forgotten and left stranded in Paris. The 120th regiment in the Prince-Eugène barracks put up no resistance as the National Guard, led by Brunel, forced their way in. The officers were taken off as prisoners, whilst some 1,500 men left behind with no orders just sat out the period of the Commune. It was the same story at the Château d'Eau barracks at the present-day Place de la République.[2] A few days later the Central Committee allowed the regiment left behind in the Luxembourg to march to Versailles, where it was given a formal welcome by the National Assembly. Other regiments followed the example of Lecomte's troops and went over to the side of the National Guard.[3] What could well have been a very serious error was directly the fault of Thiers himself. He insisted on having General Daudel's brigade withdrawn to Versailles because it was considered reliable, but this had the result of leaving the forts surrounding Paris virtually unoccupied. It was not until the following night that Vinoy prevailed upon Thiers to re-occupy at least the most strategically important fort, Mont-Valérien, which was done early on Monday, 20 March.

In Paris the revolutionaries had been slow to exploit the occasion offered them by the flight of the Government. It had been the Blanquists who as so often on that fateful Saturday had finally taken the initiative when Brunel had led the hesitant Bellevillois into the deserted Hôtel de Ville. The National Guard Central Committee

---

[1] L. Rossel, op. cit., pp. 218–19.

[2] A.H.G., Ly 19 (Zeller, op. cit., p. 200); *Annales de l'Assemblée Nationale. Compte Rendu*, vol. 43, 1875, report of General Appert, p. 252; A.H.G., Ly 20, letter from Central Committee to War Ministry saying 700–800 men at Château d'Eau should be put to some useful work such as building barricades or digging trenches to earn their keep.    [3] E.g. 110th: Dubail, *Enquête*, II, p. 356.

in its headquarters in the Faubourg Saint-Antoine did not receive news of this until 11.0 that night. Varlin wrote to Arnold telling him of the situation, but nevertheless felt the need to conclude 'keep a good look-out; all is going well, but we must be ready in case of a counter-offensive'.[1] When at last the Central Committee arrived at the Hôtel de Ville there was of course great confusion; National Guards and soldiers were wandering everywhere, and no one had the authority to give a lead. Duval, who had shown himself more capable than any member of the Central Committee, was all for immediately marching on Versailles. So were Eudes, Brunel and the Montmartre committee. There was a very good chance that the army was too disorganized and demoralized to put up a firm resistance. But the Blanquists were not listened to. The members of the Central Committee had only been elected three days previously, and the work of organizing the federation had not yet been completed.[2] One of their first acts on arrival was therefore to appoint their own Commander-in-Chief for the National Guard. They chose an ex-naval officer, Charles Lullier, who had been imprisoned several times for disobedience and drunkenness. Lullier had been a member of the short-lived military commission formed by the Central Committee of the Twenty Arrondissements immediately after 4 September.[3] He had therefore some association with the revolutionaries. Accordingly, when he finally bestirred himself from his accustomed bar around 6.0 p.m. on 18 March to present himself to the Central Committee, this past association, his impressive appearance, his grandiloquence, dazzled the members there into commissioning him to attack the Hôtel de Ville. Brunel in fact did all the work, but Lullier reaped the rewards, and even Duval's achievements of that day were passed over.

Many members of the Central Committee felt that events had outstripped them. Jourde later stated, admittedly after he had been captured by Versailles, that the Committee had never thought it could get Paris in such a short time. That evening, according to Jourde, 'we did not know what to do; we did not want to take possession of the Hôtel de Ville, we wanted to build barricades. We were very embarrassed by our authority.'[4] It was left to the bohemian literary figure of Edouard Moreau, who used on occasion to claim

---

[1] *Enquête*, III, p. 41.
[2] *Enquête*, III, p. 39, report of Arnold, 15 March.
[3] Rougerie, *'Quelques documents'*, p. 8.  [4] *Enquête*, II, p. 471 (Ossude).

aristocratic descent, to give some sense of decision. He persuaded the Central Committee, amidst shouts of 'Long live the Commune', to remain in occupation of the Hôtel de Ville at least for a few days until municipal elections could be held.

Langlois then boldly arrived to establish his claim to be Commander of the National Guard. He was an old Internationalist and friend of Proudhon, who, during the siege, had been wounded at Buzenval. He had certainly been more active than Lullier on 18 March, but on the side of the Government, making himself busy taking messages for d'Aurelle de Paladines and Thiers.[1] He had already sent off a pompous declaration to the *Journal Officiel*. The Central Committee demanded to know who had appointed him and the exalted Langlois replied, 'M. Thiers.' He was asked if he recognized the authority of the Central Committee. He refused in the name of the National Assembly, nor would he submit his name for election. The Central Committee stood firm, and Langlois backed down and resigned, departing with a warning of the danger of civil war.

Apart from this defence of its own organization the Central Committee failed to take any active measures. One of Blanqui's first acts on 31 October had been to close the gates of Paris, whereas during the night of 18–19 March almost 20,000 demoralized troops were allowed to depart for Versailles. Lullier later boasted of this at his trial. As a further disservice to the revolutionary cause he failed to pursue the occupation of Mont-Valérien with sufficient vigour, and this opportunity, so vital for the defence of Paris, was lost. Instead of passing to the offensive the representatives of the National Guard were mainly concerned with disembarrassing themselves of the power that had so unexpectedly fallen into their hands. They hoped to legalize their position by entering into negotiations with the Mayors for the election of a Commune.

[1] *Enquête*, II, pp. 517–19.

Chapter 6

# PARIS UNDER THE CENTRAL COMMITTEE

———◆◆◆———

The next day Paris awoke to a beautiful Sunday morning, the Spring-time of its liberty. The streets were quiet, particularly in the bourgeois districts, and though there was more animation in the popular quarters this was largely a market crowd. The Bourse registered no marked change.[1] It was not as if a new government had seized power ready to institute a revolutionary programme. The general feeling seems to have been one of relief that the long-feared expected attack had failed, followed by a sense of confidence that now Paris would certainly achieve its municipal rights. The central government had for some time been little more than a formal authority unable to enforce its rule within the city. In its place the autonomy of the capital was expressed by several groupings. The Central Committee of the National Guard could fairly claim to be the victors of the day, though, as has been seen, they had not directed the movement. But this committee was barely complete and its members had had no chance to forge themselves into a united body. There were still the clubs, in the main represented by the Delegation of the Twenty Arrondissements, which had been the most active form of popular organization during the siege. There were also the various political republican organizations, which were sufficiently suspicious of Versailles to be disposed favourably towards the National Guard Central Committee. And then there were the Mayors. They alone could claim any legal authority, which had been conferred by Picard's letter delegating the government of the city to them. The coming week was to be largely centred around this issue of legality.

Jules Vallès was so surprised by the peaceful nature of Paris after the revolutionary excitement of the previous day that he thought for a while that this signified the population did not support the

[1] H. Lefebvre, *La Proclamation de la Commune*, Paris, 1965, p. 302.

uprising. At the Hôtel de Ville, however, he found some signs of activity, though most of the National Guards filling the building were half-asleep, fatigued after having been up since dawn of the day before if not drowsy as a result of wine. At 8.30 a.m. the Central Committee resumed its discussion of the previous night. Edouard Moreau took the chair and again argued that their task was to organize municipal elections. Duval and the Blanquists present took up their theme of the need for immediate action in the form of preventing any more troops leaving Paris and of the National Guard marching on Versailles. They rightly realized that the victory of 18 March needed completing, and that in forcing the Government and its army to withdraw they had gained an advantage, but one that should be followed up. 'Oh, if those devoted men [of the Central Committee] had had much less respect for legality,' sighed Louise Michel, 'the Commune could have been nominated in a truly revolutionary fashion on the road to Versailles.' Louise Michel herself consulted Ferré of the Montmartre committee and Rigault about going to Versailles to try to assassinate Thiers. But the two Blanquists considered that such an act, even if she could carry it out, would only further alienate the provinces, after the murders of Lecomte and Clément Thomas. Undaunted, Louise Michel dressed herself up to look respectable and successfully made the journey to Versailles and back without being recognized and caught.[1] Allemane, the revolutionary Guardsman of the 5th arrondissement, had a similar idea, and got himself a job inside the Château as a printer on the *Journal Officiel*. He lost no time in organizing his workmates into negotiating themselves a pay-increase. Then he returned to Paris to see Billioray of the Central Committee to persuade him to send 300 men to support his small nucleus of sailors and workmen in staging a *coup* at Versailles. Allemane's idea was that they would be reinforced by 20,000 National Guards marching out to Versailles on the night of the 26th. But Billioray never even raised such warlike schemes before the Central Committee. Unsupported and in danger of being arrested by the police, who had recognized him, Allemane had to return to Paris, denouncing on his arrival at the station two police spies he had come across on the train.[2]

The majority on the Central Committee would not let themselves be pushed beyond the defensive posture they had adopted. 'No,'

[1] Michel, op. cit., pp. 143, 161–2.
[2] Allemane, op. cit., pp. 28–44; Senisse, op. cit., p. 73.

insisted Moreau against those pressing for military action, 'we have only a mandate to secure the rights of Paris. If the provinces share our views, let them imitate our example.'[1] Varlin supported this inaction, considering that the revolution had occurred too soon, before the people were ready. The Central Committee interpreted the movement, of which it was the uneasy spokesman, as essentially one for the municipal rights of Paris. This was the theme of its 'Appeal to the Departments':

> The people of Paris, after having given since 4 September an undeniable and striking proof of their patriotism and devotion to the Republic; after having supported, with a courageous resignation beyond all praise, the suffering and struggles of a long and arduous siege, has again shown itself to be equal to the present circumstances and unavoidable efforts that the country rightly expects of them . . . The existing powers are essentially provisional, and will be replaced by an elected Communal Council . . . Let the provinces therefore hasten to imitate the example of the capital by organizing themselves in a republican fashion, and putting themselves as soon as possible in contact with the capital by means of delegates . . . We have only one hope, one end: the safety of the country and the final triumph of the democratic Republic, one and indivisible.[2]

A much more stirring interpretation of the 'Revolution of 18 March' couched in class terms was presented the next day by the Committee's delegates at the *Journal Officiel*:

> The proletarians of the capital, amidst the failures and treasons of the ruling classes, have understood that the hour has struck for them to save the situation by taking the direction of public affairs into their own hands . . . The working men, those who produce everything and enjoy nothing, those who suffer poverty in the midst of the accumulation of products that are the fruit of their labour and toil, will they always be exposed to outrage? . . . The bourgeoisie, their seniors, which accomplished its emancipation

---

[1] Lissagaray, op. cit., p. 90; in a letter of 25 March, Vuillaume, op. cit., VIII, p. 131, Edouard Moreau wrote that his aim had been to prevent bloodshed: 'When I was carried to the Hôtel de Ville, I tried, in the councils, to get this people that I love to carry out their great peaceful revolution with the majesty appropriate to a lion awakening after twenty years of sleep.'

[2] J.O., 20 March.

three-quarters of a century ago and preceded them in the way of revolution, does it not understand that today the time has come for the emancipation of the proletariat? The disasters and public calamities which its political incapability and moral and intellectual decrepitude have plunged France into should rather prove to it that its time is over, and it has accomplished the task imposed on it in '89, and that it should, if not give up its place to the workers, at least let them have their turn at social emancipation . . . Why then does the bourgeoisie persist, with a fatal blindness and unparalleled persistence, in refusing the proletariat its legitimate share of emancipation? . . . The proletariat, in face of the permanent threat to its rights, the complete negation of all its legitimate aspirations, the ruin of the country and all its hopes, has understood that its imperious duty and absolute right is to take its destinies into its own hands and assure its triumph by seizing upon power.[1]

The *Siècle* commented with distaste that the revolution had finally revealed its socialist colours.[2] The Commune itself in its official pronouncements never reached this level of political class consciousness.

Even the ardent republicanism of the Central Committee did not lead it into attacking the hated monarchist Assembly at Versailles. The ease with which the Government of Versailles had melted away gave rise to the illusion that the State was about to dissolve into a federation of city-Communes, leaving Paris its own master. The first announcement of the Central Committee spoke of 'the people of Paris having shaken off the yoke that others had tried to impose on them', and went on to declare the lifting of the state of siege (in order to rid the soldiers who had deserted of the threat of courts martial), and to call for the organizing of local elections. A second poster addressed to the Paris National Guard repeated the theme that they were holding on to the Hôtel de Ville solely until elections could take place, declaring that 'our mandate has expired'.[3] A few days later Varlin told a visitor from the Swiss International that 'the movement of 18 March had no other end than the assertion

[1] J.O., 21 March. Marx quoted part of this in his *The Civil War in France*, op. cit., p. 288. In a note to the English edition, Lissagaray wrote: 'I need not justify the long quotations I shall make. The French proletariat has never been allowed to speak in books of history; at least he should do so in the recital of his own revolution': p. 103.    [2] 22 March.    [3] J.O., 20 March.

of the municipal franchise of Paris and that once it had attained
this end . . . with the electing of the municipal Council, the Central
Committee would resign its powers and all would be over'.[1] On the
20th, in the first issue of the *Journal Officiel* published under the
auspices of the new government, the Central Committee delegates
began their address with the self-denying remark, 'If the National
Guard Central Committee is a government . . .', and closed by assuring the population that 'Obscure a few days ago, we will return to the
obscurity of your ranks.' Having had power fall into their lap they
wanted to divest themselves of it as quickly as was possible, a haste
for which Marx criticized them in a letter to his friend, Dr Kugelmann: 'The Central Committee surrendered its power too soon, to
make way for the Commune. Again from a too "honourable"
scrupulosity!'[2] For the Central Committee failed to realize that it had
put itself in a state of rebellion which the Government of Thiers
would be bound to challenge. By taking over the Hôtel de Ville, by
acts such as lifting the state of siege and calling for elections, they
were claiming, however implicitly, an alternative source of authority
to that of the Assembly at Versailles. The *Père Duchêne*, one of the
most popular of the revolutionary newspapers, taking its title from
the Hébertist paper of the first revolution, claimed on 24 March that
'Every revolution accomplished with the consent of the majority of
citizens is legitimate.' The moderately republican paper the *Rappel*,
in its editorial on the day of the Commune elections, accurately
characterized the situation as a contest between two claims to
legitimacy: 'On the one hand a legal situation; on the other, a legitimate aspiration'. Or as Élie Reclus, the brother of the geographer
Élisée, asked on voting day, 'What does legality mean at a time of
revolution?'[3]

The logic of the situation pointed to the Central Committee pressing home its advantage by attacking Versailles.[4] Had they done so

[1] J. Guillaume, *L'Internationale*, vol. 2. p. 133: quoted Rihs, op. cit., p. 35.

[2] Letter of 12 April 1871.

[3] E. Reclus, *La Commune au jour le jour*, Paris, 1908, p. 39. G. Lukacs, *History and Class Consciousness*, has a chapter discussing the proletariat's sense of legality and illegality with regard to a given (bourgeois) political order. Lukacs emphasizes that the working class finds it difficult, at first, to rid itself of the notion that a revolution is 'illegal' by some absolute standard. The converse of this is that a new regime takes time to get used to seeing itself as the 'legal' government. The rule of the Central Committee illustrates Lukacs' argument.

[4] Cf. Vinoy, op. cit., p. 249: the Central Committee made 'a big and

there is every indication that they would have been victorious. The police reports for the first few days in Versailles are full of concern over the state of the morale of the troops. On the 20th, for example, it was reported that the artillery encamped in front of the Château and the men of the 48th regiment 'would join the cause of the rebellion'; similarly on 24 March with regard to the 109th and 110th regiments, who, it was said, 'had several times declared that if the National Guard came they would raise their rifle butts in the air'. On 23 March a soldier of the 113th regiment was arrested for having said that 'we won't fire on the public'.[1] Mayor Vautrain visited Versailles at this time and was greatly worried to find that the police and the army officers acknowledged that the troops could not be trusted to fire on the National Guard.[2] Thiers was equally disturbed over the morale of the army and was half-ready to withdraw to a more distant city as a meeting place for the National Assembly.[3] Had Versailles been taken this would have been a serious blow to his authority and greatly strengthened the Communal movement in the provincial cities, where the news from Paris led to numerous disturbances and the proclamation of short-lived Communes in Lyon, Saint-Étienne, Marseille, Toulouse, Narbonne and Le Creusot. Thiers was greatly relieved that these remained isolated from each other, being quickly extinguished, for he had barely enough troops to retake Paris, let alone to take on the other major cities as well.[4]

There was one strategic argument against an attack on Versailles; the fear of Prussian intervention. This Arthur Arnould afterwards called Thiers' trump card, on the grounds that the Prussians would have been bound to have supported Versailles in order to guarantee the repayment of the war indemnity.[5] In an attempt to counter this threat the first issue of the Committee's *Journal Officiel* carried an assurance by Grêlier, the Delegate at the Ministry of the Interior, that the Central Committee had 'firmly decided to ensure that the

---

irreparable mistake in not pursuing its advantage and immediately marching on Versailles'.

[1] Archives de la Préfecture de Police: Choury, op. cit., pp. 190–3.
[2] *Enquête*, II, p. 374; cf. police report that 'there are a number of troops at Versailles who have the fixed intention of refusing to fire if ordered to do so on the Paris National Guard, should the latter decide to come and attack Versailles': Archives Seine et Oise, quoted Zeller, op. cit., p. 258.
[3] A.H.G., Zeller, op. cit., p. 226.      [4] Thiers, *Souvenirs – 1871*, p. 156.
[5] Arnould, op. cit., vol. 2, pp. 46–7.

preliminaries [of the Peace Treaty] were respected, in order to safe-guard at one and the same time the safety of France and the general peace'. This assurance was repeated the next day, with the added suggestion that 'the authors of the war' should be forced to pay the indemnity. Later the Commune even expressed its willingness to pay off the indemnity itself in order to assure Prussian neutrality between Paris and Versailles, considering that the money could be raised from the Bank of France or by the sale of Church property.[1] In spite of all the popular fervour for the war during the siege, once the war was over neither the Central Committee nor the Commune nor the popular press ever suggested that Paris should restart the war against Prussia. There were a few individual exceptions. Delescluze's siding with the Commune may well have been influenced by Jacobin patriotic hostility to the Prussians. And republican mili-tary patriots such as Rossel saw in the Commune a way to get at the Prussians again once 'those who had capitulated, the shamefaced à outrance for peace',[2] had been overthrown. On the evening of 18 March a sergeant standing on a cannon outside the Saint Lazare prison had shouted out to cheers from bystanders, 'now we can start firing these against the Prussians'.[3]

Goncourt claimed to be 'disgusted' by what he called the Com-munards' attitude of 'debonair resignation' to the peace treaty, 'their friendliness almost for the Prussians'.[4] This latter remark was provoked probably by the *Journal Officiel* eagerly publishing a letter received from one of the Prussian general staff officers informing the Central Committee that the German army had been ordered 'to maintain a friendly and passive attitude' so long as the internal events in Paris did not affect the terms of the peace preliminaries.[5] Paschal Grousset replied for the Central Committee assuring the Prussian High Command that the Paris revolution was 'essentially a municipal one' and in no way directed against the German occupying armies.[6] In fact the expression 'friendly' was an optimistic mistrans-lation of the German for 'pacific', as Jules Favre, the Foreign Affairs

---

[1] *Le Mot d'Ordre*, 1 April; *Le Père Duchêne*, No. 37, 2 floréal (1 May); C. Beslay, *Mes Souvenirs*, Paris, 1874, pp. 361, 372; A.H.G., Ly 20 (19, 20 March).

[2] Rossel, op. cit., p. 258.

[3] L. Deffoux, *Pipe-en-bois*, Paris, 1932, p. 16.

[4] 1 April.

[5] 23 March; Lepelletier, op. cit., vol. 2, p. 201.

[6] J.O., 23 March.

Minister, had to assure a disturbed National Assembly.[1] To counter this false impression of Prussian benevolence Favre persuaded Mayor Tirard to spread the news of another telegram which this time Versailles had received, threatening to use force against Paris if it infringed the peace treaty in the slightest way. In this case Favre was probably over-exaggerating for effect. But he was right in implying that the Prussians were only too ready to intervene. Thiers received a very tactfully expressed offer of military help from Bismarck, which of course he wanted to try to avoid. Subsequently Bismarck several times expressed his discontent with the slow progress of the army of Versailles in reducing Paris, and the German Government did not share Thiers' confidence in his own military ability.[2] Had the Versailles troops suffered defeat there is little doubt that the German troops would have energetically intervened to guarantee order in France and the payment of the indemnity, and to prevent the spread of republican ideas in Europe. As it was, Thiers managed things in his own methodical way, and German aid was limited to being accommodating over the build-up of the new French army and to cutting off the retreat of the defeated Communards when the troops of Versailles finally entered Paris.

It was probably not the result of calculations of the likelihood of Prussian intervention or of the possibility of being able to take Versailles that decided the Central Committee's attitude immediately

[1] Favre, op. cit., vol. 3, pp. 293–4; cf. *The Times*, 28 March, reporting *Norddeutsche Allgemeine Zeitung* of 27 March, giving an official denial of the word 'friendly' and saying it should be 'passive'.

[2] Cf. Thiers, *Enquête*, II, pp. 15–16 and *Souvenirs*, pp. 157–60; G. Bourgin, 'Une Entente Franco-Allemande', *International Review of Social History*, 1956, pp. 41–53, giving telegrams between French Foreign Ministry and Thiers: e.g., 20 May, 'The German Chancellor offers to help us so as to finish it off as quickly as possible'; Tsar Alexander II told the French Ambassador in May that the Russian Government had pressed the German Government not to hinder the French in repressing the revolt, because the existing French Government was 'a safeguard for both France and all of Europe'. L. Fiaux, *Histoire de la guerre civile de 1871*, Paris, 1879, pp. 197–8, argues that the German Government was too aware of the 1848 revolutions in Europe to ever have allowed the Commune to succeed. Lord Lyons, the British Ambassador, *Lord Lyons. A Record of British Diplomacy*, London, 1913, p. 380, wrote to the Foreign Office on 30 March that Bismarck was threatening to intervene unless Thiers hurried up. On 22 April Bismarck wrote to General Fabrice in charge of the Prussian occupation in France that 'M. Thiers' faith in his own military talents causes us concern' (Dreyfus, op. cit., pp. 329–30).

following 18 March, but rather a naïve hope that civil war could be avoided, a sense of incredulity that Versailles would actually attack and bombard Paris. It was a refusal to take responsibility, a conviction that only an elected body had the right to decide what the revolution should do, partly because of uncertainty as to what the revolution was. This misplaced legalism let slip the only opportunity for widening the movement and gave Thiers all the time he needed to isolate and then attack Paris, certain that the capital would receive no relief from outside. Leaving the initiative to Versailles meant that when civil war did break out it was fought in the worst possible situation from the point of view of the Commune, making it truly a second siege of Paris.

One more immediate issue had to be confronted – the deaths of Lecomte and Clément Thomas. The *Journal Officiel*, which the Central Committee had been slow to take over, had had time to accuse the Committee of having 'assassinated in cold blood' the two generals. Babick wanted to issue a declaration dissociating themselves from the two murders and another member argued that 'the people and the bourgeoisie have joined hands in this revolution. This union must be maintained. You want everybody to take part in the elections.' To this came the retort: 'abandon the people in order to keep the bourgeoisie, then the people will leave you and you will see if revolutions are made with the bourgeoisie'. It was in line with this latter warning that Moreau drew up a statement for the by now occupied *Journal Officiel* concerning these 'regrettable facts', which though dissociating the Central Committee of any responsibility did imply that both generals deserved their fate, Lecomte for having called on his troops to charge the 'inoffensive crowd of women and children', Clément Thomas for 'spying' on the defences of Montmartre.[1] It was a compromise position and Versailles continued its calumny of the Central Committee as assassins.

Elections were fixed for the coming Wednesday. Though this avoided a military confrontation with Versailles it did mean that a decision had to be reached regarding the Mayors in Paris, who alone could legitimize in a constitutional sense any action that the Committee took. As Edouard Moreau said, 'we must come to an agreement with them to make the situation regular'. Others wanted to cut all discussion short by sending a battalion of National Guards to the Mairie of the 3rd arrondissement where the Mayors were meeting

[1] J.O., 20 March.

in order to arrest them. Instead it was decided that Arnold should go as a delegate from the Central Committee to see the assembled Mayors, more prudent spirits having again overridden the impetuosity of the revolutionaries, one of whom angrily damned the moderate majority as not being equal to their position: 'your only preoccupation is to disengage yourselves'. Babick and Arnold argued that to arrest the Mayors would have a bad effect on the rest of France and on the bourgeoisie in Paris, whereas to gain the adherence of the Mayors would make it likely that the majority of the population would support the elections. The assembled Mayors and Paris Deputies gave Arnold a poor reception, but they did agree to send a delegation to the Hôtel de Ville, composed of their most radical members.

Not without trepidation this turned up at the stronghold of the revolution around 8.0 p.m. that first evening. Clemenceau spoke first, vigorously attacking the Central Committee, saying it did not properly represent Paris, and denying the right of Paris in any case to set itself up against the National Assembly. He called on the Central Committee to submit itself to the authority of the Mayors and the Deputies. Protests arose from all sides. The National Assembly, one of the Committee members replied, could no longer claim to represent the people because its electoral mandate had expired with the passing of the peace treaty, the only reason, according to this argument, for which it had been elected. The Deputy Millière, certainly no friend of Thiers or Favre, warned the Central Committee that if they continued to defy the Government this would simply produce a repeat of the repression that had followed June 1848: 'The hour of the social revolution has not yet struck. Progress is obtained by slower marches . . . Make as much of your insurrection as you can, but don't hesitate to content yourselves with little.'[1] Millière's reference to 'the social revolution' brought out the divergence of views among his hearers, some replying that this was not the issue, which was rather simply the question of municipal elections. The Internationalist Varlin, on the other hand, went further, saying, 'we want not only the election of the municipal council, but real municipal liberties, the suppression of the Prefecture of Police, the right of the National Guard to choose its own head and to reorganize itself, the proclamation of the Republic as the legal Government, the pure and simple remittance of the rents due, an

[1] Lissagaray, op. cit., pp. 93–7.

equitable law on the overdue bills, and the army removed from the Paris region'. As it was late and the rest of the Mayors and Deputies might be beginning to think that their delegation had been arrested it was decided to continue the discussion this time at Tirard's Mairie in the 2nd arrondissement. Varlin, Edouard Moreau, Jourde and Arnold returned with the Mayors.

The Mayors and Deputies were no more a solid block than the Central Committee, and differed amongst themselves as to how far they were willing to go in holding out for Versailles against Paris. Tirard, Vautrain, Vacherot and François Favre, Mayors of the 2nd, 4th, 5th and 17th arrondissements respectively, were the most outspoken on the side of Versailles. But there were others who genuinely hoped for a reconciliation[1] between the Central Committee and the national government. The Deputy Benoît Malon actually later sat on the Commune, whilst others, including Clemenceau, Bonvalet, Millière and Mottu, whose anti-clericalist actions in the 11th arrondissement had so worried Trochu during the siege, remained in Paris working within the republican leagues for a negotiated end to the civil war. This sympathy eventually worked to the advantage of the Central Committee, though not until after a significant delay. The four National Guard delegates, a little overawed, according to some accounts,[2] at finding themselves isolated before this body of elected officialdom, simply requested the Mayors to agree to the holding of elections. Mayor Tirard, the Deputies Schoelcher and Louis Blanc, just arrived back from London, at first refused even to contemplate entering into any sort of agreement with such an irregular body. Jourde, moved to anger for once, warned the Mayors that they were 'face to face with force; beware of letting loose a civil war by your resistance'. In the end Varlin was left alone, the other delegates having given up in despair, and he agreed that if the Mayors would commit themselves by a public announcement to trying to persuade the National Assembly to grant Paris both municipal and National Guard elections within the immediate future then the Central Committee would hand over the Hôtel de Ville to them.

On Monday morning Mayor Bonvalet, of the 3rd arrondissement, and his two adjoints turned up to take possession of the Hôtel de Ville, but the Central Committees refused to consider the delegation

---

[1] Cf. Mayor Dubail, *Enquête*, II, p. 357, who spoke of the 'trying leniency' of some of his ex-colleagues.

[2] *Enquête*, II, p. 338 (Tirard); p. 524 (Ducuing).

of the previous day as having any such responsibility. In taking a firm stand the National Guard Committee had the support of the Delegation of the Twenty Arrondissements, which had met earlier that morning and strongly criticized the proposed agreement with the Mayors.[1] They called on the National Guard Central Committee to maintain its hold over both the civil administration and the National Guard until elections were held in Paris. Mayor Bonvalet, declaring he had not come to debate the issue, withdrew, the other Mayors not even having bothered to turn up, so little credit did they give the 'agreement' of the night before.[2] The Central Committee therefore again announced that Communal elections would be held in Paris on Wednesday, 22 March, calling on the electors to support them by voting for 'well-known socialist republicans' to save the capital, the Republic and France.

The Central Committee now found, even in its self-acknowledged interim role, that it had to take certain measures that in effect turned it into an alternative government. Delegates were appointed to the principal ministries, most of the administrative officials having followed the Government's order to report to Versailles. Duval had established himself at the Ex-Prefecture of Police, as it was renamed, where he was joined by Rigault, whose earlier counter-police activities during the last years of the Second Empire were now to be given official scope despite the talk of abolishing that institution. Cattelain, the newly appointed head of the Sûreté, the Criminal Investigation Department, remarked on this inconsistency when he noted that 'men once in power and whilst criticizing everything that existed before them end up by finding useful what they so desperately sought to demolish. They content themselves with replacing the name of an adversary by that of a friend, so as to continue administering in the same ways and often with the same abuses. Thus it was with the Commune, which after having attacked and taken the Prefecture immediately re-established it under the name of Ex-Prefecture.'[3] On the Sunday the long-standing republican socialist,

---

[1] Lissagaray, op. cit., p. 102; Da Costa, op. cit., vol. 1, pp. 185–6.

[2] Dubail was one such: Enquête, II, p. 356.

[3] P. Cattelain, Mémoires, Paris, 1910, p. 68; Catulle Mendès, Les 73 journées de la Commune, Paris, 1871, p. 94, asked 'Why ex-Prefecture? It seems to me that it still functions as if it were simply a Prefecture.' Da Costa, op. cit., vol. 2, p. 218, who became Rigault's assistant, said afterwards that Rigault acted as if he considered that since the Second Empire had perfected the police system over the previous twenty years 'the Commune had simply to follow its example'.

self-styled Proudhonian and 'medical student', though he was in his fifties, Paget-Lucipin, had walked into the empty Ministry of Education in the 7th arrondissement and installed himself in the minister's office: 'I took over the Ministry, which nobody else was bothering about.' The offices of the *Journal Officiel* – as its name implies, the official Government newspaper – were occupied late on 19 March, and henceforth published the decrees and views of the Central Committee and then of the Commune. Its editor for much of the time was Charles Longuet, a disciple of Proudhon, which did not prevent him being the translator into French of his father-in-law Marx's pamphlet, *The Civil War in France*. The Mairies were taken over by the local National Guard committees, which had been edging towards this since the beginning of the siege. The National Guard legion council of the 17th arrondissement had taken over the Mairie on the evening of 18 March. Jules Allix, who had founded a Women's Committee during the siege, forced out the Mayor in the 8th arrondissement. Clemenceau published a protest against his expulsion, as did most of the other Mayors in turn.

The most pressing need was for money. On 20 March it was announced that the *octroi* tax would be collected as normal, which brought in 500,000 francs the next day. There was ten times this amount at the Ministry of Finance and in the municipal coffers. But the keys had been taken off to Versailles, and rather than force the locks, which would have smacked too much of plunder, a delegation went to see Baron Rothschild, who agreed to open a credit account for them at the Bank of France. Eudes had already begun to take steps to assure some money for the National Guard, which had not been paid for the last three days. Jourde, Billioray and Varlin, the Committee's delegates at the Ministry of Finances, managed to delay any resort to force by going to see Rouland, the Governor of the Bank, on the Monday. Rouland received them with effusive protestations of friendliness, praising the 'wisdom' and 'tact' they had so far shown: 'Gentlemen, I expected your visit, we have provided money for so many governments, why not for yours.' The delegates returned through the empty evening streets in an ordinary coach, with a million francs in notes and coins.[1] By 10.0 that night the National Guard had received its pay, much to the chagrin of the hawks among the Mayors, who saw this as a Bonapartist plot

[1] See account of Eudes in J. Maitron, '*A Partir des papiers du General Eudes*', *L'Actualité de l'histoire*, October 1953, pp. 15–17; Lissagaray, op. cit., p. 106.

(Rouland having been Governor during the Second Empire) to subvert their own scheme of winning over the National Guard by distributing pay from the Bourse in the 2nd arrondissement.[1] But as de Ploeuc, the Deputy Governor, said afterwards, the Bank 'had to do all it could to avoid a collision'. On 22 March a meeting of the Bank's Council agreed that they could not pay too dearly to avoid the calamities that could be expected from an occupation by the revolutionaries. With at most only 500 employees in its own National Guard company the Bank could hardly have resisted the Central Committee had there been a conflict, especially after the end of the first week when no support could be expected from those Guards who up to then had supported the Mayor's resistance.[2] Eudes' suggestion of the Central Committee taking over responsibility for 'guarding' the Bank was not pressed in view of the seeming affableness of its Governor. Throughout the period of the Commune the Bank remained untouched, a symbol of capitalist financial respectability in the midst of Paris in revolution.

At Versailles the Assembly held its opening session on Monday, 20 March. The town, which for so long had been outside the mainstream of French political life, with grass growing in its streets bordered by houses long deserted by their former aristocratic owners, now found its German masters replaced by a sudden influx of politicians, civil servants, generals and men of letters, including Théophile Gautier and Alexander Dumas, as part of the flight of many of the bourgeoisie (although not Edmond de Goncourt) from the capital. Its population jumped from a tranquil 40,000 to a turbulent 250,000, filling up the hotels and apartments, and some Deputies had to content themselves with sleeping in stables. Prices soared with the population, and often the simplest of necessities were almost unobtainable: a bar of soap, a comb, a toothbrush. Each day the main streets were filled by a well-dressed crowd with little to do but ask news of Paris and spread rumours. The Château was in a sad state of repair, which the German occupation had made worse, but the Theatre had been converted to receive the National Assembly. Thiers cut off all communication between Paris and the rest of France, no mail being allowed through, and the

[1] *Enquête*, II, p. 358 (Dubail); p. 339 (Tirard).
[2] De Ploeuc, *Enquête*, II, pp. 487–90; Beslay, op. cit., p. 400.

trains were searched for suspects when they arrived at Versailles, just as the National Guard checked them on leaving Paris. The Government published its own *Journal Officiel* from Versailles, the tone of which was meant to reassure the provinces and arouse feeling against the 'factionists' and 'assassins' in the capital: 'The day of justice is near. To make it exemplary depends on the resoluteness of all good citizens.'[1]

The first session of the Assembly opened with an address by its staunch but conservative republican president, Jules Grévy, condemning the events in Paris as compromising the Republic. The last remark raised protests from the monarchist right, after which Clemenceau and Tirard proposed as a matter of urgency a law granting municipal elections in Paris. The other Paris Deputies proposed similarly urgent laws on the election of the head of the National Guard and for a three-month extension of overdue bills. But neither the Government nor the right-wing majority showed much sympathy for these measures meant to conciliate Paris, refusing even to add '*Vive la République*' alongside '*Vive la France*' at the foot of proclamations. Thiers expressed little hope that any concessions would satisfy Paris, which needed rather 'a firm attitude'. Jules Favre went much further in a violent impassioned diatribe against the capital, calling for 'energetic acts' to quell the revolt before the foreigner claimed the right to do so. He tried to frighten the Assembly by picturing the Central Committee as being on the verge of marching on Versailles to put the members of the Assembly to the same ferocious fate as that of Lecomte and Clément Thomas. Thiers felt the need to cover up such bellicosity with an assurance that France 'does not intend to declare war on Paris, nor do we intend to march on Paris'. It was a day of alternatively blowing hot and cold that resolved nothing. The following days were no different, the Government refusing to give any signs of its sincerity in renouncing the use of force by pressing ahead to remove the main source of discontent. Only reluctantly on 24 March did it grant a delay of one month on the maturity of bills, a measure the Central Committee had taken three days previously along with a suspension of the sale of objects pledged in the Mont de Piété, the State pawnshop, and a decree forbidding any evictions due to arrears of rent. When a shopkeeper was asked why he did not take up arms against the Central Committee he replied, 'Because they [Versailles] have

[1] J.O. of Versailles, 20 March; Lepelletier, op. cit., pp. 137–51.

made a bad law on bills of exchange.'[1] Similarly strong feeling existed over arrears of rent. A *calligraphe* (penman) told the English Methodist minister in Paris, the Rev. William Gibson, that 'after 18 March, when the insurrection broke out, I belonged to the *parti d'ordre*, and joined those who rallied around the standard of order at the Bourse. One day, on entering my apartment [on the Boulevard Poissonière], I received from the *concièrge* a paper. On opening it I found it was a *congé* [notice to quit] from my landlord [who had stayed out of Paris during the whole of the siege]. I threw my sword to the other side of the room, and there it is still.' Gibson adds that other 'respectable people have said: "Why should I trouble myself? Let the landlords come and fight their own battle." '[2]

While the Government prevaricated, seeking time to build up the army, the rural majority in the Assembly inflamed feeling between the capital and itself. The most notable occasion was on 23 March when it was announced that a delegation of Mayors had come from Paris to petition the Assembly. To the Right this raised the spectre of 1793 – Paris pressuring the Convention. When the Mayors appeared in the public galleries, wearing their tricolor sashes of office, the cry of 'Long live the Republic' was vigorously raised by the left-wing Deputies and the Mayors. At this pandemonium broke out on the Right, and the session had to be suspended. In a somewhat chastened atmosphere the session was resumed that evening and the question of municipal and National Guard elections was declared to be a matter of urgency. The Mayors presented this to Paris as a victory, but the Government had refused to grant Mayor Vacherot's proposal of immediate elections in Paris, and these were subsumed in Picard's general proposals on local government for the whole country. According to this project Paris would elect four representatives from each arrondissement, irrespective of population size, which was markedly higher in the popular districts than in the more spacious bourgeois areas, to form a municipal council. This would have the right to choose its own chairman, but the Mayors of the arrondissements and their adjoints would continue to be appointed by the Government. Paris, as Thiers put it, was to remain a special case along with the other large cities. This law was not finally voted upon until 14 April, and the elections were set for the

[1] *The Times*, 23 March, from a French correspondent.
[2] Rev. W. Gibson, *Paris during the Commune, 1871*, London, 1872, pp. 114–15, 19 April.

30th.[1] The Paris Deputies felt they had to issue a consoling statement to make the best of what they admitted was a disappointing
session. *The Times* leader of 23 March, from the vantage point of the
other side of the Channel and the comparative calm of English
political life, asked 'What promise of pacification can be found in
words like these? . . . Belleville must be moved to scorn by pledges
like these.'

At Mayor Tirard's request, Thiers had appointed Admiral Saisset
in place of d'Aurelle de Paladines as Commander-in-Chief of the
National Guard. Saisset had been popular during the siege because
he had commanded the navy guarding the forts. But he was no more
adventurous than any of the other French commanders of this time,
and his appointment was simply a stop-gap measure to gain the
Government time. Nor had he any sympathy for the Parisian National Guard and its revolution, which he regarded as passing its time in
drunken feasts at the Hôtel de Ville, and he had applauded Favre's
tirade in the National Assembly. Thiers gave him no orders, simply
telling him to support the Mayors. These latter took themselves
seriously and with several of the Paris Deputies led by Schoelcher
had organized their resistance around the Mairie of the 2nd arrondissement, suitably situated between the Bank of France and the
Bourse. They had collected additional machine guns into the adjoining Mairie of the Louvre, 1st arrondissement, and claimed to be
supported by 20,000 or more National Guards drawn mainly from
the western districts. A few of these had been strung out along the
newly named rue du 4 Septembre to Saisset's headquarters at the
Grand Hôtel by the Opera, and others guarded the Gare Saint
Lazare to keep open this link with Versailles. But Saisset himself
had no faith in the possibility of resisting the Central Committee
from within Paris. Most of the National Guard officers from the
bourgeois districts, such as Ibos who had saved the Government
on 31 October, had resigned to attend to their own affairs and out of
disgust with the way the National Assembly had behaved towards
Paris. The students of the Ecole Polytechnique had rallied to the side
of the Mayors, and had asked for their courses to be suspended

---

[1] This law determined how Paris was to be governed for the duration of the
Third Republic; Paris remains to this day the only city in France without an
elected Mayor: see E. Raiga and M. Félix, *Le Régime administratif et financier du
département de la Seine et de la ville de Paris*, Paris, 1922, pp. 155–7, 452–5; P.
Bernheim, *Le Conseil municipal de Paris de 1789 à nos jours*, Paris, 1937, p. 136.

as they did not wish 'to compromise with the revolt'. In 1830 the students had fought in 'the three glorious days'; this time they went off to join Saisset, but they only brought up the number directly under him to 11,500, most of whom seemed to the testy admiral little inclined to fight. The rest of the bourgeois battalions refused to leave their safe districts of Passy and Auteuil. 'It was insane to think that anything could be done with such a crew,' was how Saisset summed up the situation.[1]

Others were more confident. Most of the faculties of the University had been closed from the beginning of the siege, but the Faculty of Medicine held a meeting on 24 March, largely attended by professors rather than students, who affirmed their support for the Republic while vowing to aid the Mayors and Deputies 'by all possible means' against the Central Committee. A few days earlier thirty-three of the leading papers had published a collective declaration calling on the electors to consider as null and void the convocation of the Hôtel de Ville for 22 March. 'Illegality!' exclaimed Lissagaray, 'Thus the question was put by the Legitimists, twice imposed on us by foreign bayonets; by the Orleanists, raised to power through barricades; by the brigands of December; by the exiles returned home, thanks to an insurrection. What! When the upper classes, who make all the laws, always act illegally, how are the workmen to proceed, against whom all the laws are made?'[2] The continuous stream of proclamations from the Central Committee in place of any decisive action encouraged its opponents to think that it only needed a show of strength to frighten it back into obscurity. A tailor on the fashionable boulevard des Capucines named Bonne, a National Guard captain, whose clientele had come from the best clubs under the Empire, called for a demonstration by the 'good citizens . . . who want order, tranquillity and respect for the law'. On 21 March several hundred such 'Friends of Order' assembled behind their tricolor banner at the Place de l'Opéra, 'respectable well-dressed citizens . . . some of the best blood in Paris and probably some of its wealthiest citizens',[3] and then marched along the main boulevards, adding to their numbers as they went along. The demonstration culminated at the Bourse, from whence they moved to the

[1] *Enquête*, II, pp. 303–5 (Saisset); pp. 322, 327 (Schoelcher); p. 358 (Dubail); p. 375 (Vautrain); p. 340 (Tirard); Damé, op. cit., p. 315.
[2] Lissagaray, op. cit., p. 110.
[3] *The Times*, 23 March.

Place Vendôme, where the National Guard command had its head-quarters. Bergeret, the commander of the square, was howled down when he tried to speak by shouts of 'Down with the Committee; long live the Assembly'. He had to have the square cleared, peaceably this first time.

The next day a similar demonstration assembled, intending to contest the Central Committee's control of Paris by marching to the Hôtel de Ville itself. This set off, a tall West Indian carrying one of its flags,[1] determined to call the bluff of this working-men's upstart committee, confident 'that the mere exhibition of their "respectability" would have the same effect upon the Revolution of Paris as Joshua's trumpets upon the wall of Jericho'.[2] So sure were the demonstrators of themselves that they came unarmed, except for a few personal revolvers and sword-sticks. When the more militaristic Comte d'Hérisson tried to reason that this was stupid, he was told by one portly merchant, 'Sir, they will never dare fire on us!'[3] Saisset did not welcome this initiative of the 'Friends of Order', though it claimed to be acting in his name and he followed the procession from a safe distance. The first National Guards encountered were quickly forced to withdraw or be manhandled. But at the entrance to the Place Vendôme in the rue de la Paix they were confronted by three lines of Guardsmen. It was the heights of Montmartre in reverse. The demonstrators were pressing up against the National Guards; the drums were rolled as the law required in order to warn the crowd to disperse. Some accounts say a pistol shot was fired from the ranks of the 'Friends of Order', others that the National Guard first fired into the air.[4] Then, in contrast to the troops on 18 March, the Guards fired into the crowd, which at once fled, leaving some twelve or fourteen dead and up to a dozen wounded on the ground. One demonstrator saved himself by remembering the republican Arthur Ranc's remark that if fired upon

[1] Schoelcher, Saisset's deputy, during the 1848 Republic had been prominent in abolishing slavery in the French West Indian colonies: Lepelletier, op. cit., pp. 252, 260; cf. Catulle Mendès, op. cit., p. 29.

[2] Marx, *The Civil War in France*, MESW, p. 286. *The Times*, 24 March, speaks of the demonstrators' 'strange confidence in the power of purely moral influence'.

[3] Comte M. d'Hérisson, *Nouveau Journal d'un officier d'ordonnance: La Commune*, Paris, 1889, p. 99.

[4] *The Times*, 25 March, correspondent says 'a good deal of firing had evidently been in the air' because of the broken windows.

the safest line of escape was down the centre of the street away from the walls at the side.[1] One National Guardsman was killed, and several more wounded, possibly by their own men unused to quick-firing rifles and unnerved by the confined situation they were in. Amongst the casualties were a newspaper director, an editor, a regent of the Bank of France, a few army officers, an insurance agent and a café proprietor. A waiter in one of the 'best known restaurants in Paris' told *The Times* correspondent that evening that doors and windows had to be kept barred and shuttered because the men of Montmartre were quite capable of entering and butchering everyone there.[2] At Versailles the news of the 'massacre in the rue de la Paix' caused a frisson of horror, though the provinces were informed that as a result the 'party of order' had taken up its arms and occupied the main districts of the capital.

In view of the Mayor's refusal to cooperate and with demonstrations in the streets the Central Committee had to announce that because 'the reaction . . . has declared war on us' the elections were postponed until Sunday, 26 March, by which time they expected to have 'broken the resistance'.[3] Lullier was arrested, charged amongst other faults with having failed to ensure the occupation of fort Mont-Valérien. He was replaced by Brunel, Eudes and Duval, who announced 'the time for parliamentarism is past; action is required'.[4] The National Guard battalion at the Ecole Polytechnique came to an agreement with the Guards of the nearby Mairie at the Panthéon. Only the 1st and 2nd arrondissements in the centre were in the hands of the resistance, though the National Guard in the 16th arrondissement remained on the whole faithful to Thiers right until the end of March.[5] The Central Committee published a warning that 'every individual taken in the act of stealing will be shot', though crime had dropped ever since the Central Committee had taken over.[6] Another visit was paid to the Bank to collect a further 350,000 francs out of the second million that had been credited to the Central Committee. Then the International and the Delegation of the Twenty Arrondissements both came out firmly in support of the Central Committee and its elections, abandoning their earlier hesitations.

[1] Gaston Jollivet, in D'Hérisson, op. cit., p. 102.
[2] *The Times*, 25 March.        [3] J.O., 22 March.        [4] J.O., 24 March.
[5] *Enquête*, II, pp. 463-4 (Colonel Lavigne).
[6] *Enquête*, II, p. 206 (M. Claude, police chief of detective department, the Sûreté).

At a meeting on 22 March of the International, several members had expressed their distrust of the National Guard, proposing that the National Guard Central Committee should be persuaded to hand over its powers to the Mayors. But on 23 March at a joint meeting with the Trade Union Federation Frankel argued that the issue was 'no longer political, but social', a view supported by the majority of those present who agreed in the words of one member that it was time the International took up a 'militant responsibility' for what was happening. Frankel and two other future Communards, Theisz and Demay, drew up the International's manifesto calling on the workers to vote for the Commune. This listed a number of demands that it was hoped the winning of municipal liberties would make possible: 'the organization of Credit, of Exchange, and of Association in order to enable the worker to receive the whole value of his labour; free, non-religious and integral education; complete freedom of association, of the press and of the citizen; the municipal organization of the police, the army and other public services'. It went on to say, 'We have been duped by those who govern us, we have let ourselves be taken in by their game . . . Today, the people of Paris is clear-sighted and refuses the role of a child guided by a tutor.'[1]

Another working-class voice making itself heard at this time was the stone-masons and stone-sawyers' Trade Union, which announced that it would be holding a meeting on 23 March at the Corderie in view of 'the difficult epoch we are living through that should lead us to seriously reflect about our social position as workers. We must ask ourselves if we, the producers, should continue to enable those who produce nothing to live so handsomely; whether the system that has been followed until now is destined to exist for ever, even when it is completely opposed to us.' But the conclusion was less incisive, simply stating that the Trade Union would watch over and support the general interests of its members and help them in case of accidents at work. *The Times* nonetheless in its leader on this manifesto commented that it showed that 'the war not only of party against party, but of class against class, has become unavoidable'.[2]

Caught unawares as it had been on 18 March, the Delegation of the Twenty Arrondissements (the ex-Central Vigilance Committee) held a series of meetings during the week, deciding that the National Guard should act with 'energy and vigour', some even talking of

[1] Reproduced in Bruhat, Dautry and Tersen, op. cit., p. 125.
[2] 25 March.

the need for a Committee of Public Safety.[1] Vallès, on 23 March, announced in his paper that the revolutionary groups around the Delegation fully supported the Hôtel de Ville: 'We are all marching under the same flag: the *clocher* of Paris!'[2] At a meeting on this day, the same day as the International drew up its manifesto, the Delegation of the Twenty Arrondissements decided that since the Central Committee at the Hôtel de Ville had 'aimed at legality', this meant that the National Guard 'could no longer resort to revolution'. The revolutionaries, therefore, should avoid alienating the population so as to get a big turn-out as this, in the words of one member, would 'strengthen our moral force'. Vallès' paper published their electoral address, which called on the population to support the Communal elections in order that 'the rifle may be henceforth replaced by the tool, thereby assuring work, order and liberty for all'. This was followed by a 'Manifesto of the Central Committee of the Twenty Arrondissements', which now dropped its more revolutionary title of 'Delegation' adopted in January, drawn up by the Proudhonist Pierre Denis. This interpreted the revolution of 18 March and the coming elections as the consummation of the federalist principle of autonomous communes, 'pursued since the twelfth century'. There followed a list of candidates for the coming elections. These two decrees marked the return of the Vigilance Committee supported by its network of clubs and committees, as the leading popular organization.[3]

In an attempt to rally all but the most determinedly revolutionary sections of the population, Tirard on 23 March had put up a poster signed by Saisset announcing that the National Assembly had granted all of Paris's requests: municipal elections, election of the head of the National Guard, modification of the law on bills and on rents. None of this was true, except for the vague promise regarding overdue bills and rents, as all Tirard had was a note from Picard to the effect that it was probable that elections would be held around 10 April. Tirard had simply used one of the many drafts Saisset had signed to meet any eventuality, picking out the one 'that seemed

[1] Dumont, 21 March: Dautry and Scheler, op. cit., p. 217.
[2] *Le Cri du Peuple*, 23 March: *clocher*, means bell-tower; in this case it signified the belfry of the Hôtel de Ville, the medieval symbol of the municipal or communal independence of Paris.
[3] *Le Cri du Peuple*, 27 March: Dautry and Scheler, pp. 228–42; cf. Rougerie, *Procès*, p. 147.

to be the most useful'.[1] The attempt backfired, having less effect on Paris than on Versailles, where the Right talked of overthrowing Thiers if he had really made such concessions to the revolutionaries in the capital.

Then came good news for the Hôtel de Ville from outside Paris, to back up the support it was gathering within the city. On 24 March it was able to publish the report from Amouroux, its delegate to Lyon, that 'the cause of the people has triumphed and Paris alone is recognized as the capital'. The paper *La Commune*, which as its name indicated was particularly interested in the municipal movement, spoke of the news from the provinces as 'greatly resembling the liberating of the communes that occurred in identical fashion seven centuries ago'.[2] The historian Hippolyte Taine, from his country refuge, saw this in a very different light and wrote to his wife that 'never was the decomposition of society more evident'.[3] But in each case the provincial disturbances remained isolated and were easily quelled. At Lyon, where the red flag had flown over the Hôtel de Ville for most of the war, the news from Paris led to several days of tumult, culminating on 22 March in the arrest of the Prefect by the National Guard and the formation of a Communal Commission, headed by five municipal councillors. Garibaldi was nominated as head of the National Guard, and the red flag was again unfurled over the Hôtel de Ville. This was almost entirely a republican movement for local liberties, which demanded the right for Lyon 'to impose and administer its own taxes, have its own police and dispose of its own National Guard'. Mention was made of the need 'to alleviate the misery and suffering' of the working classes 'pending the final disappearance of that hideous social evil, pauperism'. But the popular battalions did not organize their own defence, and the delegates from Paris were quite unable to help. The conservative battalions rallied to the side of the Mayor and his councillors, all of whom had resigned from the Commune the day after it had been proclaimed. On 24 March the remaining members of the Commune found themselves deserted by the municipal council, threatened by the forces of order, unsupported by the popular districts. One by one they slipped away, until around 4.0 in the morning the Commune of Lyon just 'vanished away'.[4]

---

[1] *Enquête*, II, pp. 340–1 (Tirard); pp. 310–12 (Saisset).          [2] 24 March.
[3] Letter of 24 March; Taine's major work after the civil war was over was a study of this 'decomposition': *Les Origines de la France contemporaine* (1876–94).
[4] Lissagaray, op. cit., pp. 132–5; Bruhat, Dautry and Tersen, op. cit., pp. 305–6.

There were other uprisings at this time throughout France. At Saint-Étienne the Prefect was shot after the crowd had taken over the Hôtel de Ville on 25 March, but no mention was made of social reforms in the proclamation, the republicans soon backed down, and within three days order was restored. In Toulouse the National Guard movement was headed by the local Prefect, Duportal, whom Thiers had at once to replace by Kératry, the former Prefect of Police in Paris during the first part of the siege. With such a respectable head as Duportal the movement was canalized[1] into demands for purely republican franchises, though these did include the dissolution of the National Assembly because it represented a monarchist threat to the Republic. Kératry arrived on 27 March with cavalry and troops to occupy the town, where the republican leaders prevented any resistance being put up; 'the Government of Versailles triumphed thanks to the trustful loyalty of the republicans'.[2] Further south, Narbonne appealed to an ardent radical republican to lead their movement, one of the many returned political exiles of the Second Empire, Emile Digeon, who had been one of the organizers of the Ligue du Midi. On 24 March a crowd in which women played a noticeable role invaded the Hôtel de Ville, armed themselves, and Digeon proclaimed the Commune of Narbonne united to that of Paris. This lasted a week, during which time the local garrison fraternized with the popular forces, and delegates from other towns in the region arrived to try to generalize the movement. However, native troops from Algeria were sent in – the 'Turcos' – the town was threatened with bombardment, and, aided by the treacherous mediation of an old friend in exile of Digeon's, the revolutionaries were forced to surrender.

The mainly industrial town of Le Creusot, with its discontented factory workers who had been so notoriously active in the strike movement of the previous few years, did not however advance during the time of the Commune on the political autonomy gained after 4 September. Following 18 March Thiers sent a message to Le Creusot's working-class Mayor, Dumay, promising him favours if 'nothing happened' and 'the rigour of the law if he supported Paris'.[3]

[1] The expression is that of the military commander to Kératry: Bruhat, Dautry and Tersen, op. cit., p. 309.

[2] Fiaux, op. cit., p. 221; see too A. Armengaud, *Les Populations de l'Est-Aquitain*, Paris, 1961, pp. 444-50.

[3] P. Ponsot, *Les Grèves de 1870 et la Commune de 1871 au Creusot*, Paris, 1957, pp. 63-70.

DIX centimes.

1re ANNÉE — NUMÉRO 2

DIMANCHE 16 AVRIL 1871

# LE GRELOT

ABONNEMENTS :

Bureaux : 20, rue du Croissant.

POUR S'ABONNER

## FIGURES DU JOUR par BERTALL

PARIS CUIT DANS SON JUS.

5. Bismarck and Thiers: 'Paris stewed in its own juice'

6. The Commune's three Delegates of War

(a) General Gustave Cluseret: 4 April–1 May

(b) Louis Rossel: 1 May–9 May

(c) Charles Delescluze: 10 May–25 May

This did not stop Dumay supporting the 'socialist republican' committee's demonstration before the Hôtel de Ville on 26 March, which ended in scenes of fraternization between the troops and National Guards to cries of 'Long live the Commune'. The visiting delegate from Lyon, Albert Leblanc, something of a Bakuninist anarchist, declared that 'the Commune is the suppression of ministers, Prefects, and the Police. No more soldiers, only an armed citizenry. The worker must in the future enjoy all the profits of his labour, which today are consumed by a single individual.' But the revolutionary committee had been unable to win over other towns in the region, and the Prefect was able to return the next day with a thousand troops, thus preventing the holding of Communal elections. Slowly order was re-established by the making of arrests and dismissal of large numbers of workers. Dumay was forced into hiding and eventual exile in Switzerland.

The most extensive uprising was that of Marseille. Here the radical republicans and the strong local International federation led by the anarchist-inclined Bastelica were closely linked, and had supported the strikers at Le Creusot in 1870. On 23 March the ineptitude of the Prefect in calling out the National Guard, supposedly to demonstrate against the popular agitation, led to his own arrest and the forming of a Communal Commission, in this case at the Prefecture, over which the black flag was raised, the town Council continuing to hold out at the Hôtel de Ville. This movement was led by the republican clubs under Gaston Crémieux, a freemason known as 'the lawyer of the poor'. The local republicans were completely alienated by the monarchist National Assembly and were further aroused by Thiers' tactless courting of ex-Bonapartist generals to fight against Paris. They wanted, as Crémieux noted at the end of March, 'administrative decentralization with Communal autonomy through granting the local council in each large city its municipal and administrative powers'.[1] The military commander, General Espivent, the complete personification of the typical reactionary officer with his clerical, monarchist beliefs, followed Thiers' tactic and withdrew his army to a safe distance outside the city. Like Paris, Marseille suddenly found itself its own master. But as elsewhere in the south, the liberal bourgeoisie withdrew its support and the popular movement proved unable to sustain itself. The 'representatives on mission' from Paris proved utterly incompetent and

[1] A. Olivesi, *La Commune de 1871 à Marseille*, Paris, 1950, p. 137.

could not claim the authority of the name of any well-known republican figure in Paris. Marseille in turn had sent off its best revolutionary, Bastelica of the International, as a delegate to Paris. There was a
happy, festive air about the town; no measures were taken for its
defence, and most of the working-class National Guards went back
to work to get some pay. The Prefecture could probably have been
taken by a *coup de main*, as several citizens proposed, but Espivent
was determined to have his battle. On 4 April, at the news of Thiers'
opening of his attack on Paris, Espivent's troops moved in, bombarded the Prefecture into surrender, and recaptured the town after
a few hours' street fighting with the National Guard. In the days
following, Marseille provided a foretaste on a more limited scale
of the reaction that Paris was to experience. There were hundreds
of arrests and some executions, including Crémieux, and Marseille
was kept under military rule until 1876, during which time Espivent
pursued charges back to the uprising of 4 September overthrowing
the Empire!

None of the other numerous demonstrations[1] during this period
was on the scale of those just described. There were several disturbances at the stations when soldiers left to fight against Paris. This
occurred at Grenoble, for example, and at Limoges on 4 April the
troops fraternized, leaving the National Guard masters of the city
for a day. In several small towns in the south-west ammunition
trains were held up by the local population.[2] There was also Algiers,
which had been in a state of turmoil ever since the downfall of the
Empire, firstly from the white colonists against the remnants of the
Imperial administration and then by the Berbers. By April both these
revolts were under the control of the new Governor Thiers had sent
out.

All these movements are evidence of the opposition that had been
building up amongst large sections of the population during the
repression of the Empire. The breakdown of the political structures
brought about by the war meant that political and social discontent
could actively seek to establish its claims. To this extent there was
the potential of a widespread revolution, but at the same time little
likelihood that this would actually occur. The siege had intensified
the division between the capital and the provinces. As has been seen

---

[1] Bouvier in Bruhat, Dautry and Tersen, op. cit., p. 304, lists thirty-three
other towns, though this is not a full list.
[2] Armengaud, op. cit., p. 451.

with regard to Gambetta's military efforts, the provinces were tired of war, desirous of a return to normality, wanting peace. The Government at Versailles was able to monopolize propaganda, presenting a lurid picture of Paris, which the few emissaries sent out by the capital or the provincial delegations that visited the city had little chance to counteract. Apart from a few of the big cities where there had grown up some republican organization, the provinces were politically underdeveloped. There was plenty of unrest, memories going back in some cases to the resistance to the *coup d'état* of 1851,[1] but little danger of revolution unless Paris succeeded in humiliating the Government by forcing it to flee a second time. Then possibly the local supporters of social reform and of Communal liberties would have felt sufficiently encouraged to try to break completely with the central government. Even then the situation would not have been as sharp as it was in Paris. For the provincial centres of unrest had not gone through the political education the capital had experienced during the siege. In Paris those who had not left presented during February and March an almost united front against Versailles, demanding both economic and political concessions. Whereas in the other major cities the republican opposition movement was fearful of becoming a really popular revolt. When the Lyon factory workers of the Guillatière district did finally rise on 30 April, they were easily put down. Class divisions between artisans and factory workers, between shopowners, small holders and other sections of the bourgeoisie, remained stronger than any common sentiment against the central government. The war had provoked a crisis in France, but only in the capital had it brought about anything

[1] See, for example, the report of the Procureur de la République in the Basse-Alpes of 15 April 1871: A.N.; BB. 30,486. (I owe this reference to an unpublished article of Roger Price.) In his report to the National Assembly on the provincial movements, the Vicomte de Meaux suggested that there was a fair possibility of a widespread revolt, especially in the south and west: *Enquête*, I, pp. 271–9. This report, however, grossly exaggerates the amount of central direction from Paris and the role of the International. The London *Pall Mall Gazette* in its leader of 14 October was very alarmist about the state of the French provinces: 'no words could be too strong to describe the serious condition of the French cities and great towns . . . all the familiar phenomena (save one) of the first French Revolution are showing themselves at Rouen, Lyon, Dijon and Marseilles', and it quoted the King of Prussia to the effect that 'the social system of France is falling to pieces under the enormous pressure of disorderly war'.

approaching a fusion of the working and lower middle classes; elsewhere the central government could count on the fear of social change to stifle republican opposition.

Paris was left isolated, the only city where the dispute between the revolutionaries and the republican municipality ended in the latter being forced to consent to the holding of elections for a Commune. On 24 March Brunel was sent by the Central Committee with two columns of National Guards to the Mairie of the Louvre to bring an end to the Mayors' resistance. He was met by armed National Guards, and it looked as if a conflict might occur between those whose allegiance was to the Hôtel de Ville and those who supported the Mayors. Brunel and his second in command, Protot, entered the Mairie with a few others to see if an agreement could be reached over the holding of elections, whilst outside Maxime Lisbonne lined up his guns against the National Guards defending the Mairie. Brunel and Protot at first could only find the adjoint, Méline, who agreed to 30 March as a date for the elections, having persuaded Brunel that it would take a week to carry out the administrative preparations. The Mayor, Adam, then sent to the nearby 2nd arrondissement asking if the Mayors and Deputies there would agree to the compromise date of 30 March, and back came the reply that the earliest possible date was 3 April, the date the law was to be voted in the National Assembly. But Adam was forced to stick to the agreed date of the 30th, which caused great relief to the tense Guards facing each other, and there was great rejoicing all round as the news was announced that the Mayors and the Central Committee had seemingly reached agreement. The crowd, together with Brunel and his Guards, as well as Mayor Adam and his adjoint, then jubilantly marched off to the Mairie of the 2nd arrondissement, where they burst into the assembly of Mayors and Deputies debating the situation. In the end this latter body also agreed to 30 March, considering that a few days more or less did not matter if it was a question of avoiding bloodshed in Paris. The good news quickly spread throughout the city, where the crowds were soon shouting, 'No more civil war!' 'Up with Labour!' 'Long live peace!'

Saisset expressed the view that the agreement was 'the best thing that could be done',[1] and followed up this advice by dismissing all the National Guards under his command and taking himself back off to Versailles. Not all the Mayors signed – Dubail, for one, did

[1] *Enquête*, II, p. 323.

not – and the Central Committee at the Hôtel de Ville took a dim view of the agreement, considering that Brunel and Protot had no right to change the date already set. The Central Committee was tired of maintaining its undefined position, suspicious, as Assi put it, of the 'dubious attitude of the National Assembly'[1] and its representatives in Paris, the Mayors. The National Guard battalions were wearied from being constantly on the alert since the events of 18 March. So Ranvier and Arnold had to convey the news that the Central Committee insisted on its date of 26 March. The 'irrepressible' Mayor Dubail, as Lissagaray calls him, was all for armed resistance, drawing up a poster appealing to the National Guard to support the Mayors and blaming the Central Committee for causing 'civil war in Paris'.[2] On Saturday, 25 March, the Mayors and Deputies held a last morning session, at which they finally gave in to the demand of the Central Committee, knowing that they could hold out no longer. When Tirard at Versailles asked whether he should support his colleagues and agree to the holding of elections, Thiers told him that it was pointless 'to continue a useless resistance', as the army would be able to deliver Paris within two to three weeks.[3] Concession was also the theme of several of the leading republican papers, and a 'Committee of Conciliation' published an appeal to the Mayors to summon the electors; Saisset's second-in-command, the Deputy Schoelcher, held that the Mayors were aware that they were acting illegally but considered that they had the Government's tacit approval to concede in the face of force. Some justified their action by the hope that the elections might return the Mayors, thus defeating the Central Committee. Many of the more radical Mayors were influenced by the rumour that the monarchist majority at Versailles was considering replacing Thiers by one of the Orleanist princes.[4] Clemenceau described their situation as being caught between two bands of madmen, those at the National Assembly and those at the Hôtel de Ville.[5] But whatever their motives, the effect of their action was to ensure that the elections were generally regarded as legal; 'Many honest people,' according to one account,

---

[1] Lepelletier, op. cit., p. 364.

[2] *Enquête*, II, p. 358; Lissagaray, op. cit., p. 122.

[3] *Enquête*, II, p. 358 (Tirard).

[4] *Enquête*, II, p. 341 (Tirard); p. 360 (Dubail); p. 549 (Héligon); p. 378 (Vautrain); pp. 410, 412 (Desmarest); cf. *The Times*, 28 March, reports this rumour was widespread.                    [5] Damé, op. cit., p. 206.

'said that one must vote since the Mayors have accepted the situation and presented themselves as candidates.'[1]

The Central Committee posted up the news of this agreement with the Mayors, though in a way that gave itself the most credit by announcing that the Mayors and Deputies had 'rallied to the Central Committee of the National Guard', whereas the original text spoke of the Deputies and Mayors, 'reinstated in their Mairies', convoking the electors, together with the Central Committee. But such niceties mattered little at this stage. What was important was that the Central Committee had at last obtained authorization for its elections, though this had cost it four days delay. The Paris Deputies and Mayors were strongly criticized by the Assembly for having 'capitulated' to the revolutionaries, but in their own defence they rightly claimed that they had won Thiers time to build up his forces at Versailles. 'I am sure,' Mayor Vautrain told the Commission of Inquiry, 'that the eight days gained for you by the elections saved France.' Tirard, who was in touch with Thiers during this time, declared that 'the principal end we all pursued by this resistance, was to prevent the Federal forces from marching on Versailles'.[2] Yet, as has been seen, the Central Committee had rejected the idea of marching on Versailles right from the start, and it might seem as if they would have done well to have accepted Brunel's compromise of 30 March, or even the Mayors' date of 3 April. But Thiers was to declare war on 2 April, and nothing short of the complete abdication of the National Guard committee could have prevented this. Even then there would have been reprisals. Working to the advantage of the Central Committee in Paris, as in the case of the provincial uprisings, was the strong feeling that the major cities had a right to elect their own councils now the Empire had been replaced by the Republic and the war was over. But behind this unity over the demand for elections, as again the case of the provinces showed, lay a division between the bourgeoisie's support for republican political liberties and the workingmen's determination to move towards overcoming the 'social problem'. The moderateness of such demands as were formulated by those who spoke of the 'democratic social republic' was deceptive. Behind the bourgeoisie's opposition to these was the fear of the unknown; what, after all, as the Gambettist sub-Prefect

---

[1] *Enquête*, II, p. 175 (Hervé).

[2] *Enquête*, II, p. 377 (Vautrain); p. 342 (Tirard); cf. Schoelcher (p. 328); Saisset (p. 308); Desmarest (p. 409); Damé, op. cit., p. 242.

of Autun said to Dumay come from Le Creusot to ask for support, might not be expected of a government headed by unknown workers.[1] The conflict over the legality of the elections in Paris masked for both sides the underlying social conflict.

Such dark images, however, seemed far away on Sunday, 26 March, when Paris voted. The boulevards were full, the shops in the wealthy districts had reopened, and everyone was promenading as if their only 'business in life was to make the most of the glorious weather.'[2] There were about 227,000 votes cast in the all-male electorate of 480,000, which Thiers took as showing that 'the elections were deserted by the friends-of-order citizens'. But the electoral lists dated back to the plebiscite of May 1870, since when, as a result of the war and the end of the siege, there had been a big reduction in the population, and the results compare favourably to the previous mayoral elections of November.[3] This exodus worked to the advantage of the popular quarters, since it had been mainly the wealthier sections of the population that had left. The number of non-voters was highest in the bourgeois districts, those who did vote often slipping away quietly to do so, whereas the popular quarters voted with enthusiasm, often marching off to vote behind the red flag.[4] Then the proportional system of representation adopted by the Central Committee for the elections meant that the densely populated working-class districts had more representatives than the bourgeois west, instead of as previously each arrondissement having four councillors irrespective of population size.

The Central Committee published a final address announcing that 'our mission is over; we are going to give up our place in your Hôtel de Ville to those you have newly elected'. It simply asked the voters to choose 'men of sincere convictions, men of the people, resolute, active, with a clear judgement and an acknowledged honesty. True merit is modest and it is up to the electors to know their men, not for these to offer themselves.'[5] There was hardly any time for campaigning, though certain local electoral committees had been

[1] Ponsot, op. cit., p. 60.
[2] The Times, 29 March.
[3] In November the mayoral elections turnout was 218,000; in the February National elections it was 329,000. Accurate voting figures for March cannot be given: cf. Rougerie, 'Elections du 26 mars', pp. 59–68.
[4] Lissagaray, op. cit., p. 127; The Times, 29 March; Le Cri du Peuple, 27 March.
[5] J.O., 26 March.

active ever since elections had first been announced at the beginning of the week. In any case the growth of the popular movement of the preceding months had in itself been a preparation for elections. The Club de l'Ecole de Médecine was amongst the clubs dating from the siege that published a list for their own arrondissement. But the only complete list of candidates produced was that of the Central Committee of the Twenty Arrondissements, though this was simply a compilation of the lists drawn up by the local committees. As a result most likely of this pressure from below the list had been considerably widened to include prominent radical republicans and journalists such as Arthur Arnould, Paschal Grousset and Arthur Ranc, several members of the outgoing Central Committee, most notably Jourde and Edouard Moreau, as well as Blanquist revolutionaries such as Ferré and Rigault. It was no longer a party list, as that for the February national elections had been, and was accordingly very successful. Forty-nine out of its eighty-seven candidates were elected.[1] Some arrondissements chose representatives who had not even presented themselves; Arthur Arnould, for example, for the 8th arrondissement although he had only stood for the 4th. The 'party of order' decided that the only thing it could do was to support the outgoing Mayors and their adjoints.[2] Other lists were drawn up by groups of citizens, and sometimes these were passed around by hand.

The results as a whole showed an overwhelming swing to the left. There were about fifteen to twenty moderate republicans elected, mainly from the wealthy arrondissements of the Louvre, the Bourse, the Opera and Passy, fourteen of whom immediately resigned. Amongst these were Adam, the Mayor of the 1st arrondissement, Tirard of the 2nd, Desmarest of the 9th. The remaining arrondissements gave majorities to opponents of Versailles. The most working-class arrondissements were the most strongly pro-Communard, and taking the 4th arrondissement as an example, the breakdown by sections shows that the industrial districts voted more heavily for Communards than did the bourgeois areas.[3] 'It was the social revolution which, on that memorable day, came out of the poll,' wrote

[1] *Le Cri du Peuple*, 27 March; cf. Dautry and Scheler, op. cit., pp. 240–2.
[2] *La Vérité*, 27 March: 'Our candidates are known and are the Mayors and adjoints of the twenty arrondissements and the 43 Paris Deputies'; Reclus, op. cit., p. 46; *The Times*, 30 March.
[3] Archives de la Seine: Rougerie, op. cit., p. 79.

Élie Reclus.[1] Edmond de Goncourt, who had suffered from a liver attack that prevented him from noting whether or not he had voted, wrote on the evening of 28 March, 'the newspapers only see in what is happening a question of decentralization. What is happening is the even conquest of France by the working population . . . The Government is leaving the hands of those who have for those who have not' – opinions open to question, but illustrative of both the hopes and fears of this time. A voter in the 20th arrondissement was reported to have declared, 'I am voting for the reddest of the reds, but, in God's name, if I knew of something more radical than the red flag I would choose that instead.'[2] In the 20th arrondissement there had been the highest turnout in all of Paris, seventy-six per cent, with ninety per cent of the vote going to Communards; in the 18th, the local Vigilance Committee list gained almost eighty per cent of the vote, more than Clemenceau had received in November. Throughout Paris the 50,000 voters who had supported the Vigilance Committee list in the February national elections found that they were now some 150,000. This was not because of a sudden rush of converts to the 'revolutionary socialist' position, but because the republican majority in Paris was now willing to vote for the Commune as a defensive vote against Thiers and the National Assembly. In the working-class districts more particularly the victory of the socialist candidates came from 'the fact that, unlike most radicals and neo-Jacobins, they had chosen to burn their bridges behind them and stake everything on the revolutionary power of the people in arms'.[3] But political and social ideals alone would not have been sufficient to drive the Paris working class into freeing itself from its allegiance to the old forms of political rule. The impetus to do this could only have come from a more general feeling, which in this case was the frustrated popular republican patriotism arising from the siege.[4]

The duplicity of the Government of National Defence in seeking

[1] Reclus, op. cit., p. 46.
[2] E. Moriac, *Paris sous la Commune*, 1871, p. 57.
[3] Wolfe, *Past and Present*, p. 112.
[4] Cf. M. Winock and J.-P. Azéma, *Les Communards*, Paris, 1964, pp. 67, 177; C. Talès, *La Commune de 1871*, Paris, 1921, p. 21, 'The violence of Parisian patriotism explains to a great degree the 1871 revolution, political and social ideas by themselves not being enough to have moved the crowds; generally in order for the masses to think of revolt an elementary, universal and powerful feeling must be offended and violated.'

peace while professing war had deprived it of all its authority with the crowd that had carried it to power. This was the situation which the revolutionary organizations had been expecting. As the Blanquist and Internationalist Edouard Vaillant said, the Central Vigilance Committee had watched 'how the revolutionary movement had grown during the siege without, however, carrying along the population as a whole, which was duped by the lies and deceptions of its rulers; and it could foresee the anger and revolt that would occur when all illusions vanished and the Government's treachery was clearly established'.[1] The ineptitude of the National Assembly with its monarchist majority proved to be the last straw, driving most of republican Paris into accepting the Commune.

On Tuesday, 28 March, in the afternoon sunshine that continued to favour Paris's revolutionary days, the members of the newly elected Commune, wearing red sashes, lined up on the steps of the Hôtel de Ville under a canopy surmounted by a bust of the Republic, draped in red, with on high the red flag still flying from the morning after 18 March. The National Guard battalions assembled to the music of the first Revolution and popular airs from operettas and music halls. At 4.0 p.m. Ranvier read out the list of those elected and proclaimed the Commune. The drums rolled, the 'Marseillaise' was sung and cannons fired a salute from the quay. Under the direction of Brunel the National Guards, saluting the bust of the Republic as they passed by, filed off in a procession that lasted until 7.0 in the evening. It was, said Lepelletier, 'a festival of dazzling simplicity';[2] the Commune, wrote Vallès, 'was proclaimed in a revolutionary and patriotic festive day, peaceful and joyous, a day of intoxication and solemnity, of grandeur and merrymaking, worthy of those witnessed by the men of '92 and one that made up for twenty years of Empire, six months of defeats and betrayals'.[3]

[1] In the 'Enquête sur la Commune' published in the Revue Blanche, vol. 12, March–April 1897, p. 274.

[2] Lepelletier, op. cit., p. 462.

[3] Le Cri du Peuple, 30 March.

Chapter 7

# THE COMMUNE: POLITICS AND WAR

The Guards marched off, the crowds dispersed and the new representatives of Paris found themselves strangely isolated, forgotten almost. There were no precedents and the outgoing power, the Central Committee, had made no preparations for the transfer of government. They even had difficulty getting into the Hôtel de Ville, as no one knew the password, and only the better-known figures were able to argue their way past the National Guards on duty. Once inside few had any idea of the layout of the building, and they had no keys to get into the locked Municipal Council Chamber. This was dusty from disuse and lacked lamps enough to light it. Eventually late that night, after a locksmith had been sent for, there were sufficient members present to open the first session of the Council of the Paris Commune.

The oldest member was made President – Charles Beslay, born in 1795, a civil engineer by profession, who had been a Deputy in 1848 and a propagator of Proudhon's theories on mutualist associations during the Second Empire. He had held open house for leaders of the labour movement, Proudhon himself sometimes being present. At one of these meetings was broached the idea of publishing a manifesto in support of the working-class candidates in the 1864 elections, though Beslay, following his master Proudhon, was in favour of abstention. Beslay had not wanted to be elected in 1871, feeling too old and ill. He at first thought of resigning, but then decided that his influence was indispensable in helping moderate the extremer spirits so as to keep the Commune within the path of local liberties. He therefore let himself be persuaded to stay on. The Blanquists Ferré and Rigault, as the youngest members present, acted as secretaries.

Having no fixed agenda and with most of those present, just over half, hardly knowing each other, the session lasted barely two hours. An obvious task for what claimed to be a legally constituted body was to validate the election results. The law of 1848 which the Central Committee had used to conduct the elections stipulated that an eighth of the registered voters was the necessary minimum to be elected. But the Commune ignored this restriction, which if accepted would have disqualified several members, including Rigault, Vaillant, Arnould and Jules Allix of the 8th arrondissement, where the turnout had been particularly low. It could be claimed in the Commune's defence that the registers were out of date because of the war and the siege. It was also decided that no one could be both a Deputy at Versailles and sit on the Commune in Paris. Tirard took this as an excuse to resign, declaring in the face of one demand for his arrest that he preferred the regular mandate of a Deputy to the irregular situation of a member of the Commune. This latter, he added, could at most be a municipal council, yet it was beginning to act as if it were a National Assembly. Others preferred to resign by letter. But Delescluze, and Cournet – who had collaborated with Delescluze on the *Réveil* – took the opposite side, resigning from the Assembly at Versailles rather than from the Commune in Paris.

The next day, Wednesday, 29 March, there occurred the first full meeting of the Commune, which lasted from 1 p.m. until midnight, with a break for an evening meal. The Central Committee was solemnly received when it came to hand over its 'revolutionary powers'. It had published a last poster praising the citizens of Paris for having carried their revolution thus far. It called on them to support the Commune in attaining the final aim, that of the 'Universal Republic'.[1] The Commune then decided on its first proclamation, which was drawn up by Paschal Grousset, Vaillant, Tridon and Protot, all to some degree Blanquists. This justified the election of the Commune as the rejection of 'a cowardly aggressive power', a 'monarchist plot', that even now was criminally organizing for civil war.[2] In the same vein Félix Pyat's motion was passed abolishing conscription and decreeing that the National Guard was the only military force in Paris. This was simply recognizing the current state of affairs in the city, but such a decree showed that deliberately or not the Commune could not limit itself to purely municipal affairs. 'Commune in the morning,' as Lissagaray said, 'Constituent Assembly in the evening'. Replacing the regular army by the armed

[1] M.P., II, pp. 124–5.                                   [2] J.O., 30 March.

citizenry had long been a demand of the revolutionaries. The decree also justified the position of those soldiers who had deserted to the side of the Commune.

Of similar purport was the decree ordering all civil servants to stay on at their posts and ignore any orders from Versailles. Most of the top officials had followed the Government to Versailles after 18 March. But the junior personnel lacked both the inclination and the economic means to leave their homes in Paris and take themselves off to Versailles. Many considered too that they had a duty to see to the running of a city of over one and a half million people. In this attitude they were supported by some of the republican Press. The *Gaulois* on 1 April 'complimented and encouraged' officials in this attitude, as 'the well-being, the health and the safety of a large city such as Paris, its existence even, depends on the regular carrying out of a large number of services that cannot be left unattended to'. At the end of the Commune the *Tribun du Peuple* of 23 May praised 'the efforts and the prodigious administrative *tour de force* accomplished by the Commune'. Thus public services such as the post, sewers, gas, transport, continued to function more or less ably, regardless of the change of government. An additional factor was that immediately following the flight of Thiers to Versailles the Central Committee and then the Commune seemed to have more authority, being much closer, than a government that had abandoned the capital. And in general there was considerable sympathy for the Commune among the petit bourgeois, clerks included. Paul Verlaine, for example, who worked at the Hôtel de Ville, stayed on. He felt he could not leave his mother behind, he had a number of friends among the revolutionaries, Rigault having been a school fellow, and then he 'liked the activity' and 'had from the first loved, understood and in any case readily sympathized (or so I thought) with this revolution, so peaceful'. He soon came to feel alienated from the 'babbling, blundering and doctrinaire' Commune,[1] but in his case as in others the first sympathy was decisive in determining whether to remain or leave Paris.

Other decrees of this first administrative session forbade the sale of objects deposited at the State pawnshop, the Mont de Piété, its Director having announced that all unredeemed goods would be put up for sale from 1 April. Selling off articles would have been very unrealistic, considering the unemployment in Paris, and the

[1] Paul Verlaine, *Confessions*, Eng. trans., London, 1950, pp. 170–2.

Director's announcement had at once been followed by protests and letters in the popular Press. However, it took some time before the Commune could reach a decision regulating the return of some of the pawned goods. A law on overdue bills, the *échéances*, was promised, but for the time being the delay imposed by the Central Committee was left in force. Prompt action was taken regarding the other economic grief of Paris in its dispute with Versailles, the question of back rents. Public meetings had been held in February concerning this question, and a Tenants League had been formed. Generally the solution proposed was the liquidation both of all outstanding rents and of those for the coming quarter. The decree of the Commune was in line with this feeling, though it only went so far as to cancel payments for the last three quarters, covering the period from October 1870 to April 1871. Any sums already paid were to be credited to the future account of the tenant. To some supporters of the Commune this measure was too sweeping, and the suggestion was made that commercial establishments that had profited from the war or wealthy tenants should not be covered by the general exemption.[1] Clément proposed this at the Commune, on 31 March, but the majority were not willing to go back on the decision.

This decree on rents was not an attack on the principle of private property, though at the time to many of the bourgeoisie it did look, as *The Times* announced it, like 'a blow at the rights of property'.[2] In Paris it was considered an exceptional measure justified by the circumstances resulting from the war. It was only 'just' that property should be made to share in the sacrifices caused by the war, as the decree's preamble put it; or, as Arnould wrote afterwards, 'the property of the poor is as sacred as that of the rich'.[3] It was a measure that gained the Commune the continuing support of the lower middle classes, particularly because it was enacted so promptly. 'The mass of Parisian tenants, merchants, embarrassed in their affairs, small *rentiers* who have been ruined, clerks out of place, as well as workpeople out of work, awoke full of joy on the 29th when they read that three-quarters of their rents were "remitted",' reported *The Times* correspondent. 'While economists and legislators were seeking after gentle measures, and calling on time to heal one of the wounds caused by the war, the Commune, inspired with the "new

---

[1] *Le Rappel*, 4 April; *La Commune*, 31 March; *La Révolution politique et sociale*, 16 May; Arnould, op. cit., vol. 2, pp. 120–1; Lissagaray, op. cit., p. 211.
[2] 3 April.                                        [3] Op. cit., vol. 3, p. 63.

spirit", cauterized it with one word – "It is remitted".[1] Marx, watching developments from London, classified it as one of the measures 'favourable to the working class, but above all to the middle class'.[2] Seraillier, sent over by the General Council of the International, wrote to his wife that 'strangely enough, the firmest support of the Commune is the bourgeoisie'.[3] Flaubert, in the country outside of Paris, was naturally enough indignant: 'The government is interfering now in matters of natural law; it is intervening in contracts between individuals.'[4]

It was also one of the most successful measures of the Commune, many tenants taking the opportunity to leave apartments they could no longer afford without being thereby subject to the seizure of their goods. Arthur Arnould tells how women dressed in their best black clothes timidly came to the Mairies hardly daring to believe that it was really true that they could leave without paying any back rent. Such moments were among the finest in his memory of his time on the Commune.[5] The National Guard was used to enforce this measure on recalcitrant landlords, though some tenants had to fight their own battle. The poet and playwright Catulle Mendès, a republican but no Communard, came across a crowd watching a landlord and tenant struggling over a little night-table, while the removal men prudently remained neutral between the two parties. Catching the landlord off his guard, the tenant suddenly whisked the table on to the furniture cart, jumped into the driver's seat, and made good his escape to the cheers of the crowd, shouts of the removal men and curses of the landlord.[6]

The Commune's first proclamation had spoken of the 'monarchists' at Versailles organizing for civil war. This was just rhetoric so far as the first acts of the Commune were concerned. Nothing was done to prepare to meet an attack, let alone to mount one. At Versailles, on the other hand, this was the overriding preoccupation of the Government. Two weeks had now passed since the debacle of

[1] 3 April.　　　　　　　　　　[2] In his first draft of *The Civil War in France*.
[3] 12 April: given in *Lettres de communards et de militants de la Première Internationale à Marx, Engels et autres dans les journées de la Commune de Paris en 1871*, ed. J. Rocher, Paris, 1934, p. 27.
[4] Letter to George Sand, 31 March.
[5] Arnould, op. cit., vol. 3, pp. 63–4.
[6] Mendès, op. cit., pp. 67–8; see too J.O., 7 April; *L'Affranchi*, 5 April; C. Perrot, *La Politique sociale de la Commune*, D.E.S. of the Sorbonne, 1950, p. 25.

18 March. These had been spent bringing fresh troops from the provinces, who, it was hoped, would be uncontaminated by the contagion in Paris. Thiers, unhampered by having neither King nor Emperor over him, made himself both head of the Government and commander of the army. Each morning, he told the Commission of Inquiry, 'I called together all the departmental heads: I decided what should be done; everyone had his task assigned!'[1] Thiers handpicked his commanders, winning many of them over to fighting for his Republic by his considerable conversational charm. The historian of the First Empire was now to have the opportunity of conducting his own campaign. As one General said of him, 'by virtue of having studied in detail Napoleon's campaigns, he believed he was qualified to have commanded them ... Like Napoleon he laid across maps. Like him, he drew up plans. Like him, he called councils of war, at which we were never allowed to utter a word while he explained the situation and criticized the movements with inexhaustible energy.'[2] Daily Thiers visited the army camps in and around Versailles, where the troops were kept cut off from contact with the civilian population, seeing to the well-being and comfort of the men and their officers. The meat ration was increased, as was the pay, new uniforms were issued, drill was carried out regularly. Soon the men were saluting smartly again, and matters began to look less hopeless. Meanwhile Favre was negotiating with the Prussians for the return of prisoners of war. On 3 April Bismarck agreed to the return of 20,000 and to allowing the number in the French army permitted under the armistice agreement to be increased to 80,000, raised not long after to 100,000, and finally to over 130,000.

Fighting first broke out on 30 March, when in a skirmish near Courbevoie the National Guards were dislodged by the cavalry under the Marquis de Gallifet, a dashing, brave general and future friend of Edward VII. A small battery was established to cover the Neuilly bridge across the Seine. The ex-army officer, Rossel, who on joining the side of the revolutionaries had been appointed by Gérardin and Malon as head of the National Guard in the 17th arrondissement, tried to lead his legion to retake the position at Courbevoie. But someone accidentally let his gun off during the night march and the Guards panicked and fled. Rossel tried to stop them but was nearly shot by his own men, and he was lucky only to

---

[1] *Enquête*, II, p. 14 (Thiers).
[2] General du Barail, *Mes Souvenirs*, Paris, 1896, vol. 3, p. 260.

be arrested and have to spend a night in prison, where he slept soundly, so exhausted was he.[1] By now, with 50,000 men ready and under pressure from public opinion – as well as from the Prussians – Thiers decided the time had come, as he expressed it, 'to teach the rebels a lesson'. He telegraphed to comfort the provinces that 'the organization of one of the finest armies ever possessed by France is being completed at Versailles; good citizens can thus take heart and hope for the end of a struggle which will be sad but short'. A war council was held on the first of April to determine the point of attack.

On Palm Sunday, 2 April, two brigades set off early in the morning to take the improvised barricades at the Rond Point at Courbevoie (today the Place de la Défense). This was to be a test of the mettle of the fresh troops; would they remain firm or fraternize with the Parisian National Guards, leading to another disastrous 18 March? For this reason, although it was only a small military operation, the provisional Commander-in-Chief, General Vinoy, was at the head of his troops, and the usual precaution was taken of putting gendarmes into the front line.[2] An unfortunate incident preceded the opening of hostilities. Dr Pasquier, the surgeon-major, having got into the wrong brigade, tried to catch up with Vinoy, but found himself instead ahead of the army, isolated and exposed before the Communards' barricades. The federals, seeing five broad stripes on his sleeves, at once fired, thinking they had shot one of the detested gendarme colonels. This accident made excellent propaganda rather along the lines of the deaths of Generals Lecomte and Clément Thomas on 18 March, with Thiers announcing to the provinces that the army chief surgeon had been 'shamefully assassinated'. It also angered the troops as they were told that Pasquier had been shot whilst waving a white handkerchief as a truce flag in an attempt to negotiate. The first wave of the attack was not very encouraging, as the tirailleurs turned and fled under heavy fire from the Communards. This caused a few moments of general panic before Vinoy rode up to restore order with the help of a battalion of marines. But already the Rond Point had been taken and the Parisian federals were in full

[1] Rossel, op. cit., pp. 272–4; Verges d'Esboeufs, *Le Coin de Voile*, Geneva, 1872, pp. 52–7.
[2] (E. Hennebert), *Guerre des Communeux de Paris par un officier supérieur de Versailles*, Paris, 1871, p. 125; General Sesmaisons, *Les Troupes de la Commune*, Paris, 1904, pp. 7–8.

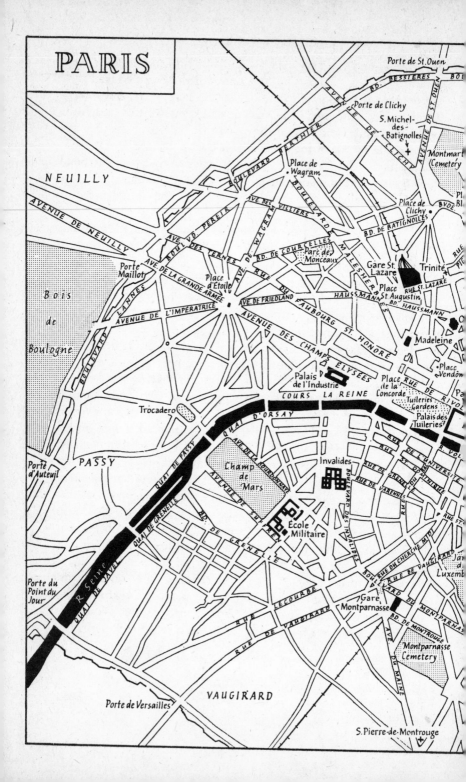

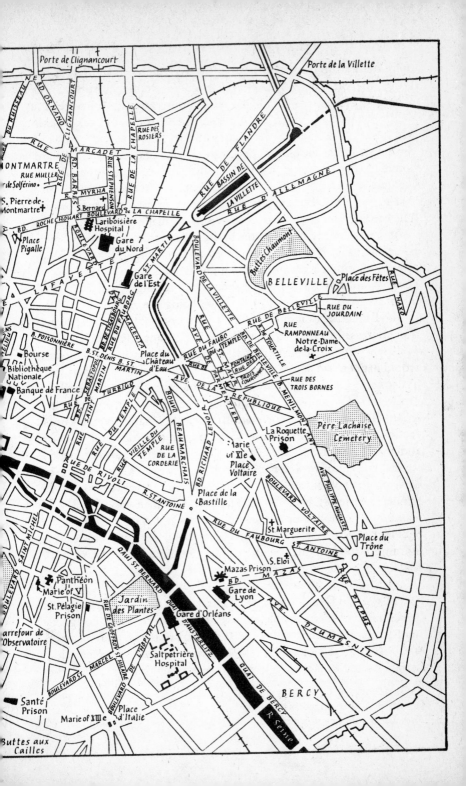

flight across the bridge and down the Avenue de Neuilly towards Porte Maillot. The Versailles troops could well have pursued the fleeing Communards into Paris, but Vinoy and Thiers were not willing to take any risks, having insufficient troops to back up this first success. Instead the Versailles army withdrew to the far side of the Seine, and at the end of the afternoon one of the National Guard commanders, 'Bergeret himself' as his chief-of-staff rather unfortunately reported it, was able to drive up the Avenue to make sure that it was clear. But already the savagery of civil war had begun. The captured federals were as soon shot as made prisoners.

At Versailles the news of this first victory came as an overwhelming relief. The National Assembly had been nervously fearful all afternoon, but at 5.0 p.m. Jules Simon assured them the action had been completely successful. It was now assumed that Paris had learnt its lesson. But this was far from being the case.

The Executive Committee of the Commune published a proclamation addressed to the National Guard expressing the indignation in Paris when it was realized that what had never really been believed would happen had actually occurred: 'The royalist conspirators have ATTACKED. Despite the moderation of our attitude, they have ATTACKED.' Even now it was not openly admitted that it was French troops that had fired on the National Guard: 'Unable to count upon the French Army, they have ATTACKED with the Pontifical Zouaves and the Imperial Police.'[1] The popular quarters were out on the streets, talking of revenge and marching off to the Champs-Elysées, carrying their rifles, singing the 'Marseillaise'. Nor was it only the popular districts. Catulle Mendès noticed that many bourgeois were marching: 'many hands are white and are not those of workers'.[2] Seraillier also remarked later in April how the bourgeoisie were fighting in the National Guard for the Commune.[3] The *grande sortie* was finally going to happen.

It was a 'spontaneous explosion' of popular anger.[4] The three generals of the Commune, Eudes, Duval and Bergeret, argued that 'the enthusiasm is irresistible, unique. What can Versailles do against 100,000 men? We must sally out.' It was left to the civilian members of the Executive Commission to criticize the lack of preparation, Lefrançais and Pyat arguing that before undertaking any such large-

---

[1] J.O., 3 April; M.P., II, p. 154.          [2] Op. cit., p. 80.
[3] 15 April, *Lettres de communards*, p. 30.
[4] Lepelletier, op. cit., vol. 3, p. 210.

scale operation it should be found out what troops they had, supplies should be organized, the troops given firing practice and artillery battalions be formed: 'One does not start at random,' said Pyat, 'without cannons, without cadres and without chiefs.' But Pyat's position was weakened by his having proclaimed the same day in his paper that Paris should march on Versailles. As a last-minute attempt to give some direction to the coming sortie Cluseret was named as the Commune's Delegate to the Ministry of War. But Cluseret felt it was too late to prevent the attack, and Pyat withdrew his opposition: 'after all, if you think you are ready . . .'

Cluseret, forty-seven years old at the time, had been decorated with the Legion of Honour in his first action after leaving Saint Cyr for taking eleven barricades in the June 1848 uprising. He had fought in the Crimea and in Algeria, until dismissed from the army in connection with a shady affair over some stores. He then went to New York to raise a volunteer corps to join Garibaldi in Italy. He was back in America during the Civil War, fought for the North and was made a brigadier-general in the army of McClellan. Cluseret was in England for a time, plotting with the Fenians, until he had to take refuge in France.[1] By this time his political views had become considerably more radical than in his young officer days. He wrote on military subjects in Vermorel's *Courrier Français* and other republican papers, and joined the International after he had met Malon and Varlin in prison in 1868. His writings on the army forced

---

[1] McClellan classified Cluseret among the many adventurers who offered their services during the Civil War. Cluseret had a letter of introduction from Garibaldi, says McClellan, 'recommending him in the highest terms as a soldier, man of honour, etc. I did not like his appearance and declined his services; but without my knowledge or consent Stanton appointed him a colonel on my staff. I still declined to have anything to do with him, and he was sent to the Mountain Department, as chief of staff, I think': *McClellan's Own Story*, London, 1887, p. 143. Washburne, op. cit., p. 107, says it was through Sumner that Cluseret eventually got his way and was promoted to brigadier-general at the end of 1862, after which he left the army. Through his relations with Sumner Cluseret then became involved in American foreign policy in Cuba and then Ireland: see A. Landy, 'A French Adventurer and American Expansionism after the Civil War', *Science and Society*, Fall, 1951, pp. 313–33, and the *Pall Mall Gazette*, 24 November 1870, p. 5. From his correspondence with Sumner it is clear that Cluseret had an idealistic picture of American intentions, considering the U.S.A. as a liberating force in Latin America and elsewhere, Europe even, against the colonialism of France and Britain.

him to leave France again for the States, where he helped in organizing the International. Returning after the fall of the Empire, he quickly became unpopular, as has been seen, because of a too realistic appraisal of the military ardour of the Government of National Defence. Leaving Paris he was active in the revolutionary movements in Lyon and became military commander in Marseille of the Ligue du Midi, but took no other part in the fighting during the war. He returned to Paris after 18 March and was on good terms with the Central Committee of the National Guard, which wanted to make him their Commander-in-Chief until Garibaldi should arrive. He had, therefore, much to recommend him for the post of being the Commune's War Delegate, and was later elected to the Commune in the April by-elections. With regard to the sortie of 3 April, however, he wisely avoided taking responsibility, leaving the other generals to see through what they had so rashly begun.

Eudes, Duval and Bergeret, the latter most unmilitarily in a coach because he was not well enough to ride a horse, were each to lead one column of the attack. This was about the limit of the planning, for most federals considered it would be little more than a promenade and were accompanied by women and children, so convinced were they that the army would fraternize rather than fire on the National Guard. Lepelletier, the republican historian of the Commune and minor participant in its events, described them more as 'a band of turbulent holidaymakers setting out gaily and unconcernedly for the country than a column of attack'.[1] Eudes and Duval with 13,000 troops between them were to march directly south through the Meudon woods to Versailles. Bergeret, supported by Flourens on his right, was to lead his 15,000 men west towards Saint-Germain-en-Laye, past Nanterre and Rueil, before moving south through the wooded country of Buzenval, Garches and Vaucresson to descend on Versailles. This route involved passing directly underneath the guns of fort Mont-Valérien, which seemed to worry no one, although Lullier had been imprisoned precisely for not ensuring the occupation of this fort immediately after 18 March. Bergeret's chief-of-staff two days before had requested the National Guard commander at Courbevoie to try to find out what troops were occupying the fort. But no reply seems to have been received.[2] Rumour had it, and rumour seemed to be considered sufficient by the crowd and the

[1] Op. cit., vol. 3, p. 231.
[2] Report of General Appert, *Annales*, vol. 43, p. 20.

commanders, that the fort had somehow reverted to the Commune, or that at the very least the Commander had given his word of honour not to fire. In any case if he did, it was felt certain he would not be obeyed and the marines would open the fort's gates to the Parisian federals. Great was the surprise, therefore, when the happy column suddenly found itself under fire. Bergeret's horses were hit, an officer killed by his side, and to the cry of 'treason' the rear part of the column turned tail and fled back towards Paris. Some at least had the bravado to bring a cannon into position and fire back. Bergeret pressed on with the front part of the column to Rueil, where he joined up with Flourens, and came to within four miles of Versailles. At Versailles this news caused many to pack their trunks ready to leave, but by now the army, after being caught by surprise, was alerted, aided by the telegraph from Mont-Valérien, and General Gallifet's cavalry were ready to attack the disorganized column. Bergeret had to withdraw his dispirited troops back towards Asnières. It was a complete rout, the federals being broken up and chased by the cavalry, being cut down if they were unlucky enough not to escape.

Flourens, worn out and very depressed at having been accused by his own men of betraying them, wandered about, lost in his own dejection, rather than returning to the safety of Paris. He eventually flopped down in an *auberge* at Rueil. The keeper and some other locals told the gendarmes of Flourens' hiding place, and they burst into the house. Cipriani, Flourens' Italian aide-de-camp, fired on them. Flourens made no effort to defend himself, but insolently walked out in his high boots, smoking a cigarette. Seeing the officer in charge, Captain Desmarets, Flourens ran up requesting him to call off his men who were beating up Cipriani with their rifle butts and bayonets. The gendarmes in their own defence accused Flourens of firing on them, whereupon Desmarets drew his sword and cleft open the bareheaded Flourens as he stood before him. A fellow officer rode up to congratulate him on a fine sword blow, and Captain Desmarets was decorated on his return to Versailles. Flourens' body was sent off to Versailles in a dung cart, from where it was collected four days later by his mother, and quietly buried in Père-Lachaise.

The other federal columns did no better, and were equally savagely hunted down. Gallifet had three prisoners shot, a practice he had picked up from fighting irregulars in the Mexican campaign, and published a proclamation boasting of his intentions regarding the Parisians: 'War has been declared by the bands of Paris. Yesterday, the day before, today, they have assassinated my soldiers. I declare a war in which there will be neither truce nor mercy upon these assassins. I have had to make an example; let it be salutary.' Eudes had to retreat back to the safety of Fort Issy, safely in the hands of the Commune, though Duval's men, after some fierce fighting, still held by nightfall the important redoubt on the plateau of Châtillon. But this was an isolated position and early the next morning they were surrounded, and Duval with 1,500 men had to surrender on promise of their lives. Vinoy stopped the column of prisoners, among whom was the geographer Elysée Reclus, on its way to Versailles and had the ex-soldiers in it shot. When the rest protested, Vinoy asked if there were any officers in charge. Duval and his chief-of-staff stepped forward, and Vinoy ordered them to be shot too. One of Vinoy's escort pulled off the boots from the corpse of Duval and rode off waving them and shouting, 'Who wants Duval's boots?'

In retaliation the Commune decreed that if 'the bandits of Versailles' continued 'to butcher or shoot our prisoners' the Commune would have to reply by shooting triple that number of hostages. A jury of accusation was formed, before which all those arrested would be tried to determine whether they would be retained as 'hostages of the people of Paris'.[1] The Commune was determined, as Protot the Justice Delegate insisted, 'to act legally' by in effect reviving the Law of Suspects of the first Revolution. The decree on hostages did not lead to anything approaching a reign of terror. A number of arrests were officially made, and many more unofficially on the initiative of the local National Guard commanders, but the Commune never carried out its threat to take reprisals until the last week when six of the hostages were ordered to be shot, and sixty or so more were executed without any official authorization.

The captured Communards found little better treatment once they reached Versailles. The successes of the army during the last three days over the 'reds' of Paris ended the state of fear that the population there had been in ever since the Government had left Paris. Once more the bourgeoisie could feel the world was unchallengeably theirs and the lines of prisoners were treated as savages, with the full implications of that term in a colonial power, as they

[1] J.O., 6 April.

dragged their way through the streets, covered in dust, worn out, wounded, their clothes in rags, to be herded into prison compounds. According to reports the elegantly dressed ladies were the most violent, especially against their own sex. The gendarmes escorting the prisoners kept them moving by using their sabres, and were barely able to prevent them from being done to death 'October'-like under the canes and umbrellas of the crowds lining the route. This performance was repeated after each victory by the army led to further prisoners. It was but a particularly spectacular example of the general fact that at this period class divisions in society were seen in racialist terms; Gautier, for example, spoke of 'the hyenas of '93 and the gorillas of the Commune'.[1] Those prisoners who could still lift their heads to look at their persecutors quickly lost all signs of anger or pride after a few days behind the despairing walls of the prison compound of Sartory.

Henceforth Versailles could dominate the battlefield, although the fire from the forts, particularly Issy, was still serious. Vinoy had to withdraw the troops from the Châtillon plateau they had taken from Duval, after one general had been wounded and another had had his horse shot from under him. But it was clear that there was no longer any danger to Versailles. 'The first three days of fighting were sufficient to give the regular army such moral superiority, such ascendancy, such confidence in its own strength, that it could truly be said that the fate of the Commune was decided.'[2] The Commune had lost the offensive and Paris was now to undergo a second siege. The next few days on the Versailles side were spent preparing for this and the bridge at Neuilly was attacked again, though it took two days of fighting and the lives of two generals before a bridge-head was secured.

On 6 April, MacMahon replaced the more elderly Vinoy, who had to console himself with a Legion of Honour and the command of the reserve army. Thiers disliked Vinoy, and Vinoy's recent successes seem not to have effaced his failure before the guns of Montmartre. But MacMahon was, after all, a Marshal of France and had been Commander-in-Chief of the Imperial Army, even if he had only led it to disaster at Sedan. Charles de Rémusat considered

---

[1] Théophile Gautier, *Tableaux de Siège*, Paris, 1871, p. 373; see further L. Chevalier, *Classes laborieuses, classes dangereuses*, Paris, 1958, p. 518.

[2] General Sesmaisons, op. cit., p. 16; cf. Vinoy, op. cit., p. 276; Hennebert, op. cit., p. 130.

MacMahon to be one of the generals 'least compromised by Bonapartism, not very inventive and willing always to carry out the ideas of others without bothering to examine them',[1] qualities that fitted him two years later as a stop-gap – or so it was intended – monarchist candidate to succeed Thiers as President of the Republic. A review was held to present the army to its new Commander-in-Chief, though because of a wound he had received at Sedan MacMahon could only manage a pony.

The change in command strengthened Thiers' own position, and it was he who determined the strategy and pace of the operations against Paris. The siege was to be conducted methodically, and nothing would be risked without the fullest preparation. Many observers chafed at Thiers' slowness, *The Times* on 9 April pointing to 'the stubborn fact that [Versailles'] efforts for these last two or three weeks have failed to gain them full possession of that left bank of the Seine which is only their first line of attack', and Bismarck from time to time made noises about the Germans taking over if Thiers did not hurry up. In May a friend of Ludovic Halévy's remarked quietly, while dining at Thiers', that Paris could have been taken by a surprise attack weeks ago. Thiers, for all his seventy-four years, had an acute ear for any criticism of himself, and browbeat his visitor into silence.

Ah, my dear sir, you are one of those who believe that Paris can be entered by surprise. Be assured, that is not so. By surprise! By surprise! I have perhaps some competence in the matter. The Paris fortifications are an immense work, a work of the first order. [Thiers it should be remembered had been largely responsible for the plans of their construction in the 1840s.] They stopped the Prussians for five months. They would have held for five years, for fifty, if Paris had not run out of food. And the Commune is not short of food, as it has no difficulty in getting provisions from across the Prussian lines. Believe me, it is no small matter to get the best of the Paris fortifications. It is a colossal, gigantic enterprise. One can only succeed after a full-scale operation, after an immense military effort, thoughtfully and deliberately worked out. Ah, the Paris fortifications! I know those fortifications better than anyone else!

The next day, Halévy's friend took his revenge in telling the story by adding that Thiers did not want to see his fortifications taken too

[1] *Mémoires*, quoted by Zeller, op. cit., p. 312.

easily or too quickly: 'it must be firmly shown that only M. Thiers is capable of taking that city rendered impregnable by M. Thiers. *Amour propre* of the author.'[1] Little wonder that even the dutiful MacMahon was driven to exclaim on one occasion, 'Let it never be said that a Marshal of France received orders from a mere civilian.'[2]

With bridges across the Seine at Neuilly and after 17 April at Asnières further to the north, opening up the way to the Porte de Clichy, the Commune's forces to the west of Paris were limited to the right bank of the Seine. The 'immense military effort' Thiers had spoken of consisted in occupying the positions vacated by the Prussians to the south and west, from which the forts of Issy and Vanves could be bombarded. Once these fell, with Mont-Valérien already in the hands of Versailles and able to turn its guns on the city it had been built to defend, the army could advance its trenches up to the walls of Paris ready for the final result. Issy fell at the end of the first week in May, Vanves a week later. During this time Thiers built up his army to 130,000 men, including 30,000 prisoners freed from Germany, made sure that his officers were satisfied by back-dating the promotions of those who had been prisoners of war, constructed a special railway station at Versailles to cope with the flow of provisions, and gathered together a thousand artillery guns from all over France. Just over two months after the Government and its army had been forced to flee Paris, the capital was retaken and a week later the fighting was over. These two months were all the Commune had to try to carry into effect some of its varied aspirations. But they were long enough to create its legend.

The Commune elected on 26 March should have numbered ninety-one councillors. Resignations of the Mayors from the predominantly bourgeois districts following the example of Tirard, double elections, the deaths of Flourens and Duval, the absences of Blanqui and Garibaldi, and the resignations of the radical republicans Ranc and Ulyse Parent left thirty-one places to be filled. Ranc's resignation showed the gap between the social revolutionaries and the Gambettists, as Lefrançais calls them, Ranc having resigned from the National Assembly along with Gambetta in protest against the Peace Treaty. Ranc had been active in the republican opposition movement at the end of the Empire, and he now joined some of the other ex-Deputies and Mayors in working within Paris

[1] Halévy, op. cit., pp. 9–10.        [2] Dreyfus, op. cit., p. 326.

to bring about an end to the civil war. After some delay, on the grounds that those fighting at the front would be unable to vote,[1] by-elections were held on 16 April. The number of voters dropped by over fifty per cent in the twelve arrondissements concerned, and in the particularly bourgeois 7th, 8th, and 16th arrondissements the number of voters was below two thousand. The 18th, 19th and 20th, on the other hand, had respectable turnouts. Two of those elected refused to take their seats because they had not received the legal minimum number required, and thirteen members of the Commune voted against ratifying the election of the others who similarly had failed to receive an eighth of the registered number of voters. As Arnould, who had opposed ratification, said afterwards, 'the time for voting has passed';[2] it was a strange and unsuccessful exercise of parliamentary formalism by a revolutionary government in the midst of a civil war. But the elections did add seventeen new members to the Commune, including Seraillier and Longuet, as well as Courbet for the 6th arrondissement where he had just failed to make it on the 26th.

The Council of the Commune finally consisted of eighty-one members, though Cluseret, for example, seldom had time to attend, and many others absented themselves with far less justification. On 9 April it was proposed to keep a register of attendance and deduct a day's pay for absences. A good attendance was around sixty. The average age was thirty-eight; only four members were in their sixties, though Beslay was coming up to his seventy-sixth birthday. Rigault, at twenty-four, was the youngest of the fifteen who were in their twenties, eighteen more having only just turned thirty. The Hungarian Léo Frankel was the only foreigner who sat, he being admitted 'considering that the flag of the Commune is that of the universal Republic'.[3]

There was no obvious leader, Blanqui being the prisoner of Thiers and Garibaldi remaining in Italy – hardly surprisingly considering the way he had been treated during the war and by the Assembly at Bordeaux. Delescluze's health had been ruined as a result of imprisonment on Devil's Island for his republican revolu-

---

[1] Motion of Vallès, Vaillant, Malon, Beslay et al., 9 April: P.V.C., I, pp. 151, 155.

[2] Arnould, op. cit., vol. 3, pp. 9–13; cf. Lefrançais, another of the opposition, Etude, pp. 248–51.

[3] 30 March: P.V.C., I, p. 64.

tionary activities. He could only speak in a croaking voice, and stayed above the personal struggles and quarrels of the Commune until called upon to play a dignified but doomed role at the end.

About eighteen members came from middle-class backgrounds, from which they had quickly broken away during their school and student days. Rigault was one such figure. Jules Vallès, another, who to the despair of his father – who had worked his way up to becoming a senior-master at the Lycée at Nantes – took part in a republican demonstration when still at school at the time of the February Revolution. In 1851 Vallès' father had him locked away in a mental asylum to try to keep him out of politics. Gustave Tridon had broken away from his rich family, becoming a Blanquist historian of the Revolution. But his health was already failing at the age of thirty, his face covered with pock-marks, his back bent. After his death in August 1871 he left his fortune to Blanqui and for the spreading of socialist ideas, but his intentions were frustrated by his mother and a supposed friend. Had he not been so physically weak, Tridon might well have provided the missing leadership, for though a Blanquist he did not side with the other Blanquists over the forming of a Committee of Public Safety, an issue that split the Commune. Beslay came of a family that had done very well during the First Empire, and had himself been a successful engineer before 'breaking with the bourgeoisie in order', as he claimed, 'to defend and help the working class'.[1] There was one dubious character, Blanchet, whose real name was Pourille, who had been a Capucin monk and worked as a secretary for the Police in Lyon. This was sufficient to lead to his arrest when his dossier was discovered by Rigault at the Prefecture of Police. Versailles nonetheless condemned him *in absentia* to death for his part in the Commune.

In all there were about thirty members of the Commune who could be classed as from the professions, belonging to *la bohème*, in many cases a term of abuse at the time,[2] half of whom had been

[1] C. Beslay, *La Vérité sur la Commune*, Brussels, 1878, p. 107.

[2] Cf. Flaubert to George Sand, May 1867, reporting a visit he paid to 'an encampment of bohemians at Rouen'. What he found so 'admirable' was that 'they excite the hatred of the bourgeois, although they are as inoffensive as sheep'. Such hatred Flaubert attributed to 'something very profound and complex. It is found among all men of order. It is the same hatred as is felt against the Bedouin, the heretic, the philosopher, the solitary, the poet, and it is based on fear.' See too the article of E. Caro, '*La fin de la bohème*', *Revue des Deux Mondes*, July, 1871.

journalists on republican papers. The others included three doctors and a vet, Régère, three lawyers, one architect, Georges Arnold, three members of the teaching profession, the 'pions' of the Commune as reactionary writers called them, as well as Vaillant, who had been pursuing scientific studies in Germany up to the outbreak of the war, and Allix, who was interested in pedagogic schemes as a means of reforming society. Eleven were in commerce or worked as clerks, the most noted of whom was Jourde, the Commune's Financial Delegate, who had been a bank clerk before working for the Ministry of Roads and Bridges.

Thirty-five on the Commune were manual workers or had been before becoming involved in revolutionary politics, as had Seraillier, Frankel, Varlin and Malon. These were mainly craftsmen in the small workshops that made up the long-established trades of the capital, including one, Champy, who had been able to set himself up in a small business making cutlery. Typical of this group were copper, bronze and other metal workers, carpenters, masons, house decorators, a dyer in a factory in the industrial belt of Grenelle, V. Clément, two book-binders, Varlin and Clémence, who was the grandson of one of the Babouvists of 1796, two fancy-leather goods makers, Mortier and Henry, whose two sons Fortuné and Emile became well-known anarchists.[1]

What is noticeable is the small number from the new heavy industries that had grown up in the outskirts of Paris. Assi of the Central Committee and then of the Commune had been one of the leaders of the strike movement in the steel works at Le Creusot. Jean-Baptiste Chardon worked in the railway workshops at Ivry before he was dismissed for absenting himself to attend and speak at public meetings. Duval, an iron worker, had been a militant in the strikes of 1864 and 1870.[2] But he was shot, as has been seen, after the first battle. Chalain, though himself not working in the Cail engineering factory at Grenelle, being a bronze-turner, had been one of the main militants of the International in the 15th arrondissement. Victor Clément and Camille Langevin had also both been active Internationalists in this district, where Langevin lived, though again neither of them actually worked for Cail. Avrial, an engineering

[1] See *Dictionnaire*; a slightly different breakdown is given in Winock and Azéma, op. cit., pp. 73–4, who give number of workers as thirty-three; Rougerie, *Procès*, p. 246, gives number of workers as twenty-five.
[2] See above, p. 39.

worker and member of the International, had been one of the founders in 1869 of the Chambre syndicale, the Trade Union in effect, of the engineers. But, taking the 2000 Cail engineering workers as typical, the workers in these large-scale industries had not yet formed their own working-class traditions of organization and combat, particularly so as most of these workers in the factories in the suburbs of Paris were first-generation immigrants from the provinces.[1] They had not taken to the Internationalist propaganda of outsiders such as Chalain, Clément and Langevin, which still strongly reflected the 'mutualist' ideas of the co-operative movement. For a time during the siege the Cail workers had begun to take part in the vigilance committee movement and the National Guard federation. But when it came to the Commune it seems as if such local leadership as had developed felt too unsure of itself, too unsuited, to play a more important role on a wider scale. In the elections to the Commune from the 15th arrondissement there was a tendency to prefer petit-bourgeois and militants from the neighbouring 17th arrondissement: Vallès, for example, rather than Langevin.

The Commune voted to pay itself fifteen francs a day, though Vallès had suggested only ten. This was well above the average daily pay of the Paris workman, three to seven francs a day (women being lucky to make three francs a day), or the 1·50 of the National Guard, but was on a par with a senior officer in the National Guard or a good foreman in certain industries.[2] More important than the

---

[1] Of the Cail workers in the National Guard in 1870, eighty-nine per cent were of provincial origin: J. Gaillard, 'Les Usines Cail et les ouvriers métallurgistes de Grenelle', Le Mouvement Social, October 1960–March 1961, p. 51. The railway workers, as another example of the new industries, had been active at the end of the siege in petitioning against the conditions of their labour. Railway engineers were a highly skilled and therefore privileged group of workers. They took no part in the Commune, though probably being sympathetic to it. An official inquiry was held into their working conditions in August 1871 as a result of their agitation, but nothing was done about this until the law of 1882 passed in the very different political climate that prevailed by then: see G. Thullier, 'La Pétition des mécaniciens et des chauffeurs des chemins de fer en 1871', Le Mouvement Social, January–March 1969, pp. 65–88.

[2] A General in the National Guard received 450–500 francs a month; a colonel 360. The average male wage in Paris in 1871 was 5·0 francs a day, and for women, 2·78. In the Mulhouse textile industry in 1870, the average male wage was 22 francs, with overseers getting 52·50 francs a day. At Le Creusot certain steel workers got 10–11 francs a day: see E. Levasseur, Histoire des classes

amount was the principle, for this was an age in which both at a municipal and a national level only gentlemen could afford to take part in public affairs. During the siege an exception had been made, and Mayors and adjoints of the arrondissements had been granted a monthly salary of three hundred francs. The Municipal Law passed by the Versailles Assembly on 14 April reverted to the previous practice of having unpaid Mayors and adjoints. It was therefore, as Clément[1] who proposed the measure put it, one 'in accordance with democratic principles', even if not with egalitarian ones.

The rule of the Commune did make a sharp contrast with the previous reign of court extravagance, scandal and financial speculation. Stories were told afterwards of orgies and huge drunken feasts at the Hôtel de Ville. But in fact both there and in the Ministries the atmosphere, though always chaotic, was more one of puritan application to duty, people taking their meals while still working and grabbing a few hours sleep on sofas. Rigault, at the ex-Prefecture of Police, stands out as maintaining something of the Left Bank ambience. The fine ladies who had to see him to try to get a passport out of Paris often came away feeling very uneasy after meeting the dark bearded young man in his splendid light-blue and gold braided uniform. But like everyone else Rigault devoted most of his energies to his work, having little time to visit the Délassements Comiques Theatre where his mistress Marie Dupin acted. Eudes' wife took over Le Flô's apartments in the Ministry of War. Here she held court to the officers as well as sometimes leading troops to the ramparts on her horse, her belt bristling with revolvers, or fighting at Issy, where her husband was in command. She and Rigault would fence together. Cluseret and Rossel both resented her presence but were unable to get her to move out.[2] Just as typical, however, was Madame Jourde, the wife of the Finance Delegate, who continued to do her washing

---

*ouvrières et de l'industrie en France de 1789 à 1870*, 2nd edn., Paris, 1904, vol. 2, pp. 707–14; Bruhat, Dautry and Tersen, op. cit., p. 32; J.O., 21 November 1875, for report on Paris industry.

[1] 31 March: P.V.C., I, p. 81. It is not said which of the three Cléments this was: Jean-Baptiste, journalist and song writer; Émile, member of the International, and one of the best shoemakers in all of Paris, having made shoes for the Empress; Victor, a dyer in a small works in Grenelle.

[2] Senisse, op. cit., p. 83; Cluseret, op. cit., vol. 1, pp. 60, 157; Maxime du Camp., op. cit., vol. 2, p. 103; Michel, op. cit., p. 192.

(a) A Women's Club in the Church of Saint-Germain-l'Auxerrois

(b) The burning of the Guillotine in front of the statue of Voltaire on the Place of the Mairie of the 11th arrondissement: 6 April

7. Popular manifestations in Paris during the Commune

(c) A concert for the wounded in the Tuileries Palace: May

(*a*) Auguste Blanqui

(*b*) Jules Miot

(*c*) Félix Pyat

(*e*) Paschal Grousset

(*f*) Raoul Rigault

(*d*) Gustave Flourens

8. Revolutionaries:
Blanquists and Jacobins

(*g*) Théophile Ferré

in the public wash-house on the Seine, or Cattelain, the head of the Sûreté, the police detective department, who moved his wife into a small room on the rue de la Montagne Sainte-Genevieve by the Panthéon, which he rented for fourteen francs a month.[1] The members of the Commune could eat at the Hôtel de Ville, paying two francs for an evening meal that included half a bottle, in Arnould's view, of 'bad *vin ordinaire*'. In May for the same price the staff-officers at the Ministry of War could eat at the Mess they had formed for themselves. But generally most of the Commune continued the normal practice of eating in local cafés. Rossel at the Ministry of War could be found eating in an old cabaret in the nearby rue Saint-Dominique with Séguin, Avrial, Gérardin and Tridon, discussing socialist ideas or more often the campaigns of the first Revolution.[2]

More extravagance was evident in the National Guard. There are the usual war stories of disappearance of battalion funds or officers claiming pay for thirty or forty men when they had only two or three. On 3 May a warning was issued to those who were doing business in selling off army equipment and clothing, dealing that is in 'the property of the people'.[3] The most obvious of the excesses was the much remarked upon 'uniform mania'. Quite junior officers and officials would deck themselves out in the most elaborate uniforms covered in gold braid and rings, with a special preference for scarlet lapels. The editors of the *Père Duchêne* designed a very fine black and red uniform for the officers of a battalion they never quite got organized.[4] The staff officers of the War Ministry had a special uniform made for themselves in a 'revolutionary' style based on uniforms from the Year II with blue, white and yellow trimmings and red lapels and cuffs. Such was the effect of this sartorial elegance that they could soon boast they had 'inherited the mistresses of the *others*'.[5] The Central Committee had to establish special patrols to close down noisy cabarets and cafés whose girls chased the glittering federal officers, who too often were more inclined to carousing than

[1] Cattelain, op. cit., p. 53.
[2] See Arnould, op. cit., vol. 3, p. 59; Senisse, op. cit., pp. 84–5; L. Barron, *Sous le drapeau rouge*, Paris, 1889, p. 154; L. Séguin, 'The Ministry of War under the Commune', *Fortnightly Review*, July–December 1872, p. 138.
[3] M.P., II, p. 406.
[4] Vuillaume, op. cit., IX, pp. 337–48; it was left to a Captain Maître to take over the organization, and the *Enfants du Père Duchêne* fought during the last week on the barricades.
[5] Barron, op. cit., pp. 60–1.

to fighting. Cluseret once pointedly had to tell one of his Generals that complaints had been received about his staff, which was 'too sumptuous and rode up and down the boulevards with their *cocottes*'. Cluseret told him to 'vigorously sweep away all that lot' as 'you are compromised by them, and with you, myself and our principle'. As an economical officer of the New World Cluseret tried to stop this costly imitation of the traditions of the French Monarchy and Empire. He sent a circular to the National Guard legions remarking on the sad fact that, 'forgetting our modest origins, a ridiculous mania for lanyards, gold braid rings and embroidery has begun to appear among us. Workers, you have, for the first time, accomplished the revolution by and for labour. Let us not deny and above all do not let us be ashamed of our origins. Workers we were, workers we are, workers we shall remain.'[1] Varlin, at the Ministry of Finance, once refused to pay the bill a National Guard General had sent in for a uniform he had had especially made by the ex-Imperial tailor; 'The Commune,' replied Varlin, 'has no money for luxury clothing.'[2]

The Commune cannot be sharply divided up into political groupings, let alone parties. Blanquists, Jacobins, socialists, remain very loose descriptions, and even so do not cover every member. Nineteen of the Commune, as a case in point, had been members of the National Guard Central Committee. With a few exceptions such as Varlin or Duval these members had had no previous experience of political activity, though a number did belong to the International. In all, some forty members of the Commune had been involved in the labour movement and in most cases had joined the International. Their own experience in Trade Unions and workers' associations had given many of them a suspicion of political power and this gave an anarchist tinge to their thinking, in the manner somewhat of Proudhon or Bakunin. Of this group the book-binder Eugène Varlin was one of the most outstanding. Aged thirty-one at the time of the Commune, he had become involved in workers' education during the 1860s and in 1869 had helped found a girls' school in the 2nd arrondissement. He shared the *ouvriériste* distrust of the radical republicans, considering that the workers should keep clear of the bourgeoisie. In 1865 he had wanted to limit membership of

---

[1] Cluseret, op. cit., vol. 1, p. 75; *Enquête*, III, p. 148. *Cocotte* is slang for 'chick'.
[2] M. Foulon, *Eugène Varlin*, Paris, 1934, p. 222.

the International to 'wage earners subject to the risks of unemployment', a view supported by the French Proudhonians but opposed by Marx and the London General Council.[1] Varlin had been arrested for founding a Mutual Credit Society of bookbinders, and again for belonging to the International. He was active in the strike movement of the end of the Empire, trying to put into practice his Internationalist principles by getting French workers to support strikers in Belgium and Switzerland. At the Congress of the International at Basle in 1869 Varlin favoured the collectivization of land and supported Bakunin's proposal for the abolition of inheritance. Varlin was always strongly anti-Jacobin, anti-State, and called himself a non-authoritarian communist, or more simply a socialist. It would be through workers' co-operative societies that men would become used to the new forms of social organization of the future that would slowly transform the existing social order. Though not military or revolutionary in a Jacobin or Blanquist sense he was one of the most courageous at the end, fighting on the last barricades before being stoned to death by a mob in Montmartre, almost on the same spot where Lecomte and Clément Thomas had been shot to death.

A few of the members of the International on the Commune were Blanquists, in all about a dozen, including Duval and Eudes, two of the Commune's generals, Tridon, the author of the study of Hébert that had made a stir in 1864, and Rigault and Ferré, who dominated the police during the time of the Commune. Rigault had taken up his position at the Prefecture of Police shortly after Duval had taken the building on 18 March. The youngest member of the Commune, at twenty-four years old, he was the son of a wealthy bourgeois family, his father having been made a member of the Prefectorial Council of the Seine after 4 September. Rigault had spent most of his student days conspiring with the Blanquists and in journalism, having collaborated with Rochefort on the *Marseillaise*. Rigault rivalled Tridon in his admiration for Hébert and had been imprisoned in 1868 for a passionately anti-clerical article. He was noted for his cynical humour and revolutionary purity. When one of the arrested Jesuits answered Rigault's formal question as to his profession with the reply, 'Servant of God', Rigault impassively continued by asking him 'Where does your master live?' 'Everywhere,' was the Jesuit's answer. Rigault then calmly dictated to one of his

[1] Foulon, op. cit., p. 55; a factor in the French attitude was their hostility to the French exiles' branch of the International in London.

secretaries: 'Write down, X, calling himself the servant of one called God, a vagrant.'[1] Cattelain, made head of the detective branch by Rigault, who was no Blanquist and showed rather a sentimental softness compared to his superior's sternness, said that though Rigault believed 'revolutionary laws are never severe enough', he also showed himself 'open to feelings of humanity'.[2] To this generosity Auguste Renoir owed his life when, unmindfully painting a sketch of the Seine, he was arrested as a spy by some National Guards. A woman in the crowd wanted him thrown into the river at once, but instead he was marched off to the Mairie of the 6th arrondissement. Rigault happened to be there and Renoir managed to catch his eye. Rigault at once recognized Renoir as the painter who a few years previously had hidden him for several weeks from the police, when Rigault on the run had come across Renoir painting in the forest at Fontainbleau. Rigault embraced Renoir 'touchingly', at once had him freed, and gave him a safe conduct pass with the warning not to get caught by the Versailles with it.[3] Rigault was shot during the last week and left dead in the gutter of the Boulevard Saint-Michel for two days, covered only with a coat thrown over his body by the patronne of one of his favourite bars.

Ferré, Rigault's second-in-command at the Prefecture, twenty-four years old, had been a legal clerk, and had met Tridon and other Blanquists when in prison for a speech at one of the public meetings in 1869. He was short, thick-set, having neither the elegant appearance of Rigault nor his humour. Behind his glasses cold eyes expressed his determination to let nothing hinder the triumph of the revolution. Cattelain, again, found him frightening: 'he would have killed, but completely without any feeling, if he thought it would help bring the triumph of his ideas'.[4] Ferré was one of the two members of the Commune to be executed afterwards. At his trial he never flinched before his judges, accepting full responsibility for his acts: 'Member of the Paris Commune, I am in the hands of its conquerors; they want my head, let them take it! I will never save my life by cowardice. I have lived as a free man, I intend to die as one! Only one word will I add: fortune is capricious; I confide to the future the care of my memory and of my vengeance.'

The Blanquists were at a loss without their leader. They had been

[1] Da Costa, op. cit., vol. 1, pp. 392–3; see too vol. 2, pp. 128–9.
[2] Chalain, op. cit., pp. 81, 110.        [3] Renoir, op. cit., pp. 118–19.
[4] Chalain, op. cit., p. 116.

among the most insistent in trying to persuade the Central Committee to attack Versailles immediately following 18 March. Having failed to do this, their main remaining hope was to get Blanqui out of jail and back to Paris, for, as Rigault said, 'nothing can be done without the Old One'.[1] One way of doing this would be by an exchange of prisoners, and the Blanquists had been quick to make arrests for this purpose. For this reason Duval had wanted to keep General Chanzy when he was arrested on 18 March. Chanzy, as has been seen, was released by the Central Committee. But other notables arrested were not so lucky. Judge Bonjean, a highly respected member of the Paris courts, was kept in prison as a valuable hostage, so it was hoped, after he had made the mistake of trying to carry on court business as normal after the Central Committee had taken over. Rigault's anti-clericalism suspected all priests of being Versailles' agents, and as soon as the war broke out he started making arrests. The most celebrated among these was the Archbishop of Paris, Monsignor Darboy, who gently protested when brought before Rigault that the clergy could not be held responsible for the horrors of a civil war since their mission was to pacify men's spirits. 'That's enough,' replied Rigault, cutting him short: 'you have been doing that to us for the last eighteen centuries, it won't wash any more.'[2] The Archbishop did agree to write to Thiers asking him to end the civil war, or 'at least to soften its character'. This Thiers in his reply denied needed doing since, as he assured the Archbishop, it was a lie that the army was killing prisoners. A second letter from Monsignor Darboy suggesting the release of Blanqui, as this was a matter only 'of people, not principles',[3] received no answer from Thiers. Nor would the Government at Versailles accede to the representations made on the Archbishop's behalf by Washburne, the American Ambassador. On the contrary, Thiers was very angry by what he called the *conduite très singulière*', of the American representative.[4] Nor had the Archbishop any friends among the monarchist Right in the Assembly, being a Gallican. He had openly been reprimanded by the Pope for

[1] Da Costa, op. cit., vol. 2, p. 194.
[2] Da Costa, op. cit., vol. 1, p. 395.
[3] Letters of 8, 12 April: Da Costa, op. cit., pp. 415, 421; also J.O., 27 April.
[4] Lord Newton, op. cit., pp. 384–5; Lyons himself had made a few tactful overtures on Darboy's behalf. *The Times* correspondent visited the prisoners: issue of 1 May.

blessing the coffin of the Grand Master of the Freemasons. As an alternative plan, therefore, one of Blanqui's closest companions left Paris to try to discover where he was and free him. But it took time to trace Blanqui's whereabouts, especially as Thiers had him transferred to another prison, and there was more delay before it was decided to take money from the police coffers to bribe the guards. Before very much could be accomplished the Commune had been defeated, and the leading revolutionary figure in France had to sit out the second revolution of his lifetime in a prison cell.

The other fervent admirers of the first Revolution were the Jacobins, and Delescluze would probably have resented Blanqui's presence in Paris. The Jacobins were not a united group, simply on the whole the older members, the men of '48, who shared a common admiration for Robespierre. In this of course they were not alone, and at least half the members of the Commune were only too willing to revive the tradition of '93. Felix Pyat was the most noted of the older Jacobins after Delescluze. But his early revolutionary passions, which had led him to become a member of the Mountain in the 1849 Assembly, had turned to rancour after years of exile. His journalism had degenerated into irresponsible revolutionary rhetoric. This in no way diminished his popularity, which had been strengthened by his fierce criticism of the Government during the siege; it was his paper, the *Combat*, that had been suppressed for publishing the rumour of the fall of Metz in October 1870. Pyat's revolutionary past, his lawyer's oratory and impressive appearance on top of his sixty years, gave him an unfortunate ascendancy over many members of the Commune. He was always trying to make sure that he was not being outdistanced on the left, seeing all issues in terms of his own suspicious pride, whilst being careful to make sure of his escape when it was clear that the adventure was over. Maxime Vuillaume, for a time an admirer of Pyat, said he was 'the devil of a romantic, living only by his "immortal souvenirs" '; Vermorel called him 'an arm-chair conspirator', and Malon, to his face in the midst of a heated row in the council, 'the evil genius of the Commune'.[1] Marx, who tried to warn the Commune against him, would have agreed with the Blanquist revolutionary Thoumieux who said to his

[1] Vuillaume, op. cit., III, p. 309; Vermorel quoted in Bruhat, Dautry and Tersen, op. cit., p. 412; Malon in P. Lanjalley and P. Corriez, *Histoire de la révolution du 18 mars*, Paris, 1871, p. 435.

friend Martial Senisse when they saw Pyat in the street: 'he needs muzzling to stop him turning our revolution into a melodrama'.[1]

Jules Miot, the same age as Pyat and with the same white beard, could be included among the Jacobins, having been a deputy in 1848. Miot, however, did have some contact with the labour movement, being a member of the International and for a time in exile a friend of Lefrançais. So too could Paschal Grousset, the Foreign Affairs Delegate, a medical student and journalist on the *Marseillaise* at the time of the Victor Noir affair, whom some called the best-dressed man on the Commune. Grousset was always favourable to the most extreme measures as a sign of his revolutionary ardour. Unlike the older Jacobins, Grousset, being only twenty-six years old, had not been through the experience of 1848. Flourens, too, was a revolutionary adventurer, always thrusting for action. But the most noble representative of the Jacobin tradition was Delescluze himself, sixty years old at the time of the Commune, whom none except Blanqui could excel in revolutionary purity, having devoted his life and ruined his health in the cause of the Republic. In 1848 Delescluze had defined his 'social democratic revolution' in terms of the Constitution of 1793 and the 'declaration of rights formulated by Robespierre'. At this time Delescluze was demanding free public education, progressive taxation, the nationalization of banks and public utilities such as the railways, the reform of the legal system and the 'establishment of the right to work with all the consequences of this'.[2] By 1871 Delescluze had not changed the basis of his position, though he had sympathized without ever associating himself with the efforts of the International in the late 1860s. During most of the Commune he played a restrained role, feeling, as he once put it, that 'we old ones should efface ourselves before the younger generation . . . Perhaps I represent the ideas of another century.'[3] In the tragedy of the last week, he walked deliberately to his death on a barricade at the Place du Château d'Eau (today the Place de la République).

'Time,' as Marx said, 'was not allowed to the Commune';[4] time in which to implement its social reforms, time in which to crystallize

---

[1] Senisse, op. cit., p. 71, 28 March.

[2] *La Révolution démocratique et sociale*, 7 November 1848: quoted Dessal, op. cit., pp. 75–6.

[3] C. Prolès, *Les Hommes de la révolution de 1871*, Paris, 1898, pp. 96–7.

[4] *Civil War in France*, MESW, p. 299.

its political nature. The first thought of the Commune had been simply to appoint Delegates to take over the various Ministries evacuated by Versailles. These were divided up into eight Commissions, though as a portent of socialist intentions a new department was created, the Commission of Labour and Exchange. These nine Commissions were to be supervised and coordinated by an Executive Commission of seven: the three 'generals' of the Commune, Eudes, Duval and Bergeret, and four civilians, Tridon, Vaillant, Lefrançais and the ever-present Pyat. The role of the Communal Council itself was never settled. The Commune refused to consider itself a parliamentary body, believing that belonged to the old order represented by Versailles. Its rambling debates could well give the opposite impression; Ledroit said on one occasion that it was a good job the public were not admitted because 'so much abuse, such insults' could only bring the Republic and the Commune into disrepute.[1] There was much personal acrimony, matters were often dropped instead of decisions being reached, and entirely unrelated points were raised in the midst of debates and then pursued. Amouroux was not the first to 'demand the floor for an extremely serious personal matter', when the assembly was supposed to be debating the formation of a Committee of Public Safety.[2] This turned out to be the daily report of proceedings published in the *Journal Officiel*, about which there were endless recriminations.

The first session of the Commune had voted that its meetings would be kept secret, on the grounds that it was 'a council of war' as Grousset described it. But under pressure from Lefrançais, Arnould, Jourde, Vallès and others it was eventually agreed that a summary of each day's proceedings would be published in the *Journal Officiel*,[3] especially as accounts were being leaked to the Press. It was also eventually decided on 3 May that the public should be admitted to all but the 'secret sessions', of which there were eleven. But there was a problem in finding a big enough room for the Commune to meet in, as the Municipal Council Chamber in the Hôtel de Ville was not suitable for such democratic procedures. Courbet and Billioray were commissioned to produce a report. They came up with the hardly revolutionary recommendation that the Commune should shift its meetings to the Tuileries Palace. Arnould was not

---

[1] 8 May: P.V.C., II, p. 254.
[2] 1 May: P.V.C., II, p. 16.
[3] 11 April: P.V.C., I, p. 172. First account published in J.O., 15 April.

alone in rejecting this suggestion on the grounds that the Commune should not 'break with tradition' by leaving the Hôtel de Ville, 'the natural seat of the elected representatives of the Paris Commune'.[1] The issue was left unresolved.

At the first full session Ranc had said the new municipal council should give itself the name of Paris Commune as being the only way of 'indicating that the great city desires its municipal franchises fully and completely, in a word, "Self-Government" '. This too was the theme of Ranc, together with Vallès and Lefrançais, when they were asked to draw up the first proclamation of the Commune. Their idea was 'to reduce' the role of the Commune to that of 'a simple executive organ', directly expressing popular sovereignty through handing over responsibility to the workers' associations and arron-dissement organizations.[2] As Arthur Arnould afterwards put it, the twenty or thirty members most concerned with social reforms wanted the revolution to be one that would overturn 'the ancient relation of governing and governed'.[3] The opening speech by Beslay had interpreted the revolution as a presage of the liberation of all 'the communes of the Republic'. The Paris Commune was to be a model for the others in its 'order, economy, honesty and strict controls', whose future was not one of war but of *Peace and Labour!*'

The same federalist theme of Communal liberties runs through the only official declaration by the Commune of its own principles. Public opinion demanded some such announcement, it being a com-plaint among the bourgeoisie that ever since 18 March they had been governed by men whose principles they did not know. Some of the revolutionary papers also called on the Commune to issue a pro-gramme. Lissagaray, on 9 April, in his paper, *L'Action*, said 'we have the right to be impatient about the programme of the Commune', and when it was published *La Commune* expressed a sigh of relief that at last it had appeared. The question of the programme resolved around whether the Commune should stay within the limits of being a purely municipal government for Paris or a revolutionary govern-ment for all of France. The Central Committee had interpreted the revolution of 18 March as simply Parisian, and had used this as a

[1] 10 May: P.V.C., II, p. 314.
[2] Lefrançais, op. cit., pp. 196–8, 300. The Commune preferred the more vibrant declaration drawn up by Paschal Grousset *et al.*: cf. above, p. 188.
[3] Arnould, op. cit., vol. 2, p. 85.

reason for not at once attacking Versailles. Billioray, one of the ex-Central Committee members on the Commune, took up this view in the discussion on the Declaration in opposition to the Blanquist lawyer Protot, who, according to Billioray, wanted a 'dictatorial power governing France'.[1] The Jacobin Delescluze was one of the committee appointed to draw up the programme, but he took little part, preferring to leave this task to the younger members. However, neither Vallès, Malon nor Thiesz seemed very interested, and finally it was left to the Proudhonian journalist Pierre Denis to draft the Declaration, which was adopted after hardly any discussion. The 'Declaration to the French People' was accordingly very federalist in tone, saying Paris had simply claimed her municipal rights and inviting the other communes to do the same: 'The political unity, such as Paris wishes it, is the voluntary association of all local initiatives, the free and spontaneous concourse of all individual energies for the common aim, the well-being, the liberty and the security of all.'[2] This echoed somewhat the October Declaration of the Central Committee of the Twenty Arrondissements, which had said communes should be 'free, autonomous and sovereign bodies'.[3] But the programme did not express the consciousness of the revolutionary districts in Paris, which were not interested in matters of federal constitutional reform. Among those who it might be expected would be interested, the feeling, according to Élie Reclus, was more one of 'irritation',[4] for the idea of France being broken up into several thousand independent communes was hardly realistic and went against the feeling of many Parisians that for far too long the reactionary countryside had prevented France from having a Republic. Had the Declaration been published before war had broken out it could have been seen as an attempt to win the sympathy of the provinces. But instead it came out in the midst of the civil war, and Picard made sure that very few copies outside of Paris escaped the notice of the police.

Régère was right when he said in the debate that the only admissible programme was 'our acts and our decrees. This demand to

[1] 8 April: P.V.C., I, p. 273.
[2] J.O., 20 April. English translation published in *The Times*, 21 April. The next day *The Times* correspondent commented that, in his view, the Declaration was a misinterpretation of the ideas of Proudhon on Communalism.
[3] See above, p. 73.
[4] Reclus, op. cit., p. 165; cf. Mendès, op. cit., pp. 190–201.

formulate a programme has come from outside; if we want to remain united we don't need a discussion that will only cause divisions among us.'[1] The ideal of a purely municipal revolution ignored the fact that almost from the start the Commune had to fight for its very existence, and the major problem quickly became that of its military organization, one it never came close to solving. As the Versailles troops progressed towards capturing the defences surrounding the capital, so the Commune found itself increasingly forced towards the Jacobin ideal of a strong directing executive, culminating in the formation of a five-man Committee of Public Safety at the beginning of May.

One of the main organizational difficulties of the Commune was the continuing existence of the Central Committee of the National Guard and the legion committees on which it was based. In appointing a military commission the Commune assumed it was going to take over the National Guard, this being the only army it had. The first act of the Commune had been to declare that the National Guard and its Central Committee 'had deserved well of Paris and of the Republic',[2] implying that its services were now over. But, although nearly a quarter of those elected to the Commune came from the Central Committee, this latter body refused to simply disappear. Had not the whole revolution arisen out of the issue of who was to control the National Guard? Having formed itself into its own autonomous federation, the Central Committee was determined to continue looking after its own interests. The delegation the Central Committee sent to the second session of the Commune announced they would 'resume the functions defined by our statutes' and refused all requests to dissolve itself. The majority of the Commune were not willing to contest this and agreed that the Central Committee should remain 'the right hand of the Revolution ... the great *conseil de famille* of the National Guard'.[3] The next day, strengthening its position, the Central Committee announced it would be holding elections to complete its own number, and that it had appointed Cluseret to the Ministry of War.[4] This was clearly the moment for the Commune to assert its own authority, as several members proposed, Grousset, for example, calling for the dissolution of the Central Committee and the assumption of all its powers

---

[1] 18 April: P.V.C., I, p. 273.    [2] 28 March: P.V.C., I, p. 21; J.O., 29 March.
[3] Lissagaray, op. cit., pp. 157-8; P.V.C., I, p. 36.
[4] J.O., 31 March; P.V.C., I, p. 76, 31 March.

by the Commune. But in the end the Commune decided that it could not engage in an open conflict with what was, after all, the basis of its power. On 3 April the Commune, on the proposition of Pyat, ratified Cluseret at the Ministry of War. This did not satisfy the Central Committee, which soon was attacking Cluseret's conduct of the war as well as criticizing its own ex-members on the Commune for paying more attention to the Commune than to the National Guard. So great was this suspicion that by mid-April the Central Committee was considering forbidding any of its own members to stand in the coming by-elections so as not to weaken itself in relation to the Commune. In the event two more from the Central Committee were elected. But there was definitely a desire that ex-Committee members on the Commune should act as representatives of the National Guard. Only the architect Arnold, one of those elected on 16 April, ever really tried to do so.

Throughout the second siege the National Guard Central Committee continued to maintain its independence, claiming that it was the military power, the Commune being only the 'political and administrative power'. Edouard Moreau, who had come to the fore with no particular revolutionary antecedents on that first night at the Hôtel de Ville, preaching at that time moderation towards Versailles, was now urging the National Guard to take charge again and force the Commune into more revolutionary paths. The Central Committee made an attempt to produce its own newspaper, and awarded each of its members a 'commemorative medal' for their part in the revolution of 18 March. Moreau's opposition to the Commune extended to more than just the running of the war. Once he claimed that 'the Commune would have taken a different direction if the Central Committee had remained in power, and many bad measures would not have been taken'.[1] Some idea of what this could have meant can be gained from the Central Committee's poster published on 5 April, which was far more vigorous than anything published by the Commune itself:

> Citizens of Paris, we are back to the great days of sublime heroism and supreme virtue! ... Workers, do not be deceived: this is the final struggle, that of parasitism against labour, exploitation against production. If you are fed up of vegetating in

[1] See meetings of 11, 12, 23 April: Enquête, III, pp. 73, 77–80, 135. Their paper, La Fédération républicaine de la Garde Nationale, had three issues in April.

ignorance and of wallowing in misery; if you want your children to be men getting the profit of their own labour, and not a sort of animal trained for the workshop or the battlefield, sweating themselves to make the fortunes of an exploiter or spilling their blood for a despot; if you no longer want your daughters, whom you cannot bring up and look after as you would like, to become objects of pleasure for the arms of that aristocrat, money; if you want an end to poverty forcing men to join the police and women the ranks of prostitution; finally workers, if you want the reign of justice, be intelligent and arise! And with your strong hands bring down vile reaction to be trodden under your feet![1]

In spite of all its claims, the Central Committee was no more able than the Commune or the Ministry of War to control the National Guard in Paris. The National Guard was never brought under any central control, maintaining its independence at the most local level. Battalions acted of their own accord, refusing in some cases to fight at all or more often simply failing to turn out on duty. Cluseret claims he had to call up 10,000 men to get 3,000, with the result that it became increasingly difficult to relieve those at the front. *The Times* correspondent noticed on 30 April that only 700 out of a battalion of 1,400 had assembled in front of the Madeleine, and 200 of these were reluctant to march to the front.[2] The anarchy of the period before March continued under the Commune. Verdure at his trial said that both the Commune and the Central Committee were 'all the time overwhelmed by the National Guard'.[3] Guards arrested anyone they suspected. Rossel was arrested by his own men in the 17th arrondissement; Ferrat of the Central Committee was nearly arrested at the Mairie of the 6th arrondissement because he had criticized the behaviour of some Guards. M. Dernière, a Manager of the Bank of France, was arrested early in April for having expressed his surprise on seeing a Guardsman wearing the Legion of Honour 'that a man who had received such a distinction should be seen with so ruffianly a band'. Beslay had him released the next day,

[1] J.O., 7 April; cf. Lissagaray, op. cit., p. 185: the Central Committee 'very distinctively set forth the character of this context, that had become a social one, and pointed out behind the struggle for municipal liberties that devouring sphinx, the question of the proletariat'.

[2] 1 May.

[3] *Procès de la Commune. Compte rendu*, 1st series, p. 100; cf. Ferrat (p. 102) and Rastoul (p. 107).

and apologized.[1] Cattelain, the chief of the Sûreté, was threatened one night in his own office by ten or so drunken Guards. Next morning, furious, he went and accused Ferré of plotting his arrest. Ferré icily replied that he had had nothing to do with the incident and that in any case if he wanted to punish Cattelain for treason, 'I would not employ anyone but kill you myself'.[2]

Part of the trouble was Cluseret's own fault, for in a military manner he had instituted conscription for every unmarried man between seventeen and thirty-five.[3] The National Guard had the task of enforcing this decree, 'each company, each battalion, each legion' being authorized by Cluseret to 'act as its own police', and he even put a whole prison at their disposal.[4] The National Guard would seal off areas and round up all the young men, stopping buses to make arrests, chasing through the streets those who tried to avoid arrest. One English gentleman, 'of good family and position', was unfortunate enough to be picked up with no passport, and so *l'anglais* became a member of the Commune's cavalry regiment. Once he had to deliver a message to Dombrowski at Neuilly, and the latter was so pleased to hear that Englishmen were volunteering, as it seemed, for service in the Commune that the young man nearly found himself in the front line. At the end he was taken prisoner by Versailles and nearly deported.[5] Most Frenchmen were more circumspect. One bourgeois of the Latin Quarter caused his arm to swell up in boils and walked around with it in a sling.[6] Catulle Mendès bought a *laisser-passer* signed with the magic name of Félix Pyat from the widow of a National Guard killed in action.[7] Conscription could not ensure devoted fighters for the Commune, and excluding those aged over thirty-five meant many revolutionaries who had fought in '48 could not join the fighting until the battle came inside Paris during the last week. One Guard defended himself to the Rev. Gibson with the rather dubious excuse that he only fired in the air; but he can well be believed when he said he wore civvies under his uniform so as to be able to seize any chance to escape.[8]

[1] *The Times*, 12 April.    [2] Cattelain, op. cit., p. 120.    [3] J.O., 5 April.
[4] Order given in *Enquête*, III, pp. 144–5.
[5] He told his story anonymously in *Macmillans's Magazine*, September–October 1871, 'A Victim of Paris and Versailles'.
[6] Dabot, op. cit., p. 193.
[7] Mendès, op. cit., pp. 277–8.    [8] Gibson, op. cit., pp. 122–3.

Other signs of the lack of any central control were the constant requisitioning, the occupation of churches, schools and other public buildings as well as sometimes the private houses of wealthy individuals. Often this expressed the revolutionary determination of local commanders to rout out reactionaries and draft-dodgers and seize any hidden arms, and was done with the agreement of the local municipality. But at the end of April the 9th and 12th arrondissements had to ask the National Guards to evacuate the churches in which they had billeted themselves.[1] And Paschal Grousset, as the Delegate for Foreign Affairs, had to apologize profusely when a battalion invaded the Belgian Consulate in the 8th arrondissement in search of some Parisians they thought had entered to escape military service.[2] Elections were also being held in the fire brigades.[3] Cluseret had to reprimand the National Guard for firing their cannons all the time as this 'reduced supplies and irritated the population'.[4] The artillery battalions were in effect a law unto themselves, having their own arrondissement committee which refused to merge itself with the main National Guard Central Committee, and presented its own candidates in the April elections for the Commune.[5] Rossel, when he took over the Ministry of War, was particularly furious that he could not get the large number of cannons theoretically available assembled together so they could be used in the defence.

The difficulty of bringing the National Guard under any central control reveals the fragmented nature of the Communal revolution in Paris, which remained entrenched at the local level of *quartier* and arrondissement. It never managed to organize itself very successfully above that level, and the resort to street barricades and fighting by *quartiers* during the last week was not just the last line of defence; it was truly in the spirit of '71, just as had been the earlier barricades of the 1830s and 1848. The 17th arrondissement, for example, though at the extreme western edge of the revolutionary movement, had become practically independent of the Hôtel de Ville during the siege. As has been seen, Malon and Varlin played a prominent part in this, and immediately after 18 March the National Guard had finally taken over the Mairie. But on the night of 22–23 March, the

---

[1] J.O., 28 April.    [2] J.O., 17, 23 April; P.V.C., I, p. 238.
[3] *La Montagne*, 2 April.    [4] J.O., 9 April.
[5] 14 April, *Enquête*, III, pp. 95–6; their electoral address is given in Firmin Maillard, *Affiches, Professions de Foi, Documents officiels*, Paris, 1871, pp. 193–4.

local 'republican committee' led by Charles Gérardin, Emile Clément and Chalain, all future members of the Commune for this arrondissement, occupied the Mairie in opposition to Malon, whom they suspected of being too conciliatory towards Versailles. At this time Malon, having just returned from Bordeaux and knowing therefore the hostility of the countryside to Paris, was trying to work for a compromise. In turn the National Guard expelled the republican committee, but Malon joined Mayor Favre in publishing a protest at the occupation of the Mairie.[1] The election of Malon and Varlin, together with Gérardin, Clément and Chalain of the local republican committee, to the Commune did not put an end to these local conflicts. Rossel, who was the commander of the 17th legion for a few days, described the local National Guard committee as 'the most idiotic little despotism imaginable'.[2] Gérardin and Malon insisted on appointing their own nominee Jaclard as head of the National Guard so as to give them control over the armed power in the arrondissement. Jaclard's first action was to clear the legion council out from the Mairie. The legion persisted in its opposition and elected a new head for itself, choosing an ex-lieutenant-colonel of an army free-corps, Muley. Such was the bitterness between the two rival commanders that Jaclard and Muley nearly had a duel. The legion also appealed to Cluseret and to the Central Committee, the latter naturally supporting Muley as the legion's own choice. Gérardin, on the other hand, tried to get the official support of the Commune declaring that 'the 17th arrondissement is in a complete state of revolution', but the matter was considered to be a purely municipal one.[3] In the end Jaclard had to retire, but the legion was in considerable disorder as a result of the dispute. Afterwards, in a letter to the papers, Muley boasted that he had only wanted the command in order to be able to deliver the Porte de Clichy and the Porte de Maillot to Versailles.[4]

Part of the difficulty came from the members of the Commune trying to administer their arrondissements by acting as Mayors. Régère and Allix seem to have been very active on the local level, but generally the arrondissements suffered from not having a

[1] D'Esbœufs, op. cit., pp. 32–9; M.P., II, p. 31.
[2] Rossel, op. cit., p. 221; cf. above pp. 192–3 on the 17th arrondissement.
[3] 1 May: P.V.C., II, p. 15; Enquête, III, pp. 130, 134, 143: 21, 22, 27 April; D'Esbœufs, op. cit., pp. 68–94.
[4] B. Malon, La Troisième défaite du prolétariat français, Neuchatel, 1871, p. 298.

representative of the central power regularly present. Municipal Commissions were chosen to see to day-to-day affairs. Arnould claims to have had good relations with the municipal commission of his arrondissement, the 4th, and with the National Guard legion council, whose second-in-command – a twenty-eight-year-old furniture designer, married with two children – he had met when they had both been on the *Marseillaise* together.[1] In the 5th arrondissement matters were far from cordial between Mayor Régère, a Catholic, and Allemane, the legion commander, an atheist.[2] The Central Committee of the Twenty Arrondissements, aware of the problem of local control, suggested that the Commune double its numbers, 'considering that the Paris Commune of 1792 had 240 members at a time when the population was barely half as large'.[3] Little wonder Arnould afterwards, in complaining of being overburdened with duties, could only recollect getting ten proper nights' sleep during his time on the Commune.[4]

The conflict between the Commune and the National Guard erupted when Cluseret in an attempt to enforce discipline set up on 16 April a Court Martial presided over by Rossel. Cluseret followed this up by personally arresting one of the members of the Central Committee, Ferrat, a battalion commander from the 20th arrondissement, for being absent from his post at Issy without permission. The Central Committee protested against the violation of what it considered was its sanctuary, Cluseret having carried out the arrest in the midst of a meeting of the Committee, for they feared they were all going to be arrested. The offending officer was released a few days later, but the Central Committee took the incident as a sign of the Commune's 'machinations' against itself.[5] In turn the Commune felt threatened when the officers of the 105th battalion of the Faubourg Saint-Germain in the 7th arrondissement were arrested for having refused to march against the enemy. Some of the Guards of the battalion tried but failed to force the prison in which their officers were being held, and the Court Martial cashiered the officers,

[1] Arnould, op. cit., vol. 3, pp. 53–8.
[2] Allemane, op. cit., p. 71.
[3] Maillard, op. cit., p. 165; cf. Lefrançais, op. cit., pp. 212–13, who makes this same criticism.
[4] Arnould, op. cit., vol. 2, p. 112.
[5] Cluseret, op. cit., vol. 1, pp. 140–1; *Enquête*, III, pp. 122–7, 19, 20 April; *Dictionnaire*, VI, p. 37.

who were disqualified from holding any civil or military office. The battalion was dissolved 'in view of the collective cowardice of all its soldiers'. But, as Rossel himself admitted afterwards, dissolving this battalion would remove the main organized political support of the Commune in the 7th arrondissement, a notably bourgeois area. Rossel's own father had commanded this same battalion during the siege. It was a straight political military conflict, and the Commune felt it had to quash the decision, in spite of the protests of Cluseret: 'You can if you wish put political matters above military, but in that case I decline all responsibility for the consequences that will result.'[1] Rossel at once resigned and thought of withdrawing completely from 'this incoherent revolution', as he could but call it.[2]

By now Cluseret himself was under attack, and the members of the Commune in an unaccustomed display of decisiveness fired questions at him concerning his stocks, number of men, state of the defences, which Cluseret could barely answer, admitting he did not know how many guns were available, nor how many men. The Commune, as a sign of its distrust of its War Delegate, decided on 23 April to appoint a commission of inquiry into the administration of the war. Cluseret was being made the scapegoat for the failure of the Commune to control the National Guard and of the National Guard to be able to organize itself. Cluseret, however, was not the sort of commander who could overcome this factionalization of the war effort. At the time his critics called him a second Trochu because of his inaction. Cluseret's own explanation was that the National Guard would never be solid enough to take the offensive against Versailles in the open field. Paris therefore would have to remain on the defensive, behind its impregnable walls, conserving its men and munitions, and wait for the provinces to rise in support. As a result of his experiences in the Ligue du Midi during the winter of 1870 Cluseret had deceived himself into thinking that this would not be long. Making the best of the situation he was faced with in Paris, Cluseret actually claimed it was a merit to have used so few men, not more than 6,500 along the whole line of the defence. He treated the demands of his commanders, who were crying out for reinforcements, as exaggerations. Nothing seems to have been able to dent his immense self-confidence in his own understanding of the war and of the Paris population, for which, again like Trochu, he considered he had a special understanding. In the midst of the frenetic activity

[1] 23 April: P.V.C., I, pp. 396-7.          [2] Rossel, op. cit., p. 231.

that surrounded the War Ministry Cluseret remained, as he put it, 'calm', showing only 'sang-froid, nonchalance or indifference, depending on the taste or urbanity of my detractors'.[1]

These latter included by the end of April practically everyone on the Commune, the Central Committee and the Military Delegation. Partly as a result of Cluseret's insistence the Commune had made an attempt in the third week of April to improve its own exercise of authority by abolishing the Executive Commission, leaving the Delegates of the nine commissions to act rather as cabinet ministers, meeting each day among themselves and reporting back to the whole Commune. Already during the debate on this reorganization the idea had been expressed of forming a 'dictatorship' of three members – or even one, and Delescluze in true Jacobin fashion had insisted on the need for a single *volonté*, will, to give unity of action. There was growing up within the Commune a fear of a military dictatorship, hardly surprisingly considering the Bonapartist tradition, and suspicion unjustifiably fell on Cluseret and his Court Martial. Better for the Commune to establish its own dictatorial body it was thought than to have one imposed by the military.[2]

Accordingly, faced with a military crisis, the fort at Issy, the key to the Paris defence, being on the verge of falling, the Commune voted on 1 May to crown itself with 'a pastiche of the Revolution', as Vaillant called it,[3] and accept the proposal sprung on the assembly by the Jacobin Miot of creating a five-man Committee of Public Safety. This was a strange anachronistic mixing of contradictory elements from the first Revolution, for it had been the Committee of Public Safety under Robespierre that on behalf of the National Convention had crushed the Commune of Paris. The Blanquists at least should have realized this, for it had been the theme of Tridon's defence of Hébert and attack on Robespierre. Lefrançais did use this as an argument in defending his opposition to the creation of a Committee of Public Safety at a meeting with his electors.[4] Everyone, as Lissagaray said, was agreed on 'the necessity of strengthening the central control and action', and there had been a unanimous vote on the need to create a tight executive committee.[5] The bitter quarrel came over the name 'Committee of Public Safety', which was

[1] Cluseret, op. cit., vol. 1, p. 180; cf. pp. 137–8, 176, 207.
[2] Cf. Billioray, 28 April, P.V.C., I, p. 558.     [3] 30 April: P.V.C., I, p. 585.
[4] Cf. below, p. 247.
[5] 30 April: P.V.C., I, p. 587.

finally adopted by a majority of thirty-four to twenty-eight.[1] Elected on to it were Arnaud, a Blanquist member of the International who had been on the *Marseillaise*; Ranvier, a decorator; Melliet, a legal clerk and Blanquist member of the International who had been active in the democratic club of the 13th arrondissement; Charles Gérardin, clerk and commercial traveller, of the 17th arrondissement and, needless to say, Félix Pyat.

The Jacobins were all in favour, Pyat saying his reason was that 'the word Public Safety is exactly of the same period as the words French Republic and Paris Commune'. Charles Longuet countered this argument by saying he was against the name because he 'no more believed in words of salvation than in talismans and amulets'. Courbet, showing the result of his friendship with Proudhon, was against the title, considering it belonged to a past epoch that was no longer relevant to 'this republican socialist movement. What we represent is the period that has passed between '93 and '71 ... Let us employ the terms suggested by our own revolution.'[2] But too many in the Commune had their heads full of the slogans of 1793 to be able to think of creating entirely new forms. The civil war made comparisons with '93 only too simple. The *Rappel*, a radical repub-

---

[1] 1 May: P.V.C., II, pp. 21–2; there was a larger majority in the vote on the project as a whole: 45 to 23 majority.

[2] P.V.C., II, pp. 33–7. Proudhon, *Le Représentant du Peuple*, 29 August 1848, had written: 'to create the new industrial forms of society does not call for the temperament of '93'. Courbet's electoral address expressed the same view, Maillard, op. cit., pp. 213–14: 'A profession of faith is asked of me. Is this because I have not been able to make my ideas understood after thirty years of public life? Nonetheless I submit to this requirement, since the language of a painter is not familiar to everyone. I have constantly been occupied with the social question and the philosophies that deal with this, taking a parallel course to that of my comrade Proudhon ... I have fought against all forms of governmental authority and of divine right, wanting man to govern himself by himself in accordance with his own needs, to his direct profit and following his own conception ... To sum up in two words and fully taking into account the American and Swiss Republics, let us consider our own as if it were born but yesterday. Consequently let us abandon vengeance, reprisals, violence, and let us set up a completely new order of things that belongs to us and is dependent solely on ourselves. I am happy to tell you that the painters, at my instigation, have just taken such an initiative. If all the groupings in society follow this example no government will be able in the future to prevail over ours ... In fact, the present Commune will become the federal council of the associations.' On Courbet's Painters' Association, see below, pp. 304–6.

lican paper going back to the election campaign of 1869, vainly pointed out on 3 May that 'we know the new Committee of Public Safety will not be the same as the old one. Why therefore does it take the same name? The revolutionaries of '92 had their creations and titles, let us have our own. Let us be, for once, men of the present.' But many of the Jacobins and Blanquists were engaged precisely in trying to play the roles of their great ancestors and were not willing to let the dead bury the dead.[1] For the Revolution in France had remained a living force and nothing was more natural than that the Commune should seek to interpret itself as a continuation of this tradition, 'an eternal messianism',[2] which in itself became an historical model for revolution in Europe in the twentieth century.

The division was not simply between Jacobins and Blanquists on the one hand and socialists on the other. Both Vaillant and Frankel supported the motion, though they disliked the name. Frankel, aware of the possibility of attacks on him for being a foreigner, voted in favour, 'since I do not wish to give cause for insinuations against my socialist revolutionary opinions', reserving, however, 'the right to revolt against the Committee'. And the Blanquist Tridon opposed the name, 'not liking useless and cast-off clothing, which far from giving us strength takes away what little strength we have'. But there was now a split in the Commune, as was shown clearly enough when twenty-five of the minority refused to take part in the elections to the new Committee, publishing instead a protest against 'this dangerous or useless, violent or inoffensive' plagiarization of the past.[3] Charles Gérardin tried to prevent this being published, implying in the tradition of '93 that the opposition group was counter-revolutionary.[4] The 'majority', as they were now known,

---

[1] Cf. Marx, *The Eighteenth Brumaire of Louis Bonaparte*, MESW, p. 99: 'The social revolution of the nineteenth century cannot draw its poetry from the past, but only from the future. It cannot begin with itself before it has stripped off all superstition in regard to the past. Earlier revolutions required recollections of past world history in order to drug themselves concerning their own content. In order to arrive at its own content, the revolution of the nineteenth century must let the dead bury their dead. There the phrase went beyond the content; here the content goes beyond the phrase.' Or again, in September 1870 in the *Second Address on the Franco-Prussian War*, MESW, p. 272: 'The French workmen . . . must not allow themselves to be deluded by the national *souvenirs* of 1792 . . . They have not to recapitulate the past, but to build up the future.'

[2] D. Halévy, *Histoire d'une histoire*, Paris, 1939, p. 21.

[3] J.O., 4 May.     [4] 1 May: P.V.C., II, p. 27.

started holding separate meetings from which the minority were excluded. This only confused matters even more, for the majority tended to act as if they were the supreme body, talking even once of arresting the Committee of Public Safety itself.[1] Nor did the Committee of Public Safety improve the running of the war, what with Pyat popping up giving orders to commanders in the field in contradiction to those issued by the War Ministry.

Outside the heated squabbles in the Commune, the middle party in Paris was centred round the League of the Republican Union for the Rights of Paris. This grouped together radical republicans, several of whom had been Mayors and adjoints during the siege, and included Clemenceau, Mottu, Rochefort and Ranc, after his resignation from the Commune. It claimed to represent the 'educated industrial bourgeoisie'. Their main fear was that the Republic would be threatened if a monarchist-dominated Assembly crushed Paris. As Clemenceau insisted, 'municipal franchises are for us the true guarantee of the Republic'.[2] These included the right of the National Guard to police the city and of Paris to control its own finances and school system. The League represented the ideal of a secular Republic which later became enshrined in the Radical Party of the Third Republic. Several of the large Paris dailies such as the *Siècle*, the *Temps* and the *National* supported the League in its efforts to bring about a negotiated end to the civil war. But their efforts met with no success. The Commune cold-shouldered them, not appreciating their demand that it should resign to make way for the holding of fresh elections. Thiers at first showed his usual civility, but he was soon talking of how busy he was and how wonderful the army was, describing it as 'the purest element there is today' in France. He continued to deny that prisoners were being shot and maltreated: 'I have given orders on this matter.' As one of the delegates who went to see Thiers remarked afterwards, 'M. Thiers believes all his orders are automatically carried out.' Thiers did promise that if Paris surrendered there would be no reprisals, except for the assassins of Generals Lecomte and Clément Thomas, but insisted that the National Guard must be disarmed, leaving it to the army to restore order in Paris, and that the capital could only have the liberties given it by the law on Municipalities passed by the National

[1] 7 May: Lanjalley and Corriez, op. cit., p. 416.
[2] A. Lefèvre, *Histoire de la Ligue d'Union Républicaine des Droits de Paris*, Paris, 1881, p. 146.

Assembly. These were hardly compromise terms, and some of the League wanted it to side openly with the revolutionaries as the Commune called on it to do.[1] But the majority of its members were more concerned with remaining within republican legality.[2]

On 8 May the Conciliation Commission of Industry, Commerce and Labour sent a delegation to Thiers bearing its proposals for a peace, which were the same as those of the League.[3] But as was remarked by the presiding officer when this was introduced as mitigating evidence at one of the trials afterwards, 'one would have to be very naïve to believe that the Government would agree to such propositions'.[4] The united workers and employers associations, with 107 representatives, came out on 21 April in support of similar demands. The Freemasons too at this time sent a delegation to see Thiers.

Schoelcher, who had been so active helping Admiral Saisset and the Mayors against the Central Committee, published his own peace proposals just after the war had begun, saying it would be criminal of any government to besiege Paris. A voice from the past at this time was that of Victor Considérant. In the 1830s and 1840s he had been the main propagandist of Charles Fourier's phalansterian ideas. Considérant had been a member of the 1849 Assembly and had then gone into exile at the time of the Empire, returning at the outbreak of war in 1870. He remained in Paris during the Commune and in April published a pamphlet, 'Peace in 24 Hours dictated by Paris to Versailles', defending the movement of 18 March as one of 'COMMUNAL LIBERTY'. He too called for new elections in Paris.

There were movements among the republicans in the provinces against the civil war. The Municipal Council of Lyon sent a delegation to Versailles, which questioned Thiers closely about his republican intentions and criticized the municipal law passed by the Assembly. However, when they visited the Hôtel de Ville this delegation only promised their moral support for Paris. In accordance with this when they returned to Lyon they reported that they had found 'a tolerable degree of calm and order prevailing in the city' and that what they had seen in Paris 'gave the lie to the absurd

[1] J.O., 15 April.
[2] Cf. *Enquête*, II, p. 297 (Floquet) and pp. 616–17 (Corbon).
[3] A.H.G., Ly 22.
[4] *Procès de la Commune. Compte rendu*, 1st series, pp. 49–50, Billioray's trial.

fables being spread about in the provinces'.[1] But both the delegation from Lyon and that of Bordeaux found the programme of the Commune as set out in the 'Declaration to the French People' too vague to be acceptable. In general the provinces sympathized with the Commune so far as it was a question of purely municipal liberties, but the social and revolutionary acts of the Commune were considered 'insane and criminal'.[2] It was in line with this first sentiment that plans were made at the beginning of May to hold a series of regional congresses at Lyon, Bordeaux, Lille and Nantes. The Government at once forbade these, using a law of 1855 forbidding municipal councils to meet together. In Paris itself there were a number of meetings of provincials residing within the city who in May formed themselves into a Federation of the Departments aimed at propagandizing the provinces in support of the rights of Paris and of ending the civil war. Paschal Grousset, the Foreign Affairs Delegate, offered the Luxembourg Palace to the Bordeaux republican committee for it to hold its proposed conference, and the League tried to send five delegates, including Corbon and Clemenceau, out of Paris. But most of these were arrested before they got very far and the Bordeaux conference never took place. Lyon did manage to hold its regional conference and sent an address to Thiers signed by seventy representatives from sixteen Departments calling for a cease-fire, dissolution of the National Assembly and of the Commune, and the holding of fresh national and municipal elections. The Government paid no attention to such appeals, Thiers assuring all those who saw him that there was no need for a new National Assembly as he was perfectly able to control the existing one. In effect Thiers was forcing provincial republican opinion to settle for his conservative Republic in preference to having a monarchist restoration. This was certainly the attitude of the republican Deputies who had stayed on at Versailles. They went no further than a mild declaration on 8 April regretting the outbreak of the civil war, but concluding with the need to preserve national unity under Thiers.

The only concrete result of all these peace efforts, apart from illusively raising hopes within Paris, was to get a truce at Neuilly in order to evacuate the houses being bombarded. Here Dombrowski

[1] Archives Municipales de Lyon: Greenberg, op. cit., p. 316; Lefèvre, op. cit., p. 94.
[2] L'*Emancipation* of Toulouse, 26 April: Armengaud, op. cit., p. 453.

with no more than 5,000 men was fighting brilliantly, holding back the Versailles army. This was the fiercest combat of the whole second siege, and the Commune threw in an armoured train and gunboats along the Seine. Dombrowski, aged thirty-five, had escaped with his wife from Russia after the failure of the Warsaw uprising of 1863. During the first siege Garibaldi had requested Trochu to let Dombrowski join him by balloon, but instead when Dombrowski did manage to get out of Paris Trochu had him arrested in the south as a Prussian spy. Like Rossel, Dombrowski was motivated by patriotic reasons, fighting against the Prussians and then for the Commune in the hope that a regenerated France would go to the aid of oppressed Poland. The same motive led other Polish officers to fight for the Commune, including two more of its generals, Wroblewski and Oklowicz. This Polish leadership of the military effort of Paris enabled Versailles to slander the Commune as a foreign-inspired revolt, especially as one of the French commanders had the Italian-sounding name of La Cecilia. Afterwards Prince Czartoryski of the one-time ruling family of Poland denounced his countrymen's marked participation in the civil war.[1] Dombrowski was the best field commander the Commune had. When Archibald Forbes, the *Daily News* correspondent, went to see Dombrowski at his headquarters at the front, it was at the risk of his life from bullets and shells, and he came away greatly impressed by Dombrowski's truly Polish aristocratic courage.[2] Picard thought it well worthwhile to try to get Dombrowski out of the way by bribing him to betray the Commune, and when this failed offering him a free pass out of France. But Dombrowski refused to go back on his word, though news of such offers gave rise to xenophobic rumours that the foreigners would betray the Commune. Until the last week Dombrowski remained at the front, having little to do with the rest of Paris and its Commune. He would occasionally appear at the Ministry of War, dramatically marching straight into Cluseret's or Rossel's office, wearing his long black cloak, white kepi and gloves, gold

---

[1] Letter to the President of the National Assembly: *Enquête*, III, pp. 323–30; it was Poles who had immigrated into France after the failure of the 1863 Polish uprising who were active in the Commune: see note on article by K. Wyczanska, in *Le Mouvement Social*, January–March 1962, p. 59, and B. Wolowski, *Dombrowski et Versailles*, Geneva/London, 1871, pp. 68, 90.

[2] A. Forbes, 'What I saw of the Paris Commune', *The Century Magazine*, October 1892, pp. 806–11.

stars on his uniform, his sword clinking across the cobble-stones.

Firing stopped at Neuilly on 25 April for the day's truce. A large crowd went to visit the ruins of what had been one of the most fashionable suburbs of Paris now 'without metaphor, a city of the dead',[1] and to look at the 'enemy' only about twenty yards across from the federal lines. The Versailles officers prevented their men from talking with the Parisians, and a few over-curious spectators who ventured too far found themselves arrested. The Commune had sent ambulance brigades to help in the evacuation, and the women's committees were active in this work of mercy. So was Sir Richard Wallace, who reputedly gave 2,000 francs to the mayor of the 9th arrondissement for the victims of Neuilly.[2] The Times correspondent went out and came across the body of a dead man who had been lying there for several days covered in fallen plaster. Two women were rescued from a cellar where they had been living for eighteen days beside the dead body of a third companion. They burst into tears when they saw the house they had lived in all their lives destroyed around them.[3] Many others had died from shock and starvation. Their only food often had come from Versailles or Paris soldiers as they fought each other amidst the destroyed buildings.

The day's truce at Neuilly was used by Thiers to transfer his artillery to increase the pressure on the forts of Issy and Vanves. Artillery was Thiers' main weapon, and the guns of Mont-Valérien could reach the Champs-Elysées. Every time a shell hit the Arc de Triomphe a crowd would run up to inspect the damage, in spite of the National Guards posted to try to keep the inquisitive at a safe distance. Little boys collected the fragments from exploded shells. Families were moving out of this area of Paris, and Edwin Child, sickened by the spectacle of Frenchmen bombarding their own capital, wrote at the end of April that the indiscriminate bombard-ment was 'deciding many hitherto neutral to join "the insurgents" although not in any way sympathizing with the Commune'.[4]

Issy was undergoing a murderous bombardment and Eudes, appointed commander in place of Mégy, showed the same interest as his predecessor in getting back to Paris. His wife, however, took her turn with a rifle, and Louise Michel, as always in the thick of the fighting, relaxed by reading Baudelaire and helping a student check

[1] The Times, 12 April.                    [2] L'Estafette, 14 May.
[3] The Times, 26, 27 April.                [4] Given in Horne, op. cit., pp. 323-4.

his calculations of the trajectory of the Versailles shells.[1] Rossel
showed his appreciation of such bravado when Colonel Leperche, in
charge of the trenches surrounding the fort, summoned the garrison
cn 30 April to surrender within a quarter of an hour, threatening to
shoot them if they refused. Eudes passed the telegram back to
Rossel at the Ministry of War. Leperche and Rossel had been at the
Ecole Polytechnique together and had both escaped from Metz, hence
the insolence and humour of Rossel's reply, which he published in
the Paris Press: 'My dear comrade, next time you permit yourself to
send a summons as insolent as your signed letter of yesterday, I shall
have your parlementary shot, in conformity with the practices of
war.' The bearer of this letter, a respectable commercial traveller,
was furious when he discovered what it contained, and the outraged
Leperche sent a copy back to his headquarters. Rossel's tone delighted his supporters, though much of the Commune Press did not like
this bandying of words by 'comrades' in the midst of a civil war.

Rossel had taken Cluseret's place as the Commune's War Delegate
on 1 May, the day the Committee of Public Safety had been formed.
The time chosen was most unjust for Cluseret had personally only
the day before recaptured fort Issy with a handful of men after it had
been abandoned by its Governor, Mégy. On entering the fort
Cluseret had found a boy of about sixteen, weeping, sitting on a
powder keg which he thought he could use to blow up the fort when
the Versailles' troops entered. Cluseret broke into tears too and
embraced him. Rossel was the opposite to Cluseret, a *polytechnicien*,
who in spite of his youth, being only twenty-six years old and having
no active military experience to speak of, immediately commanded
the respect of all those who had to work with him. Charles Gérardin
of the Committee of Public Safety, who had befriended Rossel in the
17th arrondissement, was a fervent admirer of the young army
officer, who also had the backing of the influential paper the *Père
Duchêne* as well as the admiration of Louise Michel and of André Léo
and her paper, *La Sociale*. Rossel had joined the Commune out of
pure patriotism, seeing in the armed revolt against Versailles a chance
for Paris to lead the nation once more against the Prussian invader.
This feeling had been common at the time, especially in the National
Guard, and patriotism had played a part in determining Delescluze
to leave Versailles for Paris. But in Rossel this sentiment was dominant. The young ex-army officer, Louis Barron, who arrived in

[1] Michel, op. cit., pp. 192–4.

Paris in April to join the 'social revolution', as he hoped, was surprised to be told by Rossel's second-in-command that they were fighting against Versailles, 'the capitulators', in order to be able to turn against the Prussians.[1] Rossel seemed cast for the role of military hero, the saviour of the Commune. But precisely for that reason suspicion quickly mounted against him, especially as he could not claim to represent the social aspirations of the minority on the Commune, nor the revolutionary aims of the majority, nor the confused sentiments of the local organizations and clubs. And his strictly military manner did not recommend him to the National Guard and its Central Committee.

At first, however, Rossel's appointment was welcomed on all sides. But the military situation was desperate, and Rossel decided that the only hope was to try to take the offensive. His plan was to form 2,000 men chosen from the National Guard into eight regiments, supported by forty pieces of artillery. Bergeret, Eudes, Dombrowski and La Cecilia were to take command of these and Wroblewski was to unite under his command what cavalry could be mustered. This Rossel intended would replace the 'flags and pennons so abused by the federals' with a serious, smaller military force.[2] It would also have been cheaper, and Jourde and Rossel discussed ways of reducing the allowances given to the National Guard. This army would have lived in barracks, not at home as did the National Guard. Rossel dared not attack directly the principle of elected officers, but summoned those whose elections had not yet been confirmed to the Ministry of War, where they would be given a 'regular commission' after their competence had been examined.[3] Tactfully, Arnold, a member of both the Commune and the Central Committee, was chosen to preside over the examining board. Avrial, an engineering worker and union militant, was charged with bringing some order into the confusion surrounding the supply of ammunition.[4] And to complete this reorganization, Rossel summoned all the artillery batteries that were not at the front line or on the ramparts to report to the Ecole Militaire, under threat of losing their pay.[5]

Clear directions were not enough. As Rossel realized, political

[1] Barron, op. cit., pp. 20-1.     [2] Rossel, op. cit., pp. 236-7.     [3] J.O., 2 May.
[4] *Mémoires* of Paul Martine and A. H. G.: E. Thomas, *Rossel*, Paris, 1967, pp. 327-8.
[5] J.O., 2 May.

support was necessary and this he could not get, either from the Commune or the Central Committee. His plan of forming regiments out of the National Guard was a direct threat to the Central Committee, as it would have cut across and eventually replaced the arrondissement base of the legions. On 2 May, fifteen arrondissements were represented at a meeting that decided to force the Commune to abolish the War Ministry, leaving the Central Committee solely in charge of the military effort of Paris. If this demand was refused, then, as Edouard Moreau put it, since the Commune was only 'a *communal administration*', the men of 18 March 'would act in a revolutionary fashion and take over again their Revolution'. This the legion chiefs were ready to do.[1] It is possible that some Versailles agents were encouraging the Central Committee to act in this way, hoping thereby to break up the Commune.[2] Instead of arresting the members of the Central Committee, as Rossel was considering doing, the Commune summoned their War Delegate to answer questions about his own political past and the conduct of the war. Rossel gave frank and unaccommodating answers, confident of his own superiority in military matters over a purely civilian body.

The Commune itself was showing signs of lassitude, a feeling of relief even that it had disburdened itself through transferring the responsibility for the daily conduct of affairs to the Committee of Public Safety. But the Committee of Public Safety hardly provided the unity of will Delescluze had spoken of. Instead Pyat was intriguing with the Central Committee, trying to ensure his popularity on all sides. Jourde in council on 2 May openly accused Pyat and the Committee of Public Safety of seeking to replace the Commune by the Central Committee. The situation was, in Rossel's words, both tragic and farcical. When Rossel was asked that evening to dine with the members of the Committee of Public Safety, instead of finding his advice and ideas sought for he had to put up with a long-winded discourse from Pyat on how the war ought to be fought. At the end another member spoke of the measures he had taken to improve the organization of the National Guard in his arrondissement. 'At least you have a reasonable view of matters,' replied the exasperated Rossel. To which Pyat, sensing the insult, asked Rossel if he was implying that he, Félix Pyat, had not. Rossel simply burst into laughter and they parted mortal enemies.

[1] Vuillaume, op. cit., VIII, p. 132, and X, p. 102.
[2] Malon, op. cit., p. 299; Thomas, op. cit., p. 331.

There were now at least three powers trying to run the war, and not surprisingly at a public meeting in the 4th arrondissement the commander of one battalion protested to the representatives of the Commune present that he no longer knew whose orders to obey.[1] Eudes in command of Issy was complaining directly to the Committee of Public Safety about not receiving reinforcements. Rossel was doing his best to enforce discipline and find more troops. He almost had forty deserters from Issy shot, but instead coldly told them that their uniforms would be torn, their badges ripped off, and they would be paraded back to Paris with a placard round their necks saying, 'Cowards who abandoned fort Issy'. But no sooner had a start been made with the officers than the group begged tearfully to be sent back. Many of them were killed as they tried to make their way back under fire. A similar display of sudden courage occurred when Rossel dismissed Colonel Wetzel for directing his demands directly to the Hôtel de Ville; the distressed colonel went and got himself shot. The most serious incident resulting from the multiplicity of powers occurred on 3 May when Rossel finally managed to reach Issy with reinforcements. He was surprised to find Dombrowski there as well. Dombrowski informed Rossel that he had just been made commander of all the fighting forces in the field by the Committee of Public Safety. In addition Wroblewski turned up, having also been ordered by the Committee of Public Safety to go to the support of Issy. Eudes's appeals had been only too well attended to. Rossel appealed to Gérardin, and Dombrowski was ordered back to Neuilly, which cooled relations between the Delegate of War and his ablest general. But during Dombrowski's absence Neuilly was nearly abandoned by the federals. Wroblewski's movement had even more serious effects, since that night the redoubt at Moulin-Saquet protecting fort Bicêtre to the east was taken. Rossel, furious, laid these facts before the Commune the next day, and Vermorel, who had been against the Committee of Public Safety from the start, said this showed that it was only an 'obstruction committee'.[2] Pyat at first denied categorically that any such orders had been given. But confronted by a copy of the order, Pyat had to admit that it was his signature, but excused himself by saying, 'I did not think that by adding my signature at the bottom of a note I was

[1] Meeting in *Théâtre-Lyrique* of 20 May: P.V.C., II, p. 462.
[2] 4 May: P.V.C., II, p. 150.

signing an order to General Wroblewski'.[1] Pyat was called on to resign, and Jourde said the Commune must make it clear once and for all what were the exact duties of the Committee of Public Safety. This task occupied the Commune's debates for the next few days, but as always other matters were raised and no decision was reached.

Rossel found himself therefore unable to rely on the Commune, and the Committee of Public Safety, temporarily chastened, suggested he should come to an arrangement with the Central Committee. Rossel agreed to let this latter body take over the administration, while he kept charge of the military conduct of the war. This division of powers would, as he hopefully expressed it, ensure 'not only the goodwill but the high revolutionary authority of the Central Committee of the Federation being put to work in organizing the defence of Paris'.[2] Moreau and his committee had at last an official position, in effect replacing the Commune so far as the war effort went. The Communard press was puzzled by this manœuvring, some doubting the competence of the Central Committee, others seeing it as a return to power of those who best represented the 'people in arms'.[3] Pyat in his paper insisted, however, that the Committee of Public Safety was at the top of the hierarchy of command, responsible only to the sovereign people.[4]

Hardly surprisingly there was no improvement, and Rossel, after a week at the War Ministry was in a state of despair about being able to get anything done. On 8 May he had to put up with a delegation from the Central Committee complaining of his attempts to reorganize the National Guard. Rossel pointed to the execution squad, as he called it, in the courtyard. But the delegation was not intimidated, insisting that the National Guard must not be interfered with. Rossel gave up the struggle. He challenged them to show they could get their 25 battalions of 500 men assembled by the following morning at the Place de la Concorde. At the same time he alerted Bergeret to have his men ready, in the faint hope that with such numbers an offensive could be attempted to give a check to Versailles. But in the evening Bergeret came to say his men would not fight, and several legion commanders had to admit the same thing. That night, eight

[1] 5 May: P.V.C., II, p. 171; Rossel, op. cit., pp. 239–41.
[2] J.O., 5 May, and by order of the C.P.S., J.O., 6 May.
[3] L'Estafette, 7 May; Le Réveil du Peuple, 6 May.
[4] Le Vengeur, 6 May.

days after his appointment, Rossel wrote his letter of resignation to the Commune:

> Citizen members of the Commune ... I feel myself incapable of continuing to bear the responsibility of a command which everyone discusses and no one obeys. When it was necessary to organize the artillery, the Central Artillery Committee discussed and came to no decision ... The Central Committee discusses and has not yet known how to act ... My predecessor made the mistake of trying to continue in the midst of this absurd situation ... I have no choice but to overcome the obstacle that impedes my action or to retire. I cannot overcome the obstacle, for the obstacle is you and your weakness; I do not want to do violence to public sovereignty. I retire, and have the honour to ask you for a cell in [the prison of] Mazas.[1]

The next day, 9 May, as a last hope, he went to look at the Guards assembled on the Place, but there were only seven, not twelve, thousand men. Rossel did not hesitate and galloped away; it was not enough. He had just received news from the observation post on the Arc de Triomphe that the tricolor was flying over fort Issy. Rossel immediately dispatched this news to the papers. He also had twice the normal number of posters printed announcing that 'The tricolor flag is floating over the fort of Issy, deserted yesterday evening by its garrison.' He then sent off his resignation to the Commune.

Like the Government of National Defence, the Commune had made it its policy, as had Cluseret, to give only reassuring information to the population, and many Parisians had no idea of the near military collapse of the defence. Rossel's act in publicizing such serious bad news, the fall of 'the Metz' of the Commune, without even consulting the Commune first, was at once interpreted by some as treachery. It seemed as if Rossel was vaunting in the Commune's misfortune. Delescluze tried to persuade Rossel to change his mind about resigning, but Rossel refused.

The Central Committee now suddenly rallied to Rossel. The editors of the *Père Duchêne*, particularly Charles Gérardin, who was also on the Committee of Public Safety, pressed Rossel to use the Central Committee and its battalions to overthrow the Commune to save the revolution. This idea had been in the air for some time. Rigault had been consulted. His view was that little could be done

[1] Rossel, op. cit., pp. 250–2.

Jules Vallès

(b) Léo Frankel

(c) Eugène Varlin

(e) Francis Jourde

Edouard Vaillant

(f) Louise Michel

9. Communards: socialists and anarchists

(g) Gustave Courbet

10. The Communard Press

unless Blanqui could be released, but if the Central Committee could get out a sizeable number of troops this would be something, as 'nothing worthwhile could be expected any longer from those talkers on the Commune'.[1] Dombrowski had also been approached and had replied that he would neither hinder nor help. It was even thought that the International could be brought in, but this idea was dropped since it was thought unlikely that Varlin or Frankel would countenance such an idea.[2]

Rossel's resignation and the news from Issy threw the Commune into turmoil. Delescluze tried to appeal to their sense of urgency by recalling the realities of the situation: 'You argue while the tricolor flag is floating over Issy.' The Committee of Public Safety has failed, he said, and should be removed: 'Your Committee of Public Safety is annihilated, crushed by the weight of the memories with which it is burdened. It does not even do the work of a simple executive commission.'[3] But instead it was decided to keep the Committee of Public Safety, renewing only its membership, and that the next Delegate to the War Ministry would be a civilian. The Commune went into secret session to discuss this, and immediately the majority led by Pyat, Miot and Paschal Grousset attacked Rossel vehemently, demanding his arrest as a traitor. This was pure Jacobin rhetoric, which Delescluze avoided. The Commune's own Military Commission opposed Pyat and the others, arguing instead, like Delescluze, that Rossel should be kept on. The minority voted with the Military Commission, and so great was Pyat's anger (he had not forgiven Rossel for laughing at him) that the session was suspended.

The majority then went off to decide matters among themselves, and the minority eventually had to go and search them out. The Rossel case had now become one of the majority versus the minority, and the debate was even more acrimonious. Chalain, a bronze-worker and member of the International, demanded that the minority be arrested. When Pyat tried to press this proposal Malon silenced him by shouting, 'you are the evil genius of the Commune ... It is your influence that is destroying the Commune; it is time your influence was abolished.' The architect Arnold, elected from within the Central Committee in the April by-elections, likewise blamed the old revolutionaries of 1848 for 'bringing about the downfall of the Revolution'. Pyat at least was not re-elected to the new Committee

---

[1] Da Costa, op. cit., vol. 2, p. 196.
[2] Senisse, op. cit., pp. 97–8, 27–8 April.          [3] 9 May: P.V.C., II, pp. 301–3.

of Public Safety, but Gambon, a Blanquist and man of '48 though less inclined than Pyat or Miot to Jacobin rhetoric, was chosen. Delescluze and Eudes were the other new members, Ranvier and Arnaud being kept on from the first Committee. Delescluze was also appointed to replace Rossel as the civil Delegate for War.

During this time Rossel had been kept waiting outside, supposedly under guard. But since Charles Gérardin was one of the two responsible it was easy for Rossel to escape. He and Gérardin took the coach of the Ministry of War and drove to the Latin Quarter, where Rossel hid out in a hotel on the Boulevard Saint-Michel. He remained there until the end and was arrested in June after the police commissioner of the district discovered his whereabouts.

The appointment of Delescluze to the Ministry of War on 9 May neither improved the military organization of the war nor resolved the conflict between the bodies competing for the overall direction. Delescluze tried, as had Rossel, to improve discipline, complaining that officers were neglecting their men with the result that 'abandoned to themselves, Guards were fighting completely aimlessly'.[1] The Committee of Public Safety arrested several of the staff officers of the National Guard for absenting themselves from duty 'in order to go banqueting with girls of bad repute'.[2] During the confusion caused by Rossel's departure the Committee of Public Safety had nominated Edouard Moreau of the National Guard Central Committee as 'Civil Commissioner of War', a redundant post since this was what Delescluze was supposed to be. Moreau described himself as 'the all-seeing eye of the Committee of Public Safety'.[3] Delescluze vainly protested to the Commune against this interference by the Committee of Public Safety and the Central Committee. This did not prevent the Committee of Public Safety going further in its desire to emulate the structure of its famous predecessor by delegating more Civil Commissioners of War to each of the three commanders in the field. The National Guard Central Committee was still trying to exercise its authority in the military conduct of the war, which led one paper to ask whether Paris was still under the Commune or whether the Central Committee had taken charge again.[4] On 19 May the Central Committee published a declaration on how it saw the situation. It denied there was any truth in the 'talk of a division between the majority of the Commune' and itself – the

[1] J.O., 16 May.    [2] J.O., 18 May.
[3] Enquête, III, p. 170.    [4] L'Estafette, 17 May.

minority of the Commune evidently no longer counted at all. The Central Committee also announced that it was going to take over the administration of the war. But by now there was precious little left to command.

The war had become a matter of artillery. Thiers had been a member of the Defence Council responsible for Paris at the beginning of the Franco–Prussian war, and had realized then that the weakest point was the western salient between the villages of Saint-Cloud and Meudon. Issy, with Vanves further east, covered Meudon. Mont-Valérien, in the hands of Versailles from the start of the civil war, covered Saint-Cloud. With Issy taken the approach was now opened up towards the western tip of the defences through the Porte de Saint-Cloud into Auteuil. Although this meant that Thiers had to bombard the residences of his own supporters, it also meant that once inside the walls the troops would meet with no opposition from the population of the bourgeois 16th arrondissement. The way to the heart of Paris would be clear along the Left Bank of the Seine and down the Champs-Elysées. A third of Paris could easily be occupied before having to deal with the central arrondissements and the revolutionary faubourgs to the north and east.

By using private enterprise rather than Army engineers the biggest battery of either siege was constructed on the heights at Montretout, protected to the north by Mont-Valérien. A thousand men working day and night built this up in a week, Thiers paying a visit each day to watch the progress. A poster addressed to the population of Paris tried to put a good face on this; the Government, it was explained, was not about to bombard Paris but simply to fire in order to force one of the gates. Since most Parisians considered they had been under bombardment for several weeks this was not very convincing. The Commune replied by publishing Thiers' condemnation of the bombardment of Palermo of January 1848: 'You have all shuddered with horror on learning that a great city has been bombarded for forty-eight hours. By whom? By a foreign enemy, exercising its rights of war? No, gentlemen, by its own government. And why? Because this unfortunate city demanded its rights!' It was also decided that it was only just that Thiers should personally suffer: a decree ordered the seizure of his goods and the demolition of his house. Courbet took charge of Thiers' art collection, which it was suggested should be transferred to a museum. There was some debate in the Commune by those less concerned with the sanctity of art whether objects with the coat of arms of the Orleans dynasty should not be destroyed. But the majority view was that 'we are not barbarians'.[1] An offer was received from a London Company expressing interest in buying up some of Thiers' collection and a French speculator wanted to use the bricks of the house as souvenir paperweights.[2] Rochefort had impishly suggested that it would be a good retribution to attack Thiers personally through his property, but with humouristic foresight had regretted this would not be worthwhile: 'On hearing that popular justice is pulling down M. Thiers' house, which cost two millions, the Versailles Assembly would immediately vote him another costing three.'[3] This is just what was done.

Delescluze resigned from the Committee of Public Safety on 12 May because his time was fully absorbed by the Ministry of War. Billioray, the Neapolitan-born painter, took his place. This election became another occasion of dispute between the majority and the minority within the Commune. Lefrançais, for the minority, argued that since the Committee of Public Safety had left it to the Commune to fill Delescluze's vacant seat, the Committee of Public Safety was clearly only an executive committee of the Commune. It had been Vallès who had nominated Delescluze, seconded by Lefrançais. Eudes replied for the Committee of Public Safety that in future it alone would make all appointments and there would be no need to consult the Commune. Billioray added to soften the blow that the Commune would then be free to devote all its time to 'the very important questions of legislation and social economy', matters in which Billioray himself had shown plenty of interest during his time on the Commune. The new Committee of Public Safety then used its powers to concentrate all posts into the hands of the majority. Vermorel was removed from the Commission supervising the police; Longuet from the board of the *Journal Officiel*; and the Military Commission was renewed so as to exclude the four members of the minority that until then had been on it.

The minority for some time now had been worried by Rigault's and Ferré's activities at the Ex-Prefecture of Police. Beslay had

[1] 12 May: P.V.C., II, p. 360.    [2] A.H.G., Ly 24; *Le Tribun du Peuple*, 18 May.
[3] *Le Mot d'Ordre*: Rochefort, *Les Aventures de ma vie*, Paris, 1896, vol. 2, p. 376. Nonetheless Rochefort did welcome the Commune's action, considering that Thiers had shown little respect for the property of others – a reference to the Government's seizure of Rochefort's own paper: *Le Mot d'Ordre*, 18 May.

several times tried to get some of Rigault's prisoners released, and Cluseret considered that Rigault spent too much time bothering with priests and not enough with spies. Vallès had complained to the Commune that people were being arrested for no apparent reason and kept for a week or more without ever being charged.[1] Rigault had even made it difficult for members of the Commune to visit prisoners. This had led to a passionate debate since several members of the Commune knew the inside of prisons only too well. As Arnould put it, 'I fail to understand how men who have spent their whole life fighting against despotism at once fall into the same trap as soon as they get into power.' Theisz, like Arnould, had refused to accept the argument of necessity: 'For too many years we have been told: "later". When things are over, then you will be given, Liberty, Equality, etc. We protest against such words, for it is always the same story.'[2] Rigault and Ferré had resigned, and had been somewhat surprised to be taken at their word. They had seized Delescluze's overtures that they should join the Police Commission and on 26 April Rigault had had his ambition fulfilled when he had been made Public Prosecutor, the Chaumette of the Commune.

It was in this capacity that on 17 May Rigault brought forward his project of forming a 'jury of accusation' to try the hostages and pass sentences on them. A debate ensued over whether it was in the revolutionary tradition to separate deciding guilt from passing sentence, Pyat considering that this should be done as this had been the practice in 1792. Another sign of the increasing Jacobin tempo of the majority was the suppression on 18 May of ten more papers. A number of papers had already been suppressed at the beginning of the revolution, the *Figaro* and the *Gaulois* having been the first to suffer this fate. In all twenty-seven papers were suppressed during the time of the Commune. There had been protests from papers sympathetic to the Commune against this Press censorship, including the *Vengeur*, although Pyat voted for the measures on the Commune. The early attempts at censorship had not always been very successful; street sellers would still offer those 'with reactionary looking faces' copies of the forbidden papers, producing them from under their coats.[3] The decree of 18 May affected two of the revolutionary papers, the *Commune* and the *Justice*, which were held to have

---

[1] 12 May: P.V.C., II, p. 358.
[2] 24 April: P.V.C., I, pp. 439, 441; cf. above, p. 164.
[3] Dabot, op. cit., p. 198, 9 April.

gone too far in their criticism of the Commune. This decree also forbade all new papers until the end of the war; and any attack on the Republic or the Commune would be punished by a court martial. Rastoul criticized these last two measures as making it appear as if the Commune claimed to be 'infallible'; if it was going to suppress all criticism of itself it would also have to close down the clubs and public meetings. Rochefort decided it was time he went, fearing he was likely to be arrested; but instead he was picked up by the police as he left Paris and sent off to prison in Versailles.[1]

On Monday, 15 May, the Minority turned up at the Hôtel de Ville intending to confront the majority. Jourde, Arnould and Lefrançais had each prepared a statement of their common grievances against the Committee of Public Safety, and they agreed to present Jourde's statement as a common declaration. Their point was that no military situation could justify the Commune abdicating its powers to any other body. The Commune was responsible solely to the 'social and political revolutionary movement'. Because of the attitude of the majority and of the Committee of Public Safety the minority announced they intended to devote themselves to the revolution at the local level and play their part in the decisive struggle being fought by their 'brothers in the National Guard'. The eleven members of the minority who turned up found, however, that the majority, knowing what was likely to occur, had not. So after waiting around for an hour they decided to send their declaration to the Press. It was signed by twenty-one members, in addition to Frankel, and Malon added his support.[2]

The *Père Duchêne* at once called for their arrest,[3] and Rigault had already made out their warrants by the time of the next meeting of the Commune on 17 May. But several members of the minority showed up at this session. Paschal Grousset, calling them Girondins, threatened action against them, but Delescluze and Pyat, for once, checked the more determined of the Jacobins. The members of the Commune had given up their National Guard battalion commands

---

[1] Rochefort, op. cit., pp. 79–83.

[2] Published in *Le Réveil du Peuple*, 17 May; *Le Cri du Peuple*, 17 May; *Le Rappel*, 16 May, among others. See too P.V.C., II, pp. 369–74; Lefrançais, op. cit., pp. 300–4 and '*Pieces justificatives*', No. XXIV; Arnould, op. cit., vol. 2, p. 37; Malon, op. cit., pp. 312–18.

[3] 28 floréal (17 May); but the next day it modified its tone, saying that their critique was justified though this was still no reason for deserting the Commune.

and it was doubtful if the National Guard could actually be persuaded to arrest a third of the Commune. To have tried to do so, it was finally realized, would only cause more discord and confusion. No punitive measures were taken, therefore.

The action of the minority was not on the whole well received in Paris, though Versailles of course welcomed the news that the Commune looked as if it was falling apart. The Club Saint-Ambroise called the action 'a desertion'.[1] Charles Gérardin wrote to his fellow representative from the 17th arrondissement, Malon, who had supported the minority, that he felt 'desolated ... The whole question is whether the present split will increase or decrease the strength of the Commune?' As it seemed it would do the latter, Gérardin condemned the declaration as a 'serious political error'.[2] The revolutionary faubourgs did not share the scruples of the minority about '93; on the contrary, the harking back to the first Revolution was interpreted as a sign of a revolutionary energy. Flourens had proclaimed a Committee of Public Safety when he arrived at the Hôtel de Ville on 31 October. During the siege the demand for a Committee of Public Safety had often been raised in the popular clubs, where Commune and Committee of Public Safety often seemed to mean the same thing. On 1 May a meeting of some 5,000 in Saint Nicolas-des-Champs had 'unanimously congratulated the Commune on electing a Committee of Public Safety', calling on the Commune to 'energetically and resolutely persevere on the revolutionary road, which alone could save the Republic'.[3] The Minority's seemed 'too parliamentary' a view of the military crisis the Commune was facing, as Arnould afterwards admitted.[4]

Arnould, Clémence, Lefrançais and Eugène Gérardin agreed to appear before their electors of the 4th arrondissement at a public meeting in the *Théâtre-Lyrique* (today the Sarah Bernhardt) to give an explanation of their conduct. At this meeting Clémence explained with regard to 'the memories of '92 and '93' that he considered they 'should not seek their inspiration from that epoch; the popular aspirations sufficiently indicated the line of conduct to be followed. We should not copy but innovate.' Amouroux, the fifth member of the Commune for this arrondissement, who unlike the others had voted with the majority, also took part in this debate, calling on his

[1] Meeting of 16 May: A.H.G., Ly 22 *bis*, 'Clubs'.
[2] Letter of 16 May: I.I.S.H.
[3] P.V.C., II, pp. 89–90.
[4] Arnould, op. cit., vol. 2, p. 41.

fellow representatives to unite again around the Commune. This was the sense of the meeting: faced by Versailles, and not forgetting the Prussians, Paris must remain united. The four members of the minority agreed to abide by the will of the meeting, which voted that 'The assembly of electors from the 4th arrondissement, not wishing to reproach its representatives in any way, nevertheless calls on them to return to their place on the Commune.' The wish was also expressed that the Commune should make its sessions open to the public.[1]

The International was also concerned over the split in the Commune, particularly as fourteen of the minority belonged to the Association. An extraordinary session was called for 20 May, which voted in the same way as the meeting in the 4th arrondissement, asking its members in the minority 'to maintain the unity of the Commune, so necessary for victory in the struggle against the government of Versailles'. But the International did go so far as to request the Commune to modify the powers of the Committee of Public Safety so that the Communal council could exercise some control over it.[2] Accordingly, the next session of the Commune on 21 May was attended by the minority, Arnould giving an account of the meeting in the 4th arrondissement and its request that the Commune make its sessions public, something the International had also called on the Commune to do.

This session was, however, the last time the Commune met, and the Communal Council gave way to the final heroic phase of the Commune, the street fighting on the barricades. Before passing on to this, other aspects of the Paris revolution must be looked at, for it would be misleading to see the Commune solely in terms of its government at the Hôtel de Ville. Serious attempts at social reform were proposed, particularly in the fields of education and workers' co-operatives, and these will be discussed next. Then, as has already been noticed, the local nature of the Commune was further emphasized by the formation of clubs, which tried to give some expression to the popular conception of direct democracy. For essentially the Commune was a popular take-over of a whole city, a festive revolution. Accordingly, after examining the specific social proposals of the Commune an account will be given of the popular organizations during the Commune and of the festivals of the people of Paris in revolution.

[1] Given in P.V.C., II, pp. 449–69.
[2] *Séances officielles*, pp. 189–94; P.V.C., II, pp. 375–6; Lefrançais, op. cit., p. 305.

Chapter 8

# THE COMMUNE: SOCIAL
# REFORM

The historian Taine, deeply distressed by the Commune, wrote to his wife on 5 April that 'as for the present insurrection, at bottom it is socialist: "The owner, the bourgeois, is exploiting us so we must put an end to him."' Just after the Commune was elected a correspondent from Paris wrote for *The Times* that one of the main 'streams in the bed of the insurrection . . . was the predominance of the *Proletariat* over the wealthy classes, of the workman over the master, of Labour over Capital'.[1] These are surprisingly temperate judgements compared to the general reaction of the bourgeoisie to events in Paris. More common are descriptions of the social side of the Commune in terms of pillaging and destruction by a mad band of criminals, idiots, failures, risen like a plague from the slums and prisons of the capital. This, for example, is how the poet Leconte de Lisle describes the Communards in a passage that needs to be savoured in its original:

> *Nous avons été la proie . . . d'un soulèvement total de tous les déclassés, de tous les fruits secs, de tous les singes d'Erostrate qui pullulent dans les bas-fonds des sociétés modernes, de tous les paresseux pillards, des rôdeuses de barrière, de la lie des prisons et des bagnes.*[2]

The working-class representatives of the French labour movement on the Commune saw the revolution as essentially a chance to inaugurate some of the reforms that had been the subject of discussion in the various workers' associations and in Congresses of the International. The war did not prevent attempts being made to carry through changes intended to improve the conditions of the majority of the population, particularly by Vaillant at the Education Commission and Frankel at the Commission of Labour and Exchange.

---

[1] 29 March.      [2] Letter of 29 May, to J.-M. de Hérédia.

The work of these two commissions supported by activity at the local level and a number of specific decrees constitute the socialist work of the Commune, as the term was understood at the time. These were measures that were intended to enable everyone to live with some decency, in a juster society, in which the concentration of capital and property had been broken down by means of workers' producers' associations.

The Commune, as has been seen, acted quickly over the question of rents, in itself a 'socialist' measure so far as the liberal economists of the period were concerned and something which the Government of National Defence had refused to do. On other financial matters the Commune took its time, showing an exaggerated concern for financial respectability. The Central Committee had left the Bank alone so long as it continued to provide funds for the pay of the National Guard. The Commune continued this policy. As its delegate it appointed Beslay, who had stayed on in spite of his age and health partly in order 'to conserve the Bank'.[1] The day after the inauguration of the Commune Beslay paid his first visit to the Bank, ostensibly to thank its acting Governor, the Marquis de Ploeuc, a Breton like Beslay, for the services an ambulance brigade of which de Ploeuc was the president had given to Beslay's nephew at the battle of Châtillon. After such a civil beginning to their relationship de Ploeuc had what he afterwards called 'the happy inspiration' of appealing to Beslay's sense of honour. 'The future of your country, the future of France,' said de Ploeuc, depended on whether Beslay was willing to help in the noble task of saving the Bank.[2] Such an appeal accorded with Beslay's own views, for he saw no conflict between being the representative of the Commune and what he considered were his duties to the Bank. The only threat could come from the National Guard, which on three occasions threatened to search the Bank for arms. It was only Beslay's presence on the spot that stopped this from happening. Wearing the red sash of a member of the Commune, something he considered too vulgar to do in the Bank itself, he quite falsely assured the local National Guard commander and police commissioner that he personally had searched for arms and found none. Fortunately for Versailles, the National Guard did not insist, for the Bank had insufficient forces to with-

[1] Beslay, *Souvenirs*, p. 372.
[2] De Ploeuc, *Enquête*, II, p. 491. Beslay, op. cit, pp. 427–30, naturally objected to de Ploeuc's implication that he had been won over by de Ploeuc.

stand a determined attack by the battalions of the Commune. De
Ploeuc even went to the lengths of visiting Beslay at his home in
order to encourage him to continue his duties, and persuaded him
at the end to live in the Bank so as to be available to prevent any
further attempts at invading it.

Beslay's argument was simple. If the Bank was touched, then
confidence in its notes would vanish and the basis of credit would
be gone both within and outside of Paris. This would lose the
Commune sympathy when support from the provinces was very
much needed. It would also ruin France, already in debt as a result
of the war with Prussia. And not only France, but the whole credit
system of the 'world of affairs which today ties up each nation to
the others'.[1] Beslay's conservatism has often been attributed to his
Proudhonism. Proudhon favoured free-credit banking schemes and
had a violent dislike of existing banks, becoming at times anti-
semitic in his denunciations of 'Jewish financiers'. Beslay clearly
did not welcome the revolutionary implications of attacking the
existing credit system, considering that 'in financial matters, the
Commune's only principles should be order and economy'. More
specifically, as he pointed out to one of the National Guard commanders, the very money being paid them by the Commune would
become worthless if confidence in the Bank was destroyed. The
Commune would then be forced to issue its own paper money,
which would be back to the *assignats* of the first Revolution.

The strategic value of the Bank to the Commune as its most
valuable bargaining counter with Versailles seems never to have
been considered by Beslay or by the Commune. Yet in addition to
the 500 million francs in cash, the Bank had 11 million francs worth
of bullion, 7 million worth of jewels held in deposit – though not
the royal diamonds, as the Commune at one time suspected, since
these had been removed to Brest for safety before the siege – and
most importantly over 1,000 million worth of assets, shares and
securities deposited in its vaults. In sum, a much bigger fortune than
the indemnity demanded by Bismarck at the surrender of Paris. As
such the Bank was a far more valuable hostage than any of the individuals seized by Rigault to be exchanged against Blanqui. Afterwards Lefrançais reproached himself and the Commune for not

[1] Beslay, *Vérité*, p. 80; cf. *Souvenirs*, p. 394. Jourde at his trial used a similar
argument, saying that he had been able to avert 'the great disaster of causing
a depreciation of the franc': Rougerie, *Procès*, p. 81.

having seized the Bank to put a stop to the war, and in 1881 Marx wrote to a Dutch socialist that 'the appropriation of the Bank of France would have been enough to put an end with terror to the vaunt of the Versaillais'.[1] But the Commune was by no means entirely an anti-capitalist revolution, and Beslay's attitude was shared by Jourde and the Financial Commission. Nor was the matter ever raised by the Communal assembly.

For the duration of the second siege the Bank therefore was able to buy its safety by acceding to the Commune's requests for money, in all 16,765,202 francs, of which over nine million were covered by the credit on the account of the city of Paris. The remaining seven million, so the Bank thought, was covered by the Government. De Ploeuc twice sent an emissary to the Ministry of Finance in Versailles to receive the assurance that the 'Bank ran no risk' in lending money to the Commune. But this promise was never honoured, it being held that the Bank would have to bear its own share of what de Ploeuc once called 'its ransom'. By 1891 the Bank, through internal economies, was able to close its books on the account of the Commune, except for the nominal sum of one franc, 'pour mémoire'.[2]

Orthodoxy was the mark of the Commune's finances. The Delegate appointed by the Commune was Francis Jourde, himself an ex-bank clerk. Jourde had been elected to the Commune from the Central Committee of the National Guard. When he was captured he insisted on handing over the last 9,770 francs of the Commune's finances which he was carrying on him, apart from 120 francs belonging to him personally. He could indeed claim at his trial, 'I was poor when I entered the Ministry and so was I when I left.' Next to the loans from the Bank the main source of income was the *octroi* tax levied on goods coming into Paris together with the other normal taxes belonging to the city of Paris. The railway companies had to pay over two million francs as the sum Jourde decided was owing to the city of Paris from back taxes, and a revised levy of ten per cent was imposed.[3] But when a National Guard battalion seized 183,000 francs from the municipal gas company they were made to return it and apologize.[4] The biggest item of expenditure naturally was the cost of the war. For the period 20 March to 30 April, 20 million francs were spent on the military budget compared to 3·4

[1] Marx to Domela-Nieuwenhuis, 22 February 1881; Lefrançais, *Etude*, p. 263.
[2] G. Ramon, *Histoire de la Banque de France*, Paris, 1929, pp. 357-60.
[3] J.O., 28 April.                                                    [4] J.O., 24 April.

million on everything else, and in May Rossel was asking for a further 50 million to reorganize the National Guard into fighting regiments. Without this burden, Jourde assured the Commune, the budget of the city would be cut, thus restoring credit without having to resort to raising loans in the manner of Haussmann. He was applauded in the Communal council when he announced he wanted 'to wipe out all the jobbery of the Bourse'. By economizing once the war was over, Jourde felt the day would soon come when direct taxes could be reduced, especially the *octroi*, which 'weigh so heavily on the poor'. The Commune of Paris could then look forward to a period of prosperous foreign trade that would benefit the working population. Such was Jourde's 'practical socialism', as he called it.[1]

The speed and decisiveness of the decree on rents was not repeated when it came to dealing with the other outstanding legacy from the siege, the *échéances* or overdue bills. Payment of these had been postponed by the Central Committee, and the first proclamation of the Commune on 30 March had promised, 'Tomorrow, a decision on *échéances*.' The next day, however, the Commune decided it would first have to consult the commercial and industrial interests as well as the workers' societies. On 12 April the Commune had to announce a continuation of the suspension of payments as it had not yet reached any decision. The debate began on 13 April and lasted for five sessions. 'One would have thought,' said the poet Communard J.-B. Clément, 'that the salvation of the Revolution and of mankind depended entirely upon the solution that was going to be given to this question.'[2] Jourde played a major role in determining the measure that was finally adopted, which was intended, according to Jourde, 'to give satisfaction to the commercial interests'.[3] A three-year delay was granted within which to pay off all outstanding debts. But by the time it was published on 18 April it had lost its immediacy for the middle classes, which were already beginning to desert the cause of the Commune.

The State pawnshop issue was treated with similar deliberation. There was scope here for large-scale change as the system of credit practised by the Mont-de-Piété was biased against the poorer classes: the interest rate was high on small loans and decreased as the sum

[1] 2 May: P.V.C., II, pp. 77, 81.
[2] J.-B. Clément, *La Revanche des Communards*, Paris, 1886, p. 195.
[3] 17 April: P.V.C., I, p. 259.

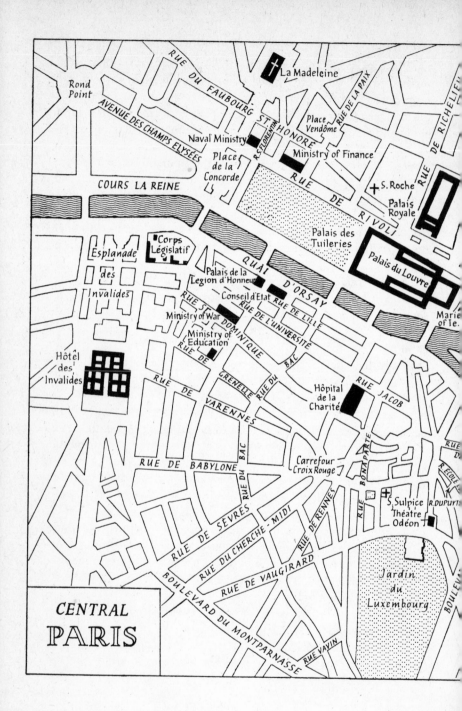

CENTRAL PARIS

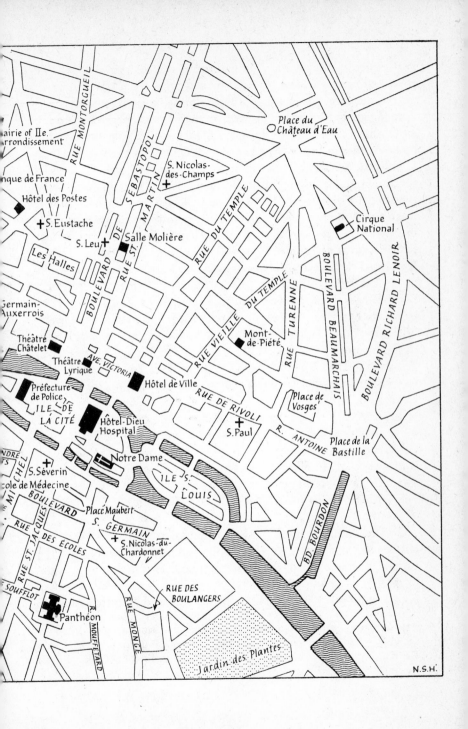

got bigger. Some of the Communard Press demanded that it be abolished completely or replaced by a Workers' Bank.[1] The report on the question produced by the Commission of Labour and Exchange did indeed look forward to the day when the revolution would have created 'truly socialist institutions' so that there would be no further need for the pawnshop system.[2] But the Commune as a whole decided it was too soon to talk of getting rid of the institution altogether, and Jourde insisted that the Commune must be prepared to indemnify the Mont-de-Piété for any financial loss it was forced to incur: 'we cannot be generous with other people's money'. The decree published on 7 May, in fact, went no further than previous governments had done at times of economic crisis. It granted the free restitution of household articles and work tools up to the value of twenty francs. The Government of National Defence only a few months earlier had declared a similar restitution of up to twenty francs, as had previous governments on thirteen other occasions dating back to the time of the French Revolution. In the case of the Commune the effect of the decree was weakened because the Director of the Institution told his employees 'to seek to resist the measure so far as possible' by slowing up the delivery of reclaimed objects. Because of this not more than 4,000 goods were handed over on any one day, and in all far less under the Commune than under the Government of National Defence or after the 1848 revolution. Little wonder one woman wrote to the Commune: 'Citizens, your decree on the Mont-de-Piété, which has long been awaited, has not been greeted with much enthusiasm by the National Guards in the poor quarters.' She called it a decree '*à la Favre, à la Trochu*'.[3]

The recommendations of the Commission of Labour and Exchange had not been accepted on the pawnshop question, but the Commission was one of the most important reforming bodies of the Commune. It was presided over by the Hungarian Léo Frankel, aged twenty-seven, the son of a doctor, who had come to France to

[1] *La Montagne*, 12 April, did propose replacing the Bank of France by something similar to Proudhon's idea of a People's Bank. The Proudhonian Pierre Denis in *Le Vengeur*, 31 March, suggested using the credit of the Bank of France to start a Proudhonian credit scheme. See too *La Révolution politique et sociale*, 8 May.

[2] J.O., 1 May.

[3] A.H.G., Ly 23: Rougerie, *Procès*, pp. 188–9; cf. Perrot, op. cit., p. 44.

complete his jeweller's apprenticeship. He joined the International by applying directly to London, though in 1870 he helped in the formation of a federation of the Paris branches. He was one of the accused at the third trial of the Association. On 30 March in a letter to Marx, Frankel rejoiced at his own election for the 113th arrondissement because it brought out the international importance of the Commune: 'If we succeed in radically transforming the social order, the revolution of 18 March will be the most effective of any up to now. In doing this we will have resolved the crucial problems of the social revolutions still to come.' Frankel added, 'your advice on what social reforms to carry out will be extremely valuable for our Commission'.[1]

The Commission's terms of reference were to 'propagate social doctrines; find ways of equalizing labour and the wage paid it; favour Parisian and French industry, and seek to develop international commerce and trade in order to make Paris a great centre of production'. The Commune never had a chance to try its hand at international trade, but an opportunity did arise to seek to regulate relations between workers and their employers. The bakery workers requested the Commune, 'the only just government and one that cares for popular needs', to abolish night work so that they might 'return to a normal life'.[2] They also demanded the abolition of the system of *placeurs*, employment agents, as this had become a monopoly to the disadvantage of the workers. These were changes that the bakery workers had been demanding for the past few years. On 20 April, though without consulting Frankel or his Commission, the Executive Commission of the Commune granted these two requests. The Mairies were also to act as employment exchanges for all workers, a popular measure that indirectly attacked the Imperial system of the *livret de travail*. This latter was a personal employment record which every worker was forced to have, and provided a means of governmental regulation. The abolition of fines and stoppages of pay worked in the same direction, and had been something workers had long complained of: three francs fine for smoking in

---

[1] *Lettres de communards*, pp. 20–1; text used here is slightly different and follows that in *Dictionnaire*, VI, p. 92. Frankel wrote to Marx again on 25 April about the attacks on him as a Prussian spy, concluding that he would ignore them and 'imperturbably pursue my objective' (p. 38).

[2] A.H.G., Ly 11, 8 April; reprinted in A. Decouflé, *La Commune de Paris*, Paris, 1969, p. 287.

one factory, 0·25 for polishing shoes or combing hair.[1] There had been serious conflicts in Paris over such matters of factory discipline.

The decree abolishing bakers' night work was strongly opposed by the proprietors, who circulated a petition that collected 850 signatures and was presented to the Commune denouncing the decree as 'an attack on the individual liberty of the worker and his employer'.[2] This latter view was upheld on the Commune by J.-B. Clément and Viard, who also warned that by so interfering between workers and their employers the Commune was encouraging violence. In the 3rd arrondissement the bakery workers were threatening to smash the windows of their employers if they continued to insist on night work.[3] Avrial and Theisz, both militant in the International, supported the Commune's decision: 'workers, men like ourselves, cannot be forced to work only at night, never being able to see the light of day', for this would be to drive them 'like miners to a form of work condemned by civilization'. Malon, Varlin and Frankel all insisted that the Commune should side with the bakery workers against their masters, Frankel calling it 'the only truly socialist decree passed by the Commune', though the execution of the measure was delayed for two weeks as a result of the employers' protests.

Frankel made a point of seeing that this delay did not result in the measure being dropped, and on 3 May he persuaded the Commune that in order to make it effective the Mairies would have to see to the confiscation of any bread baked at night in defiance of the decree. In some cases this was done: in the 4th arrondissement during the night of 19 May seven arrests were made.[4] But workers also connived with their employers to get round the decree.[5] The bakery workers, however, did hold a series of meetings in May to discuss their situation with members of the Commune. At one of these a representative of the Labour and Exchange Commission told about 2,000 workers that 'we must fight against the bourgeoisie to the end . . . Great wealth, large fortunes, must disappear for the benefit of the general well-being.' He called for the 'suppression of the ex-

[1] Duveau, *Vie ouvrière*, pp. 259–61.
[2] A.H.G., Ly 11.
[3] 28 April: P.V.C., I, pp. 538–9.
[4] Archives de la Seine: Decouflé, op. cit., pp. 289–90.
[5] Lefrançais, op. cit., p. 299; Arnould, op. cit., vol. 2, p. 192; Michel, op. cit., p. 170.

ploitation of man by man'.[1] On 15 May two delegates sent by Frankel called on the bakers' Trade Union to see to the strict enforcement of the Commune's decree on night work, and the next day some 1,500 workers marched as a deputation to the Hôtel de Ville carrying red flags and the banners of their corporations in order to thank the Commune for what it had done 'in their favour'.[2]

Food distribution, which had been a major problem during the siege, when several municipal canteens had been started, continued to be a matter of concern during the Commune. Allix as always was active in the 8th arrondissement, and he extended the system of food vouchers to cover not only bread and meat but clothes and fuel.[3] The 3rd and 12th arrondissements tried to improve the system of public assistance, and Viard for the Commune itself tried to keep prices down by distributing what food stocks remained from the first siege to the municipalities. His appointment to the Provisions Commission had been welcomed by the *Père Duchêne* as a sign that the Commune, like that of 1793, intended to do everything necessary against 'the villainous hoarders' who 'speculate on the misery of the people', for as the second siege progressed food prices had again started to rise.[4] But matters never became as serious as under the Government of National Defence, in spite of Thiers' attempts to enforce a blockade, since winter was over and peasants slipped supplies across the Prussian lines.

On 16 April came the decree entitling the Trade Unions to take over any abandoned workshops to form co-operative associations to start production up again. This resulted in some ten factories being occupied.[5] The *Vengeur* called this 'the most serious claim of the Commune to the gratitude of working men'; and the *Affranchi* was still more enthusiastic, calling it 'the glory of the Paris Commune, rallying and bringing over definitely all workers to its side' because of the way in which it had approached 'boldly and straightforwardly the greatest problem of the nineteenth century: namely, the organization of labour'.[6] The decree, however, in accordance with the

[1] 13 May: L. Michelant, '*Un Souvenir de la Commune*', *Journal des Economistes*, vol. 23, 1871, p. 268.
[2] J.O., 17 May; *Le Journal Populaire*, 17 May.
[3] J.O., 12 April; see too Decouflé, op. cit., p. 253.
[4] No. 33, 28 germinal (17 April); Gibson, op. cit., p. 102, 17 April; *Le Réveil*, 19 April.
[5] Rougerie, op. cit., p. 221.                              [6] 19 April, both papers.

traditions of the French Labour movement at that time, was a co-operative measure, not one of nationalization, though the Engineers' Union just before the fall of the Commune did suggest taking over one of the biggest engineering factories in Paris, the Barriquand works, which had been the scene of violent strikes in the 1860s. The only workshops threatened by the Commune's decree were, in its own words, those that had been 'cowardly abandoned' by owners seeking to avoid 'their civic obligations'. They were promised compensation when they returned. This idea of taking over abandoned workshops had first been raised during the siege. Part of the feeling motivating this demand was similar to that felt against absentee landlords; why should property be exempt from some sacrifices when people were out of work and starving? As Vermorel put it, such 'wealth' should be put to work, not left lying unproductive.[1] Vésinier's proposal on the Commune, however, that 'all the big factories of the monopolists' should be handed over to workers' associations was not taken up. Nor did Chalain, who had been a militant of the International in the 15th arrondissement, get any support when he proposed taking over the Cail factory in the interests of the Commune's war production. Instead Cail and the Godillot shoe factory both tactfully and profitably undertook some commissions for the Commune.

The idea of workers' co-operatives as a means of replacing capitalist production was an idea that went back to the beginning of the working-class movement in France. This was why Louis Blanc's *Organization of Labour*, published in 1839, had become a socialist best-seller. The National Workshops set up after the 1848 Revolution were a form of public assistance rather than an experiment in workers' control. But this latter idea was very alive in 1848 and over 300 meetings were held in different factories aimed at organizing labour through grouping workers together into co-operative workshops.[2] This tradition had been maintained by the co-operative movement during the Second Empire, though with great difficulty, and the repression during the last years of the Empire had broken up most of the workers' associations. The co-operative idea expressed

---

[1] *Ami du Peuple*, 24 April; cf. *Le Père Duchêne*, No. 44, 9 floreal (28 April): 'It is absurd that land and capital should continue to produce [i.e. in the form of rent] in the midst of the forced inaction of all the other instruments of labour.'
[2] See R. Gossez, '*Pre-Syndicalisme ou pre-coopération?*' *Archives Internationales de sociologie de la coopération*, 1959, No. 6, pp. 67–89.

the antagonism felt against employers, but hoped to end exploitation by the peaceful and gradual elimination of capitalist factories. This would come about, it was believed, because it was labour, not capital, that created wealth. The injustice of the existing system of production was that it deprived the labourer of his fair share. A speaker in the club in the Cour des Miracles during the siege had begun by recalling that 'the citizen Louis Blanc, in 1848, in the Luxembourg, had said to the workers: "You are the lords of the epoch" . . . Twenty years have passed – and this prophecy is about to be fulfilled. The worker is about to become the lord of the modern world, because he is its soul. The worker is everything, because nothing exists without labour. What would the rich do with their wealth if the workers did not make it fruitful?' He concluded that 'in the future, labour will no longer be the humble servant of capital; no, capital will become the slave of labour,' adding that 'all the working instruments used by labour will belong to labour. Same thing for factory buildings, same thing for the land.'[1]

Some of the co-operative ideas proposed during the Commune were overtly Proudhonian. The *Montagne* insisted that 'socialism does not deny property. On the contrary it affirms the need for individual land ownership.'[2] The *Père Duchêne* reminded its many readers that it was Proudhon who had pointed out that the interests of workers and bourgeois were the same,[3] though this conciliatory tone may have been partly prompted by the imminence of the elections as the revolutionaries wanted a high turnout to confound Versailles. But it was generally true that revolutionary language and violent acts were not incompatible with moderate and peaceful social demands. As the *Sociale* said: 'Be assured, bourgeois and peasants, there is no question of robbing you of your conquests. You legitimately possess what you have gained. But now we are reclaiming our rights just as eighty years ago you reclaimed yours.'[4] A proposal sent to the Commission of Labour and Exchange by a statuary worker suggested that the International should take the lead in grouping the workers' associations together. These could then expand 'without shocking the absurd and selfish social laws under which we are governed'.[5] There were plenty of similar schemes, all aiming at the peaceful

[1] A. Vidieu, *Histoire de la Commune de Paris en 1871*, Paris, 1871, pp. 33–4: quoted Rougerie, op. cit., pp. 215–16.

[2] 9 April.    [3] No. 10, 5 germinal (25 March).    [4] 31 March.

[5] A.H.G., Ly 11; reprinted in Rougerie, op. cit., pp. 217–19.

expansion of producers' co-operatives backed up by some form of public crediting, a 'Federal Bank'.

The militant socialist workers hoped that the services under the control of the State could be used by the Commune as one area of co-operative enterprise. This was suggested to the Labour and Exchange Commission by a member of the International's weekly study circle. The State Printer's monopoly should be broken up in favour of workers' associations, which, in addition, would be more willing to experiment with new forms of typography.[1] But the Commune did not use the opportunity of the State monopolies to effect any changes towards workers' control. The new Director of the State Tobacco industry, for example, was more concerned with ensuring discipline and preventing pillaging than with experiments in co-operative principles. His main task, after all, was to ensure that 'the courageous defenders of the Commune did not lack tobacco'.[2] The same was true of the Mint under the bronze-worker Camélinat. As a young man Camélinat had met Proudhon and had been one of the founding members of the International in France. After the Commune he had a distinguished career first in the French Socialist and later in the French Communist party. During the Commune plans were made to mint coins, and ingots were obtained from the Bank of France for this purpose together with plate from Churches, the Tuileries Palace and the Ministries. The smelter threw the Imperial plate into the furnace piece by piece, so much did he relish the task, with an appropriate remark for each object. Four hundred thousand 5-franc coins were minted, using the design of 1848 as there was no time to produce new moulds. Thus the secular Commune had to suffer its coins having the motto: 'God protect France'. Only 153,000 francs were issued, this during the last week to pay the National Guards on the barricades.[3]

The Post Office during the Commune was run by another member of the International, Theisz, a bronze-engraver who had managed to build up his own little workshop. The official Director was himself a republican with some Proudhonian sympathies, and he did not leave for Versailles until 30 March. The following day there was no post in Paris, much to the concern of those who had moved their families to the country. Theisz managed to re-establish normal deliveries within Paris, aided by the fact that many of the junior Postal

[1] A.H.G., Ly 11.      [2] A.H.G., Ly 11; Directive of 6 May.
[3] Vuillaume, op. cit., V, pp. 213–17, VII, pp. 129–30.

officials sympathized with the republican and socialist tendencies of the Commune. He also received plenty of offers of help, since there was a shortage of employment in Paris and to be a postman meant exemption from active National Guard duty. Theisz did try to make conditions of employment better, and suggestions came from below as to how to improve the postal service.[1] The *Père Duchêne* suggested that because there was a shortage of postage stamps within Paris the Commune should design its own: 'a beautiful woman, with a certain look in her eye and the air of a good *bougre de patriote*. A pretty red bonnet should be on her head.'[2] But the main problem Theisz had to face was how to get letters out of Paris, since Thiers had ordered the seizure of all mail into or out of the city. This was not easy to enforce, and postmen were sent out of Paris to do the round of the villages, dropping bundles of letters into the boxes. Representatives of the commercial interests in Paris went to see Thiers to try to persuade him to lift this ban, but Thiers would no more listen to them than to any other of the many delegations he had to receive. Private enterprise saw its opportunity here, and some fourteen agencies were founded and made quick profits getting letters through the blockade. Foreigners, having the immunity of their passports, were also much used as go-betweens. Balloons this time were not used. The only attempt to get propaganda out of Paris was on 12 May when a manned balloon was sent up carrying the 'Declaration to the French People' and other manifestoes. But these were quickly seized by the police.

War production was an area in which several attempts were made to set up workers' co-operatives.[3] It had been Avrial with 'several of his colleagues' who had first raised the issue on the Commune of the closed workshops. His union, the Engineers, was one of the biggest, having 5,000–6,000 members. They had voted at a meeting on 23 April that since the aim of the Commune should be 'economic emancipation' it should 'organize labour through associations in

[1] A.H.G., Ly 8.

[2] 3 floréal (22 April); on post see B. Laurent, *La Commune de 1871. Les Postes, Les Ballons, Le Telegraphe*, Paris, 1934, pp. 4–121.

[3] During the French Revolution arms production had come under the control of the Committee of Public Safety and new State-run factories were established. But Carnot made it clear that this State intervention was solely the result of the exceptional conditions and was not an attempt to replace private industry: see G. Lefebvre, *La Révolution Française*, Paris, 1951, pp. 389–90; D. Guérin, *La Lutte des classes sous la Première Republique*, Paris, 1946, vol. 1, pp. 324–9.

which there would be joint responsibility' in order 'to suppress the exploitation of man by man'.[1] The Tailors' Union responded to this meeting by calling on the workers' associations to meet to choose delegates to prepare an inquiry into the organization of labour, considering that 'no government has ever offered the working class a better opportunity'.[2] Two such assemblies were held during the third week of May in which members of the International played a leading role, including two women from the 'Women's Union'.[3] By the first week in May the engineers controlled most of the arms production in the arrondissements. The most important was the Louvre arms factory, where the workers drew up their own statutes. According to these the workers were to choose their own Delegate to represent them on the Commune. A Workers' Council composed of foremen and other representatives elected by each workbench were to meet every day to discuss the next day's work and any reports and suggestions sent to them. Hiring and firing was the responsibility of this Council, which also formed 'a watch council to safeguard the interests of the Commune'. A ten-hour working day was decided upon.[4] This experiment in workers' control never got very far. Avrial admitted to Rossel that there had been three directors in seven days, no work was being done, and that his own Engineers' Association spent most of its time talking. 'The next time I form an association,' Avrial sadly remarked, 'whether in America or elsewhere, it will be with a few friends that I know well, but never with the first person who comes.'[5]

By 14 May forty-three producers' co-operatives had been formed among the many craft industries of the city, though most of these were in anticipation of getting work, and thirty-four Trade Unions had re-established themselves. There were co-operative proposals from the 'State catering service', from the *charcutiers*, café waiters, concièrges, and many others. A protest was sent to the Commune

[1] *Le Réveil du Peuple*, 16 April.

[2] *Paris Libre*, 20 April.

[3] *Le Réveil du Peuple*, 18 May; cf. A. Molok, '*Les Ouvriers de Paris pendent la Commune*', *Cahiers du Communisme*, May, June 1951, pp. 619-20; Thomas, *Women*, p. 73.

[4] J.O., 21 May; A.H.G., Ly 20, gives a report to Ministry of War that most of the members of the Artillery Commission had been engineering workers in the munitions factories and that they wanted accordingly to elect their own head rather than have one imposed on them by the Commune.

[5] Rossel, op. cit., pp. 268-9, 10 May.

from the Shoemakers' Union complaining because the big footwear factory of Godillot was being allowed to supply all the boots for the National Guard. Instead, they said, the Commune should be prepared to pay more for its boots in order to support the infant shoemakers' associations. A similar though more successful protest was made by the Tailors' Union against the low wages current in the clothing industry: 'things would be very different if the workers' co-operatives were protected by those who want the emancipation of the Proletariat'.[1] Frankel appointed two active Trade Unionists to draw up a report on the system of military supplies, which he presented to the Commune on 12 May with the reminder that 'the Revolution of 18 March was made entirely by the working class. If we, who believe in the principle of social equality, do nothing for this class I see no justification for the Commune.'[2] The report criticized the Commune's Intendance for buying from the cheapest supplier with no thought about the effect this would have on the wages of the workers. 'As a result of this infamous competition,' the report pointed out, 'the Commune loses its dignity and male and female workers see their already insufficient wages drop even lower. The position, therefore, is one of exploiters profiting from the general poverty to lower wages backed up by the Commune, too blind to see what is going on.' This was not how 'a socialist government should act'. The report recommended that the Commune should deal only with co-operatives in future and that prices should be fixed 'by arbitration' between the military Intendance, the Trade Unions and a representative of the Commune. Seraillier, supporting Frankel, described this as 'a control commission to prevent the exploitation of the working class'. The final text adopted by the Commune on 12 May did not go quite this far. Instead the Labour and Exchange Commission was authorized to revise existing contracts, which the ever-cautious Jourde feared would only lead to more delays. Future contracts would have to include a stated minimum wage rate and preference was to be given to workers' co-operatives.

Clothing manufacture was largely women's work, and so Frankel's Commission proposed the creation of special workshops in each arrondissement to provide employment for women. At

[1] A.H.G., Ly 22; reprinted in Rougerie, op. cit., pp. 226-7.
[2] 12 May: P.V.C., II, pp. 348-52; published in J.O., 13 May; original in A.H.G., Ly 11.

first these would be supervised by the Commission, until they were firmly established, the eventual aim being 'to encourage the growth of genuine and homogeneous groupings by presiding over their formation and developing them in the federal spirit, all the time leaving them free and autonomous'.[1] This idea had come from a petition presented to the Commission by the *Women's Union for the Defence of Paris and for Aid to the Wounded*, in effect the women's branch of the International. The Union had been founded on 11 April by Elizabeth Dmitrieff, the daughter of a Russian hussar, and had held regular meetings throughout Paris. Its membership represented all the Paris women's trades: seamstresses, dressmakers, laundresses, linen-drapers, etc. Elizabeth had contracted a *marriage blanc* with an officer much older than herself, who believed in women's emancipation, in order to get out of Russia to study, women not being allowed in Russian universities. As a result of a stay in London in the summer of 1870 she had become acquainted with Marx. Elizabeth Dmitrieff backed up the petition of the Union by requesting the Labour and Exchange Commission to give her Committee the task of clothing the National Guard, for unless labour is provided and organized 'it is to be feared that the feminine element of the Parisian population, revolutionary for the moment, will return, because of continual deprivation, to the passive and more or less reactionary state to which it belonged in the past'.[2] But promises were not kept, and on 18 May Vallès was complaining in his paper that 'just as in the good old days' women were still being underpaid: 'This shameful exploitation must cease. We must have the women with us at any cost.'

These various attempts to introduce workers' co-operatives were envisaged by the socialist Communards, usually members of the International, as showing the answer to the social problem of how to reorganize production to end the exploitation of labour: '*sans-culotte* syndicalism' as it has been called.[3] The other side to the emancipation of labour was the question of education.

Lack of education, it was felt, was one reason why the working man remained poor. Several of the reports of the workers' delegations to the 1867 Paris Exhibition had spoken of the need for compulsory free public education: 'Only education can give us equality.

[1] A.H.G., Ly 23; Rougerie, op. cit., pp. 228–9; Decouflé, op. cit., pp. 310–12; Thomas, op. cit., pp. 68–9.
[2] A.H.G., Ly 22; Thomas, p. 70.          [3] By Rougerie, op. cit., pp. 229–30.

The educated worker is equal to anybody, because he can get anywhere, whereas the uneducated, however rich he may be, will always remain a ridiculous idiot.'[1] For many republicans it was a matter of principle that citizens of a democracy should have at least a primary education. In 1792 and 1793 there were several projects for free public primary education. This principle was restated in 1848 by Carnot, the new Minister of Education. But after the uprising in June 1849 in the field of education as elsewhere there was a return to authoritarian principles, and the *loi Falloux* of 1850 handed education back into the control of the Church. Socialists and republicans alike attacked the grip of the Church on education in France, and in 1867 certain municipalities were allowed to establish free primary schools. In Paris in 1870 72,000 children attended the 247 municipal primary schools, 87,500 were in Church schools and another 15,000 in secondary schools, out of a total population of 257,000 children between the ages of four and sixteen. Thus 83,000 children were having no schooling at all – thirty-two per cent – while non-attendance was high among those officially at school.[2] Of the 36,000 men and women arrested in Paris after the Commune, 4,000 were completely illiterate (eleven per cent), and 21,000 could only read and write 'imperfectly' (fifty-nine per cent).[3] There was therefore plenty of justification for the tailors to demand in their report of 1867 that 'for the sake of the honour and greatness of the country to which we belong, illiteracy should be abolished'.

During the siege the clubs and popular Press had given voice to the popular demands regarding education, and several Mayors on their own authority had begun secularizing the schools in their arrondissements. On 20 April Edouard Vaillant was appointed Delegate to the Education Commission, where for the next month he devoted himself to trying to put into practice republican and socialist reforms. Vaillant, aged thirty-one, came from a provincial bourgeois family and had been an engineering student before going

---

[1] *Exposition Universelle de 1867. Rapports*, vol. 3, Raffineurs; see too G. Duveau, *La Pensée ouvrière sur l'éducation*, Paris, 1947, pp. 182–212.

[2] E. Laveleye, *L'Instruction du Peuple*, 1872, p. 219: quoted S. Froumov, *La Commune de Paris et la démocratisation de l'école*, Moscow, 1958, p. 48. In London the 1870 Education Act had led to the forming of the London School Board and compulsory education from five to thirteen (or to ten if there was 'a valid reason'). But in 1871 the number of school places was worse than the situation in Paris.

[3] Report of General Appert, *Annales*, vol. 43, pp. 112–13.

on to study science at the Sorbonne, Collège de France and the Ecole de Médecine. From 1866 until forced to return because of the outbreak of the war, Vaillant studied at universities in Germany and Austria. Until this time he had not played an active part in politics, though he had joined the German section in Geneva of the International and he knew some of the German anarchist-socialists as well as some of the Blanquists. He was with Charles Longuet in Paris on 4 September, and together they sent a telegram to Marx in London informing him of the fall of the Empire. During the siege Vaillant met Blanqui, who left a decisive impression on him, and Vaillant became more active, being at the Hôtel de Ville on 31 October and signing the *Affiche Rouge* of 6 January.[1] Of the other members on the Education Commission, Verdure, aged forty-six, had been a village schoolteacher before joining the staff of the *Marseillaise*. In 1868 he had been one of the founders of a Mutual Credit Society to establish secular schools. The schoolteacher Urbain had been on the first Education Commission of the Commune prior to Vaillant's appointment; during the Empire he had tried to found a private non-religious boarding school, but a pretext was found to close it down.[2] Lefrançais, the third teacher on the Commune, was given other executive appointments. The journalist Vallès, the son of a teacher, the poet J.-B. Clément and the Jacobin Miot completed Vaillant's Commission, together with Courbet.

The task of the Commission was to coordinate the activities of the local municipalities, and Vaillant appointed a special Organization Commission to help him in this task.[3] This was not composed of members of the Commune, and included Emile da Costa, the father of the two Blanquist brothers, Charles and Gaston, a mathematics teacher who belonged to a Polytechnical Association for educating the working class. Two other members of this latter Commission had been members of the republican 'New Education' society's delegation to the Commune of 1 April. This had asked the Commune, 'considering the necessity under a Republic of preparing youth to govern itself by means of a republican education that still has to be created', to suppress all religious teaching in schools, re-

[1] See M. Dommanget, *Edouard Vaillant*, Paris, 1956, pp. 17–27.

[2] M. Dommanget, *L'Enseignement, l'enfance et la culture sous la Commune*, Paris, 1964, p. 16.

[3] J.O., 29 April; Froumov, op. cit., p. 156 reprints this and the other decrees of the Commune concerning education.

move all religious objects, and to see that only 'the experimental or scientific method be used' in all instruction. They concluded with the common demand for free compulsory public education.[1]

One of the first decrees of the Commune had been that separating Church and State, though it was not until the middle of May that Vaillant specifically called on the municipalities to close down all the Church schools. Several municipalities had already been active in trying to do this since the end of March. But first teachers had to be found to replace the nuns and priests. On 9 April the Commune appealed to those interested in teaching to offer their services, and some of those who did so were punished by Versailles. Anne Denis, a young bookseller, appeared before a War Council for having accepted a post in a nuns' school, and Jules Simon, Minister of Education at Versailles, dismissed three University professors on 13 May for having shown sympathy towards the Commune.[2] Vaillant removed all the school inspectors on 14 May, replacing them by new ones chosen by himself. The Education Commission tried to exercise its authority over the employment of teachers, but generally the arrondissements acted according to their own inclinations.

In the 17th arrondissement in April Rama of the 'New Education' society and of Vaillant's Organization Commission published with Malon's backing a set of instructions to the teachers in the arrondissement. All religious teaching was forbidden and like the 'New Education' society's manifesto Rama's instructions called for the use only of the 'experimental or scientific method' based on the 'observation of facts'. Rama also invited all those interested in teaching in the 17th arrondissement to send in their ideas on what should be the new forms of education.[3] The members of the Commune for the 3rd arrondissement announced on 23 April: 'Citizens, that which you and we have been demanding for so long and which the men of 4 September refused us, completely secular education, is now an accomplished fact in our arrondissement.'[4] J.-B. Clément, of the Education Commission, instructed his own arrondissement, the 18th, to remove all religious crosses, books, pictures and statues

[1] J.O., 2 April; Froumov, pp. 106–8.
[2] Dommanget, op. cit., p. 56; Thomas, op. cit., p. 98.
[3] See Decouflé, op. cit., p. 266, for some replies and Rama's own caustic comments.
[4] M.P., II, p. 327; Froumov, p. 135.

from the schools; prayers 'naturally were forbidden' and were to be replaced 'by more moral and more useful lessons'. These measures, Clément said, were imperfect, but they were a start, since the Commune's 'new style of education' could not be implemented because the war made it impossible to solve 'all the important questions raised by the new Revolution'.[1]

The war did not prevent Jules Allix in the 8th arrondissement from drawing up a full programme of reform based on an analysis of the number of places required and the shortage of schools to accommodate them. His hope was to be able to open enough new schools to accommodate all the children in his arrondissement between the ages of three and twelve. He proposed opening up one of the girls' schools that had been closed down as a Teachers' Training School. Children aged from five to twelve would also be received at this school, to which he eventually hoped to be able to add an infant school. He proposed similar teachers' training schools for physical education, music and art. Meanwhile 'numerous provisional classes' would be established everywhere 'they could be useful'.[2]

The secularization programme was not always welcomed. The 13th and 15th arrondissements resisted it, and in the 5th arrondissement Mayor Régère, who devoted himself as much to the affairs of his arrondissement as to the Commune, considered that it was possible to be both 'a practising Catholic and a revolutionary socialist', much to the disgust of Jean Allemane, the local National Guard legion commander. Allemane had a hard fight getting the nuns expelled from the convents. Crowds of women invaded the new secular schools, attacking the teachers. On one occasion Allemane had to rescue a Headmistress from a crowd of women shopkeepers who had pushed her down two flights of stairs. But he did manage to set up a boys' school in the Friary in the rue Rollin, after it had been given a good clean-out. On the first day Allemane made a speech asking the boys to remember, whatever happened, that the men of the Commune 'loved them dearly' and that when they became men they should 'defend the memory of the Commune against its slanderers'.[3]

Women's education was given particular attention, though it was not until right at the end that Vaillant appointed a special Commis-

[1] Dated 10 May: *Le Cri du Peuple*, 19 May; Froumov, pp. 146-7.
[2] J.O., 30 April, 8 May; Froumov, pp. 165-72.
[3] Allemane, op. cit., pp. 74-9; Froumov, pp. 135-43.

sion for Girls' Education.[1] Its all-female membership included Madame Reclus, André Léo, a member of the International who had written several feminist novels that were sufficiently popular to be translated into Russian, and Anna Jaclard, a Russian general's daughter, who had refused an offer of marriage from Dostoevsky since he needed 'a woman who would devote herself to him fully'. Like Elizabeth Dmitrieff, Anna entered into a *marriage blanc* to get out of Russia. In Paris she met a Blanquist medical student, Victor Jaclard, the future commander of the 17th legion during the Commune. They were married by Malon the day before the proclamation of the Commune. The women's society founded by Jules Allix, 'The Social Commune of Paris', held a meeting on the planning of education with the 'New Education' society. The latter met regularly in the Ecole Turgot one of the biggest and oldest primary schools in Paris. Day nurseries were suggested by Maria Verdure, the daughter of the member of the Commune, Félix and Elie Ducoudray representing the 'Society of the Friends of Education', as nurseries would be a help to working women until the time when society was 'reconstituted on new political and social foundations' and all mothers could be excused from work during the nursing period. The nurseries would have been rather like Fourierist *phalanstères*, since the women looking after the children would be periodically shifted around so that they never became tired of doing one task for too long. This would also be good for the children, 'it being important that children should be looked after only by cheerful and young women, so far as possible'. The nurseries should be scattered throughout the working-class districts, near to the factories, and have their own gardens, a play-room full of toys and even 'an aviary full of birds' to prevent the children ever getting bored, 'the greatest malady' of little children. Everything to do with religion would be excluded, and the pictures and sculptures were to be of real objects such as animals or trees. Medical supervision was to be provided for.[2]

In pressing for women's education the Communards were going against the practice of the time, which in entrusting girls' education to nuns, themselves having only a minimal education, showed the prejudice for 'elevating' women above social and public life. Proudhon was exceptional among socialist writers in sharing this

---

[1] J.O., 22 May: Froumov, p. 157; Dommanget, op. cit., p. 129.
[2] J.O., 15, 17 May; Froumov, pp. 214–19; Thomas, op. cit., p. 97.

prejudice, believing that 'woman really has no place in the world of politics and economics. Her function begins beyond these spheres.'[1] According to this view a woman's place was firmly in the home, bringing up her children, as was stressed by the Proudhonist Memoir of the French delegates to the International Congress of 1866. But such views were not expressed during the Commune, Tolain, one of the Proudhonists of 1866, remaining in any case at Versailles. After the Commune, however, one of the themes of the reaction was that education should remain limited to an elite, writers such as Flaubert, Goncourt, Renan and Taine blaming education as one of the causes of the revolution.[2] During the Commune the prevailing view was rather that of the Minority Declaration to the 1866 Memoir, which Varlin had signed, in favour of public education for both sexes. As the *Père Duchêne* said: 'If only you realized, citizens, how much the Revolution depends on women, you would have your eyes opened on girls' education. You would not leave them, as has been done until now, in ignorance! Foutre! In a good Republic, perhaps more attention should be paid to the attention of girls than to that of boys.' After all it is mothers who give us our first ideas and so it is important that these should be those of good *citoyennes*. 'Thus, citizen members of the Commune, if you want to have men, the morals of the Nation must be reformed. And in order to transform morals women must be given a good solid education.'[3] The mention of morals enabled a reference to be made to Proudhon, who was '*un crâne lapin et qui avait l'oeil*', which could be considered inappropriate in an article devoted to women's education if it did not show the loose way in which Proudhon's name was invoked by many good revolutionaries.

As in any war, widows and orphans were considered to have a special claim on the government, and the Commune, legislating with fine self-assurance, immediately announced after the fighting had begun that it would adopt the families of all those killed fighting the 'criminal royalists' of Versailles. A few days later a more detailed

---

[1] *Da la Justice*: Proudhon, op. cit., p. 255.

[2] Cf. P. Lidsky, *Les Ecrivans contre la Commune de Paris*, Paris, 1970, pp. 83–7.

[3] No. 25, 20 germinal (9 April); Froumov, pp. 158–61. The *Père Duchêne* deliberately adopted a popular style based on its illustrious predecessor of the first Revolution. Its pages therefore are liberally sprinkled with '*foutres*' and '*bougres*', which, as is usually the case with slang, cannot be given a direct translation. At the time, though not now, they had the usage and force of 'fuck' in English.

11(*a*) and (*b*) The demolition of the Vendôme Column: 16 May. 'When the imperial mantle finally falls on the shoulders of Louis Bonaparte, the bronze statue of Napoleon will crash from the top of the Vendôme Column.' (Marx: *The Eighteenth Brumaire of Louis Bonaparte* (1852))

(*a*) Barricade at the entrance to the rue de la Paix. This was one of the more substantial barricades, constructed to defend the Place Vendôme.

12. The barricades of May 1871

(*b*) Barricade on Quai de l'Hôtel de Ville: note the pavement grills

(*c*) Barricade on the rue Ramponneau, 28 May. The last barricade?

decree granted a widows' pension of 600 francs, and promised that any children left without a mother would receive an 'integral education' at the expense of the Commune. The *Père Duchêne* welcomed this '*bougrement patriotique*' decree, which it believed would greatly console those National Guards going off to battle. Special schools were established in the 3rd, 10th and 11th arrondissements for motherless children of slain National Guards and an Orphanage was opened up on the newly named Boulevard Victor-Hugo (now the Boulevard Haussmann).[1] The 11th arrondissement on one occasion organized a special outing for the eighty or ninety orphans it had taken under its charge. Five buses, especially decorated, took the children to the Vincennes woods, where they had a picnic. On the way back it was naturally felt proper that these 'victims of the odious war of the privileged against the proletariat' should pay tribute to the July Column in the Place de la Bastille before passing by the Hôtel de Ville to express 'their gratitude and attachment to the Commune that had adopted them'.[2]

The 5th arrondissement, which had had its difficulties in secularizing the schools, did see the first attempt to carry out the other side of the Commune's education programme, the establishment of 'professional schools'. Two members of Vaillant's Organization Commission, the mathematics teachers André and Emile da Costa, were successful in opening up the Jesuit house in the rue Lhomond, which had excellent laboratories and astronomical instruments. Children with sufficient primary education were admitted at the age of twelve, irrespective of whether they came from the 5th arrondissement.[3] The *Père Duchêne* in its accustomed style welcomed this news from the 5th arrondissement as '*fameusement révolutionnaire*' and '*rudement* in the interests of the people'.[4] Like so many reforms this was only just begun by the time the Commune was defeated, though according to Allemane it was restarted several years later.

This idea of what was often called an 'integral education' had been one of the most insistent demands of the French labour movement, expressing the desire both to learn a useful trade and at the same time escape from the specialization caused by the division of labour and the consequent separation into educated and uneducated classes.

[1] M.P., II, pp. 520, 510, 296, 397; Froumov, pp. 204–10.
[2] *Le Cri du Peuple*, 18 May; Froumov, pp. 213–14.
[3] M.P., II, pp. 438, 553; Froumov, pp. 190–2, 197–8.
[4] No. 54, 19 floréal (8 May); Froumov, pp. 192–5.

The editor of one of the first working-class newspapers in Paris in the 1840s, Anthyme Corbon of the *Atelier*, who remained in Paris during the Commune without taking part in the revolution, had published a book on *Professional Education* in 1859. The same idea is found in the reports of the workers' delegations to the London Exhibition of 1862 and the Paris Exhibition of 1867. Proudhon, who had had to educate himself whilst earning his living as a printer, wanted workers to receive an education that would allow them 'to go through the whole range of industrial practices, working from the most simple to the most difficult, without specializing in any one activity'; an education that would bring out 'the principles underlying these practices'. As a result, Proudhon hoped, 'the industrial worker, the man of action and the intellectual would all be rolled into one'. Both the majority and the minority of the French Memoir of the 1866 International Congress agreed on the need for 'a scientific and professional education'.[1]

On 12 May Vaillant announced the re-opening of the Art School in the rue Dupuytren by the Odeon Theatre as a Professional School of Industrial Art for Young Girls, where would be taught 'the application of the art of design to industry'.[2] Madame Manière, a schoolteacher who had organized a temporary workshop-school in the rue Turenne behind the Place de Vosges, proposed expanding this into a 'truly professional school' open to all. Girls would be taken in at twelve years old and 'practical work would alternate with the study of scientific theories and the industrial arts'.[3] Jules Allix's plans for the 8th arrondissement did not overlook this aspect of education, and the premises of his women's society, 'The Social Commune of Paris', were to be turned into a workplace for women with space set aside for an infants' school for young girls without home or work.[4] On 18 May Vaillant appealed to all the arrondissements for help in finding suitable premises to start professional and scientific methods, as it was important that the Communal Revolution should thus affirm 'its essentially socialist character' by educational reforms that would lead to social equality.

Looking back on his efforts at the Ministry of Education not long

[1] *De la Justice*: Proudhon, op. cit., p. 80; *Mémoire* given in Freymond, op. cit., vol. 1, p. 95.
[2] M.P., II, p. 486; Froumov, p. 195.
[3] *Le Vengeur*, 3 April; Froumov, pp. 188–9.
[4] J.O., 8 May; Froumov, p. 172; Thomas, op. cit., pp. 99–100.

after the fall of the Commune, Vaillant felt that because of the war little had been accomplished; 'the streets had simply been cleared and the schools filled in order to leave the population free to fight'. But he did consider that 'the main lines of an egalitarian education had been sufficiently mapped out for the idea to start to spread'.[1] In April another member of the Education Commission, the poet J.-B. Clément, had faced the issue of why the Commune bothered to pass decrees that could not be enforced. 'What will remain,' he asked, 'if the people are defeated', if not the principles enshrined in its decrees: 'They can kill us, if they wish, they can rip down our posters and remove all traces from the walls, but the principles that have been affirmed will still exist, and whatever is done, whatever is said, they are monuments that the Versaillais cannot destroy either by strokes of the pen or shots of the cannon.'[2]

This is the context in which Marx's judgement on the social work of the Commune can be seen: 'the great social measure of the Commune was its own working existence. Its special measures could but betoken the tendency of a government of the people by the people.'[3] For, and this was particularly true in the fields of education and producers' associations, the very existence of the Commune opened the way for experiments in trying to apply some of the ideas that had been developed in opposition to the economic and political repression of the French State. Proudhon's anarchist ideas, his horror of anything approaching State education or State production, were not those of the Communards. There was considerable local in-itiative, and the various co-operative workshops established did intend to manage their own affairs. But at the same time the Commune was looked to as an obvious and immediate source of help. Having made their revolution, with power for once in their own hands, the working population did not intend to let go of such a valuable ally in their battle against their capitalist masters for a juster society, one more concerned with the welfare of all. This is why the tailors looked to the Commune to provide their association with work, as did forty-nine unemployed women in a petition to Frankel; why the iron-founders co-operative requested the Com-mune to give them preference over their erstwhile employers in providing munitions for the war; why one nail-maker wrote asking

[1] Letter of 31 December 1871: Dommanget, op. cit., p. 158.
[2] Le Cri du Peuple, 23 April.
[3] Civil War in France, MESW, p. 297.

the Commune to commission him, a 'communist' and National Guardsman, rather than his employer in order to encourage other nail-makers to join him in forming a workers' federation.[1] For as the project drawn up by the Labour and Exchange Commission said · in response to the appeal of the 'Women's Union' to the Commune to organize work for women,

> the Commune is not simply the administrative municipal author-ity, but above all the affirmation of sovereign power . . . that is to say, the full and absolute right of the Communal group to give itself its own laws, to create its own political organism *as a means* towards realizing the very aim of the revolution, namely the emancipation of labour, the abolition of monopolies and privi-leges, the end of industrial feudalism, and the creation of an economic order in which the reconciliation of interests must replace the conflicts and confusion produced by the old social order.[2]

[1] A.H.G., Ly 23; Ly 22 (Rougerie, op. cit., pp. 225-7); Ly 11 (Rougerie, op. cit., pp. 213-14; Decouflé, op. cit., p. 251).
[2] A.H.G., Ly 23; reprinted in Rougerie, op. cit., p. 228.

# Chapter 9

# THE COMMUNE: CLUBS
# AND FESTIVALS

The fate of the Commune was sealed by its military incapacity, yet the atmosphere within Paris was not that of a city dominated by war. On the contrary, the war seemed something that could never really affect Parisians. There was no sense of imminent danger, although gunfire could be heard all the time. It was not felt to be credible that the troops of Versailles would ever actually enter Paris. After defeat many claimed that they had known the cause was hopeless from the start, something that became obvious before very long. But the young Louis Barron, disillusioned after several weeks at the War Ministry, was probably quite typical in just letting himself be carried along by day-to-day events. The fine weather after the winter of the first siege gave a sense of light-headedness. Stories of the massacres following the June uprising of 1848 were not taken as a warning. At worst it was thought that the leaders of the National Guard or that the members of the Commune would be arrested, but the population as a whole would surely remain unscathed. Activity kept many from thinking about the future. It was too like a game to give rise to sombre thoughts, this war and this city, which had 'all the signs of being simply on holiday'.[1] The Commune was indeed a 'festival of the oppressed', as Lenin once described it, in which the whole city became a public forum of political discussion and action. However short its duration, the Commune lasted long enough to show the possibility of new forms of social association.

The revolutionary theory of 1871 (as of 1793) regarding politics was that sovereignty lay in the people: those elected to represent them were to act as delegates of the people, not parliamentary members. This is how the Central Committee of the National Guard

[1] Barron, op. cit., p. 87; see pp. 83–7 for one of the rare descriptions of the sense of daily life under the Commune by a revolutionary.

had justified its position against the constitutional legality of the Mayors, arguing that it had a popular mandate to defend the Republic and hold elections for a Commune. In the 1st arrondissement the idea was mooted of choosing an 'advisory council' that would 'directly represent the needs of the population' to the members of the Commune.[1] On 5 May it was announced in the 18th arrondissement that there would be daily public meetings, as 'those elected by the people have the duty of keeping in constant touch with their electors in order to give account of the mandate they have received and to submit themselves to questions'.[2] But no such meetings seem to have taken place. The *Prolétaire*, 'organ of the social demands of the 11th arrondissement', published by the Club Saint-Ambroise, expressed the popular view regarding membership of the Commune when it wrote: 'The people alone have the right to be the judge of men and their acts, and the mission of its mandatories is limited to enabling the people to do this sanely and with a knowledge of the issues . . . Servants of the People, do not give yourselves false airs and pretend you are sovereigns, for that no more suits you than the Helots whom you succeeded. What does majority or minority matter to us? Your persons count for very little in the balances of the Commune. The People are tired of saviours; henceforth they intend to dispute your acts.'[3] This was the popular view of sovereignty as inalienable. No group could claim to be privileged in representing the sovereignty of the people; all alike could equally claim to represent it. Direct government was what the popular forces expected from establishing the Commune. The State, according to the 'socialist and democratic republican electoral central committee' of the 11th arrondissement, was 'the people governing themselves by a national convention made up of revocable mandatories, elected by properly constituted direct universal suffrage. The people reserve for themselves the right to debate and sanction all constitutions and organic laws.'[4] The clubs claimed to express this popular sovereignty, and to act as centres of political intelligence and education. 'People, govern yourselves by yourselves through your public meetings, through your Press,' proclaimed the 'organ of the clubs', the *Bulletin Communal*; 'bring pressure to bear on those who represent you; they will never go too far along the road of revolution.'[5]

[1] M.P., II, p. 279; J.O., 14 April.
[2] Poster in B.N.: Decouflé, op. cit., p. 106.
[3] 19 May.     [4] M.P., II, pp. 84–5.     [5] 6 May.

The Communard Press itself, however, remained largely in-
dividualistic, Rochefort, Vallès, Pyat, André Léo and others each
having their own papers. But they were used by clubs and associations to announce news of their meetings. Apart from commenting
on the days' events and on the decrees of the Commune, the Press
published letters or simply announced where cheap potatoes could
be obtained or that the public gardens would be reopened. The most
popular paper was the *Père Duchêne* of Vermersch, Vuillaume and
Humbert. This did try to speak for the people, and adopted a popular style based on Hébert's paper, whose name it had copied and
which could still be found on the quays. In May the number printed
reached 50,000, putting it on the usual level of the *Marseillaise* or the
*Figaro*. One woman wrote to it in April saying how she liked its
imitation of the original, and asked the editors to let her have a copy
of the first issue under the Commune as this was lacking in her
collection.[1] The *Rappel* in a self-congratulatory tone commented on
the flourishing of new papers under the Commune: 'Today Paris
has become truly picturesque with the cries of its paper-sellers from
dawn to dusk. It is a permanent concert, a sort of perpetual fair:
a new fair!'[2]

The Commune was ambiguous in its attitude to the revolutionary
view of its responsibilities. Holding its debates in secret was not what
was expected of a revolutionary assembly. The Central Committee
of the Twenty Arrondissements pressed the Commune to make
its sessions public, as did the International and the meeting of
the electors of the 4th arrondissement in the *Théâtre-Lyrique*.[3] *La
Sociale* asked scornfully if the Commune 'feared lest the presence of
the people might influence its decisions'.[4] Amouroux at the meeting
in the *Théâtre-Lyrique* admitted that he had been criticized by some
members of the Commune for speaking in the clubs. Yet, said
Amouroux, 'when Robespierre or Saint-Just arrived at the Convention, they were fortified because they came from the Jacobin or
Cordelier club, just as the strength of Marat came because he wrote
of what he had heard in the midst of the labouring population'.[5]

[1] 27 April: *Lettres au 'Père Duchêne' pendant la Commune de Paris*, Marx–Engels–
Lenin Institute Moscow, Paris, 1934, p. 57.
[2] 9 April.                    [3] Cf. above, pp. 247–8.                    [4] 31 March.
[5] P.V.C., II, pp. 457–8. The main studies of the clubs under the Commune
are Claude Perrot in Bruhat, Dautry and Tersen, op. cit., pp. 153–66; A. Molok,
'*Les Ouvriers de Paris pendant la Commune*', *Cahiers du Communisme*, May 1951,

Amouroux frequented the club in the church of Saint-Nicolas-des-Champs in the 3rd arrondissement, as did Johannard and Vésinier. Ferré could be seen at the Club de la Révolution in the 5th arrondissement, Vallès at the Club de l'Ecole de Médecine, Billioray at the Club Saint-Pierre and the members for the 4th arrondissement sometimes at the Club Saint-Paul. But in general the members of the Commune became consumed by their own debates and the Commissions. This was resented by the clubs. The Club des Prolétaires in the church of Saint-Ambroise complained that 'the members of the Commune have made the serious mistake of playing at being Providence. They should stick to submitting their propositions to the sanction of the people, who will tell them what to do, rather than handing down decrees.'[1] At the same club a speaker expressed the view that at least one member of the Commune should come each evening to listen to the demands of the people.[2] The same demand was expressed at the Club Saint-Nicolas-des-Champs, a speaker calling on the Commune to 'act like that of '93 and grant two hours a day to hearing petitions'.[3] The secretary of the Commune's own Executive Commission suggested that the Commune should appoint a special Commission to examine the suggestions that clubs and individuals were daily sending in: 'These suggestions are often excellent and should be seen by the Commune.'[4] Vésinier seems to have tried to rely on the Club Saint-Nicolas-des-Champs for popular support. On 3 May he deposed before the Commune the resolutions voted by 5,000 citizens at this club on 1 May. Apart from congratulating the Commune on appointing a Committee of Public Safety, the club called for further by-elections to fill the vacant seats and asked the Commune to instruct the Mairies to put churches at the disposal of the people 'in order that the instruction and political education of citizens could take place and so that they could be kept informed of the course of public affairs'. But the Communal assembly refused to discuss these proposals and Vésinier did not press them any further.[5]

The clubs were a continuation of the movement that had developed during the siege. But they suffered from the fact that many

---

pp. 608–15; E. Schulkind, 'The Activity of Popular Organisations during the Paris Commune of 1871', *French Historical Studies*, Fall, 1960, pp. 394–415.

[1] *La Justice*, 19 May.      [2] 19 May: A.H.G., Ly 22 *bis*, 'Clubs'.

[3] *Bulletin Communal*, 6 May.      [4] 26 April: P.V.C., I, p. 516.

[5] P.V.C., II, pp. 89–90.

of their leaders had passed on to the Commune without, as has been seen, maintaining close contact with the popular organizations out of which they had come. To try to exert a more effective influence on the Commune the Club of the Salle Molière in the 3rd arrondisse- ment proposed towards the end of April the forming of a federation of clubs.[1] Shortly afterwards the Central Committee of the Twenty Arrondissements announced the opening of a Club Central in Saint- Eustache in the 1st arrondissement just across from the Salle Molière.[2] During the siege a club of this name had been formed as part of the effort to group the revolutionary clubs.[3] Eleven clubs joined the Federation and listed their aims as being 'to maintain daily com- munication with the Commune in order that it may transmit daily news of activity and military events to us for distribution to the clubs by their respective delegates'. The clubs in the federation would also discuss proposals made among themselves and forward these on to the Commune.[4] The committee of this federation met for the first time on 5 May.[5] The Club Saint-Nicolas-des-Champs started on 6 May to publish a daily *Bulletin Communal* intended to circulate news of the propositions voted in the different clubs to- gether with the reports of their debates. But this had only one issue. Ten days later this same club proposed the formation of a Central Committee of all the clubs that would circulate petitions to be pre- sented to the Commune.[6] The 'majority of the Commune', accord- ing to Pyat's *Le Vengeur*, rallied to this idea, seeing in it 'an analogy to the Jacobin club' of the French Revolution. The 'majority' would use the clubs as a means of consulting 'the opinion of the people'.[7] By this date the committee of the Federation of clubs was meeting each day in the afternoon in the Public Assistance building in the Avenue Victoria opposite the Hôtel de Ville, and the clubs of the federation had begun to circulate motions among themselves.[8]

The Central Committee of the Twenty Arrondissements was less dominant as a popular organization during the second siege than during the first. But it does seem to have been intermittently active in the central arrondissements, as during the previous November.

---

[1] *Le Vengeur*, 1 May.          [2] M.P., II, p. 409.          [3] Cf. above, p. 89.
[4] *Le Vengeur*, 7 May.       [5] *Le Cri du Peuple*, 6 May.          [6] J.O., 16 May.
[7] 17 May: P.V.C., II, p. 458.
[8] *Le Cri du Peuple*, 16 May. A resolution adopted at the Club Saint-Ambroise on 19 May had been previously adopted at the Club of Saint-Nicolas-des-Champs: A.H.G., Ly 22 *bis*, 'Clubs'.

Its list of candidates was almost completely successful in the first and second arrondissements in the April elections, Vésinier, Serraillier, Longuet and Anthime Dupont having its backing.[1] By the end of April 'the delegates of the old Central Committee and of the Delegation of the Twenty Arrondissements' were meeting regularly to discuss their own re-organization, and likewise had moved their headquarters to the Public Assistance building in the Avenue Victoria.[2] This, together with the attempts of the Club Saint-Nicolas-des-Champs, where Vésinier was active, points to the Central Arrondissement Committee as being one of the leading forces helping the clubs organize themselves into a federation. The Central Vigilance Committee was also partly responsible for persuading two of the republican societies, the Défenseurs de la République and the Alliance républicaine, to come out openly in support of the Commune. Some of the local vigilance committees were again meeting regularly in May, and the Central Vigilance Committee called an extraordinary meeting for 19 May of all its present and past members, 'in view of the present circumstances'.[3]

The local sections of the International continued to function, and some new ones were formed. Jules Hamet, who had been a member of the Central Committee of the Twenty Arrondissements, was responsible for starting up the two new branches in the 13th arrondissement, naming one appropriately in memory of Duval.[4] Hamet was also a member of the liaison committee that was set up by the International in May 'to present the outcome of the efforts of its Paris branches for discussion and approval by the Commune'.[5] The Federal Council continued to meet at the Corderie.

Outside observers found the meetings of the clubs in the churches disorderly and dull. One evening Maxime Vuillaume came across André Gill feeling depressed over the prospect of defeat followed

---

[1] *Le Cri du Peuple*, 5 April, first published this list in expectation that the elections would be held sooner.

[2] *Le Cri du Peuple*, 14, 28 April; cf. Dautry and Scheler, op. cit., p. 248.

[3] *Le Cri du Peuple*, 20 May; Dautry and Scheler, op. cit., p. 250; see too *Le Cri du Peuple*, 4 May (4th arrondissement), 8 May (12th arrondissement).

[4] *Le Cri du Peuple*, 30 April, 16 May; see too *Le Cri du Peuple*, 3, 17, 20 April (Montrouge section of International, 13th arrondissement); 14, 19, 20, 29 April (Faubourg du Temple section); 22 April (Vaugirard and Grenelle section); 23 April (Batignolles section); 6, 11 May (Popincourt section), to list but some of the meetings announced.

[5] *Dictionnaire*, VI, p. 293.

by deportation or at least exile. They decided to go to a club to cheer themselves up; but Gill's aesthetic taste would have preferred the music and ceremony of the Mass to the proceedings of the hundred or so men and women they found there. They were cheered up a little at the end by the singing of the 'Marseillaise' in salute of the red flag.[1] Catulle Mendès after a visit to one of the clubs was scornful of the women he saw there, clothed in 'the heroic rags of those who swept the streets each morning'.[2] *The Times* correspondent, when he was smuggled by a newspaper-seller friend into a women's club on the Avenue d'Italie in the 13th arrondissement, likewise condemned the women there as being 'of the lowest order of society'.[3] Indeed it was the case that the clubs brought into the churches that section of the population considered by most of the bourgeoisie to have no right to so step out of their station in life. Thus sympathizers of the Commune were more tolerant of the noisy meetings held by the clubs. Villiers de l'Isle-Adam's literary sensibility found the spectacle 'thrilling': 'A whole population is discussing serious matters, and for the first time workers can be heard exchanging their views on problems which until now have been broached only by philosophers . . . a new century has just dawned.'[4] Malon of course gives an equally enthusiastic description: 'It was there in the church clubs that extempore orators preached, by profane candlelight, the sacred revolt of the poor, the exploited, the oppressed, against the exploiters, against the tyrants, and excited their energies for the decisive combat, from which would come the political and social emancipation of the nations.'[5]

One of the most striking features of the clubs, as well as one of the most frequent, was their anticlericalism. The very fact that they met in churches was one expression of this. The club in Saint-Nicolas-des-Champs called on the other arrondissements to follow the example of the 3rd and turn the churches over to 'the education of the people'. The priests could say their offices during the day and the clubs could function in the evenings.[6] The Club Saint-Ambroise made the more radical suggestion that the Commune should hire out the churches to the clergy wishing to use them as a means of

[1] Vuillaume, op. cit., V, pp. 224–8.    [2] Mendès, op. cit., p. 272.    [3] 6 May.
[4] *Le Tribun du Peuple*, 10 May; de l'Isle-Adam wrote under the pseudonym of Marius, see V. de l'Isle-Adam, '*Sous la Commune. Tableau de Paris*', *Mercure de France*, August 1953, pp. 577, 586.
[5] Malon, op. cit., p. 270.                    [6] *Bulletin Communal*, 6 May.

raising money for widows and orphans.[1] The Club des Prolétaires obtained the authorization of the Committee of Public Safety to take over Saint-Ambroise for its meetings. This same club got the support of the local municipality to occupy the church of Sainte-Marguerite, also in the 11th arrondissement in the Faubourg Saint-Antoine, in order to provide an alternative meeting place for those of its members who found it too far to walk to Saint-Ambroise.[2]

The occupation of a church was usually made a ceremonial occasion. When the Club Communal of the Salle Molière took over the church of Saint-Nicolas-des-Champs, 'a public monument that until then had served only a caste, born enemy of all progress', this was announced as 'a great revolutionary act' by the population of the district.[3] The Panthéon at the end of March had been the first such monument to be put to the service of the new religion, though it was never used as a club. Two National Guard battalions were drawn up, Jourde and Rastoul represented the Commune, and the arms of the wooden cross on top of the dome were sawn off and a red flag was attached to the stump. Another immense red flag was paraded around the Panthéon and then taken to the Hôtel de Ville to be 'blessed' by members of the Commune before it too was hoisted up.[4] Inside the churches the red flag was displayed during the club meetings, though it was often taken down in the day when the clergy performed their rites. At one church the sanctuary was boarded off, leaving the nave free for use as a club.[5] Sometimes the organ was used to accompany patriotic hymns, if an organist could be found. Often a few centimes were charged on entry towards the cost of heating and lighting, but this practice disappeared after a time.

A number of churches held out for several weeks against being taken over, the clergy often getting the support of the local municipalities against the secular ardour of the more revolutionary National Guard commanders. In the end popular pressure generally won out. Saint-Roche resisted until 11 May, when in the midst of morning Mass a National Guard commander walked in with sixty men to search for arms and carried off the offering. Another Sunday there was utter panic when a grey-bearded old man suddenly shouted out

---

[1] 12 May: A.H.G., Ly 22 *bis*, 'Clubs'.    [2] *Le Prolétaire*, 19, 24 May.
[3] *Bulletin Communal*, 6 May.
[4] Allemane, op. cit., p. 61; Dabot, op. cit., pp. 175–6; P. Fontoulieu, *Les Eglises de Paris sous la Commune*, Paris, 1873, pp. 175–6.
[5] Saint Pierre de Montrouge: Fontoulieu, op. cit., p. 203.

'*Vive la Commune! Vive la Sociale!*' Several people were hurt in the crush to escape.[1] The clergy also were sometimes vigorously supported by their parishioners. When the parish priest of Saint-Eustache was arrested just before Easter Sunday, the women of Les Halles soon had him released in time to give them Easter Mass. At Saint-Sulpice the congregation defended their priests from being expelled and it was the National Guards who suddenly found they needed protection, which the clergy provided. A second attempt was more successful, though for a time there was a stalemate as the congregation equalled the volume of the 'Marseillaise' by their singing of the 'Magnificat'.[2] As the churches were taken over, so the clubs moved back from the faubourgs where many of them had been during the siege into the old revolutionary centre of Paris around the Hôtel de Ville, the Temple *quartier* in the 3rd arrondissement, and the Latin Quarter. One count gives thirty-six clubs in Paris at the time of the Commune.[3]

Not all the churches taken over were used as clubs; some simply became National Guard posts, or were searched for arms and treasure. There were also sinister stories of orgies being held by drunken Guardsmen and sacrilegious ceremonies occurring in the churches at night.[4] In return, rumours were circulated of strange finds as a result of the National Guards' investigations. The most notable of these came when the nunnery in the rue Picpus, in the Faubourg Saint-Antoine, was occupied. Three mad women were discovered by the National Guards, locked up in small huts in the garden, where they had been for the last nine years. In another building a mattress was found, with straps and buckles, two iron corsets, an iron skull-cap, and a species of rack turned by a cog-wheel. The Mother Superior claimed the women had been mad when they arrived and that the objects were old orthopaedic instruments. The convent at once became a great tourist attraction, with the Guards on duty not failing to point out a connecting door between the nunnery and the adjacent monastery. *The Times* correspondent reported as a result of his visit that there were 'hard facts' that could not be

---

[1] Fontoulieu, op. cit., pp. 91–2.                    [2] Op. cit., pp. 247–50.

[3] Bruhat, Dautry and Tersen, op. cit., p. 158.

[4] See e.g. Fontoulieu, op. cit., pp. 35–6, 41, 77: Saint Leu; Saint-Jean-Saint-François; Saint-Vincent de Paul. Fontoulieu lists fifty-seven churches as suffering to some degree under the Commune, and fourteen as not being touched at all.

reasonably accounted for: 'the rack and its adjuncts are justly objects of grave suspicion, for they imply a use of brutal force which no disease at present known would justify'.[1] Élie Reclus thought the same.[2] Louis Veuillot in the Catholic paper, *L'Univers*, defended the nuns, saying there were only three mad women, two old orthopaedic beds and a crib.[3] The mystery of the crypts of Saint-Laurent and Notre-Dame-des-Victoires was more easily solved. The bones found there, which at first were held to be of suspiciously recent origin, turned out, when examined by a doctor sent from the Academy of Medicine, to be safely ancient.

Anticlericalism was a sentiment that went back to the *sans-culottes* of the first Revolution and had only been extended to the industrial workers during the Second Empire by the clear alliance of the Church with the State. Blanqui and Proudhon were both passionately anti-clerical. Rigault's arrests of the Archbishop and other of the clergy was fully in accord with the feelings expressed in the clubs, which often demanded the arrest of all priests. Thus one easy way to gain a hearing at a club was to begin by declaring one's atheist convictions. In Saint-Sulpice a speaker was greeted with tumultuous applause when he defied God, if he existed, to descend on to the defiled altar where a dagger would be plunged into the divine heart. At Saint-Germaine-l'Auxerrois the assembly became equally frenzied when a National Guard made a hole in the mouth of a statue of the Virgin and then stuck a pipe in. To add to his success the Guard then pulled off the infant Jesus and paraded him around on the end of his bayonet.[4] A woman at Saint-Nicolas-des-Champs proposed using the bodies of the 60,000 priests in Paris, by her count, instead of sacks of earth for constructing barricades.[5] At the Club Saint-Eloi one woman said all the nuns should be thrown in the Seine because they poisoned the wounded federals in the hospitals.[6] The Club de la Révolution in the Church Saint-Bernard shared this dislike of the nuns in the hospitals and voted they should be replaced by *citoyennes*.[7] Paget-Lucipin, who had moved from the Ministry of Education to be Director of the hospital of the Hôtel-Dieu, 'debaptized' all the wards and corridors, changing the Saints' names for those of good

---

[1] 9 May.                              [2] Reclus, op. cit., pp. 247-8.
[3] Quoted in A. Rastoul, *L'Eglise de Paris sous la Commune*, Paris, 1871, pp. 344-7.
[4] Fontoulieu, op. cit., pp. 254, 183-4. Also depicted by a contemporary en-graving.                        [5] 20 May: Fontoulieu, op. cit., p. 159.
[6] 19 May: op. cit., p. 64.            [7] 16 May: op. cit., p. 83.

revolutionaries like Blanqui and Barbès. He also forced the sisters to wear a red sash over their black habits.[1] But at least one priest openly supported the revolution, the abbé Perrin of Saint-Eloi, who was expelled by his superiors for his republican views. He used to speak in the streets in favour of the Commune, wearing at first, until he was stopped, his clerical dress.[2]

Apart from such anticlerical demands, which were particularly picked on by the Commune's opponents, mundane matters made up most of the business of the clubs. Food was again a pressing question, with the usual demand that all food and fuel stocks should be requisitioned by the Commune or the municipalities. The Club Révolutionnaire in the 17th arrondissement voted that shop-owners who had left Paris should be fined for a week, and if that did not bring them back their shops should be seized.[3] The Club Saint-Ambroise heard indignantly of a well-stocked grocer's shop that was guarded by its serving-boys armed with rifles whilst the owner was safely out of Paris.[4] The complaint was made at the Club Révolutionnaire that the municipal butchers closed for two hours for lunch whereas the 'aristocratic butchers' remained open all day. Why, it was asked to applause, could not the employees take a staggered lunch-hour?[5] The women employed in the municipal soup kitchens in the 11th arrondissement got their salaries raised after a discussion in the Club des Prolétaires.[6]

The class feeling in the clubs was that of the poor against the rich, which was often pre-industrial in its language. It was a hatred, often violent, of those idle rich, who were seen as living at the expense of the sufferings of the poor. At this level there were expressions of a popular egalitarianism. Philippe, a sculptor and ex-wine merchant, elected in the April elections to the Commune for the 12th arrondissement, declared at the opening meeting of the Club in the church of Saint-Eloi: 'We are going to found a new society, a truly social and

---

[1] Senisse, op. cit., p. 128.

[2] Fontoulieu, op. cit., pp. 60-1; Vuillaume, op. cit., IX, pp. 328-31, who says that abbé Perrin first offered his letter of complaint about his superiors to the *Père Duchêne*; it was finally published in *La Sociale*, 14 April. Perrin wanted a married clergy. He was condemned by the Military Courts after the Commune to two years imprisonment.

[3] 14 May: A.H.G., Ly 22; Rougerie, *Procès*, p. 207.

[4] 14 May: A.H.G., Ly 22 *bis*, 'Clubs'.

[5] 14 May: A.H.G., Ly 22.

[6] *Le Prolétaire*, 19, 24 May.

democratic society, where there will never be poor nor rich, since the rich, should there be any, will be forced to give up their goods to the poor.' To which a voice in the audience shouted out, 'let us begin by making the Rothschilds hand over'.[1] Héligon, a member of the International in its early Proudhonist phase, said to the Commission of Inquiry after the Commune that workers easily became communists because 'it was the simplest, the easiest to explain',[2] which indeed was how egalitarianism was seen by the clubs. At the Club Saint-Leu, citizen Boilet chaired a debate on 'whether the rich should be shot or simply made to give back what they had stolen from the people?' The conclusion was to force them to surrender their goods first and then shoot them.[3] At the mainly women's club in the Trinité a speaker first attacked the employers who got rich from the sweat of their workers; the answer was for the workers to form their own associations. Then she went on to denounce 'another vice of existing society: the rich, who spend their time amusing themselves drinking. They should be exterminated, along with priests and nuns. We will only be happy when we no longer have employers, rich, or priests.'[4] At the Club Saint-Séverin a speaker declared that 'all property had to be seized, the châteaux destroyed, the aristocrats killed until there only remained the emancipated proletariat in a purified society'.[5]

The war was naturally a major preoccupation, and as during the first siege there were plenty of suggestions as to how it could be won. Greek fire was as popular as ever, to which were added demands for the use of petrol bombs, since Versailles was shelling Paris, but Cluseret refused this form of retaliation. A speaker at Saint-Ambroise suggested setting the Bois de Boulogne on fire.[6] Talk of blowing up Paris as a final revolutionary gesture rather than surrendering was soon accepted by the Commune's opponents as an established intention of those at the Hôtel de Ville. This was the beginning of the *pétroleuses* myth, of talk of the sewers being mined.[7] The speed at which barricades were being erected was a cause of concern, and it was suggested that the 'aristocrats, the dandys, who

[1] 12 May: Fontoulieu, op. cit., p. 62.              [2] *Enquête*, II, p. 540.
[3] 6 May: Fontoulieu, op. cit., p. 78.              [4] 12 May: op. cit., p. 272.
[5] Mid-May: op. cit., pp. 282–3.              [6] 16 May: A.H.G., Ly 22 *bis*, 'Clubs'.
[7] This was suggested by an officer in the *Vengeurs de Flourens* battalion on 10 May at the Club of Notre-Dame de Plaisance (Fontoulieu, op. cit., p. 243); but nothing like this was ever attempted: *Enquête*, III, pp. 352–3.

parade up and down the boulevards in great numbers, a pince-nez on their noses, a cane in their hand, haughtily looking down on the proletarians', should be put to work digging up *pavés*.[1] There were complaints that officers in the National Guard were not leading their men to battle; it was 'those with gold braid not the citizens' who had panicked at Issy.[2] A group of citizens from this same club, Saint-Ambroise, visited fort Vanves on 16 May. They reported back that they had found the sentries asleep, but that the shell-fire from the fort was accurate. The problem of draft-dodgers was another frequent topic. Citizens at the Club Saint-Ambroise were asked to look out for those avoiding National Guard duty; it was proposed that lists be drawn up of all such so that when reinforcements were needed they could easily be picked up. Citoyenne Valentin, with regard to this problem, suggested that women should do guard duty in Paris to free men for the front line, and asked women not to hold back their men from going off to the front line. At a club in the 13th arrondissement, a 'fine looking' woman declaimed against the cowardice of the National Guards, suggesting it should be left to the women to do the actual fighting: 'Men are *lâches*, they call themselves the masters of creation, and are a set of dolts. They complain of being made to fight, and are always grumbling over their woes – let them go and join the craven band at Versailles, and we will defend the city ourselves.'[3] A woman at the Club des Prolétaires suggested as a last line of defence that women should march to the barricades with their children: 'We shall see if the soldiers dare fire on them . . . Perish our children if necessary, but the Commune must live.'[4]

Women complained of the way they were being treated when on ambulance duty. The Club de la Révolution sociale in the church of Saint-Michel called on the Municipality of the 5th arrondissement to ensure that women volunteers for this duty were treated with respect and consideration by the National Guard Commanders at the front.[5] Too often the officers had 'a petty and narrow bourgeois, authoritarian mentality',[6] and refused to let them tend the wounded.

---

[1] 'Club révolutionnaire' in 17th arrondissement, 14 May: A.H.G., Ly 22; Rougerie, op. cit., p. 204.
[2] Saint-Ambroise, 13 May: A.H.G., Ly 22 *bis*, 'Clubs'.
[3] *The Times*, 6 May.
[4] 20 May: Fontoulieu, op. cit., p. 198.
[5] 16 May: Bruhat, Dautry and Tersen, op. cit., p. 160.
[6] André Léo, *La Sociale*, 7 May; Thomas, op. cit., p. 119.

Dombrowski and his Polish staff-officers had to the full the aristocratic gallant attitude typical of the *szlachta* class. Rossel did not, and
apologized to André Léo when she complained to him of the male
chauvinism and surgeon's *ésprit de corps* that existed at a time when
on the contrary, according to her, it was necessary to move towards
'that responsible brotherhood of men and women, that unity of
feelings and ideas, which alone can form in honour, equality, and
peace, the Commune of the future'.

The clubs discussed questions of public morality. There were
expressions of revolutionary purity against street prostitutes, with
calls for their arrest together with drunkards and the closing of all
bars by 11.0 at night.[1] Several municipalities tried to enforce such
measures. Amanda, a prostitute herself, suggested at the Club Saint-
Séverin that the Commune should form a special battalion of prostitutes: 'We are 25,000 and we will rip open the guts of the Versaillais.'[2] Some of the prostitutes became nurses, though there was
prejudice against them, and many did die on the barricades at the
end.[3] Marriage came in for strong condemnation. The Commune in
its measure of 10 April adopting the widows and children of 'all
citizens killed defending the rights of the people' had included as
entitled to a pension all children whether legitimate or not. This in
effect meant recognizing the *unions libres* common among the working-
class population in Paris, putting these on an equal level to the
marriage contract. 'This decree,' said Arnould afterwards and rather
hopefully, 'delivered a mortal blow to the religio-monarchical institution of marriage as we see it functioning in modern society.'[4]
Catulle Mendès heard a woman in the club in the church of Saint-
Jacques describe marriage as 'the greatest error of past humanity'.
She went on to propose an amendment to the Commune's liberal
decree on pensions; these should be given only to the unmarried
companions of National Guards killed in the fighting: 'Everything
for the free women, nothing for the slaves.'[5] At the Club Saint-
Ambroise one of the most frequent and most listened-to speakers

[1] e.g., 15 May, Club de l'Ecole de Médecine: A.H.G., Ly 22; Allemane,
op. cit., p. 80; Thomas, op. cit., pp. 89–90.
[2] Fontoulieu, op. cit., p. 288.
[3] Michel, op. cit., p. 248.
[4] Arnould, op. cit., vol. 2, pp. 124–5.
[5] Mendès, op. cit., p. 273; J. Leighton, *Paris Under the Commune*, London,
1871, pp. 282–3.

there, noted for her violent attacks on religion, said she had a daughter sixteen years old, 'and never, while I am alive, will I let her get married. In any case she is living with someone at the moment, and is very happy without need of the sacraments of the Church'.[1]

Rigault once wrote during the Commune that he wanted 'sexual promiscuity; concubinage is a social dogma'.[2] One letter has been conserved addressed to the Central Committee of the National Guard calling on it to take inspiration from 'the Hébertists' by abandoning in a Sadian – or possibly a Fourierist – manner the idea of natural limitations:

Another prejudice that is making itself evident in the bills and decrees of the Prefecture of Police is that of modesty, decency and public morality. From what old books of religious and philosophical morality have these completely meaningless words been taken? Meaningless? No, I am mistaken. They do have a real meaning; they were created to take away the pleasures of nature from the simple, and to reserve them for the idle rich. Away therefore with your bills and decrees, citizens of the Prefecture of Police! There is no such thing as public decency, shame, vice or prostitution. Nature is not concerned with such stupidities. She has her needs, her demands, and she must be satisfied as is thought best, in her way, when and where one wishes, taking any opportunity, as one pleases, completely by chance, after waiting a long time or at the first meeting, with whoever one wants to, as we do, we other proletarians, among ourselves. Only today what we need are your girls, O idle rich, your women. What is needed is that they return for the benefit of the proletarians, and of everyone in the great communal family. Enforce this measure at once, prudish Commune, or else we will see to it ourselves, and gleefully so, I assure you. Sadly I do not speak for myself, for I am too old to do anything but simply watch the show of this great and magnificent priapic festival that will be the inauguration of the true community. Besides, even if the result will not be as grandiose as I hope, the proletariat is owed this festival.[3]

[1] Fontoulieu, op. cit., p. 128.

[2] H. d'Alméras, *La Vie Parisienne pendant le siège et sous la Commune*, Paris, s.d. (around 1925), p. 151.

[3] A.N., Séries C, carton 2885; reprinted in Rougerie, op. cit., p. 197; C. A. Daubon, *Le Fond de la société sous la Commune*, Paris, 1873, p. 189.

The clubs also shared fully in the spy mania expected in a besieged city, though this too was in the tradition of the great Revolution. All police, it was suggested, should be shot and warnings were issued against gendarmes and agents of Versailles infiltrating the National Guard.[1] Other proposals were that the wives of police agents should be arrested as hostages,[2] and 'as in '93' the guillotine should be returned for all traitors.[3] One measure often suggested by both the popular Press and the clubs was the issuing of identity cards, which the Committee of Public Safety did eventually decree. One woman told the Club Saint-Ambroise of how she had spoken to someone in front of the Bourse, addressing him as citizen. She was shocked to be told that 'in this area there are no citizens but only gentlemen and ladies'. She asked that the square should be covered by cannons to force the reactionaries to keep such remarks to themselves.[4] When the powder-magazine on the Avenue Rapp, not far from where the Eiffel Tower now stands, blew up, laying flat the whole area 'with a marvellous completeness'[5] in an explosion that could be heard all over Paris, this was at once put down to treachery. Some arrests were made by the Committee of Public Safety and an inquiry promised, but nothing further was heard. The Club Saint-Leu called for the public trial of 'the infamous authors of this catastrophe'.[6]

There was justification for the scare that Paris might be betrayed. Thiers took full advantage of the opportunities a civil war offered to try to sabotage the Parisian defence. As has been seen, offers were made to Dombrowski to sell out. Twice Thiers had troops massed in the Bois de Boulogne in the expectation that one of the western gates would be opened. Each time instead heavy fire was directed at them. This may have been an attempt by Rossel and Dombrowski to turn Thiers' plotting against him by setting an ambush for the Versailles army.[7] Within Paris there were several ex-officers who tried to rally the dissident battalions of the National Guard, seeking thereby to

[1] 19 May, Saint-Ambroise: A.H.G., Ly 22 bis, 'Clubs'.
[2] Club de la Révolution, 5th arrondissement: A.H.G., Ly 22.
[3] 13 May, Saint-Ambroise: A.H.G., Ly 22 bis, 'Clubs'.
[4] 13 May: A.H.G., Ly 22 bis, 'Clubs'.          [5] The Times, 20 May.
[6] 21 May: A.H.G., Ly 22.
[7] The accounts of Rossel and Dombrowski say some such plan was proposed to the C.P.S. but never executed: Lissagaray, op. cit., pp. 268–9, 478; G. de Moussac, Dans la Mêlée, Paris, 1911, pp. 172–4; Bourgin, op. cit., p. 337; Thomas, Rossel, pp. 349–50.

hinder the military effort of the Commune, with always the hope of being able to deliver one of the gates. Barral de Montaud got himself made legion commander in the 7th arrondissement, but could not win over the 105th battalion to his side, the battalion Rossel had court martialled and wanted to dissolve. This plotting kept the Blanquists at the Ex-Prefecture of Police busy trying to forestall these conspiracies, and they were successful in several cases. Afterwards the Comte de Mung said of these attempts that the army did not like them: 'it was best that it should not be said that we had got in by the back door'.[1]

The most insistent cry that arose from the clubs was that the Commune was 'too soft', as a correspondent put it to the *Père Duchêne*.[2] There was a level of popular violence, which the *Père Duchêne* with its '*bougres*' and '*foutres*' deliberately aimed at capturing, the language of Year III, that separated the leaders of the Commune in general from the population of the clubs. The legalistic scruples of the Central Committee following 18 March, the monetary orthodoxy of the Financial Commission, the constitutional emphasis on municipal rights of many of the 'minority', the hope of a peaceful communal revolution, were far from the intemperate revolutionary feeling of the popular *Hébertisme* of the *enragés* expressed by the popular organs of opinion, which did not have, of course, the problems that come with responsibilities. The Montrouge section of the International rebuked the Commune, though respectfully, for its lack of revolutionary decisiveness:

> considering the time of extreme peril existing for our social institutions, and the lack of vigour among the members of the Commune in producing not only decrees but the revolutionary acts that alone can save the situation and assure the success of the Revolution, which dawned so favourably on 18 March, the members of the above-named section address themselves to you, their elected representatives, to remedy this state of affairs, which will inevitably lead to our downfall if you persist in continuing along the path on which you have embarked ... You are masters of an area of Paris, you are a government at the head of a great power, the City of Paris! Nothing is lacking. You have more arms and men than you need.[3]

[1] *Enquête*, II, p. 277.                    [2] *Lettres au P.-D.*, p. 23.
[3] 11 May: A.H.G., quoted in Rougerie, op. cit., pp. 191–2; Schulkind, op. cit., pp. 413–14 also refers to this document.

Babick of the 'minority' received a letter criticizing him for opposing the creation of the Committee of Public Safety at a time when 'revolutionary measures' were needed: 'therefore, dear citizen, do not draw back before any revolutionary measure; if you are against them on principle, at least do not be an obstacle'.[1] Benoît Malon received a letter calling for extreme measures against the enemies of the Commune: 'so far you have carried out some good reforms; but many more remain to be done. Only a dictatorship can lay the foundation of the Republic. Let us have energy, and still more energy.'[2]

By energy was meant such measures as executing the Archbishop and other hostages, or even all priests and police agents; forcing all the *fainéants*, the café dandies and idle rich, to work for the defence of Paris; the overcoming of financial difficulties by seizing the property of the rich or taking over the abandoned workshops, or seizing the Bank of France.[3] The Commune must show that it meant business, by terror if necessary: 'Our rulers,' complained one woman at the Trinité Club, 'want to make omelettes without breaking any eggs.'[4] On 21 May the Club in Saint-Pierre-de-Montrouge pronounced 'the downfall of the Commune, which is not sufficiently revolutionary', and a call was made to march on the Hôtel de Ville.[5]

Ten years later Vaillant expressed this difference between the leaders of the Commune and the popular passions when he said that 'instead of a revolutionary Commune, Paris had an elected Commune. It did its duty and it did its best. But because of its electoral origin it could not have the unity of action and the energy of a committee arising spontaneously, revolutionarily, from a people in revolt.'[6] Malon too afterwards admitted, 'the men of the Communal Revolution were not up to their task. One is never up to a people in revolt.'[7]

Who were the people in revolt, the *sans-culottes* of '71? Judging by those arrested, some 36,000, and the accounts of those who spoke

---

[1] Rougerie, op. cit., p. 190: A.H.G., Ve Conseil de Guerre, dossier 735.
[2] Rougerie, op. cit., p. 199: Fonds Centner.
[3] This latter was suggested, for example, by the President of the Club Saint-Séverin in a letter to Rigault, 14 April: Fontoulieu, op. cit., p. 287.
[4] 12 May: Fontoulieu, op. cit., p. 274.          [5] Op. cit., p. 208.
[6] In the anarchist paper, *Ni Dieu, Ni Maître,* 20 March 1881: Dommanget, *Vaillant*, p. 43.
[7] Malon, op. cit., p. 177.

in the clubs, the average Communard was a working-class Parisian (which did not exclude being born in the provinces, as were most Parisians), for the Commune was the revolt of the poorer section that made up the majority of the inhabitants of the capital.[1] A significant proportion of *employés* were among those arrested (eight per cent), clerks in offices and banks, shop assistants, salesmen. This proportion rises to thirteen per cent among the arrested National Guard officers. Altogether employees, small businessmen, merchants and the professionals made up fifteen per cent of those arrested. Unlike 1789–94, domestic servants, concierges, remained on the whole loyal to their masters and to the Government (five per cent of those arrested).[2] The highest number among the workers arrested came from either the metal industries that had grown up as a result of industrialization, or were building workers, partly a result of Haussmann's policies, or were day labourers: twelve, sixteen and fifteen per cent respectively. Thus forty-three per cent of those arrested, forty-five per cent of those condemned to deportation, came from these three groups, which only made up thirty-eight per cent of the total population of the city. The traditional Parisian industries, the luxury trades, clothing industry, shoemakers, carpenters, etc., were represented among those arrested in the same proportion as in Paris at large. Among officers in the National Guard, however, the traditional craft trades did tend to predominate.

The Commune was not particularly a revolution of the young, though they took part – children too. The latter were particularly evident during the last week, many thousands joining in the fighting on the barricades. There was a National Guard company called the Pupils of the Commune. The classic story of youthful heroism is that of a *gamin*, Parisian street urchin, about fifteen years old, captured after the fall of a barricade on the rue du Temple. He was lined up with the men to be shot, but first asked permission to go to the concierge opposite to hand over a watch so that it could be returned to its owner. The officer in charge naturally assumed the

---

[1] See report of General Appert, *Annales*, vol. 43, tables on pp. 110–13; Rougerie, op. cit., pp. 125–9.

[2] e.g., Martial Senisse's fiancée did not join the revolution, being concerned chiefly to maintain the house of her master, who was a Government official at Versailles. She was simply worried lest Senisse's revolutionary activity have a bad end: Senisse, op. cit., pp. 74–5, 78: cf. R. Cobb, *A Second Identity*, London, 1969, p. 235 (Review of Thomas).

boy was trying to escape, but out of kindness let him go. To everyone's surprise he returned a few moments later to his place against
the wall, saying 'Here I am again.' The soldiers were taken aback,
and then the officer gave him a kick in the pants and told him to
clear off, '*bougre de gamin!*' Victor Hugo used this incident in one of
the stanzas of his poem on the Commune, *L'Année terrible*.[1] But on
the whole more of those arrested were over thirty than below.[2]

Nor can it be said that the Communards were in any noticeable
sense criminals: twenty-one per cent of the 36,000 arrested, twenty-
nine per cent of the 10,000 condemned, had been convicted previously. But in working-class Paris at the end of the Second Empire
this meant very little, and is more a commentary on the political
nature of a legal system that did its best to create the myth of a
'dangerous class' than on the criminal disposition of the Communards.[3]

The first Revolution had had its '*journées*', the days that marked
the periods of its development when the crowd entered into the
historical stage, becoming itself the leading personage. The overthrow of the Empire on 4 September had been one further such day,
as attempted to be the failed revolutionary occupation of the Hôtel
de Ville on 31 October. The theme of the Commune is likewise
marked by the action of the crowd: the parade of the federated
National Guards to the Place de la Bastille on 24 February; the
seizure of the cannons before the Prussian entry; the uprising
throughout Paris on 18 March; the great *sortie* of the night of 2
April and the morning of the third; and after the entry of the

---

[1] Story first told in *Le Figaro*, 3 June 1871; Dommanget, *L'Enseignement*,
pp. 103–5.
[2] 7·5% were between 16 and 20 years old; 17% between 21 and 24; 16·3%
between 25 and 30; 16·6% between 31 and 35; 17·5% between 36 and 40;
11·8% between 41 and 45; 7·3% between 46 and 50; 4·0% between 51 and 55;
1·2% between 56 and 60; 0·5% over 60: Rougerie, op. cit., p. 125.
[3] Rougerie, op. cit., p. 132; Appert, op. cit., pp. 112–13; the same proportion,
22%, holds true of the 23,000 arrested National Guards. Chevalier, *Classes
Laborieuses, classes dangereuses*, is misleading; cf. Charles Tilly, '*A Travers le
Chaos des vivantes cités*', *Sixth World Congress of Sociology, 1966*, who argues, on
evidence drawn from the period just anterior to the Commune, that the food riots,
city riots and revolutions of nineteenth-century France were composed of those
elements of the population that were 'politically alert, organized, integrated
into the life of the city. Not, that is, the uprooted, outcast, dangerous classes.'

Versailles troops the barricade fighting and fires, especially the burning of the Tuileries Palace and of the Hôtel de Ville, during the tragedy of the last, bloody week. These were revolutionary *journées* as had been 14 July, 1789, 10 August, 1792, or February and June 1848. But during the period of the Commune there were also staged public occasions, ceremonies, in which the crowd acted more as a chorus, both observing and participating in a collective representation affirming the unity of Paris in its revolutionary struggle against Versailles. The revolution that was the Paris Commune was in one of its significations a festival of the city of Paris,[1] enacted by the populace, in marked contrast to the balls and other grand occasions of the aristocracy of the city during the preceding Imperial regime.

The first stage occasion of the Commune was its own proclamation. The dramatic emotion of this event overcame the political principles of many observers otherwise not favourable to the revolution; enemies were reconciled and girls are said to have given themselves to lovers they had until then denied.[2] The next such occasion followed the failure of the military sortie of 3 April, when on 6 April there took place the first and grandest of several solemn funerals. Three huge catafalques, each bearing thirty-five coffins covered in black crepe and red flags, drawn by eight black horses and escorted by National Guards with their arms reversed, made their way slowly along the boulevards to the Père-Lachaise cemetery. Delescluze and five other members of the Commune headed the procession. Anyone who refused to bare his head in tribute was forced by the hisses of the crowd to comply.

[1] H. Lefebvre, op. cit., pp. 21-6, 417-26; Decouflé, op. cit., pp. 56-65; Winock and Azéma, op. cit., pp. 111-25, are the authors who have singled out the festive nature of the Commune – as have done the Situationnists. More generally see J. Duvignaud, *Spectacle et société*, Paris, 1970, pp. 161-4. The most striking modern comparison is, of course, May '68; but compare too the 'carnival' nature of ghetto rebellions in the U.S., 'a community event, a community activity' (H. J. Gans, *People and Plans*, New York, 1968, pp. 350-1), or the Yippies. The Commune, however, seems to have been fairly sober in its celebrations.

[2] Catulle Mendès is a good case of someone hostile finding himself unable to resist the popular enthusiasm. Leon Cladel's novel *I.N.R.I.*, written between 1872 and 1887 though not published until 1931, tells several stories of the enthusiasm, including one girl who threw her arms around her lover saying, 'Don't worry any more, your torment is over; tonight we will sleep together and have, I hope, a child nine months from this very day' (quoted H. Lefebvre, op. cit., p. 420).

Thousands upon thousands, men, women and children, *immortelles* in their buttonholes, silent, solemn, marched to the sound of muffled drums. At intervals subdued strains of music burst forth like the spontaneous mutterings of sorrow too long contained . . . This *Via Sacra* of the Revolution, the scene of so many woes and so many joys, has perhaps never witnessed such a communication of hearts.[1]

The wrinkled, stooped and dying Delescluze was moved by the crowds to exclaim, 'What an admirable people. Will they still call us a mere handful of malcontents?' At the cemetery Delescluze ended his short speech by saying, 'Let us not weep for our brothers who have fallen heroically, but let us swear to continue their work, and to save Liberty, the Commune, the Republic!'

Another such moment of drama was provided by the Freemasons rallying to the Commune. Freemasons were to be found on both sides of the civil war: fifteen members of the Commune belonged to Lodges, but so did several of the Versailles officers and the more republican members of Thiers's cabinet, though not the Chief Executive himself.[2] A general meeting was held of the Parisian Freemasons on 26 April in the Châtelet Theatre. The majority voted in favour of the Commune, and some 2,000 processed to the Hôtel de Ville, where they were welcomed by members of the Commune. Their spokesman, Thirifocq, a republican of the generation of 1848, declared that the Freemasons intended to plant their banners on the ramparts. If the Versaillais dared to fire on these, then they would march with the Commune against the common enemy. Vallès and Lefrançais, freemasons themselves, replied on behalf of the Commune.

This promise was carried out three days later, though the Grand Orient Lodge had publicly dissociated itself from this open siding with the insurgents. There were big crowds to see the 'occult power' of Freemasonry parade publicly for the first time in its history through the streets, with their banners and insignia. It was whispered that the Venerables possessed secret powers transmitted from the time of Solomon, which Versailles would be unable to resist. The Blanquist revolutionary Thoumieux wept when he saw the procession, saying to his young stone-mason friend, Senisse,

---

[1] Lissagaray, op. cit., p. 191.
[2] J. A. Faucher and A. Ricker, *Histoire de la Franc-Maçonnerie en France*, Paris, 1967, pp. 329–39.

Look well at these respectable men, who are revealing themselves before you today. They are very old for the most part. All their lives, they have chosen silence and discretion. They occupy almost all the important situations in this society that we wish to overthrow, and yet there they are coming out to join us, taking the most heroic side, rallying to the Commune at a time when its future is dark, adhering to the revolution because it represents for them justice and they realize they can no longer remain silent.[1]

The procession was headed by the two white-haired figures of Beslay and Thirifocq and the red banner of the Commune and the white banner of the Vincennes Lodge, on which was written in scarlet, 'Love one another'. Sixty-five Lodges were represented, followed by a women's lodge. A band played solemn ritual hymns as the procession made its way from the Carrousel of the Tuileries to the Hôtel de Ville. There it was received in full splendour by the Commune, everywhere being decorated with red flags and banners. Speeches were made by Beslay and Pyat, and Thirifocq again repeated their allegiance to the Commune. A balloon with the symbolic three points on it and the inscription 'The Commune and France' was launched. The procession then made its way to the Place de la Bastille and then back along the boulevards to the Champs-Elysées, where it had to make a detour to avoid falling shells. At the Porte Maillot the first banner planted was that of the La Persévérance Lodge, founded in 1790 at the time of the federation movement throughout France. The local Versailles commander, himself a Freemason, seeing the white flags, ordered a cease fire, which enabled a delegation to go and see Thiers. Thiers made them wait and then said he was tired of receiving so many delegations, and so they had to return with nothing gained. But it had been one of the great ceremonial days of the Commune, one of the events that brought some consolation to Louise Michel during her nights in prison when she would see again 'the long line of Freemasons on the ramparts'.[2]

Ceremonies in a different way, more like exorcisms, were various acts of destruction. A local committee in the 11th arrondissement had discovered a guillotine that had been commissioned by the Government. It was decided that this should be publicly burnt 'for

[1] Senisse, op. cit., p. 100; cf. Faucher and Ricker, op. cit., p. 345.
[2] Michel, op. cit., p. 232.

the purification of the arrondissement'.[1] This was done – though the blade was made off with by a collector – in front of the Mairie by the statue of Voltaire, an enthusiastic crowd shouting, 'Down with the death penalty.' The action was not in accord with Rigault's principles, but the *Père Duchêne* welcomed it, adding that a guillotine had even been prepared to cut five heads at once![2] The Commune decided to pull down the Expiatory Chapel for Louis XVI erected by Louis XVIII. But a monarchist pretending, although he spoke no English, to be an American interested in buying it to transport to the U.S.A. delayed matters until the entry of Versailles. He was well rewarded with honours afterwards from the Pope, the Comte de Chambord and the French Government.[3] It was also decreed that the Bréa Chapel should be demolished. This had been erected to commemorate General Bréa, who had been killed in rather similar circumstances to Generals Lecomte and Clément Thomas by a mob that had seized him when he came to parley during the fighting of June 1848. At the same time the Commune amnestied the remaining survivor of those accused of causing Bréa's death, who had been in prison at Cayenne ever since. The Commune announced it would release him as soon as was possible.[4]

This indeed was an example of the revolutionary phenomenon of trying to reverse or break the continuum of history.[5] Another example was the use of the revolutionary calendar by a few of the popular papers, most notably the *Père Duchêne*. The Commune itself did not, and the *Journal Officiel* continued to be published in 1871, not in Year 79. The Committee of Public Safety, however, did tend to date its decrees Floréal, *an* 79. The same idea was expressed by taking names for newspapers from those of 1793, as was done by over twenty of the Communard journals. But the most ambitious and striking action of this sort was the destruction of the Vendôme Column.

The Column originally had been intended to glorify the Grand Army, the bronze coming from captured Russian and Austrian

---

[1] J.O., 10 April.    [2] 18 germinal (7 April).

[3] *Le Vengeur*, 12 May; Fontoulieu, op. cit., pp. 262–5.

[4] 27 April: P.V.C., I, p. 519.

[5] Cf. Walter Benjamin, *Illuminations*, Eng. trans. London, 1970, pp. 263–4, who refers to the report of the shooting of the clocks that occurred during the July Revolution of 1830 (and not during the Commune as is sometimes claimed) as symbolic of the 'conscious breaking of the continuum of history peculiar to the revolutionary classes in the great moments of their action'.

cannons, but instead it had been turned into an apotheosis of Napoleon I himself. At the Restoration the statue on top was melted down to be used for a statue of Henry IV on the Pont Neuf. The Column remained uncrowned until Louis-Philippe as part of the revival of Bonapartism ordered a new statue of the first Emperor, though in a riding coat and cocked hat as befitted the Bourgeois Monarchy. In 1864 Napoleon replaced this by a statue of the Emperor in a toga and was able to put back the original winged Victory which had come into his hands during his time of exile. This obvious reassertion of the Imperial side of the Napoleonic legend roused antagonism to the Column among republicans. Charles Longuet, for example, had called on the workers to be on their guard against military glory and 'monuments of oppression such as the Vendôme Column'.[1] The overthrow of the Empire on 4 September was followed by the removal of several monuments to the previous regime, and the question of the Vendôme Column was naturally raised. Courbet, as president of the newly formed Artists' Commission, petitioned the Government of National Defence to get rid of the Column. It had, he said, no artistic value and was only a glorification of the ideas of war and conquest, outdated by the spirit of modern civilization. He later suggested that the reliefs could be displayed in a more suitable place, the Invalides for example, since this 'lump of melted cannons' was hardly a suitable decoration at the head of a street called rue de la Paix. In any case it got in the way of the traffic, as he said afterwards at his trial.[2] The Government of National Defence did nothing, though Jules Simon once suggested that the statue at least could be melted down to replace the stone statue of Strasbourg in the Place de la Concorde by one of bronze. The armament commission of the 6th arrondissement circulated a petition to the other arrondissements calling for the destruction of the column so that its bronze could be used for new cannons.

Once the Commune was elected the question was raised again, the *Cri du Peuple* of Vallès saying it should be destroyed as it was built on 'the corpse of the Revolution'.[3] On 12 April Félix Pyat proposed the Commune should demolish the Column, 'since it was a monument of barbarism, a symbol of brute force and false glory, an affirmation of militarism, a negation of international law, a permanent insult to the conquered by their conquerors, a perpetual insult to one of

[1] *La Rive Gauche*, 18 June 1865.
[2] Cf. G. Riat, *Gustave Courbet*, Paris, 1906, pp. 282–310.      [3] 4 April.

the three great principles of the French Republic, Fraternity'. Courbet was not elected to the Commune until the April by-elections, and was then too busy on the Education Commission and the Artists' Federation to have time to take part in the execution of this decree. Nevertheless, he was held responsible, as he had gone around talking of the need to *déboulonner la colonne*, a word he gave to the French language, and which expressed the common belief that the whole Column was in bronze rather than being a stone core covered by a thin skin of bronze reliefs. Courbet received threatening letters, promising to push him into the Seine on a dark night if 'my old Emperor' fell, and he was greatly worried for a while.[1] Versailles also used Courbet as a scapegoat, sentencing him to pay the cost of its restoration, which he avoided only by decamping to Switzerland.

The ceremony had been planned for 5 May, the anniversary of Napoleon's death, but the preparations took longer and it was not until 16 May that the engineers were finally ready. A huge crowd gathered in the streets, many doubting that the column would really fall, though the shopkeepers in the area had prudently pasted strips of paper over their windows against the expected shock. Entry to the Square itself was limited to those furnished with an invitation bearing a phrygian cap on a pike. Delescluze had several National Guard battalions stationed nearby in case of any attempts to break up the ceremony. Members of the Commune gathered on the balcony of the Ministry of Justice, and Glais-Bizoin could be seen, who claimed to have been the only Deputy to have protested against the return of Napoleon's ashes in 1841. Two National Guard battalions played military and popular airs. The ceremony started an hour and a half late and at the first attempt one of the cables snapped. There was a further delay whilst this was replaced. Then to the strains of the 'Marseillaise' the Column cracked at the base where it had been partly sawn through, broke into three pieces in mid-air, and finally crashed onto a bed of brush-wood and sand prepared to receive it. 'Caesar is laid out on his back, decapitated', as Vuillaume rejoiced. The red flag was hoisted on to the empty pedestal, Bergeret made a speech and a citizen climbed on to the debris to tell the crowd that 'he who had crushed the Republic under his feet, was now lying there to be trampled by the feet of the people. It was a day of vengeance, a challenge thrown in the face of the assassins of Versailles, the moment when the people asserted its rights.' Englishmen were

[1] Vuillaume, op. cit., V, p. 173.

prominent among the collectors getting bits of the Column as souvenirs, and someone made off with the Victory again. Photographs were taken of National Guards, women and children posed around the fallen column, 'but the excitement was so intense that people moved about as if in a dream'.[1]

All on the side of the Commune welcomed the act, though many criticized it as a diversion of time and effort which could well have been postponed until the more immediate task of winning the war had been accomplished. At Versailles the significance of the event was fully realized. MacMahon denounced the deed to the army: 'Men calling themselves Frenchmen have dared to destroy that witness to your fathers' victories against the coalition of Europe, *beneath the eyes of the Germans.* Did they hope, those infamous scoundrels, to efface the memory of the military virtues, of which that glorious monument was the symbol, by this attempt upon the national glory?' In Paris Catulle Mendès disapproved of this attack on the 'heroic past' of France.[2] The Bonapartist Eugène Balleyguier was outraged by this 'disavowing of our history, insult to our soldiers, to their valour and heroism; the repudiation of the past of France, its grandeur and supremacy'.[3] This was truly the intended significance of the act for the Commune.[4]

With so much drama in the streets, the theatres could hardly compete. But neither did they try. The political censorship and entertainment standards of the Second Empire had not been any preparation for a republican theatre. The Theatre directors did not think of reviving any of the plays of the first Revolution, though the journalist Rogeard[5] did suggest this to the personnel of the Opera.

[1] Colonel Stanley: quoted in Horne, op. cit., p. 351. André Breton in associating Courbet with the Commune wrote in *Nadja* that 'the magnificent light in Courbet's paintings is for me the same as that in the Place Vendôme when the Column fell'.

[2] Mendès, op. cit., pp. 150–1.          [3] Fidus, op. cit., vol. 2, p. 446.

[4] Cf. poem published in *Le Prolétaire*, 10 May, by G. Barthélemy:

> *Toujours quand nous passions dans ces riches quartiers*
> *Près de ce monument, citoyens ouvriers,*
> *Nous détournons la tête en accusant l'histoire.*

('Every time we walk by this monument in this wealthy district, citizen workers, we avert our gaze, accusing history').

[5] Rogeard had been elected to the Commune in the April elections, but refused to take up his seat because he had not received the required legal minimum of votes: cf. above, p. 204.

After the 1848 Revolution there had been some specially produced plays, full of phrygian caps. But during the Commune the theatres simply continued with their previous repertoire: 'Froufrou', 'A Dull World', 'The Duck with Three Beaks', 'The Man with 67 Wives'. An effort was made to put on an anticlerical play, 'The Jesuit', but it was not very successful. Prices were reduced and benefit shows were held for widows and orphans. At the Porte Saint-Martin Hippolyte Richard organized two benefit shows, which included a 'discourse on humanity' taken from Esquiros, a Christian socialist writer of the 1830s.

The Director of the Opera was dismissed because he refused to put on a benefit show. Eugène Garnier took his place and tried to organize the dancers and singers into their own association to run the company. He did put on a show on 20 May of popular operettas, including the 'Hymn to Liberty' last publicly performed in 1793.[1] The uncompleted new Opera House served as a powder magazine during the Commune.

Courbet took the initiative at the beginning of April in forming a federation of artists in the capital, as it was Paris that had 'nourished them like a mother and given them their genius'. The museums had to be reopened, and an exhibition organized so that Paris could become more than ever 'the international European city', offering visitors an example in the arts, commerce and industry of citizens establishing their own order. A general assembly was held a week later in the amphitheatre of the Ecole de Médecine, under Courbet's chairmanship, which elected a committee and published a declaration of principles.[2] This was drawn up by Eugène Pottier, the author of the 'Internationale', who owned one of the most important design workshops in the city and had formed his workers into a trade union that had joined the International. The main aim of the federation was to group together painters, sculptors, architects, engravers and the 'decorative arts, wrongly called industrial arts', in complete independence of the State. Courbet, like other leading artists of his time, had suffered from the controls that went with the State patronage of the

---

[1] Le Cri du Peuple, 20 May; see on theatre, D'Alméras, op. cit., pp. 424–44; Dommanget, L'Enseignement, pp. 143–4; L'Europe, May 1951, pp. 116–18; G. Labarthe, Le Théâtre pendant les jours du siège et de la Commune, Paris, 1910. This Garnier was no relation to the architect Garnier who had designed the new Opera House.

[2] J.O., 15 April.

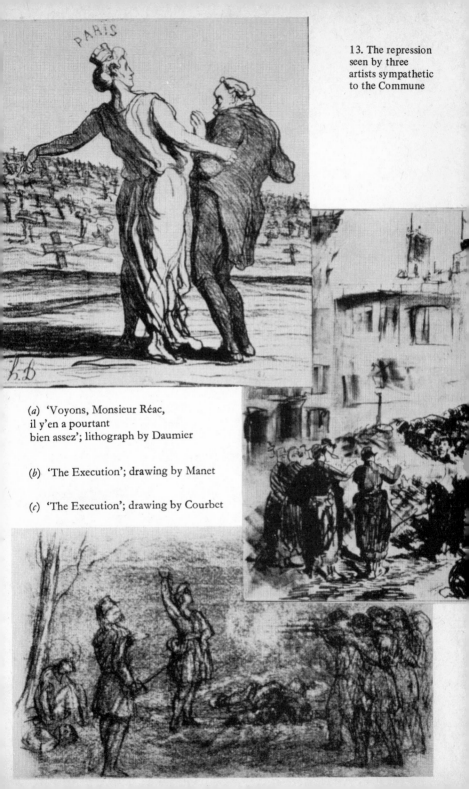

13. The repression seen by three artists sympathetic to the Commune

(a) 'Voyons, Monsieur Réac, il y'en a pourtant bien assez'; lithograph by Daumier

(b) 'The Execution'; drawing by Manet

(c) 'The Execution'; drawing by Courbet

(*a*) Paris in flames

14. The destruction of Paris

(*b*) The destroyed barricade on the rue de Rivoli at the corner of the rue Saint-Martin

arts under the Second Empire, having had his paintings refused several times by the official annual Salons for reasons of 'public morality'. In turn Courbet had made himself well known for baiting the authorities by such activities as holding independent exhibitions of his own and publicly refusing the Legion of Honour when finally it was offered him. At the same time, in February 1870, Courbet had taken the opportunity of the new liberal Government to propose that the administration of the arts be made independent of any Imperial control. After the fall of the Empire Courbet had been appointed to an official commission to inquire into the administration of the Louvre during the previous regime, and had only resigned because the Government of National Defence had refused to dismiss the officials appointed under the Empire. Being President of the Artists' Federation under the Commune, therefore, was an extension of the previous role Courbet had played as well as being in accordance with his Proudhonian dislike of State authority and his personal view that the artist 'should be his own master', art being 'a completely individual matter'.[1]

The Federation would have linked the artists together rather as in a trade union so that 'each artist would have his independence and dignity protected by all the others'. The aim of 'this government of the artistic world by the artists themselves' was 'to conserve the treasures of the past; to put into operation and make known all the elements of the present; and to regenerate the future through education'. As first steps towards this the Ecole des Beaux Arts, the Ecole de Rome and the Ecole d'Athènes were to be replaced by setting up schools in accordance with the general educational principles of the Commune. These would complete primary education by giving both a professional and an artistic training. The Federation strongly asserted the rights of the artist, as the creator of the work of art, over the commercial interests, and insisted that in the future the Federation itself would select which artists should execute any particular commission asked of it by the government. It would have its own journal as a means of publicity, 'open to all opinions and systems', as a source of information for artists. 'Finally, by word, pen, and pencil, through cheap reproductions of famous paintings, and by means of intelligent and instructive pictures that could be distributed and displayed in the Mairies of the humblest communes in

[1] Letter of 25 December 1861 to students at the Ecole des Beaux Arts: Castagnary, Les Libres propos, Paris, 1864, pp. 179–84.

France, the committee will work towards our regeneration, towards the inauguration of communal luxury, and towards the splendours of the future and of the universal Republic.'

Of the painters on the committee, apart from Courbet, the most well-known were Corot, Manet, Millet and Daumier, elected as a painter rather than as an engraver. But Millet refused to sit and Manet had been in the south-west of France since February and only returned in June, when he did two drawings of the barricades and of the dead in the streets. Corot, seventy-four years old by the time of the Commune, left Paris at the beginning of April, never having held politically revolutionary views. Daumier satirized the horrors of the civil war, and his drawing, '*Voyons, Monsieur Réac, il y en a pourtant bien assez!*', dates from the end of March. Renoir remained uninvolved in the Commune, though he knew several of the revolutionaries, including Courbet. Instead Renoir used the pass Rigault had given him together with another pass a friend had obtained for him from Versailles to cross the lines to visit his family and carry on his painting. He used the stump of an old tree near the frontier as a hiding place for whichever pass it would have been unsafe to have been found with. According to his son Jean, Renoir said of the Communards that they were 'good people. They had good intentions. But you don't play Robespierre all over again. They were eighty years behind the times. And why burn down the Tuileries? It wasn't up to much, but it was less sham than a good deal that came afterwards.' But he did add, 'they were madmen; but they had in them that little flame that never dies'.[1]

Little was done with the museums, partly because these were national institutions that could claim to be outside the jurisdiction of the city of Paris. The director of the Louvre at first refused to recognize the claims of the Artists' Federation, but on 13 May the Commune dismissed thirteen of its administrators and appointed the architect and painter Oudinot as the new provisional director. The old directors stayed on, however, and all worked together during the last week to protect the collection from the fire that burnt down the adjoining Tuileries Palace. André Gill was made curator of the Luxembourg Palace, the 'modern' collection, though here again the Director for a long time refused to open up the galleries

[1] Renoir, op. cit., p. 125. On artists see R. Boudry on Courbet in *L'Europe*, April–May 1951; Riat, op. cit., pp. 302–8; Desoné on Daumier in *La Pensée*, May–June 1950.

in spite of threats from Régère at the Mairie and appeals from the Artists' Federation. The Commune appointed its own General Inspector of the Libraries, and Élie Reclus was put in charge of the Bibliothèque Nationale. One decree of interest was that forbidding the lending out of books, since this privilege had been abused by readers to build up their own private libraries out of the national collections. The Natural History Museum showed some sense of the new spirit by announcing that it placed itself under the protection of all citizens and called on them to help its curators in assuring the common interest. Most of the colleges and the Sorbonne had been closed for the past year because of the war and the Commune had no effect on them. There were a few courses in Arabic held at the Collège de France, but only the Academies of Belles Lettres and of Science continued to hold their weekly meetings as usual.[1]

The idea of artistic freedom was strongly defended by the *Père Duchêne*, which went much further than Proudhon's ideas on the social purpose of art by arguing that there should be no restrictions on artistic expression at all.[2] The Commune itself debated the question of artistic liberty for two hours on 19 May with regard to the question of abolishing State subventions to theatres. It was decreed that these should be ended, as all theatrical monopolies, and that the Education Commission should replace the 'exploitation by a director or a company' of the theatres with associations that would enable the actors to take over the running of their own affairs.[3] Langevin, a metal-worker and member of the International, was in favour of 'a serious and severe control' by the Commune of theatres, because they were instruments of education. Pyat and Vésinier argued in favour of unrestricted theatrical freedom, limited only by the restraints of the common law. Vaillant and Frankel insisted that the Commune should intervene, not for the purpose of controlling content but as with other industries to enable them to become workers' associations, 'socialist establishments' as Vaillant put it. Frankel, in support of Vaillant, argued that artists often needed the support of the State, which need not necessarily be restrictive and harmful as it had been under the previous regime.[4]

[1] Dommanget, op. cit., pp. 110–23; Michel, op. cit., pp. 171–3.
[2] 26 germinal (15 April); cf. Proudhon, op. cit., pp. 214–17 (*Du Principe de l'art*). [3] J.O., 20 May.
[4] 19 May: P.V.C., II, pp. 425–30; an English translation can be found in *The Drama Review*, Summer, 1969, pp. 35–42.

After his election to the Commune and in the midst of organizing the Artists' Federation Courbet wrote that, in spite of all the head-aches from having to make so many decisions, he was completely 'enchanted. Paris is a real paradise . . . Paris runs itself just like clockwork. In a word it is a complete delight.'[1] Villiers de l'Isle-Adam was equally taken by the festive atmosphere of Paris during the Commune:

> Neither winter, nor the siege, nor treason, nor hunger, nor black pox, nor the bombardment accepted as the normal state of affairs, nor the pang of defeat, nor the civil war, nor the savage executions, nor the threats for the future, nothing has been able to prevail against the serenity of the ancient Capital . . . Paris fights and Paris sings! Paris is on the eve of being assailed by an unrelenting and enraged army, and Paris laughs! Paris bristles with fortresses, entrenchments and breastworks, and at the same time Paris preserves within its formidable enclosures places where one can laugh.[2]

This festivity, this gayness of the capital in its revolution and despite the siege, was typified by the concerts given in the Tuileries Palace, which all observers remarked on: 'festivals given by the soldiers in face of the enemy cannons in the most splendid palace on earth', as Villiers characterized them. The Tuileries were opened up to the public in May for a charge of fifty centimes, children half price. *The Times* correspondent on his visit noticed the ladies admiring the details of the furniture in the Empress's apartments, particularly the looking-glasses that sprang from the walls. A woman taken in admiration for these remarked, 'how foolish of them, after all, not to have done a little for us in order that they might have continued to abide in this paradise'.[3] The first public concert was given on Saturday, 6 May. Dr Rousselle, in charge of the Commune's medical corps, organized this and the succeeding ones on behalf of the wounded, widows and orphans. The throne room was packed out, decorated with red flags. Posters had been stuck up reminding the public that 'the gold that drapes these walls is your sweat and toil . . . Today, now your Revolution has made you free, you return to possess your wealth . . . here you are at home.' Those who could not get in wandered through the rooms of the Palace or out into the gardens. Louis Barron found the crowd very colourful, with National Guard officers acting as ushers, resplendent in their best

[1] Riat, op. cit., p. 301.        [2] '*Sous la Commune*', pp. 581-2, 593.        [3] 9 May.

uniforms and wearing white gloves as suited the occasion. Mlle Agar had been sent to represent the Comédie Française, the Commune demanding an artist from the State company. She sang the 'Marseillaise' and recited Hugo's *'Le Lion surpris'*, the people being of course the lion surprised from its peace by an unprovoked attack. Afterwards, Mlle Agar was bitterly attacked by the victorious Versaillais, though she had given shelter to several priests and gendarmes during the time of the Commune. The star attraction was the popular singer, La Bordas, who draped her bare arms and ample bosom in the red flag to sing the workers' revolutionary song, *'La Canaille'*, written after the funeral of Victor Noir, with the popular refrain:

> *'C'est de la canaille,*
> *Eh bien! j'en suis!'*[1]

The noise of cannons could occasionally be heard in counterpoint to the music, and from the terrace the flashes of the guns could be seen. The last concert was held on the afternoon of Sunday, 21 May, in the Tuileries Gardens filled with an animated Sunday crowd, as were the boulevards, 'desirous of enjoying the pleasures of a walk in the fine May sun'.[2] But to the west at that very moment the troops of Versailles were making their entry into Paris; the Commune was playing its own requiem.

> Thus [said Louis Barron, with regard to the concerts and ceremonies of the Commune] great and sublime movements begin by solemnities, festivals and cheerful battles. Viable revolutions begin and continue in this way. One comes down from this peak of intense excitement as one awakes from a dream. But a delicious memory remains of an instant of intoxication; it gives you the illusion of fraternity.[3]

Awakening from this dream proved to be ruder and much more sudden than anyone had expected. The battery Thiers had had built at Montretout had quickly turned the ramparts around the Point-du-Jour into a pile of rubble, making them untenable. There was no

---

[1] 'They're the rabble,
   Well, I'm one of them!'
See Barron, op. cit., pp. 114–25; D'Alméras, op. cit., pp. 446–52; Labarthe, op. cit., p. 128; *La Commune*, 14 May; *L'Estafette*, 9 May.
[2] *Le Tribun du Peuple*, 23 May.                    [3] Barron, op. cit., p. 112.

longer any real direction to the Commune's war effort; supplies were not being delivered and it was impossible to find troops to relieve those at the front. The feelings of the National Guard are indicated by a letter sent from the head of the 3rd legion to the Ministry of War in protest against plans to incorporate his legion into one of the active regiments. It was time, he said, 'to enter into a different stage of the defence in which each would fight in their own territory and defend their arrondissement'.[1] Accordingly the ramparts were left unguarded in many places, and on Sunday, 21 May, a Breton naval officer, Captain Trève, noticed that at the Point-du-Jour gate there was no sign of any activity. He crept forward across the fallen masonry, which conveniently formed a bridge, and found indeed that the place was deserted. No sooner had he returned to his trenches, than a man appeared on the wall waving a white handkerchief, shouting 'Come on!' This was M. Ducatel, a civil servant in the Department of Roads and Bridges, whom the Commune had made responsible for the construction of barricades in this sector. But instead he was firmly on the side of Versailles, for which he was rewarded afterwards, the *Figaro* opening up a public subscription on his behalf and the Government awarding him a cross of the Legion of Honour. Trève with Ducatel walked around amidst the continuing fire from Montretout to assure himself the area was empty, and then returned to his unit to telegraph the news to General Douay. The latter, suspicious that it might be a plot, first checked with Versailles on Captain Trève, and then around 4.0 p.m. the first Versailles troops marched into Paris.[2] Thiers and MacMahon were at Mont-Valérien and could see the thin black column as it spread out to open the other gates. By that evening there were 60,000 troops in Paris.

It was rather an anticlimax for the military commanders, who were irritated that someone as junior as Trève could claim to be the first into the capital. MacMahon and Thiers had an exchange of words, ending in MacMahon threatening to resign unless Thiers left him alone to carry out his command of the army. In Paris that afternoon, at the end of the Tuileries concert, a National Guard officer had been applauded when he announced: 'M. Thiers promised to enter Paris yesterday. M. Thiers has not entered, he will not enter.

---

[1] 16 May: A.H.G., 17e Conseil de Guerre, dossier 551; quoted Choury, op. cit., p. 347.

[2] L. Halévy, op. cit., pp. 52–9.

I invite you to come here next Sunday, same place, for our second concert on behalf of widows and orphans.'

Earlier that same morning Lefrançais on a tour of the sector had noted the absence of any guards, and had informed Dombrowski as well as sending off a note to Delescluze. This information did not get to Delescluze until the next day, being delivered first to the wrong Ministry. The troops Dombrowski sent to man the Point-du-Jour on receiving Lefrançais's information never got there, disbanding on the way and returning home. The Commune accordingly was caught completely by surprise in the midst of trying Cluseret when Billioray burst in from the Committee of Public Safety with Dombrowski's message: 'The Versaillais have entered by the Porte de Saint-Cloud. I am taking measures to repel them. If you could send me reinforcements I will answer for everything.'[1] But no reinforcements were available, and Dombrowski was far too short of men to be able to put up an effective resistance.

Jules Vallès, the Chairman of this, the last session of the Commune, tried as calmly as possible to continue the business of judging Cluseret, who was quickly acquitted – fortunately so for him, as this gave him a chance to hide out in Paris during the repression, disguised as a priest. But Vallès felt his blood turn cold, as he afterwards described his feelings: 'It was the end, nothingness!'[2] There was no debate as to what to do next. At 8.0 p.m. the Commune simply split up, shrugging off responsibility to the Committee of Public Safety, Dombrowski, or the Ministry of War. It was to be a case of everyone for himself – to the arrondissements and the barricades, or to try to find safety.

Delescluze had but one reaction, to the barricades. That night he drew up a revolutionary patriotic appeal to the 'people of Paris and the National Guard' which at least had the merit of finally cutting through the difficulties that had so bogged down the organization of the war:

Citizens, Enough of militarism, no more staff-officers with their gold-embroidered uniforms! Make way for the people, the combattants, the bare arms! The hour of the revolutionary war has

[1] Lissagaray, op. cit., p. 308; Malon, pp. 344–5; see too Lefrançais, op. cit., pp. 310–11; Daubon, op. cit., p. 363.
[2] Letter to Arnould, 10 May 1878: J. Vallès, Le Proscrit, ed. L. Scheler, Paris, 1950, p. 175; L'Insurgé, Ch. 29.

struck. The people know nothing of planned manoeuvres, but when they have a rifle in their hand, cobblestones under their feet, they do not fear all the strategists of the monarchist school. To arms! Citizens, to arms! It is a choice now, as you know, between conquering or falling into the merciless hands of the reactionaries and clericals of Versailles, of those scoundrels who deliberately delivered up France to the Prussians and are making us pay the ransom of their treachery! If you wish that the generous blood which has flowed like water these last six weeks be not infertile, if you wish to live in a free and egalitarian France, if you wish to spare your children your sufferings and your miseries, you will rise as one man and, before your fearsome resistance, the enemy, who flatters himself he will again submit you to his yoke, will win no more than the shame of the useless crimes with which he has befouled himself for the past two months. Citizens, your mandatories will fight beside you and will die beside you if need be. But in the name of this glorious France, mother of all popular revolutions, eternal home of those ideas of justice and solidarity which must and will be the laws of the world, march against the enemy; and let your revolutionary energy show them that Paris may be sold but cannot yield nor be conquered! The Commune counts on you, count on the Commune!

Magnificent rhetoric, which with its appeal to the spirit of the *quartiers* was only too truly in the spirit of '71. The last week of the Commune had begun.

# Chapter 10

# THE COMMUNE: BARRICADES AND REPRESSION

The week of Monday, 22 May to Sunday, 28 May, *la semaine sanglante*, was the final act of the Commune, its heroic last stand on the barricades and self-consummation in the fires of Paris – or, as its enemies saw it, the final convulsive orgy of the fevered city. This is the week that created many of the myths of the Commune, myths not because they are untrue, but because they are, rather, the apotheosis of those events: the burning down of buildings, including the Hôtel de Ville and the Tuileries Palace; the execution of the Archbishop of Paris and other hostages; the complicity of the Prussians; the massacres carried out in the name of order by the army; the deaths of the Communards on the barricades, culminating in the fighting in the Père-Lachaise cemetery at the Mûr des Fédérés, annual place of pilgrimage for French Socialists and Communists.

When the army of Versailles entered Paris the city was wide open. Few preparations had been made for such an eventuality and the much-talked-of second line of defence, a chain of barricades across the city, did not exist; there had been little enough organization in the defence of the ramparts. Rossel had invited the municipalities to assist in the task of constructing barricades. He also had put in charge of building strongholds at Montmartre, the Trocadero, Panthéon and Place de la Concorde, Napoléon Gaillard, a shoemaker, fifty-six years old, who had been imprisoned in 1869 for speaking at public meetings and had been an early member of the Central Vigilance Committee. But père Gaillard, resplendent in his new red-lapelled uniform, sword at his side, revolver in his belt, five gold rings on his sleeves, worked only too methodically, devoting all his efforts to constructing an immense barricade at the Place de la Concorde from the corner of the Naval Ministry on the rue Saint-Florentin across the rue de Rivoli to the corner of the huge wall supporting the terrace of the Tuileries Gardens. Just before the Versailles entry Gaillard had himself photographed in front of his barricade, hands on hips, whilst National Guards kept passers-by from walking into the view of the camera.[1] He did make a start elsewhere, at the Trocadero, Place Vendôme and Boulevard Ornano behind Montmartre, and several hundred workmen were on his payroll.[2] But he seemed to lack any sense of urgency; both the *Cri du Peuple* and the *Vengeur* were justified in criticizing his slowness and Chalain complained at the cost of his barricade on the Place de la Concorde – 80,000 francs.[3] In the end he was deprived of his post of Director of Barricades. But the Commune and the popular Press on the whole deceived themselves about the state of the Paris defences; Vésinier, for example, on 19 May claimed that the 'works undertaken from the Point-du-Jour to the Arc de Triomphe ... would force our enemies to a month-long siege before they could enter Paris'. This, as events were soon to show, was hardly a just appreciation of the situation.

Through the night into Monday morning troops poured into Paris by the Passy, Auteuil, Saint-Cloud, Sèvres and Versailles gates. They quickly occupied the bourgeois districts of Auteuil and Passy in the south-west corner of Paris. On the Right Bank one column pushed up to the Place Trocadero and from there on to the Etoile at the top of the Champs-Elysées. A second column worked its way along the exterior boulevards towards the Porte de Clichy, thereby threatening the rear of Montmartre. On the Left Bank Vinoy with two divisions advanced along the Quai Javel towards the 7th arrondissement and the Invalides, whilst to his right General Cissey moved along the outer boulevards in the direction of the Porte de Vanves, south of the Gare Montparnasse. It was a two-pronged attack, one along the Left Bank of the Seine and the other on the Right Bank up into the 8th arrondissement, with a pincer move-ment along the outer boulevards. Haussmann's boulevards, his *grandes percées*, were to show their value in enabling rapid move-ments of large numbers of men to outflank the revolutionary districts and their barricades.

MacMahon arrived and established his headquarters at the Troca-

---

[1] D'Hérisson, *Nouveau Journal*, pp. 295–6.
[2] A.H.G., Ly 25; see too letter of Gaillard in *Le Réveil*, 12 May.
[3] *Le Cri du Peuple*, 9, 17, 18 May; P.V.C., II, p. 418 (19 May); see too *Diction-naire*, VI, p. 115; J.O., 16 May; *Tribun du Peuple*, 17 May.

dero, and Thiers joined him shortly afterwards. By the morning of Monday, 22 May, the western third of Paris was in Government hands after hardly any fighting. The cannons at the Porte Maillot and the Parc Monceau had been overrun and some 1,500 National Guards had surrendered. There had been a few shots fired by scattered Federal detachments in Passy, and Dombrowski had tried to organize a resistance. But soon he had had to abandon the district and had arrived at the Hôtel de Ville at 2.0 a.m. badly bruised from flying stones ploughed up by gunshot. The Committee of Public Safety was so surprised that Passy was already lost that Dombrowski thought they were accusing him of treachery: 'What! The Committee of Public Safety takes me for a traitor! My life belongs to the Commune.'

Had the Versailles troops pressed on early that Monday morning they could probably have swooped down on the Hôtel de Ville, capturing the centre of the revolution before anyone would have known what was happening.[1] But this was hardly in keeping with MacMahon's cautiousness nor with Thiers' methodical plans for the reduction of Paris. Victory was too close for either Thiers or his commanders to take any chances. There had been rumours that the sewers were mined, of strange engines of war that Paris had prepared; more to the point there was a pervasive fear of fighting the Federals on their home ground where they could be expected to resist far more fiercely than they had ever done on the open field. Nor could the Government be absolutely certain that its soldiers might not become demoralized by street fighting; the fiasco of 18 March could not be completely forgotten.

On Tuesday Thiers told an excited Assembly that in view of the easy progress so far made, 'we will soon be masters of Paris'. But the resistance stiffened, and the army had missed the chance given it by its surprise entry. Brunel, who had played a major role on 18 March, was released from prison[2] and sent by Delescluze to man père Gaillard's barricade defending the north side of the Place de la

---

[1] What General Zeller has called 'the missed opportunity', op. cit., pp. 348–51; cf. Lissagaray, op. cit., p. 311; and the opinion of the American Colonel Wickham Hoffman, *Camp, Court and Siege*, New York, 1877, pp. 278–9.

[2] Brunel had been appointed commander at Issy on 9 May, but had refused to take this up considering the circumstances surrounding its defence. He had asked for a prison cell instead, where he had spent the last two weeks, Rigault having taken him at his word.

Concorde. Barricades were quickly erected in the adjoining rue du Faubourg Saint-Honoré as far up as the British Embassy and further north on the Place Saint-Augustin at the junction of the Boulevard Malesherbes with the Boulevard Haussmann, not far west of the Gare Saint-Lazare. The quay to the south of the Tuileries terrace was also solidly barricaded. As Douay's column moved down the Champs-Elysées and reached the Place de la Concorde they were met with a point-blank volley from the cannons on the terrace of the Tuileries gardens and had to scuttle back to take shelter. Meanwhile on the Left Bank Vinoy's parallel column had captured the artillery park at the Ecole Militaire. To his right Cissey's men had taken the Gare Montparnasse and entrenched themselves along the railway line between the station and the Porte de Vanves.

The Commune assembled at nine o'clock, twenty members being found at the Hôtel de Ville, and Pyat insisted a register be made of all those present. Pyat announced that their last hour had come and that his career was over; 'what more glorious end could I hope for than that of a barricade'. Tears in his eyes he signed his name, and then disappeared, not to be seen again until he emerged safely in London. The last issue of his paper, *Le Vengeur*, had to be produced without his help. No decisions were taken. Delescluze's poster was up on the walls, and the Committee of Public Safety drew up two similar proclamations calling citizens to arms on the barricades, 'because Paris with its barricades is impregnable'.

The tocsin was sounding from all the churches in the popular quarters, and sure enough barricades were springing up everywhere. On the rue de Rivoli at the corner of the rue Saint-Denis at the entrance to the Place Saint-Jacques, fifty masons on Frankel's order[1] that afternoon built in a few hours a barricade eighteen feet high and several yards deep. Swarms of children brought wheelbarrows of earth and the 'ladies of *la Halle*'[2] helped fill up the sacks. This was a real stronghold, comparable to that of the rue Saint-Florentin, which père Gaillard had been so inordinately proud of. The Place de la Bastille and the Place du Château d'Eau (today the Place de la République) had stout defences. Most of the other barricades of May '71 – one count gives over 160 on the first day, another 600 in all[3] – were at the most only five to six feet high, con-

---

[1] Senisse, op. cit., p. 137.

[2] Lissagaray, op. cit., p. 324.

[3] Hennebert, op. cit., pp. 217–22; Leighton, op. cit., p. 395.

structed simply of the square cobblestones, the *pavés*, dug up from the Paris streets, with sometimes the metal grills from the base of the trees thrown at the foot, a cannon or a machine-gun, *mitrailleuse*, behind them and a red flag wedged on top.[1]

There was a real danger of ricochets from the stones, and such barricades could be easily shoved aside once taken. Thus where there was time earth was thrown on, especially at the top, to make a real defensive obstruction.[2] The barricades in the rue du Faubourg Saint-Honoré were made largely of mattresses from a nearby warehouse, thrown down into the street by women.[3] Others were more simply obstructions of overturned buses and horse cabs, or of furniture taken sometimes from the big department stores. An English doctor describes the barricades he was forced to lend a hand on along the Avenue Friedland in the 8th arrondissement as having for foundations if possible 'two or three trolleys, cabs or cubic paving stones from the road, sandbags, bricks or anything else'.[4]

Everyone who passed by was forced to take a turn, 'Lend a hand for the Republic, citizen!' no matter how pressing an errand they might be on; staff-officers pleading urgent business on behalf of the Commune were told, 'Today, citizen, there are no more epaulettes.'[5] Archibald Forbes, the *Daily News* correspondent, had to help on the rue du Faubourg Saint-Honoré. Catulle Mendès thought it wise not to refuse the polite request asking him if he 'would be kind enough to trouble himself to go and fetch the few stones over there at the corner of the street'.[6] Sarcey's schoolteacher friend, Arthur Bary, was able to avoid such duties by binding up his arm, pretending he had been wounded.[7] Our 'young English gentleman', unwillingly enrolled in the National Guard, had to work at barricade building: 'everyone in plain clothes who went by was pressed to work at the barricade . . . if anyone refused to assist, he was escorted by a guard of four men, and compelled to work hard for an hour at least'.[8] In contrast to these recalcitrants, National Guards, women and children,

[1] Cf. Rossel, op. cit., p. 275; Lissagaray, op. cit., p. 324; Flaubert, in his *Dictionnaire des Idées Reçues*, defined *Macadam* thus: 'To put an end to revolutions; no longer any way to make barricades. Nonetheless very inconvenient.'

[2] Cf. letter to Barricade Commission from an engineer, 24 April: A.H.G., Ly 25.   [3] Forbes, op. cit., p. 815.

[4] O. C. Powell, *Reminiscences of La Commune*, privately printed, 1914: quoted in Horne, op. cit., p. 367.

[5] Lissagaray, op. cit., p. 342.   [6] Mendès, op. cit., p. 296.

[7] Bary, op. cit., p. 451.   [8] *Macmillans*, p. 392.

workers in their *blouses*, worked all day and into that night constructing the defences on which many of them were to die. On the
Place du Panthéon a barricade was built by women, wearing long
scarves and red cockades, and children singing the 'Chant du Depart'
and the 'Marseillaise'.[1] In the Place Blanche on the Boulevard Clichy
a battalion of 120 women erected the legendary barricade which they
defended vigorously on the Tuesday, many being massacred after
it fell. In the eastern part of the 18th arrondissement Josephine
Courtois, who had already earned the title, 'Queen of the Barricades', for her role in the Lyon uprising in 1848, and a member of
the clubs in her district, was requisitioning empty casks to help build
a barricade at the corner of the rue Doudeauville and the rue
Stephenson. She handed out cartridges and sent her little girl to take
ammunition to the fighters. Edith Thomas in her book on women
during the Commune lists many other similar figures, afterwards
arrested and tried for their part on the barricades.[2] Vallès, seeing
them, had his spirits raised: 'I believed that the city was going to
seem dead before being killed. And here are the women and children
joining in. A beautiful girl has just planted a new red flag, which has
the effect above these grey stones of a poppy on an old wall. Your
*pavé*, citizen!'[3]

This was the spontaneity of the Paris revolution, now the Versailles troops were upon them. It did not need Delescluze's poster
nor the call from the Committee of Public Safety to produce a city
'bristling with barricades'. The cry 'each to his *quartier*' could not be
resisted. The Federals in the 16th arrondissement had at once
retreated before the army, thinking only of getting back to their
home districts, where they would be prepared to make a stand.
Rigault had gone off to Montmartre as soon as he heard of the
Versailles entry to try to persuade his battalion to return with him
to the Prefecture of Police on the Cité in order to make a last stand
there. But they would not budge. In the 5th and 6th arrondissements
Allemane similarly tried to hold back two battalions from the 11th
and 12th arrondissements, but instead they marched off, saying they
preferred to die in their own *quartiers*.[4] Vallès, noting this pheno-

[1] A. Blancheotte, *Tablettes d'une femme pendant la Commune*, Paris, 1872,
pp. 257-8: quoted in Thomas, *Women*, p. 128; cf. Dabot, op. cit., p. 228.
[2] Thomas, op. cit., pp. 129-31.
[3] All quotations from Vallès are from Chs. 30-33 of *L'Insurgé*.
[4] Allemane, op. cit., p. 113.

menon, put it down to a desire to say farewell to their children, their women, before the supreme battle. They wanted to die defending their own homes. At the same time, as Allemane, Lefrançais, and Lissagaray, among others, regretted, this also meant that any organized defence had become impossible. Too often there occurred the 'peculiar arrangement' that Archibald Forbes came across in front of Notre-Dame de Lorette: a triangle of barricades each of which 'could be either enfiladed or taken in reverse by fire directed against the others, so that the defenders were exposing themselves to fire from the flank and rear, as well as from front'.[1] The troops of Versailles could only be seriously checked if there had been a coordinated line of barricades across Paris, covering each other and preventing any given position from being outflanked and taken from behind. Such a plan had been suggested by Gaillard himself, as well as by professional engineers at the War Ministry,[2] but, as has been seen, little had been done to effect this. 'Make some decisions!' expostulated one Guardsman telling Vallès to get back to the Hôtel de Ville; 'haven't you made any preparations then? Ah! in God's name!'

The very strong criticisms Blanqui had made in 1868 of the June 1848 uprising are very applicable to the barricades of the Commune. Blanqui condemned the spontaneous barricades of 1848, everyone fighting simply for their own district with no central organization, as the cause of the disaster, as well as facilitating reprisals and denunciations. Such tactics made it easy for the army to group its forces and take the barricades one by one. Presciently he wrote that if 'thanks to such a serious mistake, the great Paris revolt of '48 was shattered like a glass by such a pitiable government, what catastrophe is not to be feared if the same stupidity is repeated in face of a ferocious militarism that can now use the formidable conquests of science and technology, the railways, the electric telegraph, rifled guns, chassepot quick-firing rifles?' It was essential, said Blanqui, to draw up a general plan, to organize the barricades into a regular system of defence, to have leaders, workers who had been in the army or the National Guard; 'above all, not to become shut up, each in his *quartier*, as all uprisings have never failed to do, to their great loss. This mania has always been the cause of defeat and helps in the

[1] Forbes, p. 816.
[2] See Choury, op. cit., pp. 349–51.

repression afterwards. It must be cured, on pain of a catastrophe.'[1]

The Versailles army advanced during the last week in an uneven
line across Paris against the scattered forces of the Commune, closing
in at the end on Belleville in the north-east. By the Monday night
Vinoy had taken the Invalides, and the Quai d'Orsay, and established
a battery in front of the Palais Bourbon (today's Chambre des
Députés) firing across the bridge into the Place de la Concorde. The
nearby War Ministry had been hastily evacuated several hours earlier
at the first news of the army's advances. But Vinoy's progress was
checked by barricades thrown up in the 7th and 6th arrondissements,
two Communard gunboats were sweeping the rue de l'Université
with their fire, and to the south Montparnasse station was under
barrage.

The first shooting of prisoners within Paris had occurred; sixteen
Federals captured in the rue de Bac had been summarily disposed of
in the Babylone barracks. That same afternoon a chemist named
Kock prevented some children from pulling down a fence surrounding a house being built opposite his shop on the rue de
Richelieu in the 1st arrondissement. A National Guard passed by and
Kock fled into his shop. A group of Federals broke down his door
and were threatened with bottles of acid. The chemist was nonetheless captured and taken first to the Tuileries Palace and then passed
on to the Hôtel de Ville. The Committee of Public Safety seemed
uninterested, and he was returned to the Tuileries. There he was
condemned to death by Bergeret, Urbain and others and shot along
with three more prisoners. Urbain concluded his speech with, 'So

---

[1] 'Instruction for an armed uprising', Blanqui MSS in B.N. given in *Textes
Choisis*, ed. V. P. Volguine, Paris, 1955, pp. 214-20; obviously it is unlikely
this had been read by anyone, though it could be expected that Blanqui had
discussed such ideas with his followers. Blanqui, however, was not unduly
worried about Haussmann's boulevards; these, he thought, could be made use
of by the revolutionaries. In 1895, writing an introduction to a new German
edition of Marx's *The Class Struggles in France*, Engels also reconsidered the
problems of street fighting in an industrial age. Thinking particularly of the
German Social Democratic Party, for which he was writing, Engels argued that
'the superiority of better equipment and training, of single leadership, of the
planned employment of the military forces and of discipline' gave the military
a decided advantage over 'rebellion in the old style, street fighting with barricades, which decided the issue everywhere up to 1848', MESW, p. 661; see
further below, pp. 319-20, 354.

perish our Versaillais foes!' but Delescluze had already signed an order for Kock's release. It arrived too late.[1]

On the right bank Malon in the 17th arrondissement had tried to put Batignolles in a state of defence, and had sent to adjoining Montmartre for help. But again the Guards refused to leave their own district. In Montmartre, no preparations had been made all these past weeks, and this dominating position was completely defenceless. There were eighty-five cannons and about twenty machine-guns lying scattered about on top of the Butte, dirty and uncleaned, where they had been ever since March. The Hôtel de Ville had put La Cecilia in charge there on the Monday morning, and he had at once sent off for reinforcements of men and munitions. But La Cecilia was unknown to the National Guards in the district, and his orders were ignored. In the end Vermorel went to the Hôtel de Ville himself on the Tuesday, but by the time he set off back towards the heights at the head of a train of wagons it was too late. Early Tuesday morning the troops of Versailles moved along outside the fortifications through the neutral zone, the Prussians turning a blind eye, and entered Paris via Porte Saint-Ouen, taking the 17th and 18th arrondissements from the rear. Malon was nearly surrounded and only just managed to flee eastward, and by 9.0 a.m. the 17th arrondissement was in the hands of Versailles. The barricades on the Boulevard Clichy were taken, after the defenders, barely fifty in number, had run out of shells and charged with stones and chunks of asphalt. From here it was easy to encircle Montmartre and take the Butte, the heights being practically deserted. Such was the renown of this revolutionary stronghold that it still took two army corps two hours of cautious advance before at midday the tricolor was flying from the Tour Solferino. It was a serious loss to the Communards. Strategically so, because the heights could be used to fire down into the still defended central districts and across to the neighbouring Buttes de Chaumont. The psychological shock was equally serious.[2] Thiers was delighted at the news, and telegraphed off to his Prefects that it looked as if everything would be over within a day at the most.

In the general retreat Dombrowski was mortally hit on a barricade in the rue Myrha close to where Louise Michel was fighting. He was

[1] Choury, op. cit., pp. 375, 377, misdates this incident; see references to A.N., BB. 24/741 (2329: Etienne Bourdin), and A.H.G., 3e Conseil de Guerre, dossier 762 (N. Bourgeois); cf. F. Jellinek, *The Paris Commune of 1871*, London, 1937/New York, 1965, pp. 320-1.                    [2] Cf. Vinoy, op. cit., p. 320.

carried to the nearby Hospital Lariboisière, where he died a few hours later. His body was taken to the Hôtel de Ville, and laid in state on the blue satin of Valentine Haussmann's bed, his own men keeping vigil.

The massacres that were to grow more fearsome as the week advanced now began. Forty-two men, three women and four children were shot in front of the wall where Lecomte and Clément Thomas had been killed. This was but the start of the Versaillais revenge. A court martial was improvised in the fatal house on the rue des Rosiers and for the rest of the week batches of prisoners were brought there to be executed. Bareheaded, they were made to kneel down before the wall until their turn came.

In contrast to the collapse in the north the barricade at the head of the rue de Rivoli held out for its second day under Brunel's leadership. Brunel was the first to have to apply the order of the Committee of Public Safety to burn down any buildings threatening barricades by sheltering snipers. He set fire to a block of houses in the rue Royale. But by midnight on Tuesday he had to withdraw, being outflanked on his right, where the army was already taking over the Place Vendôme. This prevented him from retreating down the rue de Rivoli and his men broke down the railings of the Tuileries Gardens to gain the Hôtel de Ville by way of the quays. The whole of the rue de Rivoli was a sheet of flames by now, the Tuileries having been fired by Bergeret, and the Ministry of Finances had been burning since the previous night. It had been set on fire by Versailles incendiary shells. Firemen had been sent by the Hôtel de Ville to try to put it out, as at this stage it threatened the defenders at the Place de la Concorde. But they were unsuccessful, and its huge red and black plumes from the masses of documents rose into the sky showering the city with a fine rain of charred paper. The wind carried fragments as far as Saint-Germain, ten miles away, where crowds had assembled to watch the spectacle of Paris burning. The abandoned barricade was not finally taken until Wednesday morning, one of the last to fall being a woman who sprang on to it waving a red flag defiantly at the troops. Some thirty defenders were taken prisoner and shot, their bodies thrown into the ditch in front of the barricade. One old woman put her fingers to her nose as the firing party levelled their rifles and worked them 'after the manner of the defiant of all ages'.[1]

[1] Hoffman, op. cit., p. 279.

The capture of the Place de la Concorde together with the loss of Montmartre opened up the centre of Paris. The Bank was freed by 7.30 that Wednesday morning, 24 May, having been forced to pay out its last 500,000 francs the previous day. De Ploeuc and the Council, confronted by Jourde's demand and the very real threat at last to use National Guards, had considered that 'the definite result of an engagement with the troops of the Commune was not sufficiently certain, in spite of their confidence in the imminent arrival of the regular army' to warrant any risks being taken, and that it would therefore be more 'prudent to pay'.[1] At eight o'clock it was decided to abandon the Hôtel de Ville in favour of the Mairie of the 11th arrondissement in the midst of the Faubourg Saint-Antoine, the traditional centre of all Paris revolutions. Pindy, who had been its Governor during the time of the Commune, decided to set fire to the building to cover the retreat.

There was time for Pilotell to sketch Dombrowski's features before the body was carried away to the Père-Lachaise cemetery. The defenders on the barricades at the Bastille halted the procession at the foot of the July Column, surrounding the bier, burning torches in their hands, drums beating, to salute the dead General. Vermorel, who had been with Dombrowski when he fell, spoke at his graveside: 'This is he whom they accused of treachery! He has been one of the first to give his life for the Commune . . . Let us swear to leave this place only to die!'

Paris in flames was, and often still is, the most common picture presented of the Commune. Certainly during the last week the centre of the city presented a bonfire display that could not help but amaze all who saw it, however much they might regret its occurrence. 'The whole city was enveloped in a whirl of flame and smoke.'[2] Villagers in the vicinity stayed up all night to see the spectacle. Ludovic Halévy went to Montretout, after he had heard two Englishmen in a restaurant recommend its merits as an observation post. When he got there he found more Englishmen among the many spectators, including one with binoculars, telescope and a map, taking notes. His evident satisfaction irritated Halévy and gave him the desire 'to see London burn a little'.[3] Edmond Lepelletier from

---

[1] Meeting of Monday, 22nd; A.H.G., Ly 25, quoted in Choury, op. cit., p. 370; cf. de Ploeuc, *Enquête*, II, p. 497; Ramon, op. cit., pp. 354–5.

[2] Lissagaray, op. cit., p. 351.

[3] Halévy, op. cit., pp. 43–5.

Verlaine's balcony on the Wednesday evening saw the centre burning in 'a roar as of furnaces, splitting, crashing, rending, and the sky grew overcast with the smoke on to which were thrown gigantic crimson reflections'. Bits of charred paper rose up 'like a flight of crows or bats' to disappear from view.[1] Verlaine himself saw

a thin column of black smoke come out of the campanile of the Hôtel de Ville; and, after two or three minutes at most, all the windows of the monument exploded, releasing enormous flames, and the roof fell in with an immense fountain of sparks. This fire lasted until the evening, and then assumed the form of a colossal brazier; this in its turn became, for days after, a gigantic smoulder-ing ember. And the spectacle, horribly beautiful, was continued at night by the cannonade from the hills of Montmartre, which from 9.0 that night to 3.0 in the morning, provided a firework display the like of which is unknown.[2]

The list of buildings destroyed or damaged is enormous. The Ministry of Finance, the Tuileries, the Louvre Library, part of the Palais Royal, the Hôtel de Ville, the Legion of Honour and the adjoining Council of State and Court of Accounts, the Prefecture of Police and one part of the Palace of Justice, the Gobelins gallery and tapestry school, two theatres, the Douane and Grenier d'Abon-dance warehouses and the La Villette docks were burnt. Theisz did prevent the Central Post Office from being fired. Several railway stations were damaged in the fighting as were a number of churches and the Foreign Affairs Ministry; so too was the Magasins-Réunis Department store. Whole blocks of houses were destroyed, parti-cularly by the Place de la Concorde, along the rue de Rivoli and in the Bastille area, as well as the damage caused by the blowing up of the Luxembourg powder store.[3] Neuilly, of course, had suffered greatly, as had other suburbs.

Notre Dame was spared after a fire had been started in the nave by setting light to a pile of chairs and benches, and the staff of the nearby Hôtel-Dieu hospital helped put it out. Paget-Lucipin went

[1] Lepelletier, *Verlaine*, pp. 89–90.

[2] Verlaine, op. cit., pp. 178–9, though Lepelletier doubted whether Verlaine ever dared venture outside of his room.

[3] Nearly 1,000 private houses were burnt or damaged according to one count: Leighton, op. cit., pp. 391–5.

to see the Committee of Public Safety to get reinforcements from the National Guard, arguing that otherwise the 800 wounded Federals would be endangered. The Louvre, threatened by the burning Tuileries, also escaped, though many of the paintings had in any case been removed at the beginning of the war to the security of Brest. Not so the Venus de Milo, which because of its weight had been hidden secretly in the Prefecture of Police. Fearing, completely unjustifiably, for its safety during the Commune, its whereabouts remained concealed, and thus it was nearly destroyed with the Prefecture; a burst water-pipe saved it.[1] Courbet stayed on at the Louvre to help guard the collection, but part of the roof caught fire. The officer in charge of the Versailles troops at the Tuileries Terrace, the Marquis de Sigoyer, on his own initiative, directed his men to help put out the fire after one of them had been sent across Paris to get the spanners to undo the stop-cocks for the water pipes. De Sigoyer even delayed obeying an order to rejoin his division to complete this task. The Louvre's troubles were not quite over, for then a company of chasseurs insisted on using the Apollo Gallery to fire down on to the barricades on the Pont-Neuf, which returned fire. Hoisting the tricolor over the museum drew the attention of a battery of cannons in the east until General Vergé arrived, lowered the flag in the interests of art, and the chasseurs moved on.[2]

Not all the destruction was the work of the Commune. The Ministry of Finance fire was started by Versailles shells, which also accounted for many houses in Paris and the suburbs. The Versailles bombardment had flattened Neuilly. Some took the opportunity of the general conflagration to settle their own financial difficulties by a little private arson. One cause, the most widely held at the time, can be dismissed; the women incendiaries, the *pétroleuses*. This was simply an example of mass hysteria, 'the madness of the hour' as Colonel Hoffman of the U.S. Legation called it,[3] a similar phenomenon to the spy scares during both sieges. But the rumour spread faster than the fires it was supposed to combat, and caused the death of many innocent women. Eight were tried afterwards and condemned, with no evidence.

The bulk of the fires, however, were started by the Communards, and were done so, in most cases, as a means of defence. As such they were often successful, slowing down the Versailles advance.[4] For

[1] Gautier, op. cit., pp. 348–59.         [2] Du Camp, op. cit., vol. 2, pp. 236–42.
[3] Hoffman, op. cit., p. 282.              [4] Cf. Vinoy, op. cit., p. 326.

this reason Brunel had tried unsuccessfully to set the Naval Ministry on fire when he quit the barricade on the rue Saint-Florentin; for the same reason the Palais Royal was set on fire, and the Louvre Library. On the Left Bank, Eudes fired the Legion of Honour and adjoining buildings, and in Wroblewski's retreat the Mairie of the 13th arrondissement was burnt. The biggest fire of all, the Grenier d'Abondance warehouse, was started on the Friday to try to prevent the Bastille defences being outflanked. Houses were burnt down because they harboured snipers, or because the army used them to try to get round a barricade by breaking through the interconnecting walls of the apartments. But in some cases there were more than just strategic reasons.

The firing of the Hôtel de Ville was actually an error from the military point of view. Pindy seems to have panicked in giving the order, though he hoped it would cover the withdrawal of the Commune, Committee of Public Safety and War Delegation to the Faubourg Saint-Antoine. But instead it broke up the morale of the defenders of the 3rd and 4th arrondissements, and was greatly regretted by several members of the Commune fighting in that area. Lefrançais at the time called it the 'death' of the Commune.[1] The setting on fire of the Prefecture of Police and the Palace of Justice by Ferré was of equally dubious military value, as it made it impossible to hold the line across to the Latin Quarter and down to the 13th arrondissement, where Wroblewski was still fighting.[2]

Both these firings and the burning of the Tuileries were as much symbolic as strategic. The Prefecture of Police understandably was an object of fear and hatred, and its burning, together with that of the Palace of Justice, symbolized vengeance on a system of class justice. Lissagaray, though regretting the abandonment of the Hôtel de Ville, said of the deed once it had been done: 'The old edifice, witness of so many perjuries, where the people have so often installed powers that have afterwards shot them down, now cracked and fell with its true master.' The burning of the Tuileries Palace most of all was an act of popular vengeance against all despots: 'Fanned by an eastern wind, the blazing flames rose up against Versailles, and cried to the conqueror of Paris that he will no longer find his place there, and that these monarchical monuments will not

[1] Lefrançais, *Souvenirs*, p. 559.
[2] This was the criticism made by Champy, *Revue Blanche*, p. 271, and Allemane, op. cit., p. 114.

again shelter a monarchy.'[1] It was Bergeret at 10.0 p.m. on 23 May, whilst finishing his supper on the Louvre Terrace, who gave the command to fire the Palace, after all the hangings had been soaked in petrol and barrels of gunpowder had been stacked up at the foot of the Grand Staircase and under the cupola of the Hall of Marshals. There were some strategic interests involved, as the defences to the rear were not yet ready.[2] But in informing the Hôtel de Ville of the fact he announced that 'the last vestiges of Royalty have just vanished'. Lefrançais afterwards affirmed that he approved the destruction of this 'abhorred symbol of an execrable past' and had 'trembled with joy in seeing this sinister palace in flames, from where so often the order to massacre the people had been given and so many anti-social crimes had been planned and glorified'.[3] Or as Malon afterwards wrote, 'it is allowed to this people, avant garde of the new world, that knows how to fight and how to die so well, to burn the palace of kings', just as the Christians had destroyed the pagan temples.[4]

Many would have been glad to take Paris down with them. On the Wednesday a National Guard officer tried to persuade his men to join him in the Arsenal munitions depot, assuring them 'we will all go up together, *mes enfants*'.[5] Vallès tried to deter a group of Federals that wanted to blow up the powder store in the Panthéon, but was only mocked at for trying to preserve such monuments. But as Vallès admitted to himself, burnings were plentiful enough in the classical history taught at school: 'The last stories I heard were in honour of heroic resistances, of Numance in ruins, Carthage in cinders, Saragossa in flames', and there were plenty of more recent examples, beginning with the burning of Moscow in 1812. 'Ah!' said Vallès, 'I did not yield, I did not become an incendiary, without having taken a good look at the past, without having sought out my ancestors.' It was precisely this claim to set themselves on the level with the heroes of the past that so infuriated the bourgeoisie. 'What!' cried Lissagaray, 'this people, heroes in face of the foreigner, must therefore be called assassins, criminals, wretches, because they died for the Universal Republic, because in defence of their beliefs, their conscience, their idea, they preferred, in their fierce enthusiasm,

---

[1] Lissagaray, op. cit., p. 336.
[2] Cf. Bergeret's Chief-of-Staff's account: A.N. quoted in Choury, op. cit., pp. 378–9.
[3] *Etude*, p. 327.        [4] Malon, op. cit., p. 432.        [5] *Macmillans*, p. 393.

to bury themselves in the ruins of Paris rather than abandon it to the coalition of despots a thousand times more cruel and more lasting than any foreigner.'[1]

For if the Commune's destructions in Paris are classed with their illustrious predecessors', then instead of being the wanton destruction of property and monuments by criminal rebels, who deserved to be pitilessly exterminated for such acts, they become a heroic last stand, the obliteration of the symbols of oppression, a final revolutionary potlatch. The rebuilding of so many of the public buildings *in the same style as before* makes clear their significance. Like the restoration of the Vendôme Column this was meant to remove all signs of the Commune, to abolish it from history.

On the Monday, in preparation for the evacuation of the Prefecture, Rigault had ordered the transfer of the hostages, the Archbishop and Judge Bonjean among them, to the condemned cells in La Roquette prison. Da Costa had to carry this out, using as his tumbrils goods-carts, which he needed to protect his prisoners from the savage crowds in the Faubourg Saint-Antoine. The next day Rigault left for Saint-Pélagie prison on a personal mission of his own. The object of this was Gustave Chaudey, a violent-tempered republican journalist, editor of the *Siècle*, who had been a close friend of Proudhon's. Chaudey had been in charge of the Hôtel de Ville the day of the 22 January demonstration. He had not given the order to fire, the initiative for which had come from the military commander, but he had refused to make any concessions to the delegation headed by Delescluze. The revolutionaries held him responsible for the deaths of that day, particularly Sapia's, a friend of Rigault. Delescluze had pressed for the arrest of Chaudey as soon as the Commune took over, being an enemy of his ever since 1848, as had the *Père Duchêne*. Chaudey had taken upon himself full responsibility 'before Justice and before History for having defended the Hôtel de Ville in January', in an article in his paper on 12 April. Typical of his own stubbornness he had then stayed on in Paris, against the advice of his friends. He had been in prison ever since 13 April,

---

[1] Lissagaray, *Les Huit Journées de Mai*, Brussels, 1871, pp. 103–4. Flaubert felt that the War Councils after the Commune were not severe enough with these destroyers of property; he wrote to George Sand (around 18 October 1871) that 'all the Commune should have been condemned to the galleys, and those bloodstained imbeciles should have been forced to clear up the ruins of Paris, a chain around their neck, like common convicts'.

though Beslay had tried to get him released. His trial had not been completed by the time of the entry of the Versailles army, but Rigault decided that the deaths of Sapia and the others could not be left unavenged. In spite of Chaudey's protests that he was a republican and had a wife and children, Rigault without exchanging any more words marched him off to be shot by a very uneasy execution squad. He died crying 'Long live the Republic'. Three gendarmes, who had been held as hostages, were shot as well because, as Rigault put it, unlike soldiers they had chosen to join a force which could have only one task, the holding down of the people.[1] Rigault then went off late that night to join the fighting in the Latin Quarter.

This left Ferré in charge of the evacuation of the Prefecture, and on the Wednesday morning he had the Versailles spy Veysset shot for having tried to bribe Dombrowski and otherwise aid Versailles. Veysset had been captured on 21 May, preparing to open one of the gates of the city. His body was thrown into the Seine, and Ferré himself then hurried off to the Mairie of the 11th arrondissement. There he was met by a crowd of National Guards demanding the death of one of their officers. This was Charles de Beaufort, the cousin of Edouard Moreau of the Central Committee. De Beaufort, with his aristocratic airs, was hardly a revolutionary soldier, though his manner was not too amiss among the other staff-officers at the War Ministry, where he had spent most of his time, though he had also been with Dombrowski at Neuilly. Now he was facing the completely false charge of having been responsible for the heavy losses the 66th National Guard battalion had just suffered defending a barricade near the Madeleine. He had had the misfortune to be recognized by the *cantinière* of the 66th as the officer who had once angrily threatened to 'purge' this battalion just because a Guard had checked him outside the Hôtel de Ville. The remark had not been forgotten, and was now being used against him. In fact it does seem as if de Beaufort had lately become involved in conspiring with Versailles, though this was not known at the time.[2] Ferré tried to delay the crowd from executing its vengeance by setting up a court martial, and Delescluze appealed to the crowd for de Beaufort's life. But as several other incidents showed, the members of the Commune had little authority left, and a mob dragged de Beaufort outside and

[1] Da Costa, op. cit., vol. I, p. 444.
[2] See Lissagaray, *History of the Commune*, p. 438; Laronze, op. cit., p. 606; Thomas, op. cit., pp. 162–4.

along the streets until a few shots finished him off. He was a victim to mounting anger against all display of military privilege.

Its blood was now up and the crowd was pressing for the execution of the decree on the hostages in revenge for the massacres going on throughout Paris wherever the Versailles army had taken over. Outside La Roquette prison the crowd was trying to force the prison doors, and Genton, a skilled woodworker and one of the Commune's magistrates, said he would command the execution squad, for which there was no shortage of volunteers. Ferré agreed to sign an order for six to be handed over. The Governor of the prison, himself appointed by the Commune, refused to surrender the Archbishop, whom the crowd wanted most of all, because his name was not specifically on the list. Ferré's secretary hurried back and Ferré added to the note, 'and particularly the Archbishop'. Darboy, Bonjean and four priests were then lined up against the prison wall and shot. On this occasion the execution squad had no regrets, but when the news reached the Mairie Vallès protested against this 'horrible butchery'. Back came the reply from one Guard, 'What about the September massacres? Were you joking when you told us to act like in '93?'; and another Guard added, 'the Commune may not have been serious about the decrees it passed, but the people mean to see to it that they are executed properly'. Delescluze simply covered his face in his hands: 'What a war! What a war!'

Elsewhere in Paris a more indiscriminate slaughter was taking place. Each time a barricade fell, the defenders were put up against a wall and shot. Thirty Federals had been thrown into the ditch before the Saint-Florentin barricade. Three hundred were shot after they fled for sanctuary into the Madeleine church. Many, of course, who had been involved in the fighting were proud of having done so. A woman replied to the accusation of having killed two soldiers, 'may God punish me for not having killed more. I had two sons at Issy; they were both killed. And two at Neuilly. My husband died at this barricade – and now do what you want with me.'[1] She was undressed and shot. The seminary adjoining Saint-Sulpice had been turned into a hospital. When the Versailles troops arrived they quite falsely claimed that shots had been fired on them from the building, and proceeded to shoot all the medical staff and their patients. They left behind them eighty corpses. It was the same story in the Beaujon hospital. Walking around the Latin Quarter on the Thursday

[1] Lissagaray, *Huit journées*, p. 146; Malon, op. cit., p. 462.

morning Vuillaume found corpses everywhere; a heap against a corner of the Mairie on the Place du Panthéon; corpses in the basin of the fountain in the Luxembourg Gardens; more in a heap before the Cluny Theatre on the Boulevard Saint-Germain near the museum; still more in the rue de la Huchette, rue Saint-Jacques, on a cart in the rue des Ecoles, in the ditch of the barricade at the bottom of the Boulevard Saint-Michel by the fountain.[1]

The battle for the Latin Quarter had lasted two days, the Tuesday and Wednesday. On the Tuesday Varlin organized the defence at the western edge of the 6th arrondissement at the crossroads of the Place Croix-Rouge between the rue de Rennes, rue de Babylone and the rue de Grenelle. This linked up the barricades nearer the river with those in the rue Vavin in Montparnasse and at the Carrefour de l'Observatoire at the top of the Luxembourg Gardens, where Maxime Lisbonne held off the Versaillais from advancing on the Luxembourg. These barricades had to be evacuated during the Tuesday night, and on the Wednesday the three divisions of Cissey converged on the Panthéon. Their advance was temporarily checked by Lisbonne blowing up the powder store in the Luxembourg Gardens in an explosion that shattered all the windows of the area. Allemane was in charge of the barricades in the bottom part of the 5th arrondissement down to the Seine. There was a last council of war in the Mairie of the Panthéon at which Lisbonne, discouraged, supported Régère's suggestion of surrendering. Vallès refused adamantly to sign such an order, 'which in any case the Federals would not have obeyed'. There was nothing left but to fight to the end. An old printer of albino looks, a veteran of '48, said to Allemane as they fired together from the barricade on the rue d'Ulm, 'if you escape death, don't forget to tell your comrades that *Navret* died fighting like an old revolutionary'.[2] Shortly afterwards the barricade in the rue Soufflot fell and the Versailles rushed the Mairie and massacred the National Guards they found there. Lisbonne obeyed the Committee of Public Safety and fell back to the 11th arrondissement, the rest retreated across the 5th arrondissement to the rue Monge. The last stand in the Latin Quarter was on the rue Monge and the rue des Boulangers, at the side of the wall of the Roman Amphitheatre there, the *Arènes du Lutèce*, Allemane tying his red

---

[1] Vuillaume, op. cit., I, pp. 38–41, 78–80.
[2] Allemane, op. cit., p. 124; *Navret* means 'a turnip', and is used as a popular expression for anaemic white faces.

sash of Delegate to the National Guard Central Committee to the pole of the flag. This was abandoned during the Wednesday night.[1]

Rigault had been killed just before the Panthéon fell. He had been spotted because of his uniform as he entered his hotel in the rue Gay-Lussac to collect some documents. The hotel-keeper was forced to reveal the number of his room, and Rigault gave himself up to avoid his companion being captured. The young army officer did not recognize his prisoner, but when Rigault insolently answered his questions by saying 'Long live the Commune! Down with assassins!' he was thrown against a wall and shot in the street at the corner of the rue Collard.

Wroblewski was left defending the 13th arrondissement. His line ran from the Butte-aux-Cailles, a hill that dominated this south-east corner of Paris, near the Place d'Italie, to the outer ramparts and fort Bicêtre. Delescluze had ordered the abandonment of this fort at the beginning of the week, but Melliet, the Commune's Civil Commissioner at the fort, had called a War Council with Wroblewski and the local members at which they decided 'to consult only their patriotism and their energy to face the necessities of the situation'. Wroblewski even went to see Delescluze to try to persuade him to transfer the whole defence to the Left Bank, realizing that if this line fell the north-east would quickly be crushed between Versailles and the Prussians. The Seine, the Panthéon, the Butte-aux-Cailles and the forts, with open fields for retreat to their rear, made the south-east a safer citadel than the Right Bank. But, as Lissagaray put it, 'the heart of an insurrection cannot be displaced for military purposes and the Federals were more and more determined to defend their own quarters'.[2] Whilst the rest of the Left Bank succumbed on the Wednesday, this southern outpost held, Wroblewski's men driving back four attempts to take the hill. But on Thursday the Guards at Fort Bicêtre insisted they be allowed to return to defend their own districts, and the fort was abandoned. This left the way open to the Versailles troops to go round the Butte, threatening Wroblewski's rear via the Place d'Italie, and Wroblewski was forced to retreat towards the Seine. Just before the final withdrawal a dozen Dominicans, who had been arrested a few days previously, falsely accused of causing the loss of Moulin-Saquet,[3] were released from the prison in

[1] Allemane, p. 135.
[2] Lissagaray, *History of the Commune*, p. 331.
[3] Cf. above, p. 238.

the Avenue d'Italie. But as they emerged they were picked off by the Guards of the 101st, determined to exact revenge for the Versailles shootings of prisoners. At the end of Thursday afternoon Wroblewski crossed the Pont d'Austerlitz on to the Right Bank, where the fighting was now concentrated. The key points here were the Place de la Bastille and the Place du Château d'Eau (Place de la République) defending the approaches to the 11th arrondissement and its Mairie on the Place Voltaire.

During the past three days the Commune and the Committee of Public Safety had done very little except issue orders, ignored often by the commanders on the spot. Both these bodies and the National Guard Central Committee had published vain appeals to their 'brothers' in the army to desert to the side of the people of Paris.[1] Equally hopeless were the suggestions that a truce could be arranged between Paris and Versailles. This idea came from the rump of the Central Committee, led by Edouard Moreau and his two friends Gouhier and Grêlier, the latter being a moderate Blanquist, not having 'extreme political views' according to the workmen of the washhouse he owned who gave evidence at his trial.[2] Moreau was sickened by the fires, in despair at the massacres he saw going on around him. Their peace propositions were completely unrealistic – the withdrawal of the army, dissolution of the National Assembly and the Commune, new elections. Thiers had been refusing such proposals for the past two months. Nevertheless, Gouhier and Grêlier, claiming they were masters of the situation after the Hôtel de Ville had been abandoned, met with some of the republicans of the League of the Rights of Paris. But as both groups had to admit, it was difficult enough to get across Paris to the Mairie of the 11th arrondissement let alone out of the city to see Thiers.[3] Altogether, it was a pathetic end as the last official act of the body that had inaugurated the Revolution, something completely overshadowed by the thousands of Federals dying in the streets. It was also the end of Moreau, revolted by the cruel death of his cousin de Beaufort at the hands of a mob. Moreau made no attempt to escape when soldiers came to his home to search for him on the Thursday. He was taken to the Châtelet Theatre and quickly condemned, a friend catching a

---

[1] All three proclamations are dated 3 and 4 prairial, an 79, and appeared in the last issue of the *Journal Officiel*, Wednesday, 24 May.

[2] *Dictionnaire*, VI, p. 240.

[3] Lefèvre, op. cit., pp. 299–314; Corbon, *Enquête*, II, pp. 617–18.

last glimpse of him, looking completely impassive, waiting his turn to be led out and shot.

Delescluze had for a moment on the Wednesday thrilled the Communal council at the Mairie when he proposed in his low failing whisper of a voice that 'the members of the Commune, girded with their official sashes, should hold a review on the Boulevard Voltaire of all the Battalions that can be assembled. We will then put ourselves at their head and lead them to the points to be recaptured.' There was not the slightest possibility that such an act could be successful.

There was another attempt to get a truce on the Thursday. Arnold, the member of the Commune closest to the Central Committee, pressed the twenty-two members of the Commune assembled at the Mairie to seek the mediation of the Prussians. Arnold claimed that the secretary of the American Ambassador, Washburne, had said the Prussians were willing to intervene between Paris and Versailles in accordance with the conditions set out the previous day by the Central Committee. Some accounts say Washburne's secretary attended the Mairie to back up this suggestion.[1] Delescluze quite rightly was unwilling to credit the Prussians with such intentions, but succumbed to Arnold's pleading. A delegation including Delescluze, Arnold, Vermorel and Vaillant, the only one who spoke

---

[1] This whole affair is very unclear. Seraillier sent an account of the truce idea to Marx, saying that the American Ambassador's secretary had indeed made the suggestion and attended the meeting in the Mairie. Marx had this published as a pamphlet, 'Mr Washburne, The American Ambassador in Paris', which was reprinted in several American papers (see, *Documents of the First International*, IV, pp. 426–30). He included in the pamphlet a letter from Robert Reid, the *Daily Telegraph* correspondent, showing that Washburne had only hostile feelings regarding the Commune, which indeed was the case. Marx's conclusion therefore was that this truce attempt was a trap to get the Prussians to arrest the members of the Commune, who could then be handed over to the French Government. Vuillaume (VII, pp. 98–102), Malon, Lissagaray and Lefrançais (*Souvenirs*), all refer to the incident, linking it to the American Ambassador, or his secretary. But Washburne makes no mention of any such overtures either in his *Recollections* or in his official reports to the Department of State, and denied that any member of his staff ever had anything to do with such a scheme; (see further, Dessal, *Delescluze*, op. cit., p. 407; French edition of Marx's *Guerre Civile*, op. cit., note on pp. 308–9; Laronze, op. cit., pp. 616–17, who gives evidence from Arnold's pre-trial investigation that he was indeed in touch with a certain Mr Steinwerk of the American Embassy through a relative, Berthier, the latter saying his aim was to get Arnold safely out of Paris).

German, set off but got no further than the Porte de Vincennes. The National Guards on duty at the gate refused to let them pass, even after they fetched a written order from Ferré, because hardly surprisingly they thought the members of the Commune were trying to escape: 'No one is going to do that to us, not after having got us into this mess. We're all in this together.' Delescluze was crushed by this accusation, and returned repeating, 'I don't want to live any longer, everything is finished for me.' When he got back to the Mairie he sat down and wrote a farewell letter to his sister: 'I do not want nor am I able to serve as the victim and toy of the victorious reaction . . . I can't bear to submit to another defeat after so many others . . . Adieu! Adieu!'

After his retreat to the Right Bank Wroblewski reported to the Mairie of the 11th arrondissement, where Delescluze offered to make him Commander-in-Chief. But Delescluze could only promise him a few hundred men, and Wroblewski went off to fight as a simple soldier. Already the battle was taking its toll of the leading Communards. Elizabeth Dmitrieff, herself wounded, arrived at the Mairie supporting Frankel, hit at a barricade on the Place de la Bastille. At a quarter to seven Delescluze set out along the Boulevard Voltaire with a small group including Lissagaray and Jourde towards the hottest spot of all, the Place du Château d'Eau (Place de la République). He was dressed as always as a typical Jacobin of '48, black hat and frock coat, his red Commune sash around his waist the only spot of colour, leaning upon his cane. As he drew near the barricade he passed Lisbonne being carried away on a stretcher by the 'Pupils of the Commune' and whispered a few words in the ear of Vermorel, his legs broken, who died a few months later from lack of proper care in prison at Versailles. It was certain death to go any further. Delescluze, unmindful whether anyone was still following, walked on, the only living thing in the street. He climbed up to the top of the barricade, his thin figure silhouetted by the setting sun. Suddenly he pitched forward on to the Square, killed by three bullets. Three volunteers fell trying to rescue him, and his body was not recovered until several days later.[1]

[1] Lissagaray, op. cit., p. 361; Vuillaume, IV, pp. 35ff. Delescluze was buried in a common grave, the army wanting to avoid his tomb becoming a place of pilgrimage – another Baudin (cf. above, p. 31). But a witness planted an acacia tree on the spot, which enabled his body to be recovered in 1883 and transferred to Père-Lachaise.

At midnight on the Thursday the Mairie of the 11th arrondissement was evacuated, the Versailles troops having forced their way
into the 11th and 12th arrondissements by outflanking the defences
at the Château d'Eau and Bastille.. The July Column was a burning
torch over the Faubourg Saint-Antoine, shells having set fire to the
flags and wreaths that had decorated it ever since the National Guard
ceremonies there at the end of February. The remaining dozen
members of the Commune moved to the Mairie of the 20th arrondissement, then at the junction of the rue de Belleville and the rue
Jourdain, near the Place des Fêtes, whilst the military Headquarters,
such as was left, was set up further east in Cité de Vincennes in the
rue Haxo. Here Varlin, who had taken over after Delescluze's
death, and Ranvier sat signing orders, which the fifteen remaining
members of the National Guard Central Committee still disputed,
claiming a dictatorship for themselves. On the walls was the last
poster of the Commune, drawn up by Ranvier of the Committee of
Public Safety, addressed to the 'Citizens of the 20th Arrondissement',
calling on them to rally to the support of the 19th arrondissement.
But few read it or obeyed.

None of these official bodies could prevent popular reprisals being
taken as the Versailles troops closed in. Antoine Clavier, a commercial clerk and the Commune's Police Commissioner in the 12th
arrondissement, went to La Roquette with four National Guards
and forced the Governor at pistol point to surrender Jecker, unpopular as the financier of the Mexican expedition. They walked to
a ditch behind the Père-Lachaise cemetery where Jecker was shot,
remaining perfectly calm right to his end. That same Friday evening
the Blanquist Emile Gois,[1] who had been Eudes' aide-de-camp and
one of the judges on the Commune's court martial, went with a group
of National Guards and forced the poor Governor of La Roquette
to surrender yet more hostages, police and priests, who were then
marched back surrounded by a yelling mob to the Mairie of the
20th arrondissement. Ranvier would have nothing to do with them
and so they moved to the rue Haxo. Here Varlin, Vallès, Seraillier and
others made strenuous efforts to save the hostages, but these were
killed in batches, shots coming on all sides from the crowd of
passers-by and National Guards. Fifty-one corpses were counted,
one too many; someone in the crowd must have been hit. The

[1] *Dictionnaire*, VI, p. 208; Gois had never met Blanqui himself, but had been
part of the Blanquist group in Montmartre in 1868.

15. After the battle: the 'ruins of Paris'

(*a*) The Hôtel de Ville, June 1871

(*b*) The Tuileries Palace, June 1871

(*c*) The rue de Rivoli

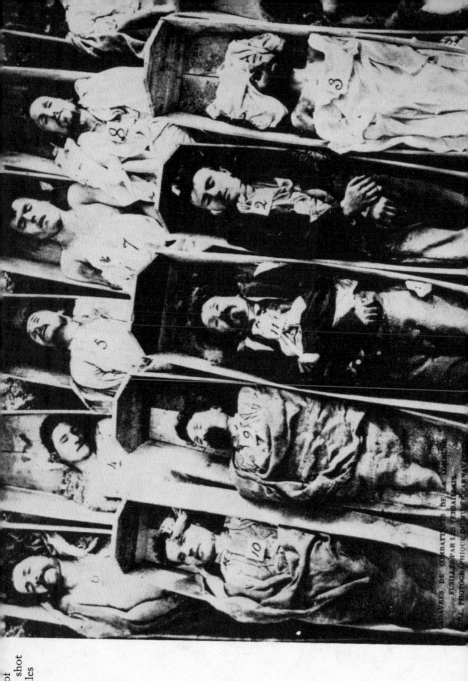

16. Corpses of Communards shot by the Versailles troops

remaining hostages at La Roquette were told they could go by the Governor, but understandably they felt it was more dangerous outside than in. They barricaded themselves in, and a few priests who did make a run for it were shot down. They were eventually released by the army.[1] In all something over seventy hostages were killed under the Commune, all during the last week after the entry of the Versailles army.

The barricades leading off the Bastille and the Château d'Eau held out until the Friday afternoon, over a hundred falling in defence of those protecting the entrance to the Faubourg Saint-Antoine. The Blanquist Thoumieux was shot when these fell. He refused to stand on a pile of rubbish to die, and walked across to the other side of the road: 'I fought bravely. I have the right not to die in *la merde*.'[2] A General was killed before a barricade in the rue du Faubourg du Temple, protecting Belleville, was taken. Here also Protot of the Commune fell, hit in the foot, though he was saved by some local women carrying him off to receive medical attention. During Thursday night and Friday morning the Prussians had moved up 10,000 troops to strengthen their forces at the back of the Communards, with orders to prevent any fugitives from escaping. They refused to let pass a Freemason delegation leading 3,000 Parisians, wounding one woman when she tried to force her way over the bridge.[3] But they did agree to transmit to the American Ambassador a final effort by Arnold to obtain mediation. During Friday night fighting still continued around the Place du Trône (Place de la Nation today).

Saturday morning dawned foggy and raining, for the second day running. The fighting was now confined to Belleville. There was little ammunition left, though the Buttes de Chaumont continued firing all day. In the afternoon the remaining ten or so members of the Commune, including Vaillant, Eugène Gérardin, Vallès and Allix gathered in the rue Haxo. Vaillant, supported by Vallès, took up a suggestion first made by Dr Rastoul earlier in the week. This was that they should offer, through the Prussians, to surrender themselves to the Versailles Government in return for an end to the

---

[1] Vuillaume, op. cit., II, pp. 183–217; Abbé Lamazou, *La Place Vendôme et la Roquette*, Paris, 1871, pp. 201–36. Lamazou raises number of hostages taken out to fifty-four; his account, significantly enough, found an English translation almost at once – 1873.                    [2] Senisse, op. cit., p. 146.

[3] Senisse, op. cit., p. 147; Lissagaray, *Huit Journées*, pp. 141–2.

shooting and reprisals. But at this last moment the Central Committee of the Twenty Arrondissements in the person of Constant Martin decided them against making any such tentative. To do so, argued Martin, would tarnish the reputation of the Commune; the greatness of the Commune in the future would lie in its having fought to the end, without ever surrendering.[1] The Place des Fêtes fell after the defenders had been distracted by Ferré marching a column of 1,333 soldiers from the Prince Eugène Barracks, where they had been ever since 18 March, to their new prison in the Church of Belleville. Being soldiers, not gendarmes or priests, they were in no danger from being mobbed by the crowd. Some of the last fighting this day took place in the Père-Lachaise cemetery, which the two hundred National Guards there had foolishly failed to put into a proper state of defence. The army blew open the gate, and there was bitter hand-to-hand fighting among the tombs in the heavy rain and failing light, enemies falling and dying in the same grave. The last of these combatants fell by the busts of Charles Nodier and Balzac. Those not killed in the fighting were lined up against the wall in the eastern corner of the cemetery and shot. The killings continued here for several days afterwards.

On Whit Sunday, 28 May, in the smoky rainy early morning the Mairie of the 20th arrondissement fell, leaving only a few pockets of resistance, mainly the square in the 11th arrondissement bounded by the rues du Faubourg du Temple, des Trois Bornes, des Trois-Couronnes and the Boulevard de Belleville. Varlin, Ferré and Gambon, wearing their red sashes and headed by a gigantic Garibaldian carrying an equally enormous red flag, led a column of fifty men down from the 20th arrondissement to the barricade at the corner of the rue du Faubourg du Temple and the rue de la Fontaine, just east of the Place du Château d'Eau. But this barricade was turned, and the defenders only just managed to get away. It was the final appearance of any semblance of the Communal Council. Varlin wandered around the streets, dazed and lost, until in the afternoon, recognized by a priest in civilian clothes and arrested, he was dragged up to the rue des Rosiers, beaten by rifle butts and stoned by the crowd. He was almost dead by the time he was sentenced. He was dragged out again into the streets, until his face was smashed to

---

[1] Vaillant in *L'Humanité*, 18 March 1908; quoted in Dommanget, *Vaillant*, p. 49; Choury, op. cit., p. 410. Rastoul's suggestion is in A.H.G., Ly 26: see Decouflé, op. cit., p. 200; Choury, op. cit., pp. 399–400.

jelly, one eye out of its socket. He still tried to hold himself up straight. He was shot at the second attempt, point-blank, still finding sufficient force to cry out 'Long live the Commune'. About noon the last cannon shot was fired, and two hours later, in Belleville, on the rue Ramponneau where it crosses the rue de Tourtille in the 20th arrondissement, the last barricade held out for a quarter of an hour, defended by a single man. He fired his last shot and walked away.[1] The Commune 'died in its bed'.[2]

The next day the fort of Vincennes with 374 men was forced to surrender, having been immobilized by the Prussians cutting it off from the city. Nine of the officers were shot, although they had been promised that their lives would be spared, and their bodies were thrown into the moat of the fort.

The savagery with which the civil war was fought emphasizes the impossibility of the Commune's position, once Paris had been entered and the Communards had retreated to their barricaded *quartiers*. Both Blanqui in 1868 and Engels in 1895 pointed out that barricades are essentially a moral, not a military tactic.[3] Blanqui was confident they could still be used, and in recommending a more efficient use of barricades in organizing the defence, his expectation was that before such determined resistance the morale of the army would crack whereas the insurgents would be upheld by their revolutionary ardour. When the army first entered Paris, many Communards did indeed believe the troops would fraternize, and this expectation persisted for some time. On the Wednesday, on one of the last barricades on the rue Soufflot, the army tried to trick the defenders into showing themselves by shouting 'Long live the National Guard'. Allemane had to hold back those 'naïve' enough to be taken in by this seeming act of fraternization.[4] But the difference between 18 March and the last week in May lay in the fact that the army remained firm, and so the revolution was crushed.

Of course, it could be argued that if the Commune had organized its defences properly, if the cannons on Montmartre had been brought into play at the start – Vinoy admitted this would have severely hampered the occupation of the Place du Trocadero on the

---

[1] This is Lissagaray's account, *History*, p. 379. Da Costa, op. cit., III, p. 118, says that the last barricade was in the 10th arrondissement on the rue du Faubourg du Temple between rue Saint-Maur and the Avenue Parmentier.

[2] Winock and Azéma, op. cit., p. 148.

[3] Cf. above, pp. 319–20.      [4] Allemane, op. cit., p. 126.

Monday morning[1] – then Paris could have held out much longer. But the aim would still have been the same, as it had been ever since the Central Committee and then the Commune had taken over, namely to win over the provinces into forcing the Government to back down and to make the troops in the army change sides.

Neither of these possibilities was very likely. In the provinces the republican bourgeoisie feared the social passions of the clubs, the popular Press, the Communal Council itself, which outweighed their sympathy for Paris's claims to municipal liberty. Thiers was easily able to keep the provincial municipalities quiet by his assurances regarding the Republic, as well as the judicious use of troops to quell any popular movements. In Paris, unlike the situation in March, the soldiers in May had been kept clear of all possibility of contact with the insurgent population. They had little idea and certainly no sympathy with what had driven Paris to revolt. Instead they had been carefully nurtured on a diet of patriotism against those who dared to dishonour France any further after the humiliation of the defeat against Prussia, and of righteousness in crushing the assassins of Clément Thomas and Lecomte together with many other similar horror stories. As the American Colonel Hoffman wrote, the soldiers acted as men 'heated with battle' and had been 'taught to believe every prisoner they take an incarnate devil'.[2]

If the battle was over, the shooting was not. Thiers had told the Assembly on the Monday after the army had first made its entry into the capital that 'the cause of justice, of order, of humanity, and of civilization has triumphed', and that the restoration would be 'in the name of the law and by the law'. In his *Memoirs* Thiers insists that he gave strict orders that 'the anger of the soldiers must be restrained', and MacMahon likewise claimed he had given orders against any summary justice being taken. But the Versailles entry quickly became a bloodbath, which neither the Government nor MacMahon tried to stop. The 'expiation', as Thiers had also said, was 'to be complete'. The big dailies were encouraging the Government and the army in this attitude. The *Figaro* spoke of the need 'to purge Paris. Never has such an opportunity presented itself for curing Paris of the moral gangrene that has been consuming it for the past twenty years ... Today, clemency equals lunacy ... What is a republican? A savage beast ... We must track down those who are

[1] Vinoy, op. cit., p. 310.
[2] Hoffman, p. 280; cf. Lissagaray, *Huit Journées*, pp. 40–1.

hiding, like wild animals. Without pity, without anger, simply with the steadfastness of an honest man doing his duty.' The *Moniteur Universel* said they should be treated as 'brigands', as 'the most appalling monsters ever seen in the history of humanity'. The *Bien Public* spoke of the need for a 'Communard hunt'. The images were all racialist and animal; the Communards, the whole Paris population even, were no longer regarded as human and so the normal laws of civilization could be ignored.

During this week, accordingly, Paris was put to the sack by the French army, 130,000 troops – or, to adapt a contemporary term, it experienced an army-riot. The enemy, in Paris as in Marseille where General d'Espivent saw to the repression, was not simply the Commune, but republicanism in general; in short, all the progressive forces of the time. Thus, for example, on the Thursday, after the Latin Quarter had been taken, troops searched the house of Eugène André, the mathematics teacher whose only crime had been to help set up the professional school in the Jesuit house in the rue Lhomond.[1] Nothing incriminating was found, but he was arrested and marched off. An officer coming across the company in the street ordered André to be shot 'all the same'. Another officer ordered the execution of the banker Cernuschi, picked up grieving beside his dead friend Chaudey, because he was known to have given a large sum of money to combat the 1870 plebiscite of Napoleon III. He was only saved by the last-minute intervention of a monarchist Deputy who happened to be on the spot. Equally outrageous as having nothing to do with the Commune was the execution of the Deputy Millière on Friday, 26 May. He had not supported the Revolution, although he had strongly condemned the National Assembly for fighting a civil war against Paris. His position was similar to that of Clemenceau, whose friend he was. He was arrested and General Cissey ordered him to be shot 'on his knees, in order to demand pardon of society for the evil he had done to it'. The captain carrying out this sentence replied to Millière's protests that he personally had been 'revolted' by an article of Millière's he had read, and that Millière was 'a viper that should be stamped out'. Millière was taken to the steps of the Panthéon, forced to kneel by two soldiers, and died crying 'Long live the Republic! Long live the People! Long live humanity!' The repression was to be a moral purge of all those considered politically dangerous.

[1] Cf. above, p. 273.

This attitude among the officers shows the shift to the right that had occurred within the French army. The tradition of the revolutionary armies, the people's army, liberating Europe, had maintained its hold well after the end of the Napoleonic wars, as the revival of the Napoleonic legend had shown in the 1840s. For this reason the conservative upper classes had tended to refrain from patronizing the Napoleonic military establishments. The use of the army in putting down the June revolt of 1848 followed by the *coup d'état* and subsequent repression marked a shift within the officer class. Sons of good families now attended the Saint-Cyr officer training school and the Ecole Polytechnique.[1] In fact many army N.C.O.s stayed on in Paris and joined the Commune because they felt they had been unfairly treated by a promotion system that favoured those of the right family background.[2] In turn, republican opinion turned against the idea of a permanent army as it became clear that this would be used for internal repression or in foreign adventures such as the unpopular Mexican expedition or the support of the Papacy in Rome. In short, the authoritarian State of the Second Empire had an equally conservative, anti-democratic, anti-egalitarian officer class. It was such officers as Gallifet, whose promotion had been the result more of his wife's talents on the ballroom than his own on the battlefields, who relished putting down the Commune. The big review of the victorious army held on Longchamp in July 1871 was taken by many observers as marking the beginning of the resurgence of France; the victory over the Commune made up for the defeat by the Prussians.[3] One of the main themes of the succeeding reaction was the army as a stabilizing moral force in the country. Not surprisingly, therefore, the socialists opposed the idea of a regular standing army. This was one of the points of the 'minimum programme' of Guesde's Parti ouvrier drawn up with the help of Marx in 1880. In 1911 Jean Jaurès, the leader of the French Socialist Party,

[1] See R. Girardet, *La Société militaire dans la France contemporaine (1815–1939)*, Paris, 1953, pp. 24–39, 122–38; P. Chalmin, *L'Officier français de 1815 à 1870*, Paris, 1957, pp. 264–8, 364, and '*La Crise morale de l'armée française*', *L'Armée et la Seconde République: Bibliothèque de la Révolution de 1848*, vol. 18, La Roche-sur-Yon, 1955, pp. 73–6.

[2] e.g., see Baron, op. cit., p. 63.

[3] General du Barail, op. cit., p. 291; Bary, op. cit., p. 461 (30 May); Sarcey in *Le Gaulois* said 'How nice are our little soldiers'. See too P.-M. de la Gorce, *The French Army*, Eng. trans. London, 1963, pp. 7ff; Girardet, op. cit., pp. 163–175; Girard, *Garde Nationale*, pp. 358–70.

restated the republican conception of a citizen army in his book, *L'Armée nouvelle*.

The Versailles entry was accompanied by the setting up of special military courts which for days divided the prisoners into those to be shot and those to be sent to Versailles – no one, of course, being set free. Vuillaume was picked up in the Latin Quarter on Thursday, 25 May, and taken to the Luxembourg. His over-curiosity in venturing out nearly caused his death, although he was wearing a red-cross arm band. The examining police official asked him what it was he had on his arm, and Vuillaume replied that it was the badge of the International Geneva Convention. This was a mistake, for the official seized on the word 'International'. Vuillaume protested it was not the Workingmen's International, but in his panic addressed him as 'citizen'. This was his immediate undoing, and he was sent off to join the 'queue' of 300 waiting to be shot. He was only saved by a young sergeant passing by who had been a medical student and recognized his arm band.[1]

Anyone who was in Paris was thereby considered suspect, guilty even. General Valentin, the Prefect of Police since March, whose brutality in Lyon had led to his arrest there when the revolutionaries took over for a time, said after the defeat of the Commune that 'the simple fact of having stayed in Paris under the Commune is a crime. Everyone there is to blame, and if I had my way everyone would be punished.'[2] At the Châtelet Theatre the death sentence was 'transfer to the detachment', which meant being taken to the Lobeau barracks, where the prisoners were not even lined up against a wall but shot down anyhow, often only being wounded the first time. Goncourt, more naïve than many in such matters, was surprised to hear from these barracks an 'explosion, like a violent noise enclosed within walls, a fusillade, with something of the mechanical regularity of machine-gun fire', followed by 'the reverberating crack' of the *coup de grace* finishing off those still not dead.[3] The corpses were thrown into shallow graves in the Square Saint-Jacques or along the river banks. Blood was running down the streets into the gutters and out as a thin line along the surface of the Seine. Women wandered round, poking at the corpses, with their sunshades; men boasted, quite falsely, of having executed their quota of insurgents, or, more truly, of the number they had denounced. The Government received

[1] Vuillaume, op. cit., I, pp. 42–75.
[2] Quoted by Arnould, op. cit., III, p. 78.                    [3] Sunday, 28th.

nearly 400,000 denunciations – all but a twentieth unsigned. Anyone in the streets, anyone denounced, was likely to be arrested and often ended up being shot. 'Any lieutenant,' Wickham Hoffman noted with disgust, 'ordered prisoners to be shot as the fancy took him, and no questions were asked.'[1] Women, even if they were well dressed, were liable to be seized as *pétroleuses*, for carrying a milk bottle or offering a soldier a swig from a bottle of wine. On the Sunday, the American Ambassador had to rescue an American lady who had been arrested, accused of harbouring Communards who had fired from her house.[2] Many were shot for having watches as probable 'officials' of the Commune. The wearing of a pair of army boots was sufficient to lead to arrest and often execution, or a discoloured right shoulder from a rifle butt or simply blackened hands, assumed to be the result of having been an incendiary or having used a *tabatière* rifle, which left tell-tale powder marks. One chimney sweep at least is known to have been shot for having dirty hands. He had just finished sweeping the chimney of a good *bourgeoise* in the rue Saint-Honoré.[3]

The Marquis de Gallifet, that 'Swine' as Clemenceau continued to call him long afterwards,[4] was in his element being in charge of the cavalry conducting the prisoners to Versailles. Before they set off from the Bois de Boulogne he exercised his self-appointed right of judgement by walking slowly along the lines of prisoners, eyeing them, playing with them, picking out to be shot those he found particularly ugly, the wounded, the old, exactly those whom any humane sentiment would have spared. As he told one woman pleading for her life, 'Madame, I have visited every theatre in Paris; your acting will have no effect on me.'[5] One time he had 111 prisoners shot for having white hair, on the grounds that they were of an age to have taken part in the 1848 revolution. As he told two prisoners he had condemned at Montmartre, his fists defiantly on each hip, 'I am Gallifet. You may think me cruel, but I am far more cruel than you think.' None of this impeded his political career afterwards; in 1899 he became Minister of War in Waldeck-Rousseau's Government of 'Republican defence', which also included the first Socialist Minister in a French Cabinet, Millerand. But opinion

[1] Hoffman, op. cit., p. 281.                    [2] Washburne, op. cit., p. 160.
[3] Story recounted by Horne, op. cit., pp. 414–15.
[4] Martet, op. cit., p. 340.
[5] *Daily News*, 8 June 1871.

did prevent Gallifet being made Military Governor of Paris when this was once suggested.[1]

Many prisoners died on the way to Versailles, shot because they were too exhausted to walk any further, killed sometimes by being dragged behind the cavalry horses, ropes under their arms or tied to the horses' tails. At Versailles they were greeted by hostile crowds, which had turned out for the daily sport of taunting the prisoners, pelting them with mud and stones, hitting them with canes and parasols.

In Paris the dead began to take their revenge. There was a danger of pestilence if the streets continued to be filled with corpses. There was a stack of 1,100 near the Trocadero; in the yard of the Ecole Polytechnique they were piled three-deep in a line a hundred yards long. Limbs were sticking out of the ground in the Place Saint-Jacques. Flies were swarming over the bodies and the burial grounds. The city looked as if it had been struck by the plague. The English Press, which was not without influence in France, was condemning the continual slaughter. *The Times* on 29 May spoke of 'the inhuman laws of revenge under which the Versailles troops have been shooting, bayoneting, ripping up prisoners, women and children during the last six days', and on 1 June that 'the wholesale executions inflicted by the Versailles soldiery, the triumph, the glee, the ribaldry of the "party of Order", sicken the soul'. Foreign observers such as Archibald Forbes of the *Daily News* were 'saddened and sickened' by the spectacle of the Versailles soldiers 'enjoying the cheap amusement of Communard hunting'.[2] The French Press too began to call for an end to the indiscriminate killing. The *Temps* on 29 May

[1] The fact that Gallifet was in the same Cabinet added greatly to the crisis Millerand's appointment caused the French Socialists. The Blanquist and Communist Deputies withdrew from the Socialist Parliamentary Union, refusing to support a Government that contained, as Vaillant put it, 'the assassin of the Commune and the massacrer of the Communards'. At the Socialist Congress of that year Millerand was driven out of the hall to shouts of 'Down with Gallifet'. (See M. Perrot in *Le Socialisme français et le pouvoir*, Paris, 1966, p. 75; A. Noland, *The Founding of the French Socialist Party*, Harvard, Cambridge, 1956, pp. 93–6.) Similar discontent had earlier been felt against Brousse, the leader of the Possibilist Socialists, when as Vice-President of the Paris Municipal Council in 1890 he approved a motion calling for the holding of a reception of honour for the men and officers of two Marine battalions that had taken part in the repression of the Commune (Noland, op. cit., p. 22).

[2] Forbes, op. cit., p. 54.

recalled to the Government that 'the first duty of those who govern is the re-establishment of the rule of law . . . To abandon to the first-comer the task of being judge is to maintain anarchy.' The *Paris Journal* on 2 June asked 'Let us kill no more,' as had the *National* on the previous day: 'Enough executions, enough blood, enough victims.' So out came carts, buses, any form of transport to take away the bodies to the cemeteries and to the outskirts of Paris, where graves of lime swallowed up the corpses until even these were full and they had to be carted off to be burnt in the forts, turned into crematoria for the occasion. But these worked imperfectly and the charred bodies had to be soaked in petrol and burnt in the open air.

Far more had died during the last week in May than in any of the battles during the Franco–Prussian war, than in any of the previous 'massacres' in French history. Neither the Terror of the French Revolution, which accounted for 2,627 in Paris and up to 17,000 throughout France during the eighteen months from March 1793 to July 1794,[1] nor the White Terror that followed the Restoration in 1815, caused as many deaths. There is no exact figure, but something in the order of 25,000 Parisians[2] were killed, compared to the Versailles losses in battle of 877 dead and 6,454 wounded.

There remained something like 40,000 prisoners still to be tried, crammed into the Orangerie of the Château of Versailles, the riding schools, the cellars of the stables or in the open in the mud at the docks of Satory, where elegant crowds would come to inspect the prisoners as they grovelled for biscuits thrown to them. It was a human zoo. Some went mad, dashing their heads against the walls; others howled, tearing their beards and hair. However innocent, once arrested it needed a lot of influence to get out. One Mayor of a village outside of Paris, missing his firemen sent to fight the fires in the capital in response to the Government's request, found them in prison at Versailles. Elise, the fiancée of Martial Senisse, had been

[1] See D. Greer, *The Incidence of the Terror during the French Revolution*, Harvard, Cambridge, 1935. A much larger number were imprisoned, probably in the region of half a million, and this caused many thousands of deaths from the bad conditions. Many thousands were also executed without a trial, especially in the winter of 1793 following the collapse of the Vendée civil war.

[2] This is the figure of Winock and Azéma, op. cit., p. 165. Estimates vary from the 17,000 given by General Appert in his report, which was also the number buried at the expense of the City of Paris, to 30,000 or 35,000: see Lissagaray, op. cit., p. 393; Jellinek, op. cit., p. 370; Bourgin, *La Guerre*, p. 384; Bruhat, Dautry and Tersen, op. cit., pp. 276–7; Zeller, op. cit., p. 399.

arrested running in the streets frantically searching for Martial. She was denounced as a *pétroleuse* by a wine merchant. She was lucky not to be shot on the spot. But though her employer, whose house she had faithfully protected during the Commune, was an important official in the Ministry of Justice at Versailles, it took weeks to find her and longer still to get her out.[1] Suspicion, once it had fallen, could not easily be removed.

The exact number arrested is not certain: General Appert gives 39,000 but the actual number was probably higher than this – maybe 50,000.[2] To relieve Versailles 28,000 were dispatched to the harbours, forts and oceanic islands on the west coast of France, where they suffered a cruel regime, being penned in cages on pontoons or packed into the forts. In Paris and the surrounding region twenty-six courts martial tried the prisoners, dragged back often all the way across France. Many had no lawyer to defend them and were quickly condemned. Twenty-three Communards of those arrested were actually executed between November 1871 and January 1873, the first being Ferré and Rossel, the latter in spite of pressure from public opinion and student demands that he be reprieved. Genton was shot for his part in the shooting of the Archbishop and the five other hostages. Three were shot, Herpin-Lacroix, Lagrange and Verdaguer, supposedly for having taken part in the killing of Lecomte and Clément Thomas, although their only role had been to distinguish themselves from the crowd by trying to defend the two victims. The same reasoning led to the execution of François, the Director of the prison at La Roquette, who had done his best to save the lives of the hostages in his charge. Philippe was the other member of the Commune to be shot. In addition to these twenty-three, Gaston Crémieux was executed for his part in the Marseille Commune, and three soldiers, the last in 1875, were shot for the death of Vicenzini, the police agent stoned to death in February 1871.[3] Apart from Ferré and Philippe, and Delescluze, Durand, Rigault, Varlin and Vermorel, who died during or as a result of the fighting of the last week, a further twenty-two members of the Commune were arrested and condemned to varying sentences from deportation to a few months in prison; one, Descamps, was

[1] Senisse, op. cit., pp. 171, 206–7.
[2] This is Lissagaray's estimate, op. cit., p. 404; General Appert, op. cit., p. 96, says the Military Courts passed 50,000 sentences.
[3] See above, p. 123–4.

acquitted, having restricted his activities to his municipality. Most of these, Ferré and Trinquet being notable exceptions, did not defend themselves very boldly, seeming shocked almost that their respectability could be attacked.[1] Louise Michel, on the other hand, defiantly demanded to be shot: 'Since it seems as if every heart that beats for liberty has only the right to a little lead, I too demand my share.' She was sentenced to deportation. Rochefort was condemned to deportation to New Caledonia, although his only 'crime' was his journalism. But the reaction was determined to get him, as much for his attacks on the Empire as for his writings during the Commune. Like Millière, shot during the last week, he had to be removed for the health of society.

Of the remaining prisoners, some 20,000 were liberated without even being formally tried, after long winter months in the appalling prison conditions; over 10,000 were condemned, including 1,169 to transportation in a fortified place, 3,417 to simple deportation.[2] Many died on the transports, others when they got there, especially in New Caledonia near Australia, torrid, rocky isles, where the deportees lived in huts under a brutal regime. Only a few escaped – Rochefort and Paschal Grousset in an attempt planned by Jourde. But this only made matters worse for the others.

Of the Communards who escaped death or arrest, many fled and stayed hidden in the provinces, protected by republican feeling in their local districts. This is how Martial Senisse lived to tell his story. He escaped from Paris with the help of a doctor friend. When he got to his home town in the Limousin he had good protection, and was even able to smuggle food to comrades hiding in the woods. But in October, he had to go into hiding for a couple of weeks because of an anonymous denunciation, even though the Prefect was a friend of his uncle. For, as the Prefect confessed, 'the military authorities are very strong at this time'.[3] Many who escaped from Paris eventually made their way out of France into exile in Switzerland, Belgium, Britain, or further afield. Frankel escaped to Switzerland, then to London for a few years before returning to his native Hungary in 1876. In all there were over 3,300 in exile, con-

---

[1] Cf. Rougerie, *Procès*, p. 64; Jellinek, op. cit., pp. 374–5; Da Costa, op. cit., I, p. 447, calls it a 'cowardly attitude'.

[2] Appert, op. cit., p. 96. In the end this number was reduced to 696 and 2,879 (Bourgin, op. cit., p. 408).

[3] Senisse, op. cit., p. 218.

demned to death or transportation if ever they returned to France.

Those in London lived generally in poverty, usually in Soho, constantly surveyed by the police, though Gladstone refused the French Government's demands for extradition. A few found compensation for 'the most appalling city that I know' in the facilities of the British Museum, that 'most admirable library,'[1] where Vallès could see Lissagaray, Regnard, Pilotell and naturally enough Pyat. Several were able to get some money from journalism – Paschal Grousset, for example, who also translated *Treasure Island* and became something of an authority on English literature when he eventually returned to France. Vaillant became a lecturer at University College, Longuet at King's College, London; Eudes and Brunel at Dartmouth Naval College. Skilled workmen such as Langevin and Camélinat (the Commune's Director of the Mint) had little difficulty in finding employment.[2] Though Longuet and Lafargue married Marx's two daughters, none of the exiled Communards adopted Marx's ideas with any completeness. As Marx wrote to Engels once in November 1882, 'Longuet is the last Proudhonist, Lafargue the last Bakuninist. The devil take the two of them'; this of Lafargue, who tried to popularize Marxism in France and with Guesde founded the Parti Ouvrier Français, the first French Communist Party. Vallès found *Capital* 'so difficult to read';[3] Vermersch, though made welcome enough by Marx in 1873, was offended by what he considered was Marx's German prejudice against the Latin races.[4]

One way of estimating the total effect of the repression after the Commune is by comparing the July 1871 elections with those of the previous February. Although many of the bourgeoisie had returned to Paris by July, there were 40,000 less voters.[5] Another indication is the acute labour shortage in the months following the Commune. Industries were having to refuse orders; half the shoe-makers of

---

[1] Vallès, letters to Arnould in Switzerland, August 1876; 20 July 1877 (*Le Proscrit*, pp. 97, 135–6).
[2] Gordon Lewis, 'The Paris Commune. Then and Now', *Monthly Review*, November 1968, p. 88.
[3] Letter to Arnould, 18 April 1878: op. cit., p. 174.
[4] Letter to Vuillaume, 4 September 1873: *Cahiers Rouges*, X, pp. 57–8.
[5] J.O., 16 July 1871, gives 290,823 voters in July against the 328,970 of February. Lissagaray, op. cit., p. 404, quotes the *Journal des Débats*, to the effect that the insurgents had lost 100,000 in dead and prisoners.

Paris were missing, and when employers went to Versailles to try to get their workers released they were told they could have soldiers instead.[1]

Nine years later, in 1880, a few days after the first time 14 July had been celebrated as a national holiday, and after several previous attempts had failed, a general amnesty was voted. This was as a result of republican and socialist electoral victories, culminating in the election of the shoe-maker Trinquet, ex-member of the Paris Commune, as a socialist Deputy for Belleville in June, 1880. Just previously, on 23 May, 25,000 had responded to the appeal of Guesde and the socialists, in spite of police attacks, for the first demonstration at the 'Wall' of Père-Lachaise.

[1] Bourgin, op. cit., p. 403.

# EPILOGUE

The immediate consequences of the defeat of the Commune were disastrous for the French labour movement, a period of severe repression coming on top of the trauma of the blood-letting of the last week. The Republic itself was nearly lost, something moderate republicans had feared all along. That it was not was due as much as anything to disagreements among the Monarchists themselves. Paris remained under martial law until April 1876, and the International was outlawed by the Dufaure Law of 1872. Armed with these powers the police were very active in rounding up political activists, who were given heavy sentences. Jules Guesde, who had not participated in the Commune itself, was forced into exile to avoid a five-year prison sentence for writing an article favourable to the Commune. The *Emancipation* of Toulouse was seized in January 1872 for printing an article by Frankel.[1] The International was forced out of existence practically, except for a few secret sections that managed to survive for a time, mainly in the south. The leaders of the working class were either dead, imprisoned or in exile. At the 1876 Parisian Trades Congress only two of the delegates had been active in the working-class movement of the period before the Commune.[2]

Following the Commune, therefore, the French working class in the big cities found itself struggling under a regime as restrictive as that of the first period of the Second Empire. The only form of organization that managed to continue was the co-operative

[1] This was published in *La Revue Socialiste*, 1952, pp. 471–6; Frankel concluded his article by quoting 'the brave and intelligent Louise Michel' to the effect that she was for the Commune because ' "it wanted the Social Revolution". In these words is all the programme of the Commune.'

[2] See Aimée Moutet, '*Le Mouvement ouvrier à Paris du lendemain de la Commune au premier congrès syndical en 1876*', *Le Mouvement Social*, January–March 1967, pp. 3–39.

movement. By 1876 some hundred mutualist societies had been re-
formed, but they were considerably weaker than those of the 1860s.
This movement was non-revolutionary, resuming the earlier *ouvriérist*
tradition of peaceful reform. They sought to keep clear of all political
activity, distrusting the State, as had the similar movement under the
Empire. When, for example, the Legislative Assembly voted a sub-
sidy to help send a workers' delegation to the Philadelphia International Exhibition of 1876, several sections refused to accept this
assistance from the State and sent a separate delegation of their own.
The demands formulated by the reports of the delegations to this
Exhibition and to the earlier one at Vienna in 1873 were similar
in content to those of the 1867 Paris Exhibition, including the right
to organize workers' associations and the provision of free compulsory professional education. It was a movement that kept clear of the
strikes that did occur, which generally it condemned. As a result of
this 'wise' attitude the workers' societies were praised by the republican press.

Socialist political activity began at the end of the decade around a
small group of intellectuals meeting in a café in the Latin Quarter.
It was here that Jules Guesde was won over to Marxism by Karl
Hirsch, a journalist and member of the German Social Democratic
Party. In 1878 appeared Guesde's paper, *L'Egalité*, which set out
Marxist doctrines for the first time in France. Guesde gained great
publicity from being imprisoned, and at the Marseille Congress of
1879 he was largely instrumental, together with Paul Lafargue, in
forming the first Marxist political party in France, the French Socialist Workers' Party Federation. But this attempt to form a party in
France along the lines of the successful German S.P.D. met with little
success. It was not until 1905 that this aim was finally achieved, the
French socialist movement remaining for the first quarter of a
century of its existence divided between Marxists such as Guesde
and Lafargue, Blanquists led by the ex-Communard Vaillant,
anarchists, Possibilists and Independent socialists such as Miller-
and and Jaurès. In Paris particularly the Guesdists made little progress, the still predominantly artisan working population preferring
the Possibilists and Allemanists. The ex-Communard Malon was one
of the leaders of the Possibilists, who proposed the gradual conquest
of power and defeat of capitalism by means of municipal socialism.
Allemane, who had been the National Guard legion commander of
the Latin Quarter during the Commune, was the leader of this party

in the Paris region until he split from it in 1891, on the grounds that the Possibilists were compromising themselves too much with the bourgeois State. His group, which in addition to himself included the ex-Communards J.-B. Clément and J.-B. Dumay, emphasized the need for economic action in the form of trade unions as much as political action through parties and elections.

This economic tradition, syndicalism, remained strong in France, providing a distinctive flavour to the trade union and socialist movement. It also best maintained the revolutionary tradition, often having links with the anarchists, who scorned the political forms of activity of the socialist parties as inevitably involving compromise with the State and bourgeois parliamentarism. This indeed was what was happening to the socialists. Once they had accepted participation in elections they found that they had to accept alliances with the radicals, supporting Ministries and measures which seemed most favourable to some degree of social reform in contrast to outright conservatives, and having to defend republican institutions against the monarchists. The early messianism of Guesde, Lafargue and the other revolutionaries, who in the 1880s had expected the revolution to break out at any hour, had given way by the 1890s to an acceptance of the need to work for limited improvements, at least until the final overthrow of capitalism, whether this came by revolution or an electoral victory. A similar development had taken place in Germany, which on the ideological plane was represented by Bernstein's attempt to replace revolutionary Marxism by doctrines of social reform. By the first years of this century the whole European socialist movement, the Fabians in England being another example, was trying to work along parliamentary lines.[1]

On 20 July, 1870, Marx had written to Engels that 'if the Prussians win, the centralization of the power of the State will be useful for the centralization of the German working class. German predominance, moreover, would shift the centre of gravity of the European working-class movement from France to Germany, and comparing this movement in the two countries from 1866 onwards is sufficient to show that the German working class is superior to the French working class on both the theoretical and the organizational level.

---

[1] A useful account in English of the forming of the French Socialist party is the opening chapters of Aaron Noland, op. cit.; see too Michelle Perrot in *Le Socialisme français et le pouvoir*, and the major study of the first French Marxists, C. Willard, *Les Guesdistes*, Paris, 1965, pp. 11ff.

The predominance on the world's stage of the German working class over the French would also mean the predominance of our theory over Proudhon's.' This in fact was the effect of the Franco-Prussian war on the European socialist movement. The Commune simply made this more certain by setting back the development of French labour. The period from the Commune to the Russian Revolution was marked by the predominance of the German social democratic ideology, which paralleled the political and economic domination of Germany in Europe. In the 1890s, after Marx's death, Engels was boasting that by the beginning of the next century the German socialists were likely to win an electoral majority that would bring 'our party' into power.[1] It was in line with this that he had written the Preface to Marx's *Class Struggles in France*, already referred to, arguing the need for a change of tactics away from barricade fighting towards using the legal means of electoral parties. In France there were no theoreticians, Marxist or otherwise, to compare to Kautsky, Rosa Luxemburg or Bernstein, the Leninist interpretation of Marx only gaining wide acceptance after the Bolshevik victory of 1917. Marxism in France never really caught on, and the independent traditions of French socialism remained very influential. Partly it was a question of language, for the only works of Marxism available in French before 1889 were the first volume of *Capital* and a translation of part of Engel's *Anti-Dhüring*, which had been published as *Socialism: Utopian and Scientific*. Guesde simply accepted from Marx the idea of economic materialism, which he interpreted more in terms of French eighteenth-century materialism than the dialectic, and the idea of the imminent collapse of capitalism. The Blanquist Vaillant, who at least could read German, or Jaurès understood Marx better than his self-declared followers. Little wonder that Marx, thinking of the French, denied in 1882 that he was 'a Marxist'.[2]

[1] Interview in the *Daily Chronicle*, 1 July 1893. In his correspondence with Paul Lafargue Engels was more careful over such formulations, emphasizing that all compromise must be avoided, and he criticized the French parliamentary socialists for failing precisely on this score. Engels also complained bitterly of the German S.P.D.'s cutting and altering of the text of his *Introduction* to Marx's *Class Struggles* so as to reduce its revolutionary tone even further.

[2] Reported by Engels in a letter to Bernstein, 2–3 November 1882. See further, Willard, op. cit., pp. 596–601. Jaurès is a difficult figure to generalize briefly about as he maintained a skilful balance between Parliamentary action and revolutionary theory. He tried to assimilate various themes from earlier French socialists and from Marxism to the republican tradition going back to the great

The balance between political and economic forms of action, between socialist political parties and the revolutionary syndicalism of the trade unions, can also be seen in the ambiguity of Marx's own position towards the Paris Commune. The period of the late 1840s up to the *coup d'état* of Napoleon III, the time of the *Communist Manifesto* of 1848 and the *Address* of the Central Committee of the Communist League of 1850, was a time of revolution in Europe. The 1860s on the other hand, had been the time of the first international organization of the labour movement. Marx had become fully involved in the First International, seeking, with some success, to control it through the General Council in London. This was primarily a labour movement concerned with working conditions, the formation of trade unions to bargain over working hours and rates of pay. The French particularly were concerned at first to avoid any form of political action. Although Marx never accepted this limitation to purely economic activity, he did consider that a social revolution could only come in a situation in which there was a large, organized working-class movement. This, he realized very well, was not the case in France in 1870, and he was at pains to counsel against any attempt to seize the opportunity of the collapse of the Empire to have a revolution. Immediately following 4 September Marx, in the International's *Second Address on the Franco-Prussian War*, wrote that 'Any attempt at upsetting the new Government in the present crisis, when the enemy is almost knocking at the door of Paris, would be a desperate folly. The French workmen must perform their duties as citizens...Let them calmly and resolutely improve the opportunities of Republican liberty, for the work of their own class organization. It will gift them with fresh Herculean powers for the regeneration of France, and our common task – the emancipation of labour.'[1] This remained Marx's theme throughout

---

Revolution: there is a good biography of Jaurès in English by Harvey Goldberg.

[1] MESW, p. 272; E. Dupont, on behalf of Marx, wrote at this time to the Lyon Internationalists, saying 'in the circumstances, the role of the workers, or rather their duty, is to let the bourgeois vermin make peace with the Prussians (because the shame of this act will stick with them for good), not to weaken it by uprisings, so as to be able to profit from the liberties that circumstances will bring for organizing all the forces of the working class': cited in M. Moissonier, '*La Commune et la mouvement ouvrier Lyonnais*', *La Nouvelle Critique*, April 1961, p. 116.

the war, and through the intermediary of Seraillier he warned the
Parisian Internationalists against what he called such 'stupidities' as
'overthrowing the Provisional Government, establishing the Paris
Commune, nominating Pyat as French Ambassador to London,
etc.'[1] Marx actively campaigned in London to try to get the British
Government to recognize the new French Republic, and wrote to
his German friends attacking the Prussian demands for territorial
gains, especially the annexation of Alsace-Lorraine. Marx had no illusions about the conservative nature of the Government of National
Defence in Paris and its 'middle-class heroes' such as Trochu, who
'considered it much more important to keep down the Reds in
Paris . . . than to defeat the Prussians'.[2] But this did not lead Marx
to advocate revolution. His hope rather was that if the French put
up a stiff resistance, and with diplomatic pressure possibly from
Britain, then the resulting peace would not be such as to strengthen
the imperialist forces in Germany. This would open up a favourable
climate for the development of the working class in Germany (and
in France) after the war.

Twenty years later, at the end of his life, Marx restated this theme
in a letter to the Dutch socialist Domela-Nieuwenhuis. Socialism
could only come to power when the conditions for it had sufficiently
developed. The Paris Commune, said Marx, was not a counter example; 'apart from the fact that this was merely the rising of a city
under exceptional conditions, the majority of the Commune was in
no way socialist, nor could it be. With a modicum of common-sense,
however, it could have reached a compromise with Versailles useful
to the whole mass of the people – the only thing that could be
reached at the time.'[3]

The lesson Marx drew from the Commune, and Engels and Lenin
following him, was political not social. In the development of world
history, according to Hegel, the State represented the fullest realiza-
tion of the Idea, the embodiment of philosophy on earth. Marx had
interpreted the 1851 *coup d'état* in France and Bonapartism as the
example of how capitalist exploitation would develop a bureaucratic,
military executive power, an oppressive 'State machine'. When the
executive power had been perfected, then the preliminary stage of
the revolution in Europe would be completed, its target being the

[1] Marx to Engels, 6 September 1870.
[2] Marx to Kugelmann, 14 February 1871.
[3] 22 February 1881.

destruction of the State: 'well grubbed old mole!'[1] As soon as the Commune broke out Marx returned to this idea. Writing on 12 April, 1871, he referred Dr Kugelmann to 'the last chapter of my *Eighteenth Brumaire*' where 'you will find that I say that the next attempt of the French revolution will be no longer, as before, to transfer the bureaucratic military machine from one hand to another, but to *smash* it, and that is essential for every real people's revolution on the Continent. And this is what our heroic Party comrades in Paris are attempting.'[2] This is the central theme of his essay of May 1871 on the Paris Commune, *The Civil War in France*. In this Marx emphasizes the federalism of the Commune, its abolition of the standing army and the police (though this was hardly how Rigault or Ferré interpreted their position), the disestablishment of the Church, the election of the Judiciary. Marx saw the Commune as the antithesis to the Empire, the breaking up of the modern State, being in itself the

[1] *The Eighteenth Brumaire of Louis Bonaparte* (1852), MESW, pp. 170–1. There is an added complexity to Marx's analysis since he sees the State machine in France as a continuation of the feudal traditions of France and its monarchist centralization. The class basis of this in 1851, says Marx, was not the bourgeoisie but the small-holding peasantry, which was incapable of enforcing its class interests except through being represented by an individual authoritarian master. Thus the subordination, in Hegelian terms, of society to the State is a result of pre-capitalist not post-capitalist development. This, Marx seems to imply, is a contradiction that will prove to be fatal for Bonapartism (op. cit., pp. 171–2, 177–8).

[2] Lenin, in his commentary on this letter in *State and Revolution*, noted that Marx limited his comments to 'the Continent', excluding England. At this time Marx does seem to have considered that the working class in England might be able to achieve political power by means of universal suffrage, thus avoiding the need for a violent revolution: see Marx's interview in the American journal, *Woodhull & Claflin's Weekly*, 12 August 1871, and his speech at Amsterdam of 18 September 1872 summing up the Hague International Congress: the relevant passages are given in S. Avineri, *The Social and Political Thought of Karl Marx*, Cambridge, 1968, pp. 215–17. Care has to be taken in interpreting Marx's remarks of this time, particularly his public interviews, as he was very concerned to avoid giving Governments an excuse for banning the International, as had occurred already in France. The other important passage on England is Marx's confidential circular on the International enclosed in his letter to Kugelmann of 28 March 1870, in which he says that 'although the revolutionary initiative will probably come from France, England alone can serve as the lever of a serious economic revolution', without specifying how politically such an economic revolution might occur. Marx simply regrets the English 'lack' of the 'spirit of generalization and revolutionary ardour'.

new political form of society, the 'social republic' and not just a
reproduction of the medieval Communes.

> The unity of the nation [wrote Marx] was not to be broken, but,
> on the contrary, to be organized by the Communal Constitution
> and to become a reality by the destruction of the State power
> which claimed to be the embodiment of that unity independent of,
> and superior to, the nation itself, from which it was but a parasitic
> excrescence. While the merely repressive organs of the old govern-
> mental power were to be amputated, its legitimate functions were
> to be wrested from an authority usurping pre-eminence over
> society itself, and restored to the responsible agents of society.

The Commune was the political form of society 'under which to
work out the economic emancipation of labour'.[1] This, twenty years
later, is how Engels interpreted the Commune. It was the beginning
of the process of the destruction of the State, 'until such time as a
generation reared in new, free social conditions is able to throw the
entire lumber of the state on the scrap heap'. Engels, therefore, could
give the Paris Commune as an example of 'the Dictatorship of the
Proletariat'.[2] Marx's judgement of 1871 accordingly remained, in
spite of his remarks about the impossibility of it being a socialist
revolution; 'whatever the immediate results may be, a new point of
departure of world-historic importance has been gained'.[3]

As stated in 1871, Marx's notion that the social revolution meant
the destruction of the State seemed close to the anarchists. James
Guillaume, one of the leading members of the Swiss Federation of
the International, considered in January 1872 that the dispute between themselves and the London General Council under Marx's
influence could probably be healed, as both the Swiss Internationalists, including its French exile members, and the French in London
wanted the 'destruction of the centralized State and its replacement
by a federation of autonomous Communes'. This, said Guillaume,

---

[1] MESW, pp. 292, 294. The same emphasis is found even more strongly in
the first draft. For further interpretations of Marx and the Commune see
M. Rubel, *Karl Marx devant le Bonapartisme*, Paris, 1960, pp. 146–59; Collins and
Abramsky, op. cit., pp. 185–210, 292–6; Avineri, op. cit., pp. 185–201, 239–49.
[2] 1892 Preface to the *Civil War*, MESW, p. 262. Marx himself never publicly
made this connection, and in the context Engels is using it the term is being
used in contrast to the idea of a revolutionary regime of terror.
[3] Letter to Kugelmann, 17 April 1871.

was not because of any Proudhonist ideology, and he regretted that their language had misled Marx into thinking this. In any case, it looked to Guillaume as if Marx, 'since the Paris Commune, was tending to modify' his ideas on the State.[1] Reading the *Civil War in France* it is easy to see how Guillaume could have thought this, but in fact the gap between Marx and the anarchists only became more accentuated, and certainly Lenin's interpretation of the 'dictatorship of the proletariat' in the form of the Bolshevik party was closer to Blanquism,[2] with its emphasis on the need for a revolutionary conspiratorial vanguard, than to the anarchy of the Commune.

Trotsky in 1921 said that 'the great error' of the Commune was 'the autonomy of the sections, of the arrondissements, of the battalions, of the cities', which 'for certain revolutionaries was the best guarantee of true activity and individual independence'.[3] Yet this was the essence of the Communal revolution in Paris. The seizure of the cannons and other events preceding 18 March, as well as the events of that day, were largely the unorganized and spontaneous reaction of the population and its National Guard against a Government it hated more than it feared. As the Russian anarchist, Kropotkin, put it, on 18 March 'the Government evaporated like a pond of stagnant water in a Spring breeze'.[4] The federal structure of all the popular organizations reflected this insistence on local control. Elected representatives were supposed to act as mandatories, referring matters back to the local population in their clubs and National Guard battalions. The Commune remained most firmly established at the local level, and never really got above this. But the dynamic of the situation of the Commune, because of the war, was towards tighter forms of organization, something that was obscured by the

[1] Given in M. Vuilleumier, '*La Correspondance du peintre G. Jeanneret*', *Le Mouvement Social*, April–June 1965, p. 98.
[2] This was Rosa Luxemburg's criticism of Lenin in her pamphlet, *Leninism or Marxism?* (1904). The Commune played a decisive role in Lenin's political thinking: see particularly, *The State and Revolution* (August 1917), Ch. 3, where he uses Marx's study of the Commune as the basis for an attack on parliamentary Social-Democracy, as well as evidence of the need to 'smash the bureaucratic machine of the modern state'.
[3] Preface to C. Talès's history of the Commune, op. cit., p. xiii. Trotsky's main criticism of the Commune was that it lacked the central direction a revolutionary party could have given it; see too Trotsky's attack on Kautsky, *Terrorism and Communism* (1910).
[4] P. Kropotkin, *The Commune of Paris*, London, 1895, p. 3.

Jacobin insistence on outmoded forms and the resulting struggle over the title of Committee of Public Safety.

There was, therefore, a contradiction between the federalist nature of the Communal revolution and the realities of having to face a situation of civil war. The Commune lacked the time in which to develop socially and politically; it was unable to organize itself efficiently in order to win the war; but it did know how to die heroically in the streets. Its ending eclipsed what had gone before, and the Commune went out with a bang that long reverberated throughout Europe.[1] The effect was to ensure that the Commune was enshrined as part of the European socialist movement, although it contained many elements foreign to what might be regarded as the hoped-for proletarian revolution. For, as has been seen, the Commune was not a revolt of an industrial proletariat. This had only just begun to be formed in Paris, and the workers in the factories of the outlying districts were not the main forces of the Commune, any more than they had been of the International. The Communards belonged more to the past tradition of Paris revolutionaries than presaging the industrial struggles of the future. It was an alliance of artisans, the workers in the Paris craft industries, and the petit-bourgeoisie, the shopkeepers and traders threatened, for example, by the Assembly's decrees on rents and maturities, that provided the unity for action in defiance of Versailles. Other elements played their part: foreign adventurers and Latin Quarter revolutionaries, the journalists, writers, students in law and medicine of *la bohème*, joined by some of the returned exiles of '51 such as Delescluze and Félix Pyat. And there were leading figures who had been thrown up by the working-class movement itself – Varlin and Frankel, for example. But the distinguishing feature of Paris in the Spring of 1871, which marked it off from the other big cities in France, remains the reforging during the siege of the old *sans-culotte* alliance of the lower middle classes and upper working classes. Elsewhere, in contrast to the capital, these two classes remained apart.

[1] Henry Maret, a collaborator of Rochefort on the *Marseillaise* and the *Mot d'Ordre*, said afterwards that 'the massacre was not only a crime, it was for the reaction itself a grievous fault. The Commune, which would have faded out in ridicule, assumed a tragic grandeur': quoted in Mason, op. cit., p. 282. Elisée Reclus, who had spent most of the time of the Commune in prison in Versailles, said of the Commune that 'through its defenders rather than its rulers it had raised up an ideal for the future far superior to all the revolutions that had preceded it': interview in *La Revue Blanche*, 15 March 1897, p. 298.

The social measures of the Commune expressed much of this social background. Rather than an attack on property as such, there was an attempt to shift some of the benefits of the industrial expansion of the previous period away from the large-scale financial and industrial capitalists back to the small entrepreneur and individual working man. Education was meant to broaden the opportunities of those with few prospects; co-operative workshops to give working men a juster share in and greater control over what they produced. Tenants were to benefit against landlords; the poor rather than the rich. The social ideals of the Commune were those that had been developed by the early labour movement confronted by the first effects of industrial capitalism; ideas of social reform that had for the most part been first openly proclaimed from a public platform by the 'workers' parliament' in the Luxembourg in 1848. But in 1871, as in the earlier period, these attempts by workers' societies to develop less repressive forms of social organization were still considered to be too dangerous to be tolerated. To say in this way that the Communards were still in many ways ahead of what their time allowed simply expresses the cruel slowness of social change. They were indeed 'storming heaven';[1] it is hardly surprising that they failed.

In a sense they were lucky to have got as far as they did. Lucky in that the Government showed such ineptitude in dealing with Paris that it practically made the gift of a revolution to the city. Rather than Machiavellian cunning in the actions of Thiers and the other Ministers, there was lack of understanding, lack of finesse, and of course the same military bungling as had lost France the war against Prussia.[2] It can only be regretted that the revolutionaries were not able to seize on this weakness and turn it even more to their own advantage. For if the members of the Government showed a low level of political skills, the leading figures of the Commune too often were even less able. Blanqui perhaps might have made an important difference, but it is by no means certain that he could have provided the missing leadership, especially considering he was sixty-five years old. He had not done so during the time of the Second Republic nor during the siege. Certainly no one else could, which is not to denigrate *en masse* all the Communards, for there were, as should have become evident, very fine figures both within and outside the

[1] Marx to Kugelmann, 12 April 1871.
[2] Which naturally the two official Inquiries into the Government of National Defence and the Revolution of 18 March tried to cover up.

Communal Council. But no revolutionary leader of genius emerged, and as subsequent revolutions have made clear that was an important lack. To look back into France's own past, Paris in 1871 did not produce any Danton, any Robespierre, any Marat; there was no Hébert or Jacques Roux.

Incompetency on the side of the Commune was not just a question of personalities, as if it were just a matter of chance that no figures were thrown up of the stature of those of a hundred years earlier. There simply had been no long maturing political movement under the Empire. The strikes, the French section of the International, the co-operative movement, had all been largely attempts at 'economic' reform, The last few years had witnessed an intensification of political consciousness, but this was still in its early stages, and was as much inclined to social democracy as to political revolution. The small group of out-and-out revolutionaries, Blanquists often, though there were others who claimed no particular allegiance, were not the advance guard of the labour movement but, on the contrary, often hostile to it. These revolutionaries looked to the past, and this weight of a revolutionary tradition, both Jacobinism and Hébertism, was not an unqualified asset. The 'professional' revolutionaries did see the realities of the situation with regard to the necessity of civil war. But they also too easily became lost, and the Commune with them, in parodying the past by applying formulas extracted from '93.

The siege both provided the opportunity for Paris to have a revolution, whilst ensuring it would have little chance of success. It provided the opportunity because of the economic crisis it brought about in Paris together with a breakdown of the social and political structures. The siege as experienced within the capital was one of increasing disillusionment with the Provisional Government, primarily arising from a frustrated patriotism. Because the Government of National Defence, necessarily in its own terms, had to deceive the population over the conduct of the war, professing resistance whilst pursuing peace, it lost its credibility, its authority, its respect in the eyes of the Paris population. Eventually the mask of government was destroyed. But this same patriotism checked the revolution from coming during the war; the attempt was only made when the fighting was over, when the French Government was free to use its army against the revolutionaries and when a victorious Prussia was entrenched outside the city, ready to intervene if necessary. It was as if the Bolshevik revolution had taken place in 1919, not 1917.

The siege also emphasized the separation of Paris from the rest of France, where the experience of the war had had the opposite effect, creating a desire for peace and a lassitude regarding any further political change. The provincial revolutions were never serious enough to threaten the Versailles Government and prevent it from concentrating all its efforts on putting down the capital. If there were plenty of causes for discontent and outbreaks of unrest in the cities, the countryside remained quiet, even in the mountain regions of the south and east where there had been major revolts against Louis-Napoleon's *coup d'état*. Isolated, cut off from all communication with the rest of the country, there was no chance, once Versailles had had time to recover from the first shock of 18 March, that the Paris Commune would end other than in military defeat.

The repression itself is also part of the history of the Commune. The fury of the reaction seems out of all proportion to the moderation of the social measures the Commune actually enforced, the naïvety almost of the Paris revolution. That the conservative government of Thiers and the reactionary Assembly did lash back so unrestrainedly shows as surely as does the reaction abroad, with its talk of the 'reds' and 'communists', the fright the Commune gave to the European bourgeoisie. Faced by the threat of the Commune, of a working-class government, the French bourgeoisie forgot the political differences that for the past half century had divided Legitimists from Orleanists, Bonapartists from Republicans. This temporary junction lasted sufficiently to give birth to the Third Republic and to the establishment of parliamentary democracy in France.

Because the Commune was the end of a century of revolutions in France, the last eruption seemingly of an otherwise extinct volcano, it is easy to see it as the patriotic reflex of a revolutionary tradition confronted by the special circumstances of the war. Particularly so as history tends to see events more in terms of their antecedents than their future possibilities. It is the practical man desirous of changing the existing order, the revolutionary or the reactionary, who seizes events for their future implications. Many of the Communards themselves did think in this latter way and were aware that they were creating more for the future than re-living the past. Vaillant, for example, over a quarter of a century afterwards considered that 'the struggle and fall of the Commune, its history and its legend, were as the universal evocation of the revolutionary socialist consciousness'.[1] And it was in this spirit that the meeting held in Hyde Park on 16 April in support of the Commune declared that 'we, the people of London, believing you to be fighting for the liberty of the world and the regeneration of mankind, hereby express our profound admiration for the grandeur of your enterprise'.[2] The innovating element in the Commune, as both Marx and his anarchist opponents saw, was its political form, the very lack of central control and direction that proved so disastrous for conducting a civil war. For this did express a real determination to liberate the worker and the rest of society with him from all forms of repression. As a result Paris under the Commune was a mosaic, and it was this local popular variety that refreshed its supporters, Arthur Arnould for example, in contrast to the muddled debates and quarrels of the Communal Council itself.

Individual writers of the time, the intellectuals of the Second Empire and of the new Republic, in most cases reacted with hostility often to the extreme as did Flaubert, Gautier or Feydeau. Zola, Anatole France and George Sand were less immoderate, though still condemning the Commune and justifying the repression afterwards of what they could only describe in terms of psychological abnormality; a 'mad saturnalia' as George Sand called it. Of the established figures only Victor Hugo showed sympathy for the Communards, and then only after they had been defeated. It was younger, as then unrecognized writers such as Jules Vallès who became caught up in the events of Paris. Verlaine was not an enthusiastic partisan of the Commune, yet he found it impossible to resume his old life again after it was all over, though he could always have gone back to his clerical job. It was in the October after the Commune that Rimbaud came to stay with him in Paris, marking a new period in Verlaine's life. Rimbaud himself had been at home in the country during the time of the Commune. But he had visited Paris shortly before the revolution began, and the events in Paris had a very great effect on his imagination, something more extensive than the result of being raped, if indeed he ever was, by National Guards (or just as probably by regular soldiers) during his wanderings in Paris at the end of February, 1871. For it has been in the realm of the imagination, which is not to say the imaginary, that the Commune has exercised

[1] Interview in *La Revue Blanche*, 15 March 1897, p. 275.
[2] As reported by *The Times*, 17 April 1871.

its most powerful influence as a sign of the rejection of all that is repressive in society. French artisans in the early part of the nineteenth century did not hesitate to trace their ancestry of revolt back to Spartacus; since 1871 the Commune has become firmly part of that tradition.

Paris in revolution was a festive Paris. Festivals traditionally meant reversing the normal order in society, the creation of a topsy-turvy world. But such a reversal usually compelled a return to established norms because it took place within a structure of rules. The antithesis between leisure and work in an industrial society also operates in the same way; play is a safety valve for the serious business of work. The festive nature of the Commune, however, was not just a ritualistic acting out of repressed desires, but the active conquest of urban time and space; a restructuring of the city. The progress of the Commune was marked by the advance of the crowds from the outlying districts, whither they had been driven by Haussmann's rebuilding projects, back into the streets of the centre, where there were no longer any police or army to keep them back. For a time, too short to make any lasting conquests, a large section of the population became actively involved in the public affairs of their districts, of the whole city even. Order, as repressively understood, was only restored when this population was driven off the streets and its barricades destroyed. Once the city was again under its control, the National Government could celebrate its victory by voting its own monument in 'expiation' of the 'crimes' of the Commune, the Sacré-Cœur, a white basilica to dominate what had been red Paris. The Commune as a revolution was not just one stage in a gradual social progress, but a 'tiger-leap', one of those moments that cancel historical time.[1] This is why the Commune can be seen as a success in spite of its failure. Judged in terms of Fabianism, of the notion of gradual reform, of politics as the art of the possible or of the necessary compromise, the Commune was a senseless, mad revolt in impossible circumstances. But the Commune was also the upsurge of a repressed population against such conventional wisdom with its counsel of prudence. The legend is greater than the actual event and its failure more important than anything moderation could have gained, for without such 'failures'

[1] Benjamin, op. cit., pp. 263–5: 'Theses on the Philosophy of History', Nos. XIV–XVIII.

all vision would be lost. This is why the Communards were genuinely 'heroic', with the 'spark' Renoir praised them for having.[1] As such the Commune was a truly revolutionary event, the breakthrough into a new realm where what seemed barely to be possible becomes, however fleetingly, actual, thereby revealing all other forms as condemned. In this the Commune was a revolution of more than just its own time.

[1] Cf. above, p. 306.

# APPENDICES
# BIBLIOGRAPHY
# INDEX

Appendix I

# CHRONOLOGY OF EVENTS FROM THE FRENCH REVOLUTION TO THE COMMUNE

———◆◆◆———

1789 Meeting of the States-General. Nation-wide disturbances. Fall of the Bastille. Abolition of feudal dues. Formation of a Constituent Assembly. Declaration of the Rights of Man.

1791 Flight of the King and his arrest. New Monarchical constitution. Election of a new Legislative Assembly.

1792 Outbreak of war between France and Prussia and Austria. 9 August, formation of a revolutionary Commune to replace the elected legal Communal Council of the city of Paris. Tuileries Palace invaded on 10 August by the revolutionary crowd. September massacres in the prisons. New elections for a National Assembly, the Convention. First French victories over Prussians at Valmy, leading to invasion of the Netherlands. Abolition of the Monarchy.

1793 Execution of the King. Declaration of war against Great Britain and other European powers. Food riots in Paris led by Jacques ROUX and the *enragés*. First law of the *maximum*. Measures voted by the Convention against counter-revolutionaries, including the sending of 'representatives on mission' to the provinces. Formation of the COMMITTEE OF PUBLIC SAFETY in April. June: invasion of the National Convention by the Paris *sans-culottes*, organized by their Sections into the revolutionary Commune. Arrest of the moderates, the Girondins, and victory of the Jacobins of the Mountain. July: election of ROBESPIERRE, St-Just and other Jacobins to the Committee of Public Safety. New Constitution and a second Declaration of the Rights of Man. ROUX criticizes Robespierre and the Jacobins for failing 'to assure bread to those who have none and to banish beggary from the Republic'. Charlotte Corday stabs MARAT to death. Execution of Marie-Antoinette. *Sans-culottes* uprising in September led by HÉBERT, editor of the most popular of the revolutionary newspapers, *Le Père Duchêne*, and deputy-*procureur* of the Commune. This uprising also supported by CHAUMETTE, the *procureur* of the Commune. Demand economic measures to relieve distress of the poor and greater revolutionary vigour in the prosecution of the war. The Convention and the Committee of Public Safety have to make concessions: Law of Suspects; decree on the price and wages *maximum*; adoption of the Revolutionary Calendar, backdated to 22 September, 1792 (Year I). Festival of Liberty on the Champs de Mars. Anticlericalism. But Committee of Public Safety strengthened to take measures against Paris revolutionaries. September, Jacques ROUX arrested, and

1794 HÉBERT executed in March. Fall and execution of ROBESPIERRE in July and the counter-reaction of *Thermidor*.

1795 Constitution of the Year Three (The Directory).

1796 Small communist uprising in Paris of BABEUF and his Conspiracy of the Equals.

1799 10 November, the eighteenth *Brumaire*, *coup d'état* of Napoleon Bonaparte. The Consulate.

1804 Napoleon declared Emperor.

1814 Defeat of Napoleon. Congress of Vienna meets.

1815 Hundred Days. Waterloo. Second restoration of Louis XVIII.

1824 Accession of Charles X.

1830 July Revolution. Constitutional monarchy of Louis-Philippe, Duke of Orleans.

1831 First uprising of Lyon silk-workers.

1834 Further workers' uprisings in Lyon and Paris, massacre of the rue Transnonain.

1840 Thiers Premier. Crisis between Britain and France. National Assembly votes to build fortifications around Paris. Guizot replaces Thiers.

1848 February Revolution. Overthrow of Monarchy. Declaration of the Second Republic from the Hôtel de Ville, after the crowd invaded the Assembly. Provisional Government formed that includes Lamartine and Ledru-Rollin together with Louis

Blanc and the worker Albert, who had been demanded by the crowd in front of the Hôtel de Ville. Blanc put in charge of Luxembourg Commission, but Government refuses his idea of National Workshops and the 'right to work'. Instead name only taken and Workshops become a form of unemployment benefit. April elections of a Constituent Assembly, with a conservative majority. 15 May, invasion of the Assembly by the clubs led by BLANQUI and Barbès, demanding 'abolition of property'. Closure of the National Workshops leads to June uprising of Paris working classes. Severe repression. December election of Louis-Napoleon as President of the Republic.

1849 May elections return a more divided Assembly, with a strong conservative majority. Left-wing republican uprising of 13 June easily put down and Ledru-Rollin, Félix Pyat, Delescluze and others of the Mountain had to escape into exile.

1850 March by-elections see radical republicans elected, and conservative majority in Assembly revise franchise law to reduce electorate.

1851 December: *coup d'état* of Louis Napoleon.

1852 Proclamation of the Second Empire and plebiscite endorses this.

1857 First republicans elected to the Legislative Chambre; formation of the opposition group of the 'five'.

1859 General amnesty for political prisoners; many exiles, though not all, return.

1860 Haussmann annexes outlying Communes to Paris administration.

1864 Tolain stands as a working-class candidate in elections; 'Manifesto of the Sixty'. Foundation of the First International in London.

1865 Tridon's articles on the *Hébertistes*.

1866 First Congress of the International at Brussels; presentation by the French delegates of their *Memoir*. Arrest of Blanquists at the Renaissance café.

1867 Workers' delegation sent to the Universal Exhibition in Paris. Strike of the Paris bronze-workers.

1868 Condemnation of the first and second Paris Council of the International. More liberal Press law. Delescluze founds the *Réveil*; is defended by Gambetta at his trial for articles on the Deputy Baudin killed in 1851 in the resistance to the *coup d'état*.

1869 National elections; republican victories in big cities; Gambetta elected for Belleville district in Paris. Troops sent in against strikers in Saint-Etienne and Aubin. Rochefort founds *La Marseillaise*, and is elected Deputy in by-elections for Belleville. Conference at Lyon on Decentralization.

1870 JANUARY

Formation of 'Liberal' cabinet under Ollivier. Assassination of Victor Noir and big demonstration at funeral. Troops called in against strikers in Le Creusot.

MAY

Plebiscite on the liberal reforms gives Napoleon III big majority.

JULY

Hohenzollern candidacy for Spanish throne. Declaration of war between France and Prussia. *Address* of Paris International against the war.

AUGUST

First French defeats. Parliament recalled. Blanquist attempt to seize arms at La Villette fire station.

SEPTEMBER

**4th** News of French defeat at Sedan and capture of the Emperor. Crowd invades Legislature and the Republic proclaimed from the Hôtel de Ville. Formation of the provisional Government of National Defence.

**6th** Second and more bellicose *Address* of the Paris International on the war.

**7th** Paris International calls for the formation of vigilance committees, which leads subsequently to formation of the Central Committee of the Twenty Arrondissements.

**18th** Siege of Paris begins. First meeting of Favre and Bismarck.

**19th** French defeat outside Paris at Châtillon.

**20th** Protests in Paris against news of negotiations and Central Committee of Twenty Arrondissements leads a delegation to the Hôtel de Ville.

**28th** Bakunin's attempted revolution fails in Lyon.

OCTOBER

**5th** Demonstration led by Flourens against conduct of the war.

**7th** Gambetta leaves Paris by balloon to head Delegation at Tours.

**8th** Failure of demonstration led by the Central Committee of the Twenty Arrondissements.

**27th** Bazaine surrenders Metz.

**30th** Thiers negotiating with Bismarck for an armistice; French defeat at Le Bourget.

**31st** News of surrender of Metz leads to uprising in Paris; occupation of the Hôtel de Ville, where several members of the Government including Trochu are held. Proclamation of a new government, which includes moderates as well as Blanqui. Government promises elections. Revolts in Marseille, Toulouse and Saint-Etienne.

NOVEMBER

**1st** Government decides to arrest revolutionaries of previous day.

**3rd** Plebiscite in Paris strengthens position of Government of National Defence. Uprising in Lyon.

**4th** Election of arrondissement mayors.

**5th** Success of Army of the Loire under d'Aurelle de Paladines at Coulmiers, making reoccupation of Orleans possible.

**29th** to

DECEMBER

**1st** Failure of attempt to break out of Paris at Champigny.

**4th** Orleans evacuated; Provincial Delegation has to move to Bordeaux.

1871 JANUARY

**5th** Bombardment of Paris begins.

**6th** *Affiche Rouge* of the Delegation of the Twenty Arrondissements.

**19th** French defeat at Buzenval; first and only time National Guard used.

**21st** Release of Flourens from Mazas prison.

**22nd** Vinoy replaces Trochu as commander of Paris. Demonstration in front of the Hôtel de Ville dispersed by firing on crowd.

**23rd** Closure of clubs and suppression of revolutionary papers.

**28th** Armistice signed.

FEBRUARY

**8th** Elections for National Assembly.

**12th** National Assembly opens at Bordeaux.

**20th** and **23rd** Delegation of the Twenty Arrondissements adopts declaration of principles forming itself into a 'revolutionary socialist party'. Thiers forms a ministry.

**24th** Vauxhall meeting of the National Guard Federation and demonstrations at the Place de la Bastille, which continue for several days.

**29th** Crowd seizes the cannons at Place Wagram and transports them to eastern suburbs.

MARCH

**1st** Prussian ceremonial entry into Paris. Assembly votes in favour of the peace treaty.

**10th** Last session of the Assembly at Bordeaux; votes to move to Versailles; votes decrees on rents and overdue bills.

**11th** Vinoy suppresses six more revolutionary papers; Blanqui and Flourens condemned to death for events of 31 October.

**15th** National Guard elections for its Central Committee.

**16th** Thiers arrives in Paris.

**18th** ATTEMPT TO SEIZE CANNONS ON MONTMARTRE FAILS; Thiers and Government flee Paris; killing of Generals Lecomte and Clément Thomas in rue des Rosiers; Central Committee of National Guard takes over the Hôtel de Ville.

**19th** Central Committee of National Guard proclaims elections in Paris for a Commune.

**22nd** Second demonstration of the 'Friends of Order'; National Guard fires on demonstrators in the rue de la Paix. Commune proclaimed at Lyon.

**23rd** Commune proclaimed at Marseille.

**25th** Collapse of the Commune in Lyon.

**26th** Elections in Paris for the Commune. Commune at Le Creusot.

**28th** PROCLAMATION OF THE PARIS COMMUNE FROM THE HÔTEL DE VILLE.

**30th** Commune's first decrees; clash between troops of Paris and Versailles at Courbevoie.

APRIL

**2nd** Versailles troops drive Paris federals from Courbevoie.

**3rd** *Grande sortie* of the Communards; Mont-Valérien fires on Bergeret's column; death of Flourens.

**4th** General retreat of Communards; death of Duval; many prisoners. Cluseret becomes Delegate of War; decrees general conscription into National Guard. Defeat of the Commune at Marseille.

**6th** MacMahon made Commander-in-Chief of army of Versailles. Commune's decree on hostages.

**16th** By-elections to the Commune. Decree on abandoned workshops.

**18th** Decree on overdue bills.

**19th** Commune's 'Declaration to the French People'.

**21st** Reorganization of the executive power of the Commune and choice of new delegates to the Commissions.

**25th** Truce at Neuilly. Requisitioning of vacant apartments.

**28th** Miot proposes format.on of a Committee of Public Safety. Decree forbidding bakers' night work. Creation of a Commission on Education.

**30th** Municipal elections throughout the rest of France.

MAY

**1st** Cluseret dismissed and arrested. Rossel replaces him at the Ministry of War. Creation of the first Committee of Public Safety. Bombardment of the capital begins.

**4th** Fall of the redoubt of Moulin-Saquet.

**5th** Suppression by Commune of seven pro-Versailles papers.

**7th** Decree on the Mont-de-Piété.

**9th** Fall of fort of Issy. Changes on the Committee of Public Safety. Rossel resigns.

**10th** Delescluze appointed civili Delegate of War. Peace Treaty between France and Prussia signed at Frankfurt.

**11th** Decree ordering demolition of Thiers' house. Six more papers suppressed.

**13th** Fall of fort of Vanves.

**15th** Declaration of the 'minority' of the Commune published. First meeting of the committee of the Federation of the Clubs.

**16th** Fall of the Vendôme Column.

**17th** Commune decides to enforce decree on hostages. Distinction abolished between legitimate and illegitimate children regarding National Guard pensions.

**18th** Committee of Public Safety suppresses ten papers. Versailles Assembly ratifies Treaty of Frankfurt.

**19th** Vaillant of the Educational Commission decrees the secularization of education.

**21st** Last full session of the Commune; Cluseret freed. Troops of Versailles enter Paris.

**22nd** to **28th** *Semaine sanglante*.

**23rd** Death of Dombrowski. First fires. West of Paris occupied by troops of Versailles.

**24th** Execution of six hostages, including Archbishop of Paris. The rump of the Commune and the Committee of Public Safety moves from the Hôtel de Ville to the Mairie of the 11th arrondissement. Rigault shot after fall of the Latin Quarter.

**25th** Last session of the Commune in Mairie of 11th arrondissement. Wroblewski evacuates the Left Bank. Death of Delescluze.

**26th** Executions in the rue Haxo. Defence now limited to Belleville.

**27th** Fall of the Buttes-Chaumont, and execution of fallen Communards in the Père-Lachaise cemetery.

**28th** Last barricades fall. Death of Varlin.

NOVEMBER

First execution of condemned Communards.

1872 MAY

First deportation of prisoners. Dufaure law makes the International illegal.

1880 General amnesty.

# MAIN ORGANIZATIONS
# AND PEOPLE

————◆◆◆————

ORGANIZATIONS

*CENTRAL COMMITTEE OF THE NATIONAL GUARD.*
This was formed between February and March 1871 as a republican and patriotic organization of the Paris National Guard. It was
this Committee that was carried to power by the events of 18
March, and it 'ruled' Paris for the following week until elections
could be held for the Commune. During the Civil War it continued to function, led by Edouard Moreau, helping towards the
disorganization of the Paris forces.

*CENTRAL COMMITTEE OF THE TWENTY ARRON-
DISSEMENTS.* Formed in mid-September out of delegates
from the locally organized vigilance committees. This, with fluctu-
ations, was the main revolutionary organization during the siege.
At the beginning of January 1871 it changed its name to 'Delegation of the Twenty Arrondissements' and published the *Affiche
Rouge* of 6 January calling for the Commune. In February, after the
elections, it organized itself into a 'revolutionary socialist party'.
After 18 March, apart from supporting the National Guard
Central Committee against the Mayors, it does not seem to have
played an important role. In May it started helping group the clubs
into a new federation.

*COMMITTEE OF PUBLIC SAFETY.* The first C.P.S. was
formed in 1793 and was the main executive agent of Robespierre
and the Jacobin Terror. At the suggestion of Miot the Commune
voted to form a Committee of Public Safety on 1 May. This was
renewed on 9 May. It hardly increased the efficiency of the
Commune's war effort.

*THE INTERNATIONAL.* The International Workingmen's
Association, to give it its English title, was founded at a meeting

in St Martin's Hall in 1864, called to protest against Russian repression in Poland. Marx attended, but did not speak, though he soon came to dominate its General Council, which met in London. The French delegates were against political forms of action, in any case made impossible by the censorship of the Empire, and tended towards Proudhon's ideas. This did not stop the police arresting the Paris Council three times between 1867 and 1870, with the result that it became more revolutionary. The Paris International, with its offices in the Place de la Corderie, played no official role during either the siege or the Commune, its organization having been gravely affected by the war. But individual members of the International were very active in forming the vigilance committees at the beginning of the siege. Internationalists were elected as delegates to the Central Committee of the National Guard, and then to the Commune. Afterwards the International was blamed for the Commune and itself made illegal by the Dufaure Law of 1872. By then the First International had ceased to function because Marx, faced with opposition from Bakuninist anarchists, French exiles and British trade unionists, decided to have the General Council transferred to New York.

*THE TRADE UNION FEDERATION.* This was a loose organization of the *chambres syndicales*, the equivalent at the time to the later trade unions, of the Paris region. Its offices were in the same building as the International – the Corderie – with which it was closely linked.

## PEOPLE

ADAM, Edmond. Aged 54 in 1870. Republican. Had been journalist on the *National* in 1840s. Adjoint to Mayor of Hôtel de Ville and then Conseiller d'Etat. Banker during Second Empire. Made Prefect of Police in place of Kératry on 11 October 1870. Resigned after 31 October uprising. Elected as a Republican Deputy in February 1871 elections. Later became a Senator.

ALLEMANE, Jean. Aged 28 in 1871. Printer and active in printers' strike of 1862. Organizer of the National Guard in 5th arrondissement during the Commune. Deported. After the amnesty he first joined the Parti Ouvrier, then split, along with the Possibilists. In 1890 broke with these to form the more revolutionary Allemanists.

Active in the Syndicalist movement. Supported the war in 1914, and belonged to the Communist majority at the Congress of Tours of 1920. Was one of last survivors of the Commune.

ALLIX, Jules. Aged 53 in 1871. Was a 'communist' candidate in the 1848 elections. Supported the June days, and then took part in republican plots against the Emperor. Imprisoned in an asylum for a time. Elected to the Commune by the 8th arrondissement, of which he was also the Mayor. Attempted a number of reforms in his arrondissement, particularly in education and women's employment.

ARAGO, Etienne. Aged 67 in 1870. Playwright in 1820s and friend of Balzac. Fought in 1830 revolution along with La Fayette. Became head of the Paris Post Office during the 1848 revolution. Elected to the National Assembly, but forced into exile for his part in the June 1849 republican revolt. Became Mayor of Paris on 4 September 1870, until replaced by Jules Ferry after 31 October.

ARNOLD, Georges. Aged 31 in 1871. Architect. Very active member of the National Guard Central Committee. Elected to the Commune for 18th arrondissement in April by-elections.

ARNOULD, Arthur. Aged 38 in 1871. Son of a Professor at the Sorbonne. One of editors on *La Marseillaise*. Member of the Commune for the 4th arrondissement. One of the main members of the 'minority'. Escaped to Switzerland, where he wrote a useful history of the Commune.

ASSI, Adolphe. Aged 30 in 1871. Member of the International and one of the leaders of steel-workers' strike in Le Creusot at the beginning of 1870. Active in the National Guard and member of its Central Committee. Member of the Commune for 11th arrondissement. Deported.

D'AURELLE DE PALADINES. Aged 66 in 1870. Fought in Algeria and Crimea. Actively supported Louis-Bonaparte's *coup d'état*. Made Commander-in-Chief of the Loire army in November 1870. Won victory of Coulmiers on 9 November and thus recaptured Orleans. But failed to follow this up and Orleans had to be abandoned, d'Aurelles losing his command. Elected to National Assembly in February 1871. Appointed by Thiers on 3 March to head Paris National Guard, which refused to recognize him as their chief. Supported the Right in the Assembly after the Commune.

BAZAINE, Marshall. Aged 60 in 1871. Had been made a Marshal by

Napoleon III for commanding the Mexican expedition from 1862 to 1867. Appointed to command the Rhine army in August 1870, but was shut up in Metz. Surrendered the fort on 27 October. Court-martialled after the war, found guilty of treachery and imprisoned. Escaped in 1874 to Spain, where he died.

BERGERET, Jules. Aged 31 in 1871. Bookshop assistant. Member of the National Guard Central Committee. Member of the Commune for the 20th arrondissement. One of first three War Delegates and Commander of the Place Vendôme. Led one column of the unsuccessful *grande sortie* of 3–4 April. Supported 'majority' on the Commune. Exile in U.S.A.

BESLAY, Charles. Aged 76 in 1871. Engineer, republican Deputy in 1848. Friend of Proudhon, and kept in touch with workers' organizations during 1860s. Oldest member of the Commune, and its Delegate to the Bank of France. Allowed to escape to Switzerland, where he died.

BILLIORAY, Alfred. Aged 31 in 1871. Painter. Member of the National Guard Central Committee, and of the Commune for the 14th arrondissement. Elected to the second Committee of Public Safety. Died in deportation.

BLANC, Louis. Aged 60 in 1871. Republican journalist in 1830s and 1840s. Published the *Organization of Labour* in 1839, which made his name as a socialist writer. Made a member of the Provisional Government formed in 1848, and put in charge of the Luxembourg Commission (the 'workers' parliament' and the National Workshops). Was accused of having taken part in the revolutionary invasion of the Assembly on 15 May 1848 and went into exile in London. Returned to Paris after 4 September 1870. Headed the Paris list in the February 1871 elections. Opposed the Commune, but defended republican liberties during repression afterwards.

BLANQUI, Auguste. Aged 66 in 1871. Revolutionary. Member of republican secret societies after 1830 Revolution, and imprisoned. Freed after 1848 Revolution, he was active against the new Government, and led invasion of the Assembly on 15 May 1848. Imprisoned, until 1859 amnesty. Again imprisoned in 1861, until he escaped in 1865. Fire station at La Villette affair in August 1870. Founded paper, *La Patrie en Danger*, that pressed the Government of National Defence to take more active measures during the siege. Condemned for his part in 31 October uprising, he was captured and imprisoned on the eve of the Commune. Thiers refused to exchange him for the Archbishop of Paris and other hostages. Freed in 1879, and died two years later.

BRIDEAU. Aged 26 in 1870. Son of a lawyer. Student and engraver. Was condemned to death for attack on fire station of La Villette. Pardoned.

BRUNEL, Paul. Aged 41 in 1871. Had been regular army officer. Patriotic member of the National Guard during the siege. Played an important role on 18 March. Member of the Commune for the 7th arrondissement. Wounded during last week, but escaped to London.

CHANZY, General. Aged 58 in 1871. Replaced d'Aurelles de Paladines as commander of army in south in December 1870. Arrested in Paris on 18 March as he was on his way to take up his seat at Versailles. Freed by the National Guard Central Committee, on condition that he did not fight against the Commune. He opposed the signing of peace with the Prussians, having been one of the few active republican Generals during the war. Later became Governor-General of Algeria, a Senator and the French Ambassador to Russia.

CLEMENCEAU, Georges. Aged 30 in 1871. Doctor and militant republican. Had been imprisoned for one year for his opposition to the Empire, and spent some time in the U.S.A. Mayor of the 18th arrondissement during the siege. Elected as a Deputy for Paris in February 1871. Unable to prevent executions in rue des Rosiers on 18 March. French Premier, 1917–20.

CLUSERET, General. Aged 48 in 1871. Regular army officer, and decorated for his taking barricades in putting down June 1848 uprising. Opposed Second Empire, and fought in the American Civil War. Afterwards acted as a professional revolutionary in South America and Ireland. Returned to France, and during the war was active in the League in the South and uprisings in Lyon and Marseille. Was the Commune's first Delegate of War from 3 April to 1 May. Arrested, but freed in time to escape to London. The last few chapters of his *Memoirs*, concerning the street battle during the final week, were translated with a short analysis by Lenin in *Vperiod*, 23–30 March 1905.

DA COSTA, Gaston. Aged 21 in 1871. Blanquist student. Assistant to Rigault during the Commune. Deported. Wrote an important account of the Commune.

COURBET, Gustave. Aged 52 in 1871. Painter, whose pictures had often been a cause of scandal during the Second Republic and Empire. Friend of Baudelaire and Proudhon. Elected to the Commune in the April by-elections by the 6th arrondissement. President of the Artists' Federation. Condemned afterwards for the destruction of the Vendôme Column, and had to flee to Switzerland, where he died in 1877.

CREMIEUX, Gaston. Aged 35 in 1871. Lawyer, and supporter of Gambetta during the war. Led the Marseille Commune. Executed.

DELESCLUZE, Charles. Aged 62 in 1871. Jacobin republican journalist. Commissioner for the north of France during the Second Republic. Condemned for his part in June 1849 revolt. Escaped to England but returned after *coup d'état* to try to plot against Napoleon. Captured and deported to Devil's Island. Freed in 1859. Founded the *Réveil* in 1868. Patriotic during the war; took part in 31 October and arrested after 22 January. Elected by Paris to the National Assembly in February 1871 and then to the Commune for the 19th arrondissement. Resigned from the National Assembly. Member of the Committee of Public Safety, and made Civil Delegate of War when Rossel resigned. Died on a barricade.

DEMAY, Antoine. Aged 49 in 1871. Stone-carver. Member of the International, and of the Commune for the 3rd arrondissement.

DMITRIEFF, Elisabeth. Aged 20 in 1871. Daughter of a Russian nobleman. Married a Russian Colonel to escape Russia and study in Switzerland. Joined the International; met Marx in London. During the Commune she organized the Women's Union for the Defence of Paris as a branch of the International. Returned to Russia in October 1871, married someone condemned to deportation to Siberia, where she died.

DOMBROWSKI, Jaroslav. Aged 35 in 1871. Son of impoverished Polish aristocracy. Joined in attempted Polish uprising against Russia of 1863, but arrested. Escaped from Moscow before being deported and went to Paris. Was prevented from taking part in the war, and joined the Commune, being its ablest commander. Defended Neuilly fiercely for almost two months. Killed during the last week.

DUCROT, General. Aged 53 in 1870. Escaped after being taken a prisoner at Sedan to become the most active commander during the siege. Strongly anti-republican, and monarchist Deputy after February 1871.

DUVAL, Emile. Aged 30 in 1871. Steel-worker, Blanquist and member of the International. Active in the National Guard during the siege, and on 18 March. Member of the Commune for 13th arrondissement, and made one of first War Delegates. Led a column during *grande sortie* of 3 April. Made prisoner on 4 April, and killed by order of Vinoy whilst being taken a prisoner to Versailles.

EUDES, Emile. Aged 27 in 1871. Blanquist student. Took part in attack on La Villette fire station. Arrested, and then freed after 4 September. Member of the Commune for the 11th arrondissement. Member of the Committee of Public Safety. One of the commanders, and took part in *sortie* of 3 April. Put in charge of the defence of the forts at the end of April, particularly that of Issy. His wife also took part in some of the military action. Escaped to Switzerland.

FAVRE, Jules. Aged 61 in 1870. Republican lawyer. Deputy in 1848 and briefly Minister for Foreign Affairs. Opposed *coup d'état*; famous for his defence of Orsini, the Emperor's would-be assassin. Elected as a Deputy for Paris in 1863, and one of the 'Five' of the opposition in the Chambre to the regime. The senior member of the Government of National Defence after Trochu, and Minister of Foreign Affairs. Continued this post in Thiers' first cabinet.

FERRÉ, Théophile. Aged 24 in 1871. Blanquist, and member of vigilance committee in 18th arrondissement. Member of the Commune for this district. Next in command to Rigault at the Prefecture of Police. Executed.

FERRY, Jules. Aged 38 in 1871. Republican lawyer. Attacked Haussmann's financing. Deputy for Paris in 1869. Member of Government of National Defence and Prefect of the Seine. Took over from Arago at the Hôtel de Ville after 31 October. Minister of Education in Thiers' first cabinet.

FLOURENS, Gustave. Aged 33 in 1871. Son of a professor at the Collège de France, where he also taught for a short time. Fought in Greece. Worked on *La Marseillaise* after 1868. Strongly patriotic during siege and opposed Government of National Defence, being one of the leaders of 31 October revolt. Arrested, and freed just before 22 January demonstration. Member of the

Commune for the 19th arrondissement. One of leaders of *sortie* of 3 April, when he was taken prisoner and executed.

FRANKEL, Léo. Aged 27 in 1871. Son of a Hungarian doctor. Arrested in Germany. Freed, came to London, where he met Marx. In France one of the founders of Lyon branch of the International. Practised as a jeweller in Paris, until imprisoned after the second trial of the International. Freed after 4 September. Member of the central Council of the International, and then of the Commune for the 13th arrondissement. Played a leading role on the Commission for Labour and Exchange. Escaped to London. Afterwards was active in the socialist movement both in Hungary, until arrested, and then in Paris again, where he died and was buried in a red flag in Père-Lachaise.

GALLIFET, Marquis de. Aged 41 in 1871. Famed for his gallantry and for his severity during the Mexican campaigns. Made a prisoner after Sedan. Returned to France in March 1871 to command the cavalry against the Commune. Notorious for his savage treatment of the Communard prisoners. Became Minister of War in Waldeck-Rousseau's cabinet in 1899.

GAMBETTA, Léon. Aged 32 in 1870. Fiery republican lawyer, elected by Belleville in 1869 elections but preferred to represent Marseille. Refused any compromise with the Empire. Member of the Government of National Defence, and in October sent to head the Delegation at Tours. Vigorously tried to pursue the war, and resigned over the armistice. From 1871 to 1881, when he formed a short-lived government, he was one of the most active of the republicans, opposing any attempt at a monarchist restoration.

GÉRARDIN, Charles. Aged 28 in 1871. Commercial traveller. Member of the Central Committee of the Twenty Arrondissements. Member of the Commune for the 17th arrondissement, and friend of Rossel. Exile in London.

GROUSSET, Paschal, Aged 26 in 1871. Journalist on the *Marseillaise* (Victor Noir affair). Member of the Commune for the 18th arrondissement, and Delegate for Foreign Affairs. Jacobin. Escaped from deportation and later became a socialist Deputy.

HAUSSMANN, Baron. Napoleon's Prefect of the Seine and carried out the rebuilding of much of Paris.

JACLARD, Anna (born 1844) and Victor (born 1840). The wife was daughter of a Russian general. Friend of Dostoevsky. Joined

Russian section of the International in Geneva whilst in exile with Victor. During Commune member of the women's vigilance committee of 18th arrondissement, and of the women's education Commission formed by Vaillant at end of May. Victor: Blanquist, doctor, mathematics teacher, freemason. Adjoint to Clemenceau in 18th arrondissement during the siege. During Commune in charge of National Guard, after some dispute, in 17th arrondissement. Later active in the socialist movement.

JOURDE, Francis. Aged 28 in 1871. Bank clerk. Member of National Guard Central Committee, and then of the Commune. Financial Delegate. Deported.

LANGLOIS, A.-J. Aged 52 in 1871. Had collaborated with Proudhon during 1848 Revolution, and remained a close friend during Second Empire. Joined International, though he had independent means. National Guard commander during the siege. Elected to the National Assembly. Appointed on 18 March by the Mayors to head the National Guard in a last attempt to assert their authority. But he was rejected by the Central Committee.

LECOMTE, General. Aged 53 in 1871. Fought under Ducrot during siege. Was one of the two generals massacred in Montmartre on 18 March, after his troops had failed to capture the cannons.

LEFRANÇAIS, Gustave. Aged 45 in 1871. Schoolteacher, until forced into exile by the *coup d'état*. Returned to France and worked as a clerk. Militant republican and 'socialist'. Member of the Commune for the 4th arrondissement. Member of the 'minority'. Escaped to Switzerland, where he wrote a history of the Commune. Anarchist member of the Swiss branch of the International.

LÉO, André. Aged 39 in 1871. Literary name of novelist Léodile Champseix. Exiled after *coup d'état*. Active in women's organizations during the siege and the Commune. Became the wife of Benoît Malon whilst in exile in Switzerland.

LISSAGARAY, Prosper. Aged 33 in 1871. Republican journalist. Supported the Commune and edited paper, *L'Action*. Escaped to England. Published in 1876 his classic *History of the Paris Commune*.

LONGUET, Charles. Aged 31 in 1871. Republican journalist and Proudhonist. Member of the International, and of the Central Committee of the Twenty Arrondissements. Elected to Commune in April by-elections, and became its Delegate to the *Journal Officiel*. Escaped to England where he married Jenny Marx in 1872. Was a socialist militant on his return to France, though supporting Possibilists rather than the more communist Parti Ouvrier.

LULLIER, Charles. Aged 33 in 1871. Naval officer. Appointed by the Central Committee to command the National Guard on 18 March, but was incompetent, if not treacherous. Quickly arrested by the Commune. Afterwards deported by Versailles.

MACMAHON, Marshal. Aged 62 in 1870. Made Marshal after 1859 Italian campaign. Commander of the French army that surrendered at Sedan. Appointed by Thiers to command troops against Commune. Became President of the Republic in 1873 on downfall of Thiers. Resigned in 1879 because of republican opposition.

MALON, Benoît. Aged 30 in 1871. Member of the International. Adjoint Mayor in 17th arrondissement during siege, and elected to National Assembly in February 1871. Resigned. Member of the Commune for the 17th arrondissement. Supported 'minority'. Escaped to Switzerland, and wrote a history of the Commune. In 1880s joined Parti Ouvrier until he broke with this to become an 'independent socialist'.

MELLIET, Léo. Republican lawyer, and close to Blanquists. Member of Central Committee of National Guard; of Commune for 13th arrondissement; of the Committee of Public Safety. Deputy in Radical Party from 1898 to 1902.

MICHEL, Louise. Aged 41 in 1871. Schoolteacher and revolutionary. Delegate for Montmartre to Central Committee of Twenty Arrondissements. Fought during the Commune. Deported. Anarchist revolutionary in 1880s and forced into exile in England.

MILLIÈRE, Jean-Baptiste. Aged 54 in 1871. Cooper and then became a lawyer. Socialist journalist in 1848. Deported for opposing the *coup d'état*. On the *Marseillaise*. Deputy for Paris in February 1871. At first tried to conciliate Paris and Versailles before returning to Paris in April 1871. Did not take part in the Commune but was nonetheless shot during last week.

MIOT, Jules. Aged 61 in 1871. Chemist. Republican Deputy in 1848; deported in 1851. Blanquist and member of the International in 1860s. Adjoint Mayor in 8th arrondissement during siege, then member of the Commune. Escaped to Switzerland.

MOREAU, Edouard. Aged 33 in 1871. Man of letters and in commerce. Not involved in politics before 1870. Active in the National Guard during the siege. Played a leading role on its Central

Committee after 18 March and during the Commune. Shot during last week.

MOTTU. Aged 40 in 1871. Banker. Radical Mayor of 11th arrondissement during the siege. Did not support the Commune, joining the League of the Rights of Paris.

MURAT, André. Aged 38 in 1871. Son of a journalist and himself a journalist in Lyon, before the Second Empire. One of founders of International in Paris. Adjoint Mayor in 4th arrondissement during the siege. Did not support the Commune. Afterwards took part in workers' movements of 1870s.

OLLIVIER, Emile. Aged 45 in 1870. Republican lawyer, and administrator during Second Republic. One of the 'Five' of the 1857 opposition in the Legislative Body. Directed the Government formed in January 1870, the 'Liberal Empire', until forced to resign in August after first French defeats.

PALIKAO, Comte de. Aged 74 in 1870. Gained his title from commanding French troops in China. Replaced Ollivier as head of Government on 9 August until Empire overthrown on 4 September.

PICARD, Ernest. Aged 49 in 1870. Wealthy republican lawyer and had financial interests in the Press. One of the 'Five' of the opposition to the Imperial Government in the Chambre. Minister of Finance in the Government of National Defence, and then Minister of the Interior in Thiers' first cabinet.

PROTOT, Eugène. Aged 32 in 1871. Son of a peasant family and became a lawyer. Close to both the Blanquists and the International. Active in the National Guard during the siege. Member of the Commune for the 11th arrondissement. Delegate of Justice. Escaped to Italy.

PROUDHON, Pierre-Joseph (1809–65). Leading French socialist and anarchist thinker. Imprisoned in 1849 for articles against the newly elected Louis-Napoleon. Opponent of the political republicans, and came into contact with the newly emerging working-class movement of the early 1860s. Main writings: *What is Property?* (1840); *System of Economic Contradictions* (1846–attacked by Marx in his *Philosophy of Poverty*); *Justice in the Revolution and the Church* (1858); *War and Peace* (1861); *The Federal Principle* (1863); *On the Political Capacity of the Working Classes* (1865).

PYAT, Félix. Aged 61 in 1871. Trained in law, but republican journalist instead in 1830s. Deputy in 1848 and member of the

'Mountain' in 1849 Assembly until had to flee to Switzerland after June 1849 revolt. Did not return to France until 1869. Attacked the Government of National Defence vigorously in his paper, *Le Combat*, until it was suppressed. In February founded *Le Vengeur* and elected to National Assembly. Resigned at beginning of March. Member of the Commune for 10th arrondissement, and of Committee of Public Safety, where he favoured extreme Jacobin position. Escaped to England. Republican Deputy in 1880s.

RANC, Arthur. Aged 40 in 1871. Law student, deported in 1853 and Blanquist journalist. Mayor of 11th arrondissement during siege. Elected to National Assembly in February 1871. Resigned over signing of peace treaty. Member of the Commune for 11th arrondissement, but resigned on 6 April. Had to flee to Belgium on defeat of the Commune. Afterwards became a radical Deputy and founder of the Society of the Rights of Man.

RÉGÈRE, Dominique. Aged 55 in 1871. Vet. Had to flee after *coup d'état*. Returned after 1859 amnesty. Member of the Commune for 5th arrondissement. Deported.

RIGAULT, Raoul. Aged 24 in 1871. Latin Quarter revolutionary and Blanquist. Member of the Commune for 8th arrondissement. Delegate at the Prefecture of Police. Killed during the last week.

ROCHEFORT, Henri. Aged 40 in 1870. Most successful journalist opponent of the Second Empire, notably in *La Lanterne*. Elected as a Deputy for Paris in 1869 by-election, and founded *La Marseillaise*. Member of the Government of National Defence, until he resigned after 31 October. Elected to National Assembly in February 1871, until resigned over peace treaty. Journalist, *Le Mot d'Ordre*, under the Commune, but arrested by Versailles when he fled from Paris. Deported, but escaped. In 1880s published one of most popular newspapers and again Deputy.

ROSSEL, Louis. Aged 27 in 1871. Army officer, escaped from Metz after its surrender. Joined Paris after 18 March out of patriotic disgust with the National Assembly. Delegate of War from 1 May until he resigned on 9 May. Escaped arrest by the Commune, but was picked up by Versailles after the Commune and executed.

SAISSET, Admiral. Aged 51 in 1871. In charge of the forts of Paris during the siege. After 18 March replaced d'Aurelle de Paladines as head of the National Guard until he returned to Versailles when the Mayors agreed to elections.

SIMON, Jules. Aged 57 in 1871. Philosophy professor at the Sorbonne; Deputy in 1848. Republican opponent of the Empire. Deputy in 1863. Member of the Government of National Defence, and Minister of Education in Thiers' first cabinet, until he resigned because he could not get his law on public education passed. Premier briefly in 1876.

THEISZ. Aged 32 in 1871. Bronze-worker. Member of the International, and of the Commune for the 18th arrondissement. In charge of the postal service during the Commune. Escaped to London.

THIERS, Adolphe (1797–1877). Lawyer and historian. Belonged to liberal opposition under Charles X, and played an important role in getting the crown offered to Louis-Philippe in July 1830. Premier and Minister of Foreign Affairs in 1836 and 1840. In latter year crisis between England and France. Proposal of fortifications of Paris. Thiers replaced by Guizot. Defended conservative cause after 1848, but opposed *coup d'état*. Deputy again in 1863 and elder statesman of the opposition and leading Orleanist. Acted as negotiator between Government in Paris and Bismarck during the siege. Made 'Chief Executive of the Republic' in February 1871. Resigned in 1873.

THOMAS, Clément. Aged 62 in 1871. Radical republican of the 1830s and in the 1848 revolution. Made Commander-in-Chief of National Guard of the Seine region for his role in repressing the June 1848 uprising. Opposed *coup d'état*, and in exile until after 4 September. Appointed to head National Guard after 31 October until he resigned in March. Captured and killed on 18 March in Montmartre.

TIRARD. Aged 44 in 1871. Civil servant and then in export business. Well known in Paris for his opposition to the Empire. Mayor of 2nd arrondissement during siege. Elected Deputy in February 1871. Led the 'resistance' of the Mayors to the Central Committee after 18 March until the elections to the Commune. Elected but immediately resigned and went to Versailles. Minister of Agriculture and Commerce in successive governments after 1879.

TOLAIN, Henri. Aged 43 in 1871. Engraver. Proudhonist and one of founder members of the French International. Attended first Congresses. Condemned in first trial of International in 1868. Adjoint Mayor in 11th arrondissement during siege. Deputy in February 1871 and did not resign over the Commune, for which he was expelled from the International by the Paris section. Republican Senator afterwards.

TRIDON, Gustave. Aged 30 in 1871. Journalist and historian of the *Hébertistes* of the first Revolution. Son of a wealthy landowner. Blanqui's second-in-command. Elected Deputy in February 1871; resigned over peace treaty. Member of the Commune for the 5th arrondissement, but already very ill. Escaped to Brussels, where he died shortly after.

TROCHU, General Jules. Aged 55 in 1870. Had been *aide-de-camp* to Bugeaud in Algeria. Fought in Crimea, but disgraced for his book on the army of 1867; Legitimist rather than Bonapartist. Made Governor of Paris in August 1870. President of the Government of National Defence, and in charge of the French forces during the siege. Replaced by General Vinoy on 22 January. Elected to National Assembly in February 1871. Resigned his seat over the military law of 1872.

VACHEROT. Aged 62 in 1871. Professor of Philosophy at Ecole Normale from 1838 until he lost his post because of his opposition to the *coup d'état*. Mayor of the 11th arrondissement during the siege. Resisted the Central Committee after 18 March. Opposed the Commune and was member of the League of the Rights of Paris.

VAILLANT, Edouard. Aged 31 in 1871. Engineer and science student. Studied in Germany until outbreak of the war. Had joined International and was in contact with the Blanquists during the siege. Member of the Central Committee of the National Guard, and of the Commune for the 8th arrondissement. Delegate of Education. Met Marx in London in exile, but on return to France after 1880 became leading organizer of the Blanquist Party. Deputy for Paris from 1893 and leading figure next to Jaurès in the Parti socialiste unifié formed in 1905.

VALLÈS, Jules. Aged 39 in 1871. Journalist and novelist. Part of the revolutionary opposition to the Empire. National Guard commander during the siege and arrested for his part in 31 October uprising. Founded the *Cri du Peuple* in February 1871. Member of the Commune for 15th arrondissement. Escaped to London.

VARLIN, Eugène. Aged 32 in 1871. Son of peasant farmers. Book-binder. Active in strike movement of 1860s, and joined the International, becoming one of its most militant members.

Member of the Central Committee of the National Guard, and of the Commune. Killed during the last week.

VAUTRIN. Aged 52 in 1871. Lawyer, and Mayor of the 18th arrondissement during the 1848 revolution. Resigned after the *coup d'état*, and returned to law. Mayor of the 4th arrondissement during the siege. Opposed the Central Committee after 18 March and went to Versailles.

VERMOREL, Auguste. Aged 30 in 1871. Journalist and writer. Edited the *Courrier Français* in the 1860s, which he made into a socialist paper. Imprisoned after 31 October uprising of the siege. Member of the Commune for the 18th arrondissement. Opposed the Jacobins. Wounded during the last week and died in prison shortly after.

VINOY, General Joseph. Aged 68 in 1871. Had helped in the repression after the *coup d'état*. Replaced Trochu as Commander of Paris in January 1871. In charge of the attack on the cannons of 18 March. MacMahon succeeded him to command of the army, and Vinoy put in charge of the army of the reserve.

# BIBLIOGRAPHY

There is no complete bibliography of the Commune. The best available is that of Giuseppe del Bo, *La Commune di Parigi*, Istituto Giangiacomo Feltrinelli, Milan, 1957. Jean-Léo has published a *Bibliographie de la Commune de 1871*, Grenier du Collectionneur, Brussels, 1970. J. Rougerie and G. Haupt, *Le Mouvement Social*, Nos. 37–38, October–December, January–March, 1961–2, give a comprehensive survey of the literature on the Commune between 1940 and 1961. For the history of the International there are the three volumes of the *Comité International des sciences historiques. Répertoire international des sources pour l'étude des mouvements sociaux au XIXe et XXe siècles. La Première Internationale, 1864–1877*, Paris, 1958–63. Bruhat, Dautry and Tersen have a good full descriptive bibliography; R. Williams has a bibliographical essay on the period from the Second Empire to 1875.

The basic sources for the history of the Commune are the reports and depositions of the two official Inquiries into the *Acts of the Government of National Defence* and the *Insurrection of March 18*. The *Journal Officiel* of the Commune published all the decrees of the Commune and of the Committee of Public Safety, and is full of other information about clubs and events in Paris during the Commune. Vallès' *Cri du Peuple*, which has been reprinted, is another valuable source, especially for meetings of the various popular organizations. The second volume of *Les Murailles politiques françaises*, is the best published collection, running to several hundred, of the posters of the Commune, the Mairies and the various other organizations as well as of the Government at Versailles. The first volume covers the period of the siege. Firmin Maillard gives a much smaller collection. A critical edition of the proceedings of the Communal Council has been produced by G. Bourgin and G. Henriot. This has useful appendices and notes. Part Two of the *Dictionnaire biographique du mouvement ouvrier français*, edited by Jean Maitron, is a tremendous source of information.

Lissagaray's history is by far the best and most detailed of the contemporary accounts. Marx's daughter, Eleanor, translated it into English in 1886, though the English and French texts sometimes differ. The English text does, however, have certain notes not found in the French editions. Lissagaray can be supplemented on some points by the history of Lanjalley and Corriez, both supporters of the Commune, who had to go into exile afterwards. Other useful Communard Memoirs are the accounts of Lefrançais; Gaston da Costa, especially for the Prefecture of Police; Arthur Arnould (the history Stalin relied most on, though this should not be held against Arnould's work, which is written from a partly anarchist point of view); Benoît Malon; and the ten little volumes of Vuillaume, mainly concerned with personages and anecdotal details, though nonetheless valuable for that. The *Carnets* of Martial Senisse, though never published by the author, are a fascinating day-by-day view of events by a young revolutionary. A less enthusiastic view is that of Louis Barron, though he makes several very original points. The un-completed three volumes of Lepelletier provide a detailed, but wordy, history of the period up to early April. More specifically as printed sources for the clubs and popular movements (which need to be supplemented by archival and newspaper material) are the accounts of the clubs during the siege by the Liberal economist Molinari, and, less satisfactorily, for the Church clubs during the siege by Fontoulieu. For the 17th arrondisse-ment a strangely neglected source is V. d'Esbœufs' *Le Coin de Voile*.

The most important of the recent studies that have used archival and newspaper material is the collective edition produced by the French Communist Party, edited by Bruhat, Dautry and Tersen; the study of the central arrondissements by M. Choury, *La Commune au cœur de Paris* (his volume on the Latin Quarter lacks references); the study of women dur-ing the Commune by Edith Thomas, and the same author's biography of Rossel. On the politics and social measures of the Commune, again using archival and newspaper sources, there is the excellent doctoral thesis of A. Decouflé, published as *La Commune de Paris (1871)* J. Rougerie has been most responsible for throwing new light on the popular or-ganizations of the Commune and hence on the whole interpretation of the revolution: see his articles listed below. His little book, *Le Procès des Communards*, as well as providing a commentary giving his as yet un-completed interpretation of the Commune, is a very good collection of extracts from archival documents. Henri Lefebvre's sociological account of the proclamation of the Commune has been influential on several later accounts, including that of Decouflé and the valuable little book by Winock and Azéma. For the politics of the war and the siege, a subject largely neglected by English histories, see the superb three-volume account of H. Guillemin, which is based very much on the official inquiries and the writings of the members of the Government of National Defence.

The five-volume history by G. Soria, *La Grande Histoire de la Commune*, Paris, 1970-1, came too late to be used here; as did the anniversary col-lection of essays published by the International Institute for Social History at Amsterdam.

The following is a list of the works referred to in the footnotes, with some additional general accounts not specifically mentioned in the text.

OFFICIAL REPORTS AND ANONYMOUS PUBLICATIONS

*Les Actes du Gouvernment de la défense nationale, du 4 septembre 1870 au 8 février* 1871, *enquête parlementaire.* Versailles, 1872–5.

*Annales de l'Assemblée Nationale. Compte Rendu in extenso des séances.* Paris, 1871–5, vols. 1, 2 (1871); 43 (1875), containing the report of General Appert.

*Dictionnaire biographique du mouvement ouvrier français,* ed. J. Maitron. Part Two, 1864–1871. *La Première Internationale et la Commune,* vols 4ff. Paris, 1967–71.

*Documents of the First International,* vol IV, 1870–1. Moscow/London, s.d. (1967).

*Enquête parlementaire sur l'insurrection du 18 mars,* 3 vols, Versailles, 1872.

*L'Europe,* April–May 1951, Special issue on the Commune. June–August, 1968, issue on Vallès.

*Exposition Universelle de 1867 à Paris. Rapports des délégations ouvrières, dirigées par M. Arnould Desvernay.* Paris, 1869.

*Guerre des Communeux:* see Hennebert.

*Histoire Critique de siège dè Paris par un officier de Marine.* Paris, 1871.

*Letters from Paris,* written by C. de B., a political Informant to the head of the London House of Rothschild. Translated and edited by R. Henrey. London, 1942.

*Lettres au 'Père Duchêne' pendant la Commune de Paris.* Marx–Engels–Lenin Institute, Moscow. Paris, 1934.

*Lettres de communards et de militants de la Première International à Marx, Engels et autres dans les journées de la Commune de Paris en 1871,* ed. J. Rocher. Paris, 1934.

*Macmillan's Magazine,* September–October 1871. 'A Victim of Paris and Versailles'.

*Les Murailles politiques françaises,* vols 1–2. Paris, 1871.

*Procès de l'Association Internationale des Travailleurs. Première et deuxième Commissions du Bureau de Paris.* Paris, July 1870.

*Troisième Procès de l'Association Internationale des Travailleurs de Paris.* Paris, 1870.

*Le Procès de la Commune. Compte rendu des débats du Conseil de Guerre. Paraissant tous les jours par livraison de huit pages, avec illustrations.* Paris, 1871.

*Proces-Verbaux de la Commune de 1871,* ed. by G. Bourgin and G. Henriot, 2 vols. Paris, 1924, 1945.

*La Revue Blanche,* vol 12, nos 91, 92, 15 March, 1 April 1897. 'Enquête sur la Commune'.

*Les Séances officielles de l'Internationale à Paris pendant le siège et pendant la Commune.* Paris, 1872.

AUTHORS

ALLEMANE, Jean, *Mémoires d'un Communard*. Paris, s.d. (1910).

D'ALMÉRAS, H., *La Vie Parisienne pendant le siège et sous la Commune*. Paris, s.d. (1925).

ANDRIEU, J., 'The Paris Commune. A Chapter towards its Theory and History', *Fortnightly Review*, vol. X. New Series, November 1871, pp. 571–98.

ANDRIEUX, L., *La Commune à Lyon en 1870 et 1871*. Paris, 1906.

ARIÈS, P., *Historie des populations françaises*. Paris, 1948.

ARMENGAUD, A., *Les Populations de l'Est-Aquitain au début de l'époque contemporain*. Paris, 1961.

ARNOULD, Arthur, *Histoire populaire et parlementaire de la Commune de Paris*. Brussels, 1878.

AVINERI, S., *The Social and Political Thought of Karl Marx*. Cambridge, 1968.

BALLEYGUIER, Eugène: see Fidus.

DU BARAIL, General, *Mes Souvenirs*, vol. 3, 1864–79. Paris, 1896.

BARRON, Louis, *Sous le drapeau rouge*. Paris, 1889.

BARY, A., 'Lettres écrites pendant la Commune de Paris. 1871', *La Revue hebdomidaire*, vol. 9, August 1904.

BAX, E. Belfort, *A Short history of the Paris Commune*. London, 1903.

BENJAMIN, Walter, *Illuminations*. Eng. trans. London, 1970.

BERNHEIM, P., *Le Conseil muncipal de Paris de 1789 à nos jours*. Paris, 1937.

BESLAY, Charles, *Mes Souvenirs 1830–1848–1870*. Paris/Neuchatel/Brussels, 1874.

— *La Vérité sur la Commune*. Brussels, 1878.

BLANQUI, Auguste, *Textes choisis*, ed. V. P. Volguine. Paris, 1955.

— *La Patrie en danger*. Paris, 1871.

BOURELLY, General, *Le Ministère de la Guerre sous la Commune*. Paris, s.d. (1902).

BOURGIN, G., *La Guerre de 1870–1871 et la Commune*. Paris, 1939.

— *Les Premières journées de la Commune*. Paris, 1928.

— 'Une Entente Franco-Allemande: Bismarck, Thiers, Jules Favre et la répression de la Commune de Paris', *International Review of Social History*, vol. 1, 1956, pp. 41–53.

BOUVIER, J., 'Des Banquiers devant l'actualité politique en 1870–71', *Revue d'Histoire Moderne et Contemporaine*, vol. 5, 1958, pp. 137–51.

— 'Aux origines de la 3ème Republique. Les réflexes sociaux des milieux d'affaires', *Revue Historique*, vol. 210, December 1953, pp. 271–301.

BRABANT, F. H., *The Beginning of the Third Republic in France*. London, 1940.

BRUHAT, J., DAUTRY, J., and TERSEN, E., *La Commune de 1871*. Paris, 1960.

BURY, J. P. T., *Gambetta and the National Defence. A Republican Dictatorship in France*. London, 1936.

BUSCH, Moritz, *Bismarck in the Franco-German War*. London, 1879.

CAMERON, R. E., 'Economic Growth and Stagnation in France, 1815–1914', *Journal of Modern History*, vol. 30, March 1958, pp. 1–13.

— 'French Finance and Italian Unity. The Cavourian Decade', *American Historical Review*, vol. 62, April 1957, pp. 552–69.

DU CAMP, Maxime, *Les Convulsions de Paris*. Paris, 1878–9.

CARO, E., 'La fin de la bohème', *Revue des Deux Mondes*, vol. 94, July 1871.

CAROLUS, F., *Organisation du travail et du crédit social. Projet présenté à la Commission du Travail et de l'Echange de la Commune de Paris*. Paris, 1871.

CASE, L. M., *French Opinion on War and Diplomacy during the Second Empire*. Philadelphia, 1954.

CASTAGNARY, *Les Libres propos*. Paris, 1864.

CATTELAIN, P., *Mémoires inédits du chef de la sûreté de la Commune*. Paris, 1910.

CERF, M., *Le d'Artagnan de la Commune*. Paris, 1967.

CHALMIN, P., *L'Officier français de 1815 à 1870*. Paris, 1957.

— 'La crise morale de l'armée française', *L'Armée et la Seconde République. Bibliothèque de la Révolution de 1848*, vol. 18. La Roche-sur-Yon, 1955.

CHAPMAN, J. M. and B., *The Life and Times of Baron Haussmann*. London, 1957.

CHEVALIER, L., *La Formation de la population parisienne au XIXe siècle*. Paris, 1950.

— *Classes laborieuses, classes dangereuses, à Paris pendant la première moitié du XIXe siècle*. Paris, 1958.

CHOURY, M., *La Commune au Cœur de Paris*. Paris, 1967.

— *Les Origines de la Commune. Paris livré*. Paris, 1960.

— *La Commune au Quartier Latin*. Paris, 1961.

— *Les Poètes de la Commune*. Paris, 1970.

CLARETIE, J., *Histoire de la Révolution de 1870–1871*. Paris, 1872.

CLÉMENT, J.-B., *La Revanche des Communards*. Paris, 1886.

CLUSERET, G.-P., *Mémoires du Général Cluseret*. Paris, 1887.

COBB, R., *Les Armées révolutionnaires. Instruments de la Terreur dans les Départements*. Paris, 1961–3.

— *A Second Identity*. London, 1969.

COLLINS, H., and ABRAMSKY, C., *Karl Marx and the British Labour Movement*. London, 1965.

DA COSTA, Charles, *Les Blanquistes*. Vol. 6 of *Histoire des partis socialistes en France*, ed. A. Zévaès. Paris, 1912.

DA COSTA, Gaston, *La Commune vécue*. Paris, 1903–5.

COULLIÉ, Abbé, *Saint-Eustache pendant la Commune*. 2nd edn. Paris, 1872.

DABOT, Henri, *Griffonnages quotidiens d'un bourgeois du Quartier Latin*. Paris, 1895.

DAMÉ, F., *La Résistance. Les Maires, les Deputés de Paris et le Comité central du 18 au 26 mars*. Paris, 1871.

DAUBAN, C. A., *Le Fond de la société sous la Commune*. Paris, 1873.

DAUTRY, J., and SCHELER, L., *Le Comité central républicain des vingt arrondissements de Paris*. Paris, 1960.

DECOUFLÉ, A., *La Commune de Paris (1871). Révolution populaire et pouvoir révolutionnaire*. Paris, 1969.

DEFFOUX, L., *Pipe-en-bois*. Paris, 1932.

DESSAL, M., *Un Révolutionnaire jacobin. Charles Delescluze*. Paris, 1952.

DOMMANGET, M., *L'Enseignement, l'enfance et la culture sous la Commune*. Paris, 1964.

— *Hommes et choses de la Commune*. Marseille, s.d. (?1938).

— *Blanqui et l'opposition révolutionnaire à la fin du Second Empire*. Paris, 1960.

— *Blanqui, la Guerre de 1870-1871 et la Commune*. Paris, 1947.

— *Les Idées politiques et sociales d'Auguste Blanqui*. Paris, 1957.

DREYFUS, R., *Monsieur Thiers contre l'Empire, la Guerre et la Commune 1869-1871*. Paris, 1928.

DUBOIS, J., *Le Vocabulaire politique et social en France de 1869 à 1872*. Paris, 1962.

DUCROT, General, *La Défense de Paris (1870-1871)*. Paris, 1877.

DUPONT, L., *Souvenirs de Versailles pendant la Commune*. Paris, 1881.

DUPUY, A., *1870-71: La Guerre, la Commune et la presse*. Collection Kiosque, Paris, 1959.

DUVEAU, G., *La Vie ouvrière en France sous le Second Empirer*. Paris, 1946.

— *La Pensée ouvrière sur l'éducation*. Paris, 1947.

— *Le Siège de Paris*. Paris, 1939.

DUVIGNAUD, J., *Spectacle et société*. Paris, 1970.

D'ESBŒUFS, Verges, *Le Coin de Voile*. Geneva, 1872.

FAUCHER, J. A., and RICKER, A., *Histoire de la Franc-Maçonnerie en France*. Paris, 1967.

FAVRE, Jules, *Gouvernement de la défense nationale. Simple récit*. Paris, 1873.

FIAUX, L., *Histoire de la guerre civile de 1871. Le Gouvernement de l'Assemblée de Versailles. La Commune de Paris*. Paris, 1879.

FIDUS (Eugène Balleyguier), *Journal. La Révolution de septembre*, vols 1, 2. Paris, 1889.

FLAUBERT, Gustave, *Correspondance*. Paris, 1930, vol. 6.

— *Correspondance*. Supplement. Paris, 1944, vol. 2.

FLOURENS, G., *Paris livré*. Paris, 1871.

FONTOULIEU, P., *Les Eglises de Paris sous la Commune*. Paris, 1873.

FOULON, M., *Eugène Varlin*. Paris, 1934.

FORBES, A., 'What I saw of the Paris Commune', *The Century Magazine*, October 1892, vols 44-5.

FRIBOURG, E. E., *L'Association Internationale des Travailleurs*. Paris, 1871.

FREYMOND, J., *La Première Internationale. Recueil de documents*. Geneva, 1962.

FROUMOV, S., *La Commune de Paris et la démocratisation de l'école*. Moscow, 1958

GAILLARD, J., 'Les Usines Cail et les ouvriers métallurgistes de Grenelle', *Le Mouvement Social*, No. 33-4, October 1960-March 1961, pp. 35-53.

GANS, H. J., *People and Plans*. New York, 1968.

GARNIER, F., *Le Siège de Paris. Journal d'un officier de marine*. Paris, 1871.

GAUTIER, Théophile, *Tableaux de siège. Paris 1870–1871*. Paris, 1871.

GIBSON, Rev. W., *Paris During the Commune. 1871*. London, 1872.

GILL, André, *Vingt années de Paris*. Paris, 1883.

GIRARD, L., *Les Elections de 1869. Bibliothèque de la Révolution de 1848*, vol. 21. Paris, 1960.

— *La Garde Nationale. 1814–1871*. Paris, 1964.

— *Etude comparée des mouvements révolutionnaires en France en 1830, 1848 et 1870–71. (1870–71)*. Fascicules 1, 2. Les Cours de la Sorbonne. Paris, 1961.

GIRARDET, R., *La Société militaire dans la France contemporaine (1815–1939)*. Paris, 1953.

DE GONCOURT, Edmond, *Journal des Goncourt*, vol. 4. Paris, 1890.

DE LA GORCE, P.-M., *The French Army*. London, 1963.

GOSSEZ, R., '*Le 4 septembre 1870*', *Actes du 77e Congrès des Sociétés savantes. Grenoble, 1952*. Paris, 1952.

— '*Pre-Syndicalisme ou pre-coopération? L'organisation ouvrière unitaire et ses phases dans le département de la Seine de 1834 à 1851*' *Archives Internationales de sociologie de la coopération*, 1959, No. 6, pp. 67–89.

GREENBERG, L. M., '*The Commune of 1871 as a decentralist reaction*', *Journal of Modern History*, vol. 4, No. 3, September 1969, pp. 304–18.

— *Marseille, Lyon and the Paris Commune*. Unpublished Ph.D. thesis, Harvard, 1963.

GREER, D., *The Incidence of the Terror during the French Revolution*. Harvard, Cambridge, 1935.

GUERIN, D., *La Lutte des classes sous la Première République*. Paris, 1946.

GUILLEMIN, H., *Les Origines de la Commune*. Paris, 1956–60: vol. 1, *Cette curieuse guerre de 70;* vol. 2, *L'Héroique défense de Paris (1870–1871);* vol. 3, *La Capitulation (1871)*.

HALÉVY, Daniel, *Histoire d'une histoire esquisée pour le troisième cinquantenaire de la Révolution française*. Paris, 1939.

— *Le Courrier de M. Thiers*. Paris, 1921.

HALÉVY, Ludovic, *Notes et souvenirs. 1871–1872*. 5th edn. Paris, 1889.

— *Carnets*. Paris, 1935.

HAUSSMANN, Baron Joseph, *Mémoires*. 3rd edn. Paris, 1890.

D'HAUSSONVILLE, Comte, *Mon Journal pendant la guerre (1870–1871)*. Paris, 1905.

(HENNEBERT, E.), *Guerre des Communeux de Paris par un officier supérieur de l'armée de Versailles*. Paris, 1871.

D'HÉRISSON, Comte Maurice, *Journal d'un officier d'ordonnance*. Paris, 1885.

— *Nouveau journal d'un officier d'ordonnance. La Commune*. Paris, 1889.

HOBSBAWM, E., *Labouring Men. Studies in the History of Labour*. London, 1964.

HOEFFEL, G., *Some Aspects of Reformist Socialism in France. 1870–1914*. Unpublished D.Phil., Oxford University, 1971.

HOFFMAN, W., *Camp, Court and Siege*. New York, 1877.

HORNE, Alistair, *The Fall of Paris*. London, 1965.

HOWARD, Michael, *The Franco-Prussian War*. London, 1961.

L'HUILLIER, F., *La Lutte ouvrière à la fin du Second Empire*. Paris, 1957.

DE L'ISLE-ADAM, Villiers, '*Sous la Commune. Tableau de Paris*', *Mercure de France*, August 1953, pp. 577–98.

JELLINEK, Frank, *The Paris Commune of 1871*. London, 1937/71; New York, 1965.

JELOUBOVSKAIA, E., *La Chute du Second Empire et la naissance de la Troisième République en France*. Moscow, 1959.

JOHNSON, Douglas, *Guizot: Aspects of French History 1787–1874*. London, 1963.

KATZENBACH, E. L. Jnr, 'Liberals at War. The Economic Policies of the Government of National Defense, 1870–1871', *American Historical Review*, July 1951, pp. 803–23.

KRANZBERG, M., *The Siege of Paris, 1870–1871*. Ithaca, New York, 1950.

KRIEGEL, A., '*Syndicalisme révolutionnaire et Proudhon*', *L'Actualité de Proudhon*. Centre Nationale d'études des problèmes de sociologie et d'économie européenne. Brussels, 1967.

KRIEGEL, A., and BECKER, J.-J., *1914. La Guerre et le mouvement ouvrier français*. Paris, 1964.

KROPOTKIN, Peter, *The Commune of Paris*. London, 1895.

KULSTEIN, D. I., 'The Attitude of French Workers towards the Second Empire', *French Historical Studies*, Spring, 1962.

LABARTHE, G., *Le Théâtre pendant les jours du siège et de la Commune*. Paris, 1960.

LAMAZOU, Abbé, *La Place Vendôme et la Roquette*. Paris, 1871.

LAMBER, Juliette (Mme Adam), *Le Siège de Paris*. Paris, 1873.

— *Mes Sentiments et nos idées avant 1870*. Paris, 1905.

LANDY, A., 'A French Adventurer and American Expansionism after the Civil War', *Science and Society*, Fall, 1951, pp. 313–33.

LANJALLEY, Paul, and CORRIEZ, Paul, *Histoire de la révolution du 18 mars*. Paris, 1871.

LARONZE, G., *Histoire de la Commune de 1871 d'après des documents et des souvenirs inédits. La Justice*. Paris, 1928.

LAURENT, B., *La Commune de 1871. Les postes, les ballons, le télégraphe*. Paris, 1934.

LAZARE, Louis, *La France et Paris*. Paris, 1872.

LEFEBVRE, Georges, *La Révolution Française*. Paris, 1951.

LEFEBVRE, Henri, *La Proclamation de la Commune*. Paris, 1965.

LEFÈVRE, A., *Histoire de la Ligue d'Union Républicaine des Droits de Paris*. Paris, 1881.

LEFRANÇAIS, Gustave, *Etude sur le mouvement communaliste à Paris en 1871*. Neuchatel, 1871.

— *Souvenirs d'un révolutionnaire*. Brussels, 1902.

LEIGHTON, J., *Paris under the Commune*. London, 1871.

LEPELLETIER, E., *Histoire de la Commune de 1871*. Paris, 1901–13.

— *Paul Verlaine. His Life – His Work*. Eng. trans. London, 1909.

LEVASSEUR, E., *Histoire des classes ouvrières et de l'industrie en France de 1789 à 1870*. 2nd edn. Paris, 1904.

LÉVY-LEBOYER, M., 'La Croissance économique en France au XIXe siècle', *Annales E.S.C.*, July–August 1968, pp. 788–807.

LEWIS, Gordon, 'The Paris Commune Then and Now', *Monthly Review*, November 1968, pp. 84–93.

LIDSKY, P. *Les Ecrivains contre la Commune*. Paris, 1970.

LISSAGARAY, P.-O., *History of the Commune of 1871*. (Brussels, 1876.) 2nd edn. New York, 1898.

— *Les Huit journées de mai*. Brussels, 1871.

LUKACS, G., *History and Class Consciousness*. London, 1971.

MAILLARD, Firmin, *Affiches, professions de foi, documents officiels, clubs et comités pendant la Commune*. Paris, 1871.

MAITRON, J., *Histoire du mouvement anarchiste en France (1880–1914)*. Paris, 1951.

— 'A partir des papiers du Général Eudes', *L'Actualité de l'histoire*, October 1953.

— 'La personalité du militant ouvrier français dans la seconde moitié du XIXe siècle', *Le Mouvement Social*, October 1960–March, 1961.

MALON, B., *La Troisième défaite du prolétariat français*. Neuchatel, 1871.

MARTET, J., *Clemenceau*. Eng. Trans. London, 1930.

MARX, Karl, *La Guerre Civile en France 1871. Edition nouvelle accompagnée des travaux préparatoires de Marx*. Editions sociales, Paris, 1968.

— *On the Paris Commune*. Moscow/London, 1971 (This volume includes the preparatory drafts of Marx's *Civil War*.)

— *Letters to Dr Kugelmann*. London, 1934.

MARX-ENGELS, *Selected Works*. London, 1968.

— *Selected Correspondence*. Moscow, 1954.

— *Correspondance Friedrich Engels–Paul et Laura Lafargue, 1868–1895*. Paris, 1956, 1959.

MASON, E. S., *The Paris Commune*. London, 1930.

MCCLELLAN, General George B., *McClellan's Own Story*. London, 1887.

DE MEAUX, Vicomte, *Souvenirs politiques*. Paris, 1905.

MENDÈS, Catulle, *Les 73 journées de la Commune*. Paris, 1871

MICHEL, Louise, *La Commune*. Paris, 1898.

MICHELANT, L., 'Un Souvenir de la Commune', *Journal des Economistes*, vol. 23, 1871, pp. 264–71.

MOISSONIER, M., 'La Commune et le mouvement ouvrier Lyonnais', *La Nouvelle Critique*, April 1961, pp. 104–24.

DE MOLINARI, M. G., *Les Clubs rouges pendant le siege de Paris*. Paris, 1871

MOLOK, A., 'Les Ouvriers de Paris pendant la Commune', *Cahiers du Communisme*, Nos 5–6, May, June 1951, pp. 608–22, 728–75.

MORIAC, E., *Paris sous la Commune*. Paris, 1871.

DE MOUSSAC, Georges, *Dans la melée*. Paris, 1911.

NEWTON, Lord, *Lord Lyons. A Record of British Diplomacy*. London, 1913.

NOLAND, A., *The Founding of the French Socialist Party (1893–1905)*. Harvard, Cambridge, 1956.

OLIVESI, A., *La Commune de 1871 à Marseille*. Paris, 1950.

PERROT, C., *La Politique sociale de la Commune*. D.E.S. of the Sorbonne, 1950.

PERROT, Michelle, and KRIEGEL, Annie, *Le Socialisme français et le pouvoir*. Paris, 1966.

PINKNEY, D. H., *Napoleon III and the Rebuilding of Paris*. Princeton University Press, 1958.

PONSOT, P., *Les Grèves de 1870 et la Commune de 1871 au Creusot*. Paris, 1957.

POSTGATE, R. W., *Out of the Past*. London, 1923.

PRICE, R., 'Ideology and Motivation in the Paris Commune of 1871', *The Historical Journal*, 1971/2.

PROLÈS, C., *Les Hommes de la révolution de 1871. Charles Delescluze*. Paris, 1898.

PROUDHON, P.-J., *Selected Writings of Pierre-Joseph Proudhon*, ed. Stewart Edwards. New York/London, 1969, 1970.

RAIGA, E., and FELIX, M., *Le Régime administratif et financier du départemente de la Seine et de la ville de Paris*. Paris, 1922.

RAMON, G., *Histoire de la Banque de France*. Paris, 1929.

RANC, E., *Souvenirs-Correspondance. 1831–1908*. Paris, 1913.

— *Sous l'Empire*. Paris, 1872.

RASTOUL, A., *L'Eglise de Paris sous la Commune*. 1871.

RECLUS, Elie, *La Commune au jour le jour*. Paris, 1908.

RECLUS, Elisée, *Correspondance*, vol. 2. Paris, 1911.

RENOIR, Jean, *Renoir, My Father*. London, 1962.

RIAT, G., *Gustave Courbet*. Paris, 1906.

RIHS, C., *Le Commune de Paris, sa structure et ses doctrines*. Geneva, 1955.

ROBERTS, J., 'The Myth of the Commune', *History Today*, May, 1957, pp. 290–300.

ROCHEFORT, Henri, *Les Aventures de ma vie*, vols 2, 3. Paris, 1896.

ROSSEL, Louis, *Mémoires, procès et correspondance*. Paris, 1960.

ROUGERIE, J., *Procès des Communards*. Paris, 1964.

— 'La Commune de 1871: Problèmes d'histoire sociale', *Archives Internationales de Sociologie de la Coopération*, No. 8, 1960, pp. 45–68.

— 'Quelques documents nouveaux pour l'histoire du Comité central des vingt arrondissements', *Le Mouvement Social*, October–December 1961.

— 'Composition d'une population insurgée: l'example de la Commune', *Le Mouvement Social*, July–September 1964, pp. 31–47.

— 'Belleville', in L. Girard, *Elections de 1869*, Paris, 1960 (see above).

— 'La Première Internationale à Lyon (1865–1870)' Istituto Giangiacomo Feltrinelli, *Annali*, vol. 4, 1961, pp. 126–61.

ROUGERIE, J., 'Sur l'histoire de la Première Internationale', Le Mouvement Social, April–June 1965, pp. 23–45.

— Les Elections du 26 mars à la Commune de Paris. D.E.S. of the Sorbonne, 1955.

RUBEL, M., Karl Marx devant le Bonapartisme. Paris, 1960.

RUDÉ, G., The Crowd in History. London, 1964.

SARCEY, F., Le Siège de Paris, Paris, 1871.

SCHULKIND, E., 'The Activity of Popular Organisations during the Paris Commune of 1871', French Historical Studies, vol. 1, No. 4, Fall, 1960, pp. 394–415.

— 'La Commune de 1871 à travers sa littérature', La Pensée, Nos. 35–6, 1951.

SÉE, H., Histoire économique de la France. Paris, 1939.

SÉGUIN, Léo, 'The Ministry of War under the Commune', Fortnightly Review, vol. 12, New Series, July–December 1872, pp. 136–50.

SENIOR, Nassau, Conversations with distinguished persons during the Second Empire. London, 1880.

SENISSE, Martial, Les Carnets d'un Fédéré 1871, ed. J. A. Faucher. Paris, 1965.

SESMAISONS, General, Les Troupes de la Commune. Paris, 1904.

SIMON, Jules, Souvenirs du 4 septembre. Origine et chute du Second Empire. Paris, 1874.

— Souvenirs du 4 septembre. Le Gouvernement de la Défense Nationale. Paris, 1874.

— Le Gouvernement de M. Thiers. Paris, 1878.

SOBOUL, A., Les Soldats de l'An II. Paris, 1959.

TALES, C., La Commune de 1871 (Preface by Trotsky). Paris, 1921.

TCHERNOFF, I., Le Parti républicain au coup d'état et sous le Second Empire. Paris, 1906.

THIERRY, Augustin, Narratives of the Merovingian Era and the Historical Essays. Eng. trans. London, 1845.

— The Formation and Progress of the Tiers Etat in France. Eng. trans. London, 1855.

THIERS, A., Notes et Souveniers (1870–1873). Paris, 1903.

— Notes et Souveniers – 1848. Paris, 1902.

— Discours parlementaires. Paris, 1882.

THOMAS, E., The Women Incendiaries. New York/London, 1966–7. (English translation of Les Pétroleuses, Paris, 1963.)

— Rossel. Paris, 1967.

TILLY, Charles, 'A Travers le chaos des vivantes cités', Sixth World Congress of Sociology, Evian-les-Bains, September 1966.

— 'How Protest Modernised in France: 1845 to 1855', Conference on Applications of Quantitative Methods to Political, Social and Economic History, University of Chicago, June, 1969.

THULLIER, G., 'La Pétition des mécaniciens et des chauffeurs des chemins de fer en 1871', Le Mouvement Social, January–March 1969, pp. 65–88.

TINT, H., The Decline of French Patriotism 1870–1940. London, 1964.

TROCHU, General Jules, *Pour la vérité et pour la justice.* Paris, 1873.
— *La Politique et le siège de Paris.* Paris, 1874.
— *Œuvres posthumes.* Vol. 1, *Le Siège de Paris.* Paris, 1896.
— *L'Armée française en 1867.* Paris, 1867.
VALLÈS, Jules, *L'Insurgé.* Paris, 1886.
— *Le Proscrit: Correspondance avec Arthur Arnould. Œuvres complètes,* ed.
L. Scheler, vol. 4. Paris, 1950.
VERLAINE, Paul, *Confessions.* Eng. trans. London, 1950.
VERMOREL, J., *Auguste Vermorel (1841–1871).* Paris, 1911.
VINOY, General Joseph, *L'Armistice et la Commune.* Paris, 1872.
VUILLAUME, Maxime, *Mes Cahiers rouges au temps de la Commune.* Cahiers
de la Quinzaine. IXe séries. Paris, 1908–14.
VUILLEUMIER, M. 'La Correspondance du peintre G. Jeanneret', *Le Mouve-
ment Social,* April–June 1965.
WASHBURNE, E. B., *Recollections of a Minister to France, 1869–1877.* New
York, 1887.
— *Franco-German War and Insurrection of the Commune. Correspondence.*
Washington, 1878 *The Executive Documents printed by order of the Senate
of the United States.* 45th Congress, 2nd Session, Executive Document
No. 24, vol. 1.
WEILL, G. *Histoire du mouvement social en France 1852–1924.* Paris, 1924.
— *Histoire du parti républicain en France 1814–1870.* Paris, 1928.
WILLARD, C., *Les Guesdistes.* Paris, 1965.
WILLIAMS, Roger L., *The French Revolution of 1870–1871.* London, 1969.
— *Gaslight and Shadow.* New York, 1957.
WINNACKER, R. A., 'The French Election of 1871', *Papers of the Michigan
Academy of Sciences, Arts and Letters,* vol. XXII, 1936, pp. 477–83.
WINOCK, M. and AZÉMA, J.-P., *Les Communards.* Paris, 1964.
WOLFE, R. D., *The Origins of the Paris Commune: The Popular Organisations
of 1868–1871.* Unpublished Ph.D. thesis, Harvard, 1966.
— 'The Parisian Club de la Révolution of the 18th arrondissement 1870–
1871', *Past and Present,* April 1968, pp. 81–119.
WOLOWSKI, B., *Dombrowski et Versailles.* Geneva/London, 1871.
ZELDEN, T., *The Political System of Napoleon III.* London, 1958.
— *Emile Ollivier and the Liberal Empire of Napoleon III.* Oxford, 1963.
ZELLER, General A., *Les Hommes de la Commune.* Paris, 1969.
ZÉVAÈS, A., *De l'Introduction du Marxisme en France.* Paris, 1916.

# INDEX

# ABOUT THE AUTHOR

STEWART EDWARDS was born in Lincoln, England, in 1937. He studied at Cambridge University and at the London School of Economics, where he received a Ph.D. For five years until 1970 he lectured in Political Theory at the University of Southampton. Mr. Edwards has also edited *Pierre-Joseph Proudhon: Selected Writings*.